BrutalProof!

Table of Contents

Forward

It would have been great to include much more material but, due to the urgency of finishing this project and my desire to keep it within 200 pages; I am keeping it at its current length in consideration. For those readers who have limited time and means. I tried to address the most critical issues and make these issues clear in a simple way.

Thanks to my mother for her support, Bill Glynn for his encouragement and Kevin Annett for his generous sharing material and Tiffany Aliano for her patient editing and hard work.

Prologue

Brutal terror engulfs me nightly as I struggle to sleep. As I close my eyes, I see butcher knives flashing around me and I open my eyes in terror, hoping I'm not reliving this nightmare. My life has become terror and pain, which I cannot escape from, a daily torture that will not subside. I cling to the hope that one day this condition will end and I will have a happy, normal life. I cling to this hope through decades of suffering and carrying a heavy cross; the weight of which, I no longer feel since I am so used to carrying it. Extreme fear and pain, I will do anything for relief; anything that will ease the terror and numb the pain. My life spirals down into an involvement in illegal activities for with the money gained safety can be bought. I know the horror has brought me here. It does work for the money buys me safety. I am no longer living in dangerous neighborhoods where total strangers follow me up to my apartment while I frantically unlock doors with shaking hands. I am no longer living in places being burglarized in broad daylight as I watch sitting on my couch terrified. I am safer now and I no longer think of the lives others take for granted. I don't have boyfriends or think parties are fun. My life is totally geared to finding safety. I no longer care about entertainment or social mores. These did not save me from the brutal attack and the ensuing insanity. And I do feel the insanity of living this crazy life and not caring. I have lost the life I had and found trauma and terror. I buy a Smith and Wesson revolver. At the gun shop I make sure it will kill. I have come to the brutal realization my government does not care about me. This torturer-killer has done this before. He will do this again. And who will care? Certainly, not the middle class I was raised among living in comfort and safety. He is a serial killer and loves what he does. I could see it in his eyes as he pondered murdering me. I could feel the evil in his soul possessed by the powerfully demonic as his eyes turned black. I will carry this with me to my grave. My soul is shattered into painful pieces. The pain pervades every moment of my continuing nightmare life. This nightmare never ends. I do not fear death, for I am in hell. Death would be a welcome relief. I know every feeling of the women who die and are still dying along the Highway of Tears and all over Canada. The betrayal, terror, feeling of abandonment; pain is my daily life. This book is dedicated to the thousands of murdered and missing. My hope is that they will not be forgotten and that Justice will finally prevail. My God, why did I live this life? My torture has lasted a lifetime. In the end my experiences are the defining reason I am so drawn to the Canadian Holocaust and its' horrific connection to the missing and murdered minors & women connected to the snuff porn rings and the Highway of Tears. Willie Currie is now the replacement for Willie Picton. He commits his murders on Jingle Pot Road creating snuff films in Nanaimo, British Columbia. If nothing else, I want to see him get the death sentence. It is for the murdered that I write this. It is for the missing I will expose this.

My incentive is my own stolen life. Exposing these sadistic torturers gives me a grim satisfaction. I'll make sure the world knows the horrific details of your rapes and murders.

Preface

This is about Rape, Torture & Murder of Women & Children: the Depopulation Agenda Being Enacted on the Public via Withholding of Cancer Cures, Financial Crimes & Genocides Resulting, Serial Killers & Mass Murderers Created by Governments Being Allowed to Rape & Murder Vulnerable Women, Homeless & Hitchhikers, MK Ultra and the very synergistic cocktail of Aluminum, Mercury, Lead Poisons, Fluoride, etc. neurotoxins in our vaccinations, chemtrails, water, GMO's and dental amalgams leading to an eventually lethal 100% mortality rate sponsored by the Rothschild Zionist Khazarian Mafia who own America via their social engineering charities like B'nai B'rith & AIPAC as well as their bagman's George Soros's social engineering charities (he has hundreds), their fraudulent Big Pharma and our beyond corrupt politicians & lobbyists who live like the bestial Romans in their heyday during the fall of the Roman Empire. This is about the Depopulation Agenda of Satanic Zionists (Synagogue of Satan) in America & their Satanic Freemason Colleagues. What You Can Do About it.... Time to get Active!

This is the result of my research starting from the day I knew something was seriously wrong in the world and found out why the horrors go on. That there are so many missing children is a clue. It has been a mostly horrific journey involving world class psychics, serial killers and leading to icons in politics, government, & entertainment.

It all started one day as I was watching Nancy Grace and she was saying that there were 750,000 missing children every year in the United States (US Dept. of Justice): 15.000 missing children in every state every year!!!! Huge! I thought to myself that if the government could see license plates

(797,500) by satellite they could certainly find these missing children. Strange that there were so many!

I was also embarking on a journey to find the identity of the one who had viciously attacked and almost murdered me at age twenty. It was a festering wound in my psyche that never healed affecting every cell of my being and every day of my life. I was burdened with the heavy cross I carried.

I could never feel safe even with every window and door covered with iron bars-I could not feel safe. In a motel parking lot an old beater sent me into a panic attack while intrusive thoughts of being kidnapped and tortured saturated my mind. Working with an orderly who resembled my attacker would almost immobilize me in terror. I left Florida after a Florida serial killer left seven dead, while in a one night killing spree at a hospital off Jupiter Beach. Newspaper inserts with a dozen pages of sexual predators made me want to vacate North Miami immediately, which I did the same day my lease was up.

My life has been a daily battle just trying to feel safe. It had been so stressful I thought I might've been better off murdered than to live like this. I didn't have a strong network of long term relationships. Excessive moving as a child had interfered with building them. I had only a will to survive and a festering wound that would never heal. In time, I was to realize my injuries were the same as the wounds of the tortured in Guantanamo Bay, the wounds of children robbed of innocence whose pleas for justice have never been heard nor seen the light of day; the massive psychic trauma of concentration camp survivors. In my search for the truth and longing for closure I began enlisting the aid of known psychics. One was a police psychic, another had written a book about her bizarre Harry Potter-like experiences of bi-location, astral travel, visions, and medium ship abilities to hear, see, and feel spirit. I figured a gifted psychic would have strange and bizarre experiences so I contacted her. In her trial reading she was amazingly accurate even getting the correct name of the person pictured. Later she would give me an accurate physical description of my attacker and tell me I would never be rid of the PTSD. She described how he had gone to the next level (of murder) and wasn't even on the FBI's most wanted list. She said it was a miracle I was alive. She asked me if I had any questions. I had one: What was that swirly creature I saw in my dream? It was a male spirit. What was really fascinating was the way the light glinted off of it as it swirled around like light reflects off the facets of a diamond. She stated: It's a Djinn. And in my confusion and curiosity, I asked 'What's a Djinn?" She said "It's a male spirit. They're very powerful and rare and from the Middle East. You will see more. They work both sides so I wouldn't advise having one as a guide. I've given hundreds of readings and I can count on one hand the people who've seen a Djinn" she stated matter of fact. Reading culminated as she made very clear Djinn's were not her favorite subject. I found out later, 90 percent of Djinns are demonic. Since then I've asked God to protect me. I remember at the point I was taken over completely by terror my assailant's eyes turned black as if they were filling up with ink. I felt the presence of malevolent evil. It was as if he were under a spell of something so evil that he was capable of anything. I saw it & felt it. Maybe the smoky black thing shining through his eye was the Djinn-the thing that exorcists expel.

Years later when the same psychic gave spiritual development classes she emphasized looking at David Icke's website. David Icke wrote about the black-eyed beings and how deadly they were. They are the ones possessed by evil Djinns. He wrote about PM Heath and his torture and murder of boys and seeing Heath's eyes turn black.

The injury seemed to break my assailant out of the spell he was under. He actually seemed to become human again. I was so paralyzed by fear. I think the evil ones are attracted to those in deep fear. The Djinn dream happened after I'd just completed nine weeks of exposure therapy for severe PTSD. The nightmares of serial killers have continued for months. In one dream, I opened the door to a man with pure evil coming out of his eyes and realized he was there to kill me. I knew he was hiding a knife behind his back. In another dream, I was alone in my car frantically trying to lock the door with a broken lock as footsteps walked up to my car. I froze in terror for my murderer had arrived. I woke up in terror with my heart pounding. In another dream a black-haired woman was being stabbed to death by a nice looking black-haired assailant who looked like a conservative office worker. A month later I would see someone who looked the same on the front page of the Atlanta newspaper. He had stabbed eight women to death and his eyes emanated the blackest evil. In another dream, I watched a beautiful 6-year-old boy's body being pulled out of a trunk by a Latin man. He appeared to be asleep, but I knew he was dead and murdered by a pedophile ring and this man was disposing of the body. I knew his body would be cut into pieces and the pieces thrown into different regions. I suppressed all thoughts of what had happened in almost thirty years and now after exposure therapy I was inundated with these dreams. For thirty years, I had no memories of any dreams at all and now I was inundated. And a supernatural Djinn had appeared!

With the psychic's emphasis on David Icke I felt this was something BIG. It was. I began reading of protected sadistic pedophiles who tortured children to death-George Bush Sr. and PM Heath. They were connected and wealthy and never were prosecuted for their horrific crimes. The victims were shunned by society and discredited by our media that claims to care so much about human rights while 1,000,000 children disappear to never be seen again. They cared so much about human rights that all these missing children never had any human rights here at home! And our government, while putting on this big fake show of caring about human rights is directly involved in the abductions and murders of these missing children. It was all in David Ickes website and Kevin Annett's websites: itccs.org and hiddennolonger.com. What a bunch of fakes and charlatans these politicians are! The most criminal of them all was my own government, the self-appointed democracy spreader and very vocal human rights "advocate." Nothing could be further from the truth! With the media busily spreading human rights lies my government was busy killing Iraqi children with embargos. I'm sure I will be attacked by self- serving idiots, truth deniers and most of all those who have profited off of all this evil. The ones who are committing these evil acts and remain protected by the delusional who can't handle the truth, the idiots, the corporations & political connections. In other words, the criminals in high positions remain protected by an ignorant public who uphold a criminal and corrupt political establishment. Welcome to Satan's America! Ten years of intensive research has shown me this truth. David Icke's twenty plus years of research has shown him this truth. Those who dismiss it, dismiss it at their own peril for their children and grandchildren will live in everlasting slavery for the luxury of their denial. Kevin Annett has been trying to reveal this truth too of how Satanists have infiltrated the Catholic churches and infested the government. How they are the reason for all the missing kids and young women. John DeCamp wrote a book: *The Franklin Cover-Up* about Satanic rings operating all over the US and in DC. You, reader, can go to davidicke.com and go to the Archives, then to Satanism and see exactly what I'm telling you about. You can YouTube Kevin Annett/Satanism and watch the YouTube videos on how the murdered children were ritually sacrificed by the elite in Canada and abroad. Yesterday I read in *Veteran's Today* an article about all the missing people and "where do the rest of us think all of these missing people go?" Then the article described Piggy's Palace, a snuff film production site in Canada run by the Picton brothers fronting for elite consumers. If you don't believe me, go to the hiddennolonger.com website and the pdf book there. Go to the **Synopsis in bold print** at the end and read it. You will see that icons like Eddie Murphy are connected to these snuff film rings. (Ann Parker's testimony) That's why there aren't prosecutions. Money and power are the reasons the victims see No Justice. It's the same all over the EU and Western Europe, America and Canada. It's all one mass Nazi Holocaust of sex trade workers and children. It's like the movie: *The Girl with the Dragon Tattoo* and *The Girl Who Played with Fire* and *The Girl Who Kicked the Hornet's Nest.* It is like the movie *Whistleblower* whose NATO-UN worker blew the whistle on the UN's-NATO's pedophilia sex rings with underage sex slaves. It's like the internet movie Conspiracy of Silence taken off of TV in America because it exposed a child sex ring in D.C. It is like the movie 8 mm with Nicholas Cage-more truth than fiction. These people are like pigs at the trough raping children and even eating human flesh. One book is almost unavailable. It is called *Lucifer's Lodge: Satanic Ritual Abuse and the Catholic Church.* $399 for anyone with the money at Amazon.com, but free at **brutalproof.net** under pdf books. It goes on in English speaking countries the most: England, USA, Canada, Australia, Etc. People don't realize that in certain African countries (Sudan?) pedophiles are put to death after a thorough investigation. At least that was what an African veteran told me. We consider ourselves civilized, but our government gives the most vicious criminals the freedom to rape and murder hundreds of children each especially if they are connected to elite Luciferians/Satanists. To believe this freedom fiction every American has to look the other way as almost a million children disappear every year! I guess if the public really cared and we had an honest media it would not be happening. No one cared about what happened to me either-they seemed to resent my disability status more. Only people who care will read David Icke or Alex Jones or Hiddennolonger.com or listen to Kevin Annett's YouTube webcasts. But, the truth is so horrifying, they prefer not to look at this monster and they abandon these tortured and murdered children and people to their horrific deaths. But, looking the other way doesn't solve anything because the pedophilia and Satanism and sadism are addictions, which become bigger and bigger monsters requiring more and more blood, and more and more brutal killings to quench their sick desires. Did the Queen of Bathory quit killing? Only when forced to by being imprisoned. I pity the world being left to the children and grandchildren of these people in denial of the truth. For they are leaving a legacy of brutal child sex slavery, a legacy of a completely enslaved human race where the white man will become the new American Indian as Russell Means has stated. His race was used in Mind Control "torture" experiments and exterminated in "Christian Residential Schools" that were actually Nazi death camps-70% death rate in some schools- double the death rate of Auschwitz! It's lonely and uncomfortable work passing out thousands of flyers, but that is what I've done. Flyers about George Bush's pedophilia and Satanism, the child sex ring exposed in *Conspiracy of Silence* and always mentioning David Icke's and Kevin Annett's websites hiddennolonger.com and itccs.org I've probably passed out about 50,000 flyers. I've also mentioned Alex Jones's website Prisonplanet.com as well as JohnnyGosch.com. This book will show all my flyers, which you can download for your own self and pass out if you wish. Research what I tell you. Tell others. Word of mouth is powerful. I always seem to attract the blind who don't believe me, but invariably they know someone who does and wants to see the flyers and read David Icke's books. I feel like I AM getting this information out. It needs to be gotten out so much more!!!

I remember working in a San Francisco Hospital. A violent rapist was nearly let loose with absolutely no follow-up. Only because of a conscientious RN was there follow up. She caught the lack of follow up and corrected it. She made sure I helped him pack his items in the lobby within full view of the nursing station. Recently Kevin Annett stated on his itccs.org website that a NYC cop told him a child rapist must rape the child about 15 times before anything is done about it otherwise the violent, assaultive child rapist goes Scot free. See RAINN.org statistics. The system is all for the worst offenders by design. And if you dare challenge it beware! You WILL pay some way, somehow. The system is ALL for the Child ABUSERS, ESPECIALLY FOR CHILD RAPISTS AND SATANIC CHILD KILLERS! The USA is one of the most Satanic countries of all and that is why one million children go missing every year and nothing is done about it. The same situation is in Europe of one million additional Europeans missing too. The situation can't be examined too closely by our media because it goes straight to the top: The Monarchies, the Parliaments, Congress, the PM's, the State Departments, Pentagon, NASA, Presidents, Vice Presidents, the Intelligence Agencies especially, etc. etc. etc. David Icke, Alex Jones, and Kevin Annett especially tried to expose this and they all live under death threats. Kevin Annett has repeatedly been beaten up and is not safe in his own house. He left Vancouver and then Nanaimo. Vancouver must be one of the worst of all places! Yet, it is so beautiful as is Nanaimo one of the most beautiful places I have ever seen. Now, reader, do you understand why child porn is posted so freely on the web? It's protected by our "elite" who basically control all of our systems: the media, drug/medical system, courts and injustice systems, social welfare systems, our propaganda corrupted news, educational systems that are mainly rote memorization of truly useless information and irrelevant non-historical histories while the truth is edited out (Search: the inventor of peanut butter-George Washington Carver-where is he in the history books?) etc. etc. etc. I could go on and on, but I don't want to lose you in the details. Instead I'll make it simple and short. This is a Luciferian world controlled by pure evil and unless we all wake up to this and do something about it this problem will worsen. Evil is Addicted to evil acts and the monster grows bigger and bigger all the time. I am shouting out a warning to the rest of you. There is still time, but the sands of time are running. Get off your duff and do something! Turn off the TV to look on the internet instead. Health Freedom News has older magazines that you can order and distribute ($3 each) to waiting rooms at doctor's offices, dentist's waiting rooms as well as gyms (to read on the elliptical machines) or Coffee shop tables. READ!! Tell everyone you know what you learn by researching. You could download and copy some of these movies and give a few out. Or buy some $1 DVD patriot packs at Republic Media Broadcasting Network under *Sponsors* **Dollar DVD Project Liberty and give them out.**

Our "systems" don't care about missing kids. I read about a little German boy named Manuel, who was raped and tortured to death in a snuff film, which sold for 5000 pounds-about $7,500. His killer only got 5 -6 years in prison for kidnapping and raping 2 homeless runaways. We live in a world ruled by the most malignant narcissists. There is no telling how many lives this one vicious criminal ruined. Poor Manuel had his penis cut off and was cut open while still alive. The pedophile seeing this snuff film turned it off to vomit and could absolutely not look at any more of it.

I think the sadistic psychopaths that did this to Manuel should die.

I know the royals are involved in all of this degeneracy and sickness. They have surrounded themselves with sadistic & Satanic pedophiles like Jimmy Savile, PM Edward Heath, etc. I hope the nest of vipers around them pay too. Sleazy criminals have the same arrogance. I guess if someone gets away with making money off of murdering children, Satanism, insider trading, stealing land from aboriginals and murdering them and their children, Nazi war crimes, etc. etc. like they do, they would develop a cold arrogant attitude. Only David Icke exposed them for the longest time and then Kevin Annett and now Bill Mahoney and Chris Everard. The Sex Pistols tried to expose them as fascists. I hope they get locked up! Let there be justice for their victims and may they pay. See Chris Everard films, which document their crimes and look at itccs.org with "Toos Nijenhuis testimony".

R.I.P.

Manuel Schadwald

Tortured to death by sadistic pedophiles protected by EU

One day I know this evil will be overcome. I am sure of it. I KNOW I WILL TELL THE SHOCKING TRUTH THAT A NATIONAL HERO LIKE HARRY LEE WAS AN INVESTOR IN A MASSAGE PARLOR and his vice used to viciously go after anyone setting up shop or sending "escorts" to Jefferson Parish. Yup, Sheriff Harry Lee allegedly was a part owner in Tokyo Massage parlor in Fat City. We live within a cult of popular opinion where anyone deemed an outsider telling truths no one wants to hear is viciously attacked and condemned by cowards. It doesn't change the truth, but usually makes for dirtier truths because problems unresolved always cascade into bigger ones. I'm here to reveal the dirty little secrets the fat pedophiles in America don't want revealed. Or the sexual sadists like Eddie Murphy, who tortured to death more than two women and had their bodies discarded by his private security. My source is Hiddennolonger.com (**synopsis**). Read it! The truth is brutal beyond imagining! The good news will start with the criminal convictions of these child murderers and when the streets begin to be safe for children.

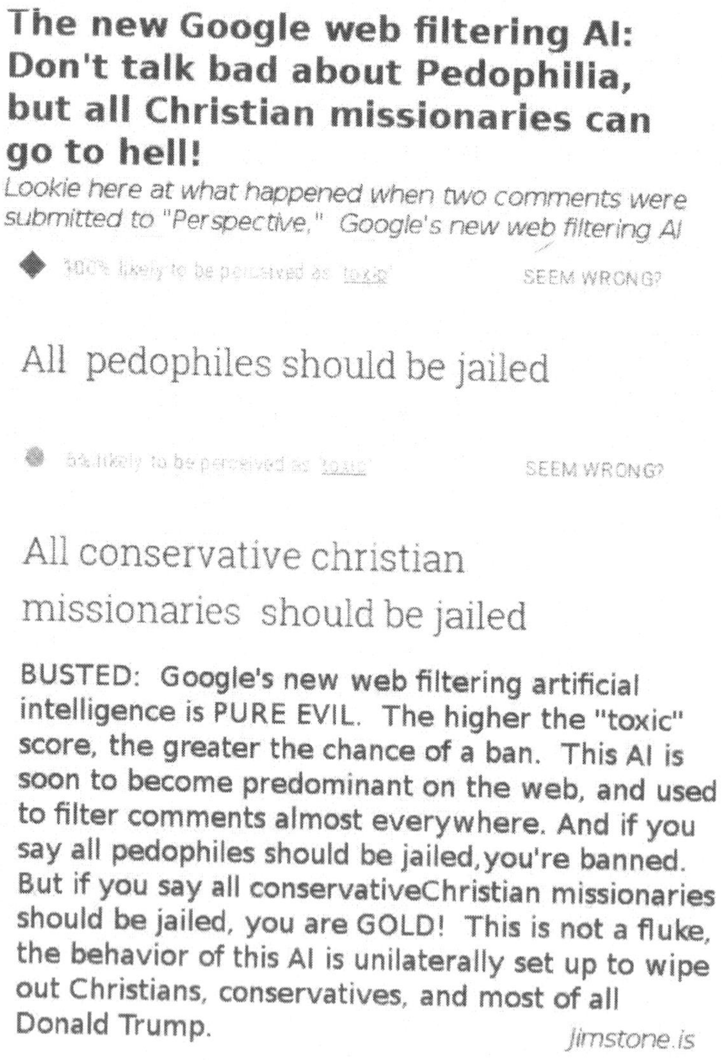
The new Google web filtering AI: Don't talk bad about Pedophilia, but all Christian missionaries can go to hell!
Lookie here at what happened when two comments were submitted to "Perspective," Google's new web filtering AI
100% likely to be perceived as "toxic"
SEEM WRONG?
All pedophiles should be jailed
5% likely to be perceived as "toxic"
SEEM WRONG?
All conservative christian missionaries should be jailed
BUSTED: Google's new web filtering artificial intelligence is PURE EVIL. The higher the "toxic" score, the greater the chance of a ban. This AI is soon to become predominant on the web, and used to filter comments almost everywhere. And if you say all pedophiles should be jailed,you're banned. But if you say all conservativeChristian missionaries should be jailed, you are GOLD! This is not a fluke, the behavior of this AI is unilaterally set up to wipe out Christians, conservatives, and most of all Donald Trump.
Jimstone.is

50 000 CANADIAN CHILDREN MURDERED

Hiddennolonger.com

(pdf book)

19. Witness claims that MICHAELSON provides security for foreign diplomats in Vancouver and film industry stars, including Eddie MURPHY, to whom MICHAELSON introduced the witness in 2002. Witness claims that MURPHY raped and sadistically assaulted her, slicing her skin with a knife and leaving permanent scars on her shoulder and neck. *(see videotaped interview)* Witness states that MURPHY was also responsible for the death of two women during the years 2002-3 in Vancouver : a 21 year old Asian porn actress and a prostitute, both of whom were provided to MURPHY by MICHAELSON, and whose bodies were disposed of by the latter after MURPHY had tortured and raped them, and then overdosed them on drugs.

20. Witness states that she reported the attack on her by MURPHY to a Detective SCOTT with the VPD, along with the claim of MURPHY's murder of the two women, but when MICHAELSON learned of the complaint he tortured the witness with a knife, carving her neck and face, *(see videotaped interview)* and threatened to kill her if she pressed charges against MURPHY. Witness then withdrew her complaint. Detective SCOTT subsequently confirmed to the witness that MURPHY was responsible for the murders but they had not enough evidence to prosecute him.

21. Witness believes that MICHAELSON and his associates are *"hunting prostitutes of intelligence"* and are engaged *"in a kind of ethnic cleansing … they target Indians and girls as young as twelve or thirteen."* She

Health

Cancer "Charities" (Hoaxes)

These should also be on your list of toxic charities since they are basically a fraud. Want proof? Well, here it is. The cure for cancer is not allowed in the US for the US government that cares so deeply about its citizens does not allow the many cures for cancer to be marketed here. Take a look at this documentary: Cancer: The Forbidden Cures. Mistletoe juice, turmeric, Sour Sop Fruit aka Graviola Fruit, Dr. Burzynski's neoplaston's (he is always under attack by the FDA for his forbidden cancer cure), Romanian Cancer Tea, the Hoxsey Clinic (driven out of the USA by the FDA to Mexico), Pau d'Arco tea, the immune booster tea (Whole Foods who no longer sells it), Laetrile, the list goes on and on and on.... there are so many cures I can't keep up with them all, but I personally do not believe in Chemo or Radiation. For one thing Chemo is so poisonous that Chemo nurses must wear gloves so their skin doesn't absorb these poisons, which destroy a person's immune system and radiation causes cancer. Marie Curie discovered radium and died from cancer from working with this radioactive element. By the way sea cucumber is supposed to be 95% effective with breast cancer courtesy of NaturalNews.com. Furthermore, Natural News just wrote an article about how the Cancer Industry is locking up profits in advance by contaminating their vaccines with Nagalase, which is a protein made by all cancers causing immunodeficiency. This would virtually guarantee the cancer industry's profits later on as the Nagalase vaccinated patients get cancer from the injected nagalase! Dr. Bradstreet and Dr. Gonzalez both had proof it was being injected via vaccines. They are now both dead (dead doctors don’t give speeches and publish papers) as well as six other doctors who were all Holistic doctors.

Illuminati, Big Pharma is unforgiving if anyone dare interfere with their profits!

THE FDA IS NOW SUPRESSING A GROUND-BREAKING GENE-TARGETED CANCER TREATMENT, LEARN MORE!

BURZYNSKI
the movie

"No one appears to contest the efficacy of his treatment; the problem ... is a pharmaceutical industry with nothing to gain — and much to lose — from the introduction of a highly successful, nontoxic competitor to chemotherapy and radiation."

The New York Times - June 4, 2010

"a wonderful movie" "grippingly told ... compelling"

Dr. Mehmet Oz - The Dr. Oz Show - May 17, 2011

*"**Burzynski** charts how a Texas medical doctor and biochemist developed Antineoplastons ... only to bring down the full force of the medical establishment, which has laid assult to him in the most stupefying, devious and costly manner."*

Los Angeles Times - June 3, 2010

WINNER! HUMANITARIAN VISION AWARD
NEWPORT BEACH FILM FESTIVAL 2010

CANCER IS SERIOUS BUSINESS

See it on Netflix, Documentary Channel, or get the DVD at www.burzynskimovie.com

BrutalProof!

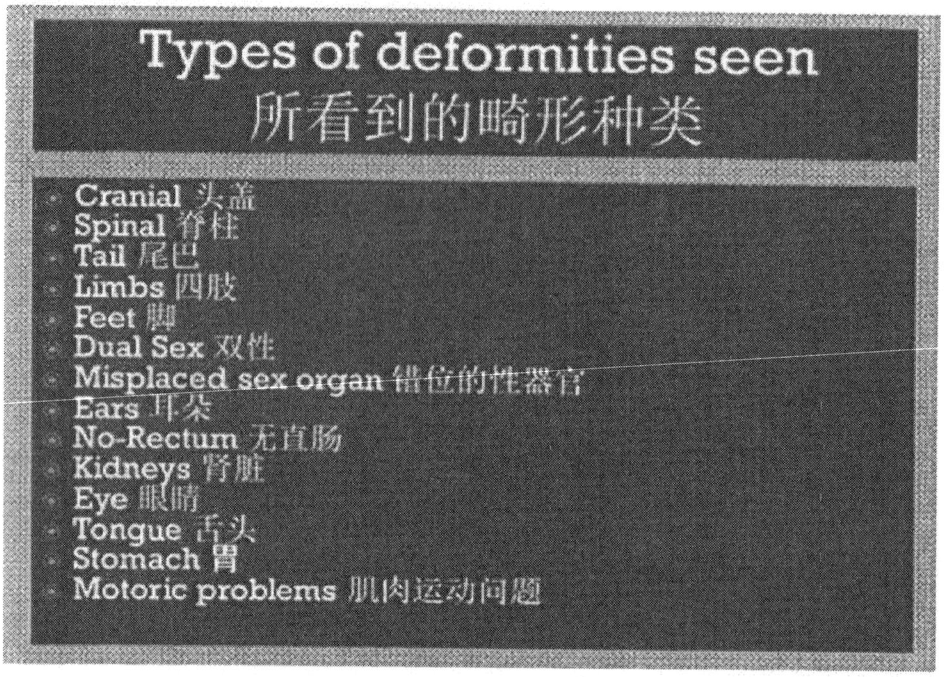

Glyphosate weed killer unleashes grotesque chemical deformations in farm animals... two...

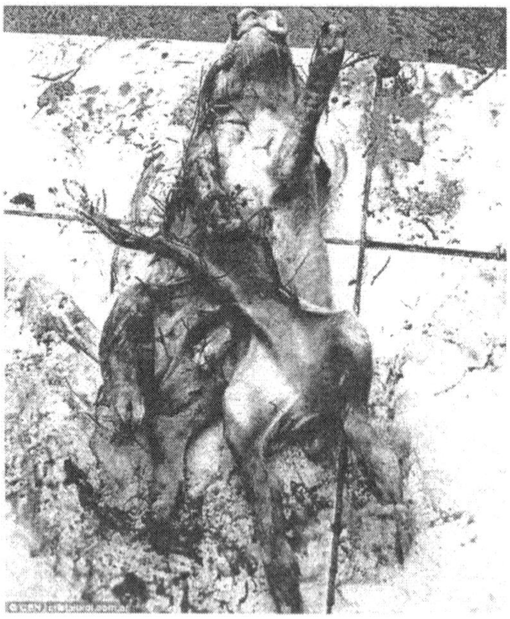

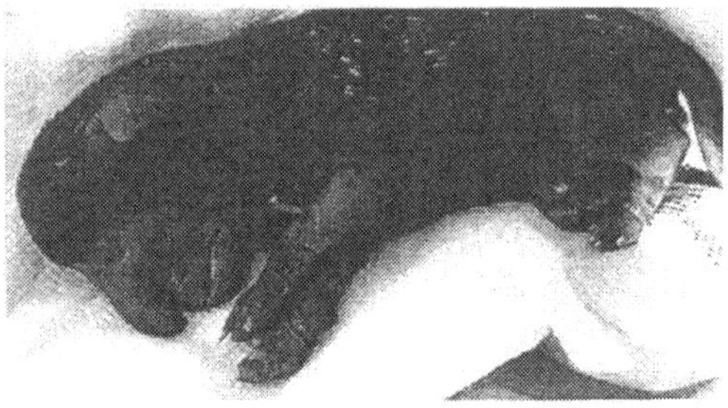

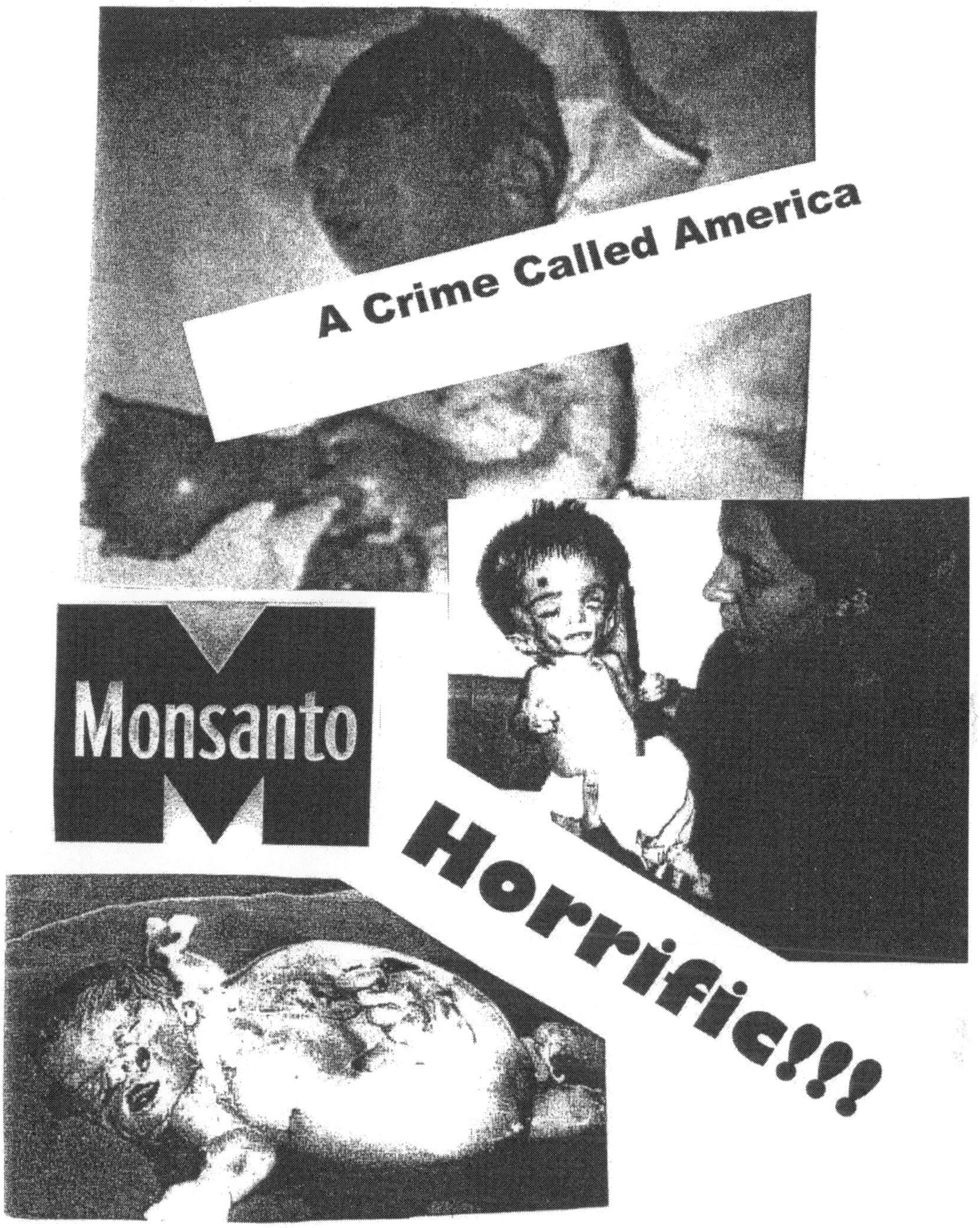

BrutalProof!

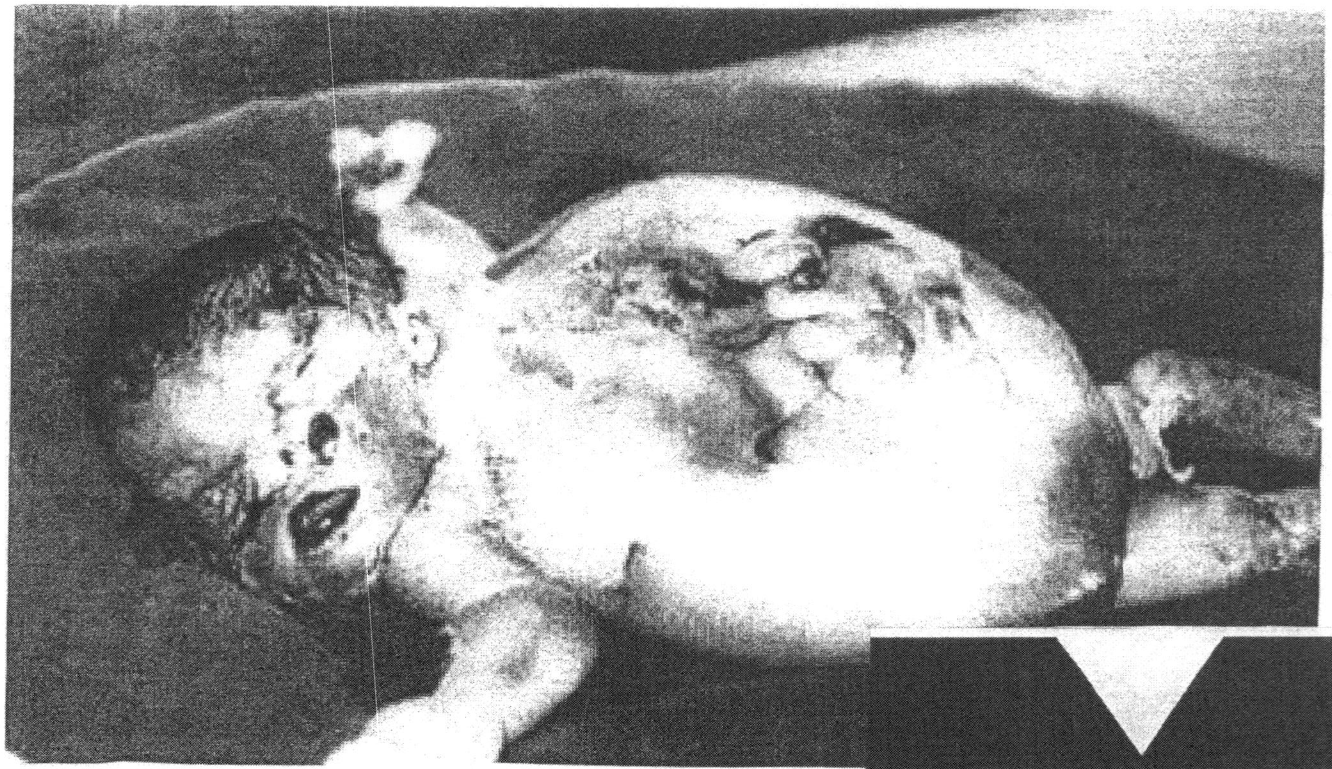

Depleted Uranium Babies Courtesy of Monsanto

MONSANTO

Genetically Modified Food Courtesy of Monsanto

This is a Rumsfeld (he pushed it through when studies showed it was clearly unsafe) Trojan horse that every time you stick it in your mouth you are playing Russian roulette with your health. A French study showed how Monsanto rats all died within 2 years from fist sized cancers and this has been met with a media blackout in the United States. No need to worry! Just don't eat processed foods like bakery goods or fast foods: McDonald's, BK, Taco Hell, Church's Fried Chicken, Popeye's, Kentucky Fried Chicken, Domino's Pizza, Pizza Hut, Panda's, or any other fast food or convenience food such as TV dinners, artificial coffee creamer's, artificial sweeteners, etc. etc. etc. We live in the land of the free and cancer is free. Also, if you are of the 70% of the unfortunates who have sodium fluoride in your tap water, buy a filter that gets the rat poison out of your water. Calcium fluoride is the good fluoride; sodium fluoride is the rat poison. It is the rat poison fluoridating our water. This is a distinction worthy of the movie Erin Brockovich with Julia Roberts. Grace Co. told the people of Hinckley that they had an organic, safe chemical in their water when really the company was leaching hexavalent chromium- a very cancerous substance classified as a hazardous waste. This is just as bad as GMO's and fluoride causing our water to be cancerous and is also the subject of the John Travolta movie: A Civil Case. Buy a filter or pay 50 cents a gallon to filter the fluoride out of your water. You can detoxify yourself with blue and or green algae, spirulina, chlorella and probably even with the sushi algae. Fortunately, for me, I like seaweed better than land veggies and it is super-good for you and to detox you from all the poisons our government lovingly allows to be put into our water and vaccines. Ancient Aliens even mentions the manna from heaven was most likely Chlorella algae!

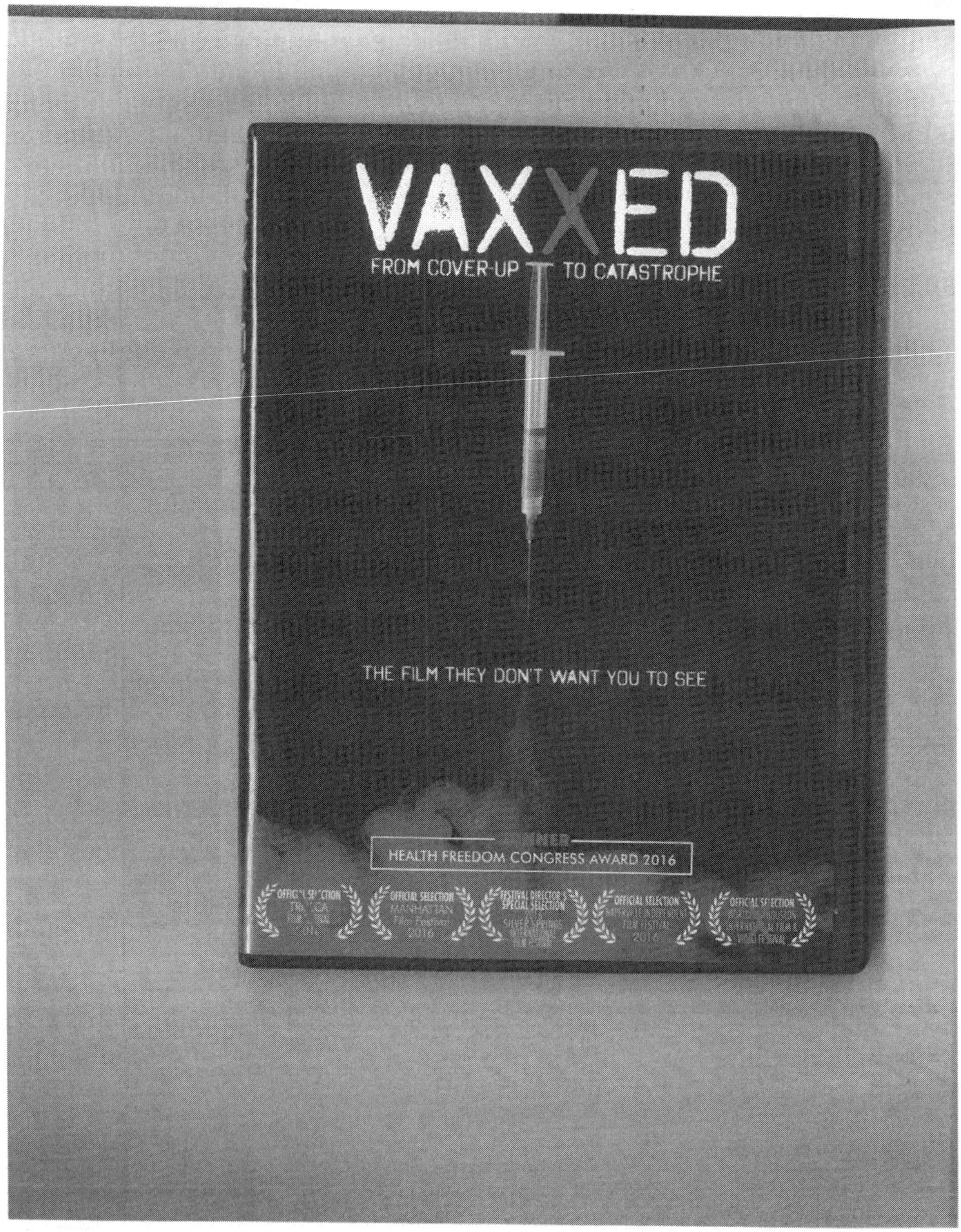
VAXXED
FROM COVER-UP TO CATASTROPHE
THE FILM THEY DON'T WANT YOU TO SEE
HEALTH FREEDOM CONGRESS AWARD 2016
OFFICIAL SELECTION
MANHATTAN
Film Festival
2016
FESTIVAL DIRECTOR'S SPECIAL SELECTION
OFFICIAL SELECTION
OFFICIAL SELECTION

BrutalProof!

Vaccines/Neurotoxins in a Needle & the Carbon Emissions Scam

Poisons in a needle containing thimerosal/thimerosal (a mercury product) and formaldehyde at about 400 times the safety level young children can absorb, which by the way is illegal. No wonder the skyrocketing rates of autism (measles, mumps, rubella vaccine), (flu vaccine too). Dr. Wakefield, a real doctor, who cared about his patients and tried to warn them is a must search. His movie VAXXED! Has just been released and it is a bombshell exposing a CDC whistleblower Dr. Thompson's phone calls leaking the CDC distortion and actually destroying clinical results proving the Autism link to multiple dose measles mumps rubella vaccines! Now, this information is exploding on the alternative media. Wow! You MUST search Dr. Wakefield! No wonder Bill Gates is such a huge proponent of vaccines whom by the way, is autism/Asperger's damaged himself! He has publicly stated: "The world today has 6.8 billion people.... that's headed up to about 9 billion. Now if we do a really great job on new vaccines, health care, reproductive health services, we could lower that (surplus population) by perhaps 10 or 15 percent." Vaccines are a vital part of the Depopulation Agenda. He also presented the CO_2 formula as CO_2=P X S X E X C trying to get the CO_2 emissions to zero meaning to get there we need to Depopulate! The P stands for People and he mentions reducing people with vaccines! (S stands for Services per person and the E stands for Energy Per Person.) (The C stands for CO_2=Carbon Dioxide per person, which all plants need and they then produce Oxygen, which we need so I hope no one falls for this scam!) Scarily if people do fall for this SCAM and carbon dioxide levels fall, the plants will be forced to compete with us for Oxygen to produce CO_2! This is right out of yahoo.com Answers when searching plant respiration.

BrutalProof!

Carbon Emissions Scam

Ignores plants need carbon dioxide and then emit O2 for us to breathe

The more carbon dioxide-the more rapidly plants will grow and the more deer, wild pigs, squirrels, turtles, wild turkeys who will eat these plants…this is BAD? It's a trillion dollar scam that will destroy industry, and force plants to use O2 reducing the atmospheric O2 which will affect human ability to live…Ouch..we're under attack!

Thank God for Dr. Mercola, a real doctor, and if you go to his website drmercola.com you will see how much he focuses on nutrition. He is a prolific writer and has lots of good articles and he is doing a really good job at educating the public. Subscribing to his website is free and so are the newsletters. Recently he had an article on Ayurvedic medicine, which is the real medicine as were the Edgar Cayce healings. Personally, I think the American diet is saturated with sugar, which is akin to poison and the artificial sweeteners are poisonous too. Anyways, Dr. Mercola was a BIG funder of labeling GMO products (about one million dollars!) The psychiatrists are the biggest drug dealers around, but they have the cloak of protection of Big Pharma as well as persecution by Big Pharma & AMA if they don't write prescriptions. The selective serotonin reuptake inhibitors (SSRI's) work for some, but do not work for many and for a few results in lethal killings. Note the black box warnings on these prescription drugs: homicidal or suicidal ideations. Ideations is another word for ideas. When under the influence of this drug you will have ideas about suicide or killing others. Now, anyone can be 5150'd (to be involuntarily restrained) or baker acted into psychiatric confinement if deemed to be a danger to self and/or others. Isn't it malpractice and criminal negligence to give patients drugs, which make them into killer assassins on innocent children or themselves? The information out there is legion for anyone who cares to look. I have many sources: Dr. Breggin's Toxic Psychiatry, Citizen's Commission on Human Rights (who put the black box warnings on these SSRI's by lawsuit) (cchr.org), and a native American type of healing for a schizophrenic in Coyote Healing, which was a great read. By the way the Native Americans taught a dangerously violent schizophrenic to cope with his schizophrenia and in the process made him a productive member of their tribe. He said he felt the community supported him and, in a way, the whole story feels like he was inspired to go to these people for their help.

He did not take any prescription drugs anymore either. I wonder if he was taking all of these dangerous antidepressants when he had the idea to kill his family? A man I met in NYC told me he almost murdered someone while on a psychiatric drug dispensed by the Veteran's Administration hospital and his mother called his doctor and said "take my son off of this drug!" He had severe PTSD from war trauma and mentioned the last word of the drug name was hydrochloride. I am quite sure this was an SSRI antidepressant and he had no more episodes after being taken off of this drug. The VA is a notoriously illuminati-controlled entity and they are doing a fantastic job of depopulating us. Recently they were in a class action lawsuit with the Legionnaires for killing veterans with poisonous cocktails of psychiatric drugs. I could not make this up. The New York Post did a front-page article about a woman who almost or did murder her teenage daughter under the influence of these antidepressants. WeAreChange.org recently had a list of about 60 mass shootings whereby the shooters were on these psychiatric drugs and John DeCamp made the connection decades ago with the Columbine shooting in his latest edition of The Franklin Cover-Up. David Icke has had numerous articles on his website about the same. There is even a website named doctorsaredangerous.com written by a (you guessed it) doctor exposing our illuminati-controlled sickness industry! You didn't really think they would want us well when there is so much more money in our being ill would you??? You can also research at brutalproof.net!

There are many cures for cancer and more keep popping up all of the time. Recently I saw an article on David Icke about a whistle-blowing scientist who wanted the world to know about Sour Sop fruit aka Graviola. It is sold in Asian and African markets since it is a tropical fruit. The drug company had hired the scientist since they had heard about this miracle fruit and wanted to make money off of it in patented cancer cures. Apparently, this fruit has to be eaten fresh to work and therefore once the drug companies realized they couldn't make money off of it they wanted all knowledge about this cure covered up. It is reportedly 10,000 times more effective than chemotherapy. (NaturalNews.com) I remember seeing this green, prickly oblong fruit in a dream years ago, and wondered what its significance was. I thought maybe it was from another planet or from the future; it was so strange looking. Smoothie King has a Pau d'Arco tea brewed from the bark of a South American tree that is supposed to be anti-viral and anti-bacterial. It is only $10 for a kilogram bag that has two months minimum worth of tea. The man who brought it to the US went through a great deal of difficulty getting it in. The Hoxsey Clinic, which has been run out of the US by the food and drug administration (FDA) now operates in Mexico. Their formula was created by a veterinarian who observed his horse healing himself of cancer by eating burdock. There is an immune booster tea sold at organic coops known as Essiac tea with the same or similar formula, but they are not allowed to market it as a cancer tea. It has Burdock root, Sheep Sorrel, Slippery Elm bark and Turkey Rhubarb root in it. Dr. Burzynski has a clinic in Houston that cures cancer with neoplaston's, but he has been almost shut down by the FDA on some technical issue (prescribing drugs without FDA approval, among other "issues" the main unspoken issue being that since neoplaston's turn on cancer suppressing genes and turn off tumor causing genes Big Pharma, whom TX AMA really represent would lose money hand over fist) because cancer is BIG business and no one is allowed to interfere with Big Pharma's profits. Dr. Burzynski is truly independent. He has no affiliations with Big Pharma or the US Government is being a Polish immigrant who set up his own clinic. He has spent millions of dollars and fifteen years defending against the FDA's harassment lawsuits and his patients have repeatedly testified for him, but the harassment goes on when big profits are being interfered with. Suzanne Somer's book, Knockout! Is a good resource (available for 1 cent on the internet) and she writes about the many doctors doing research on cancer cures. (About eight of them are now dead in the most suspicious circumstances.) Dr. Burzynski is in this book too. An excellent internet movie is Cancer: The Forbidden Cures, which also mentions Burzynski's clinic and also mistletoe juice, which is very popular in Germany. Germany has doctors prescribing herbal cures and remedies. Nowhere is any country following the Rothschild Big Pharma culture of synthetic drugs more than the English-speaking countries. Dr. Mercola at drmercola.com recently wrote about Ayurvedic medicine, which is 5000 years old and based on Indian tradition. Chinese medicine is also ancient and based on herbs and oil massages typical of Edgar Cayce's cures, which worked 99% of the time. Dr. Mercola also wrote a fascinating article about Dr. Burzynski finally winning after 15 years of harassment from the FDA & Texas Medical Board whose Director, Roberta Kalafut, resigned after a class action lawsuit from a bunch of pissed off doctors. Dr. Hulda Clark, PhD and N.D. have a free eBook and YouTube video: The Cure for All Diseases. She states that lack of proper nutrition is responsible for 900 Nutritional Deficiency Diseases. Exercise and diet are extremely important. A cured cancer patient who worked at Texas Collision in San Antonio gladly told me her oncologist sent her to Mexico, where she was told to eat organic (pesticides like Round-Up cause cancer) had vitamin C infusions and met with nutritionists. She appeared to be in glowing good health and very satisfied. Pesticides are manufactured by the petrochemical industry who have an elite status with our government. They not only kill bugs; they kill us too. It just amazes me to see the gall of fake charities like the Cancer Cure Foundation. Most of them care only about the money and nothing else. They are the worst. Dr. Mercola sells many a nutritional supplement and is a big advocate of turmeric for its cancer fighting ability. Natural news recently mentioned sea cucumber, as being 95% effective against breast cancer and the Romanians even had an herbal tea, they sold for cancer that cost about 80 cents a box. An old man recently got on the internet telling how he cured his stage IV prostate cancer with baking soda-alkalizing his body. He drank baking soda water once or twice a day with a teaspoon of baking soda because cancer thrives in an acidic environment and it loves, loves, loves sugar! Another English man relayed to davidicke.com how he cured his cancer by eating 10 servings a day of fresh fruits and vegetables-this also alkalizes the body. No matter how hard Big Pharma stonewalls the cures they WILL get out. Once people realize alkalizing the body is the key that will be it for Big Pharma. Who wants to pay hundreds of thousands of dollars for painful chemo and radiation when a 53-cent box of baking soda allegedly works about one hundred times better without the distress! More cures are flooding in and this information is just the beginning.

Soursop Fruit

knockout! by Suzanne Somers

Cancer: The Forbidden Cures

Soursop Fruit (most powerful anti-cancer)

google: Hoxsey clinic

davidicke.com

Post-Traumatic Stress Disorder

A very debilitating anxiety condition underlying many addictions and addictive behaviors PTSD is treated with exposure therapy, cognitive behavioral therapy, eye movement desensitization recovery (EMDR), and anti-depressant and anti-anxiety drugs. Massive Psychic Trauma details a doctor's experience working with massively traumatized concentration camp survivors. Basically, he stated, practically, that the best thing for these massively traumatized individuals was to try to live as normal a life as possible. I agree, but I do know it IS difficult. People, meaning the public, have no clue what massive trauma does to a person. They know nothing about panic attacks, intrusive memories, extreme fear crippling your everyday life, depression from an overwhelming condition that never ceases, pacing all night because you are too afraid to go to sleep, living in a house with iron bars across every window and door and still feeling unsafe, the teeth grinding, backpain from extreme muscle tension, death fantasies to escape your hell-life, etc. My sympathy goes out to anyone who has this condition. It is straight from Hell and no amount of money can be used to un-devastate the sufferer's life. I personally think it is one of the absolute worst conditions anyone can have. Like a Dementor it sucks all the joy out of your life and only leaves you with the horrific memories in a black hole. In Newsmax, it was listed second as the most debilitating condition. Number one was a stroke. No wonder so many with PTSD end up addicts; it's the only way they can feel "normal" again! Because of the "survivors" lifelong difficulty coping with stress many wind-up homeless and in the streets. PTSD people are often very nervous and highly agitated people and homelessness only adds to the agitation, suffering, and stress. PTSD is the residual of brutal rapes, brutal near murders, sexual assaults in the military and in childhood, war trauma, gang rapes, tortures, and some horrific trauma perpetrated by a monster upon a victim as well as horrific catastrophes. Think Hurricane Katrina, bombings of Hiroshima and Nagasaki, and tsunami floods where the victims lost everything and almost died or saw others die horrifically.

The extreme trauma causing this debilitating condition causes structural changes to the brain's hippocampi and amygdala caused by the glucocorticoids flooding the brain in a fight or flight panic. The adrenals go into overdrive at time of trauma overproducing these chemicals. The brain will be forever anatomically changed and the survivor's cortisol levels will stay unregulated and out of whack. This is probably why PTSD is so difficult to treat and so very resistant to treatment. How is therapy going to cure massive brain damage? This massive brain damage can be physically measured too. The problem is that even though the trauma can last for minutes it leaves forever brain damage resulting in unregulated moods; out of control stress reactions and rage. Survivors often live in extreme poverty or homelessness and are usually very isolated due to the misunderstanding of the public and the inability for other people to understand what they're dealing with. Many survivors have maladaptive coping stress responses and in many cases of massive trauma a tendency to commit crimes. Child rape "survivors" have a way higher tendency to wind up in the porn industry or prostitution. Their boundaries have already been destroyed and their coping mechanisms annihilated; for many prostitution, will be an easier choice than working a normal job with all of its inherent stresses. The public seems to have an impossible time understanding the devastating effects of trauma-suffice it to say the trauma equals massive brain damage that never goes away leading to permanent mood dysregulation. If you look at the statistics on porn stars many have early demises from suicides, murders, drug overdoses and cancer. It is not only a destructive lifestyle, but clearly the porn actresses have horrific lives. We seem to have the attitude that if someone else's child is being molested it's no one's business but condemn that child as an adult for being a porn star. Do we still feel uninvolved if that raped child becomes seriously PTSD'd and in an attempt to "feel normal" resorts to using drugs, becomes a drug addict, and burglarize homes? Do we believe as a nation, we should turn our backs on these seriously damaged people and blame them for their dysfunction or perhaps child protection laws should be ENFORCED and all child rapists locked up forever? Whatever the cost is the children need to be protected. A school teacher once stated that if every child filled out a one-page questionnaire all students could be easily screened for child abuse. So why isn't this being done? I guess it's not being done so that the elite pedophiles can continue to have their meat market in children. All of this is possible by not prosecuting organized pedophiles, allowing children to remain in extremely abusive homes, and having almost no outreach for the resulting runaways and staffing the homes (think Boystown) with pedophiles. Where is the protection for children? This guarantees the huge underground networks will continue to have their meat market in children. It also guarantees that the Dutrouxs of this world will always be able to find more children to kidnap and the Satanists like Larry King of The Franklin Cover-Up will continue to traffic children, which by the way, he has never been prosecuted for most likely due to his Bush-Reagan connections. Cathy O'Brien writes how she was trafficked to Bush and her daughter Kelly was trafficked to Herbert Walker Bush, Sr. among others. Bryce Taylor (Thanks for The Memories) writes about how she was trafficked to Ronald Reagan and how his bedtime stories involved bestial child pornography. Sick elites WILL have their sicknesses indulged and we, as a society, are paying for it in lost productivity, increased crime, and the devastated lives of their victims.

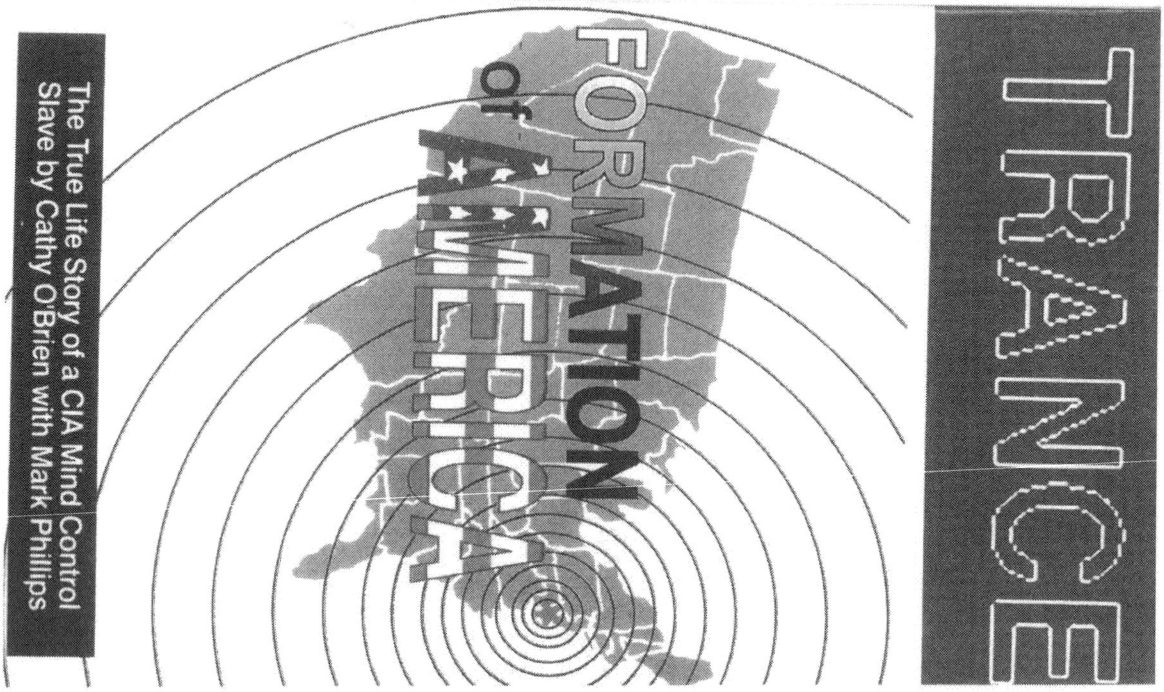
TRANCE
FORMATION of AMERICA
The True Life Story of a CIA Mind Control Slave by Cathy O'Brien with Mark Phillips

THE FRANKLIN COVER-UP
Child Abuse, Satanism, and Murder in Nebraska
by John W. DeCamp
SECOND EDITION with NEW STARTLING REVELATIONS

BrutalProof!

Hillary knew I was a mind-controlled slave, and, like Bill Clinton, just took it in stride as a 'normal' part of life in politics. [She] was fully clothed and stretched out on the bed sleeping when Hall's wife and I arrived.

'Hillary, I brought you something you'll really enjoy. Kind of an unexpected surprise. Bill ordered her out of the meeting and I took her to my bedroom and made an interesting discovery. She is literally a two-faced (referring to my vaginal mutilation carving) bitch'.

'Hmm?' Hillary opened her eyes and sleepily roused herself. 'Show me'. Hall's wife ordered me to take my clothes off while Hillary watched. 'Is she clean?' Hillary asked, meaning disease free.

'Of course, she's Byrd's', [Hall's wife] responded, continuing the conversation as though I were not there. 'Plus, I heard Houston say something about her being a Presidential Model, whatever the hell that's supposed to mean'.

'It means she's clean', Hillary said matter-of-factly as she stood up.

I was not capable of giving thought to such things back then, but I am aware in retrospect that all Presidential Model slaves I knew seemed to have an immunity to social diseases. It was a well known fact in the circles I was sexually passed around in that government level mind-controlled sex slaves were 'clean' to the degree that none of my abusers took precautions such as wearing condoms.

Hall's wife patted the bed and instructed me to display the mutilation. Hillary exclaimed, 'God!' and immediately began performing oral sex on me. Apparently aroused by the carving in my vagina, Hillary stood up and quickly peeled out of her matronly nylon panties and pantyhose. Uninhibited despite a long day in the hot Sun, she gasped, 'Eat me, oh, god, eat me now'. I had no choice but to comply with her orders, and Bill Hall's wife made no move to join me in my distasteful task. Hillary had resumed examining my hideous mutilation and performing oral sex on me when Bill Clinton walked in. Hillary lifted her head to ask, 'How'd it go?'

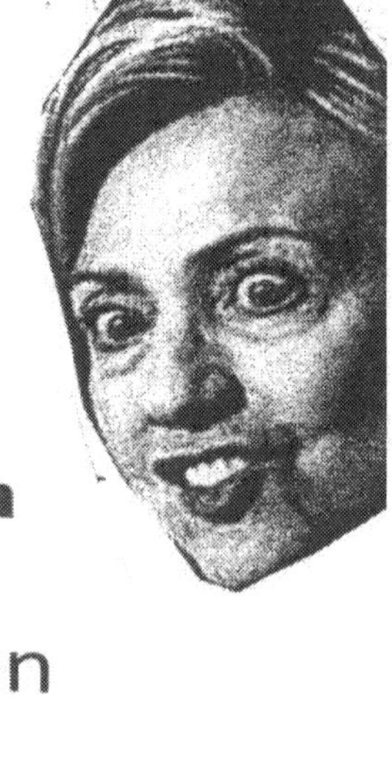

Book: Trance-Formation of America

Hillary Clinton & Sex Slave Cathy O'Brien

It's time for these truths to be told and for society to quit tolerating these horrific crimes being done to the most vulnerable. Child sex abuse results in the most extreme trauma similar to the massive trauma of concentration camp survivors. Most have obsessive-compulsive behaviors and intrusive memories, which they try to self-medicate for by drug use. They are trying to self-medicate their PTSD symptoms and the sad thing is once they are off drugs then they are dealing with the extremely painful PTSD symptoms and life does NOT SUDDENLY BECOME BETTER!!! They are suffering through the very painful, depressing, anxious discomfort that drove them to drugs to begin with. Many prostitutes are products of incest, which is a very nice word for the very unpleasant words' child rape. We have pretty words like incest and molestation for brutal child rape. The words themselves get these perpetrators off the hook because they imply it's not such a big deal after all, so the person can easily get over it. This is a LIE. It is one of the biggest lies of all. I have even seen a well- known TV psychiatrist imply that a woman could get over her Katrina caused PTSD with a therapist and I can honestly say my orthodontist told me she has PTSD from Katrina and just the fact that she mentioned it shows me she is not getting over it just like that. If a highly intelligent professional orthodontist finds PTSD a struggle what is the prognosis for the rest of us?? It's like telling me your worst nightmare and then LIVE THROUGH IT. Then come back and tell me you were strong enough to recover on your own. Our society and all societies are so full of judgement and condemnation for the most injured among us. Most people assume nurses like working with patients, but many burn out very quickly working in Psychiatry and Alzheimer's wards. Some are in the profession for a paycheck. Some do care but burn out with the stresses of the job and understaffing. The measure of the greatness of a nation is in how they protect and treat their most vulnerable. Our nation has failed miserably in protecting its kids and part of this is in all of the child rape and Catholic church involvement. The Vatican (that international criminal corporation) is on the website vaticancrimes.us for over ten million documented crimes against children. (It has since been taken down.) Most of the crimes involve child rape and sodomy, but many also involve slave labor, neglect, child kidnapping, starvation and even Satanic Ritual Abuse. Many people still support this vast criminal organization, which is beyond my comprehension how they can. Still, this criminal organization collects $50 billion a year and still has Crimens Solicitanus as a policy, which basically means no prosecuting of child rape or reporting it. The newest Pope Francis has reinforced this policy with the threat of imprisonment for whistleblowers- he is a criminal too. On the one hand, he has made himself very popular, promising financial reform and telling everyone what they want to hear about the greed and corruption of the bankers and on the other hand he has slyly gouged any child protections out of the Vatican policies. These are evil geniuses and they know how to manipulate the masses with extremely clever PR. No one seems to look at their actions vs. their words. The ONLY thing the Vatican cares about is money and they will say anything to keep the money flowing in; the Vatican is now run by Jesuits, who have the blackest history anyone can have with the exception of the British Monarchy! These criminals know they are safe due to 99.99% of the people never doing any research whatsoever, but just swallowing every lie on TV. The British Monarchy does not hold up to scrutiny either for anyone doing any research at all. They are actually descendants of PIRATES! Queen Elizabeth took 10 Indian children out of Kamloops "residential school" in 1969 and none of these children has ever been seen again. She has never accounted for these ten missing children and William Coombs, the last living witness, was murdered in a very suspicious medical mistreatment scenario in a Vancouver hospital. Vancouver is the hub of international child sex trafficking (one of the top three in the world according to UNESCO in 1999) and along the Highway of Tears hundreds of native women and children have disappeared or been found murdered. Many remains have been found by hunters, hikers and even motorists by the side of Highway 16. Most recently a 26-year-old honors student, Loretta Saunders, was found murdered with the cover story being that her tenants murdered her. It resembles the killing of the graduate student in Girl with the Dragon Tattoo when she gets very close to the core of the human trafficking and is murdered in her own apartment; she also was working on her thesis. It seems when one gets very close to the truth of the child sex trafficking and snuff film networks one winds up dead or in hiding (Kevin Annett) especially when one is getting ready to publish the truth. Another sadistic pedophile-murderer was Gordon Northcott, who fled Vancouver and relocated to Riverside, California to avoid the law. He allegedly was running a child prostitution network for the elite pedophiles in Los Angeles and there "wasn't enough evidence to prove" this, but it would have been very lucrative for him and would have provided him with the funding to build the chicken ranch and pay the bills too. He claimed he had been sexually abused as a young boy, which is believable because sometimes severely traumatized people go into repetition compulsion of the original trauma meaning he would've committed the same traumas done to him to other young boys. A very red flag is how the police tried to cover the missing boy up (Walter Collins) by claiming he was returned to his mother and forcing a runaway on her. When she insisted, the runaway wasn't her son the Captain forced her into a lockdown psychiatric unit. This reek of complicity and maybe the higher ups in the police department were involved (as they often are), which would explain why Northcott evaded responsibility for his vicious crimes for years. David Icke writes at length about the pedophilia, Satanism and human sacrifices by the elite and how people do not get into the elite inner circles unless they are willing to do homosexual acts and swear allegiance to he who has no name. Sandusky got away with his pedophilia crimes for many decades with Paternos full knowledge and consent; the assistant coach reported seeing Sandusky rape a little boy in the locker room and stated he reported it and still nothing was done. I wonder where this little boy is and is he an addict now or dead?? If you search male prostitution and the elite, you'll see how young runaways have to prostitute themselves for food to eat and how they are preyed upon by married men in professional positions. The really sick and sad part of this story is how so many of them are abused to death and how they are abused by society in every way: by their families, the police, johns, foster care systems; by everyone they come into contact with. When you research child snuff films you go into the heart of the darkness and into Satanism. Not only are young, street boys raped and murdered routinely, but if they somehow manage to get out of street life they are forever damaged by the memories and the trauma and have difficulty having a normal life. Many are driven to drug addiction. Their problems are compounded by the lack of vocational training, the lack of an education and the lack of the financial wherewithal to obtain them as well as the supreme psychological damage done by life on the streets. Two young boys in this video were murdered and mutilated after being interviewed presumably for talking; one admitted living in a major corporate apartment! What was even more horrific is how the cop said that the only customers interested in the black male prostitutes tended to be sadists! The child has a choice of death by torture by a fellow inhuman sadist or the agonizing death by starvation! This is truly Satan's America and we are all complicit by our doing nothing. I saw this film when I "search-engine'd" Hillary's Peril. The numbers of 666 are within the name of Vancouver in Chaldean numerology. The child trafficking is the reason there are so many missing children in the USA and millions more missing in Eastern Europe. The trail leads to the Pope, the Monarchies and Royalty, elite Luciferians and satanic businessmen, doctors, lawyers, judges, police chiefs, famous actors, writers, musicians, and the military elite. These people are icons in these positions, wealthy & powerful. Defense agency employees at DARPA, the Pentagon, NSA, State Dept. and others have been investigated for downloading thousands of pictures of child pornography. Many bodies of murdered children have been found at the Windsor's properties not only at Kensington, but also at Windsor owned land at Haut de La Garenne, where the corpses of at least six small children were found and at least 140 children abused with up to 100 suspects. Haut de la Garenne is on Jersey Island, which is a haunt of the rich and famous as well as being a banking center. When Lenny Harper started doing a real investigation, he was taken off the case. This investigation was covered up, naturally, and the honest police chief was quickly replaced with a do-nothing police chief who would not investigate these horrific crimes against children. It was the same with the Belgium Monster except this case involved removing an honest magistrate and replacing him with another who would do as he was told. I am quite sure Ian Watkins, front man for the Lost Prophets, never believed he would be charged with child rapes due to his connection to pedophiles in Wales. He also had the emblematic Satanic cross on his ear and black dragon tattoos symbolic of evil incarnated. When the victims are the bottom 1% the top 1% who victimize them are seldom charged. The perpetrators of child sexual abuse are the most likely to turn sadistic and then go to the next level of sadistic killers. Frequently, these disturbed individuals were sexually abused themselves as children: Gordon Stewart Northcott allegedly was sexually abused by his whole family as a child and his behaviors by having a raging libido, and taste for physical abuse bear testament to some type of sexual abuse; similarly, in Choreography Corey Haim's abnormally sexualized behavior spoke volumes to the author, Corey Feldman, that something had been done to Corey Haim. The serial killer, John Martin Crawford, who murdered multiple native women in Canada also had a voracious appetite for food and sex constantly eating and masturbating in his jail cell. Again, this serial killer was allegedly sexually abused at least twice as a little boy in the extraordinary book: Just Another Indian. Clearly, the sexual abuse suffered by these young boys has permanent damaging effects. The early sexual abuse of these victims turned them into obsessive adults with food addictions, alcohol addictions and drug addictions----obsessive-compulsive behaviors typical of severe PTSD. When John Martin Crawford was on his killing sprees he would obsessively drink massive quantities of alcohol and shoot up drugs constantly the whole day or night long. The same behaviors were typical of Corey Haim minus the murders. Obsessions & Compulsions take over these damaged personalities or perhaps the demons of gluttony, lust, and bacchanalian drinking. They enter during the traumatic sexual abuse that opens the child's soul to these entities as described in Dr. Modi's book: Remarkable Healings. This may be a controversial book in the psychiatric profession, but entities in one's soul is backed up by another psychiatrist who did hypnosis and regressions: Louise Ireland-Frey in Freeing Captives. At one point, she even describes a lizard entity within her patient's energy field. She writes of child molestations due to dark forces. Roxana Shirazi writes in The Last Living Slut how she lived a groupie life having sex with entire rock bands without any concern of their treatment of her until she hit an all-time low with Dizzy Reed. His vicious texts like: "I'm gonna tell him what a slut you are" or "I hope you have many more abortions you piece of shit!" I guess are the underlying attitude many rock stars have to groupies. I don't care how polite the words during seductions; the behaviors say it all. Groupies are disposable. Dizzie Reed hit the nail on the head when he asked her if she was molested. She was molested by two men as a child as young as five and became as hypersexual as Corey Haim and John Crawford. Once again, the out of control compulsions reign. PTSD is an annihilation of one's soul and I can't put it any other way. In the sexual abuse treatment, counseling center (Fort Lauderdale) there were masks and on every single one of them lines showing faces cleaved in two. The split faces show the damage that is unfixable and surely when I saw Roxana Shirazi interviewing Michael Monroe I thought she had that PTSD look of an annihilated soul. Today I read how she spent a month in a psychiatric unit and was diagnosed with PTSD. It hasn't taken away her talent for writing. The book was a great read and I couldn't put it down. I'm willing to bet groupies have been one of the most sexually abused people on earth BEFORE they became groupies as are porn stars and prostitutes. It's difficult to find a prostitute or porn star who hasn't been sexually abused and when you are speaking about a high-strung group of very emotionally fragile people you are talking PTSD. I really think PTSD is a form of a nervous breakdown where your defenses are so hammered you can no longer cope. The resulting hormone stress response causes long term brain damage to the hippocampi and amygdala actually changing the sizes of these structures. Now add the epigenetic changes caused by the rush of adrenal corticosteroids bathing the brain in chemicals and you've got a dizzying array of changes - all permanent. Brain damage that's permanent! Anyone with two active brain cells should be alarmed at this information because in the United States alone legions of children are sexually abused and damaged for life. Not only is this a horrific crime, but the terrible effects of post-traumatic stress disorder have lifelong effects of diminished productivity resulting in trillions of dollars in lost productivity in the U.S. Legions of PTSD sufferers wind up on disability due to their inadequate stress coping and this alone is a huge part of the entitlement expenditures. PTSD also causes bruxism, or teeth grinding, which can result in very expensive dental bills. The constant tension can result in arthritis. PTSD sufferers have double the rates of arthritis and hepatitis of the normal population. My suspicion is that they also suffer from much higher rates of heart attacks and strokes. They tend to die of cancer for cancer is a stress related disease with the stress damaging the immune system response. We are creating the sickest society of all with our trauma culture. Roxana Shirazi described her PTSD symptoms as so horrific it was as if they were sent by Satan. Dr. Modi writes in Remarkable Healings that there are literally demonic forces involved in psychological attack on these victims. These negative energies hold pieces of the sufferers shattered soul and massage it or put devices onto it to keep them in pain. Evil thrives on pain. To think Vancouver is rated one of the top three places in the world for child rape by UNESCO in 1999 and that the Chaldean numerology of Vancouver includes three sixes. The letters v and u are equivalent to the number 6 each and every one. A New York policeman stated to Kevin Annett that a child had to be raped at least 15 times before anyone took the complaint seriously. This makes shattering a child's soul and demonic activity legal here. Rape IS demonic and child rape is very demonic and accepted ritual with Satanists. The policeman went on to say that child rape is basically legal in the United States and these children do not fare well as adults in any way, not socially, not vocationally; not health-wise. Can we afford to keep enabling demonic pedophiles? Can we afford to keep erring on the side of the demons? What about the souls of these little ones? Is it any surprise that many of the child rapists commit their acts under alcoholic or drug influences or that many of them are practicing Satanists? The Canadian & American governments willfully and viciously depopulate/kill off natives without much of any outcry from the Europeans who moved in and took over. It's the story of America, Canada, the rainforests, Africa, Asia and about 50 more countries who have lost their sovereignty due to CIA and Economic hit men and takeovers to place US puppets in the wake of the destruction. Think Iraq, Chile, Iran, Japan, Philippines, the breakup of Yugoslavia and the Bosnian Serbian war, etc. It goes on now in the Ukraine and Victoria Nuland's cell phone conversation about paying $5 billion for a regime change in Ukraine is exactly what's been going on all over the world for decades' courtesy of the USA and the NATO nations. Victoria Nuland should be prosecuted for her violating the rights of a sovereign nation, but she gets away with her crimes as does everyone else in a position to do so in the USA who does the bidding of the shadow government (Rothschild Khazarian Mafia/Zionists/British Monarchy/Military-Industrial Complex). Certainly, Barney Franks and Christopher Dodd, both of whom promptly retired after creating the bail-in Dodd-Franks law should be prosecuted for treason. Maybe it will take a bank bail-in to finally wake up the sleeping public—*ZZZZZZZZZZZZZZZZZZZZZZZZZZZZZZZZZZZZZZZZZ*. Barney Franks, former congressman was major league involved with the Franklin Cover-Up child sex ring coming out of

Nebraska. In fact, Paul Bonacci describes being raped by him in a Washington, D.C. townhouse multiple times. Barney Franks was clearly beholden to Wall Street and the bankers and they have him firmly in their clutches for anyone photographed with children can always be threatened with the scandal later on. Same old politician's stories centuries later…it was much like this with the Roman empire with Tiberius and his minnows of whom many were thrown into the ocean to their deaths after he was through with them. Another serial rapist morphed into a serial killer. Sounds like Jersey Island of the Channel Islands in the UK for Edward Heath also would have the boy's bodies thrown into the water after he was finished raping them and then murdering them. Jimmy Saville (constantly spending time with Margaret Thatcher & Prince Charles) was involved in the raping of children as well as procuring them for other elite pedophiles who needed to remain undercover. They were free to do anything they wanted with these Care Home Kids for they had no one to protect them. Social Workers, nurses, aides and all staff at hospitals and care homes were complicit in the abuse even if they did not actively abuse these kids by covering the abuse up and allowing it to go on unimpeded.

FREEING
the
CAPTIVES
The Emerging Therapy of Treating Spirit Attachment
Louise Ireland-Frey, M.D.

REMARKABLE
HEALINGS
A Psychiatrist Discovers Unsuspected
Roots of Mental and Physical Illness
SHAKUNTALA MODI, M.D.

"The nexus between homosexuality and violence is notorious. We have motorcycle gangs, black leather boys and rough trade addicted to chains, torture, slaves, and sadism." *Excerpt from Violence and Homosexuality by Dr. Paul Cameron* who also noted the "**top serial killers were all homosexuals.**"

"Rape in prison is not a joke....Some inmates can no longer deal with the sexual abuse and commit suicide. Others....become "alternative women" in order to survive. **Studies have shown that victims of prison rape attempt to regain their manhood by raping women and children when released from prison."**

Excerpt: Corruption Behind Bars (Inmates' Boy Toy)

by Gary York

—

The retired New York City cop stared at me with the eyes of someone who knew too much. He said matter of factly,

"It's standard practice here not to prosecute child rapists for a first offense. They have to rape a kid ten, maybe fifteen times before there's a good chance of conviction".

"You mean it's not a crime to rape a child, in practice?" I replied.

"Not really. Not under our legal system it isn't"

Whenever people ask me why we've established our own common law court of justice, I simply tell them that story.

New Yorkers engage strangers with a familiarity unknown to most Canadians, and so it wasn't long before I fell into a conversation with the cop in question during my all-night vigil at JFK airport last week, awaiting my flight home. He was a Brooklyn precinct veteran who knew the score. At one point, to emphasize what he'd told me about child rapists, he handed me that day's New York Times.

"Small world" he remarked, pointing to one article.

The story was about a network of Catholic priests and bishops in central Germany who had for years targeted the same children for rape and trafficking. None of them had ever been convicted.

"People are going to have to take the law into their own hands" I said to him, after skimming the article in disgust.

Child Rape

97% not prosecuted

"Damn straight" the cop replied.

Someone once said that if the sun comes up every morning, it is only because of people of good will. I disagree. There are more than enough of us with good will; that has

Laws to Protect Children Always Created by Victim Child's Family Not D.C. Politicians As A General Rule-Laws Protecting Children Not Enforced

Except to Remove Good Children From Stable, Good Families

Archon Laws-Do the Inversion Of What They Are Supposed to Do

Geoengineering aka Chemtrails (Billboards Going Up All Across America!)

Geoengineeringwatch.org is an excellent website exposing chemtrails (not to be confused with contrails), which are laced with barium, white blood cells, aluminum, and other radioactive elements, and are linked to asthma, and Morgellons's Disease. The Department of Defense is involved and there is an excellent YouTube video that exposes the DOD spraying chemtrails all over the USA. It is now being done on a massive scale all over the world and Europe too. There is now technology for weather warfare (HAARP), seeding storms, causing blizzards and earthquakes (fracking), causing tsunamis, etc. A new class action lawsuit can be seen on YouTube regarding the chemtrails and the Death Agenda is openly admitted in court. (Depopulation) This video was posted in Dec, 2013. Public awareness was nil when I marched to expose this three years ago, but has rapidly increased. Geoengineering was written about in this magazine: Health Freedom News, which is doing a phenomenal job exposing Vaccines, Monsanto GMO poisons, the Cancer Industry, and many other health topics. Health Freedom News is clearly not illuminati for they are really exposing them and if I were a teacher it would be required reading for my class.

Wealth

The Arbitration Scam (against the little guy and for the big corporations)

Nowadays, many companies (to avoid class action lawsuits) have written arbitration agreements into their contracts. Gold dealers have these arbitration clauses as well as cell phone companies. Unbeknownst to the hapless consumers for the privilege of convenience they sign their rights away and agree to pay the salaries of the arbitrating judges and other arbitrating employees, which can cost upwards of $5,000 a day. The arbitration proceedings are kept in strictest confidence acting like a seal on the courtroom records. I don't see arbitration benefitting you the little guy in any way!!!! Thank God for me the arbitration person in charge told me my problem belonged in small claims court where it could be resolved by one appearance and the $50 filing fee. Small Claims Courts are really people's courts! There are great Small Claims Court books available on the internet and in libraries. (alibris.com, thriftbooks.com, etc.)

Glass-Steagall & Joining the BRICs Nations to Save Ourselves!

Glass-Steagall is now on the table in the majority of states and all parties' platforms. It would separate commercial banking (depositor's accounts) and investment banking (Wall Street Gambling in stocks, bonds, and especially derivatives contracts). The Zionist Federal Reserve has over printed the Federal Reserve dollar to the tune of $4 trillion. With the BRICs countries now dealing in their own currencies officially starting on October 1st, 2016 all these dollars they were previously forced to use will be floating back to the US en masse. Expect inflation and then hyperinflation. Without Glass-Steagall Banksters can grab your savings and any money not FDIC insured and keep them to bail themselves out-they're insolvent. Call your Congressperson and insist he/she support this law-your life depends upon it-your life savings/deposits/checking accounts are at stake. 1-202-224-3121 and ask for your congressperson by name. Web of Debt is a good read and webofdebt.com is a good website to visit. Ellen Brown is an attorney who knows how to research and she shows us how we wound up in this fiscal mess and how we can get out of it. Be sure to see the Takedown of Glass-Steagall either on youtube.com or larouchepac.com. When Bill Clinton did not want to repeal Glass-Steagall he was hit with the Zionist/Monarchy manipulated Monica Lewinsky scandal and endless litigation. He also had Zionist owned Congress against him so he finally gave in and the Graham-Leach bill was passed. The results are the bank bail-ins, dot-com and housing bubbles, endless printing of Federal Reserve notes, derivatives scams, which are nothing more than financial contracts whereby the banks having them are going to have to come up with large sums of money they don't have to honor these contracts and then they intend to steal money from depositors to make up the difference. I would not advise having large sums of money in any bank because of this treasonous law.

Ellen Brown covers Glass-Steagall and State Banks too, which are largely credit institutions to fund state projects and private businesses in opposition to the Wall Street Gambling type casino banks we have now. For a banker to go into the casino business is exactly what Wall Street has done! I don't agree with paying their gambling debts off; they can sink or swim on their own. The big six banks have tons of derivatives contracts and I mean these banks: Chase Bank, Bank of America, Wells Fargo; Citibank. The Bank of North Dakota is the only state-owned bank in the country. It provides privately owned banks and credit unions with lending and capital support to improve their performance. Many say the state-owned bank has lent quite a bit of money opposed to the Wall Street banks hoarding of their bail-out funds. North Dakota has a low unemployment rate. A point to make is that there is nothing federal about the Federal Reserve; it is privately owned like Federal Express. The Federal Reserve is destroying the value of the Federal Reserve note (aka our "dollar") by overprinting it in Quantitative Easing Scams to the tune of $85 billion a month. This note is backed by nothing, which is why countries want to get away from our "dollar" for self-preservation. Eventually Weimar style hyperinflation will result. Our dollar is tanking like the Titanic and other countries see no need to tank with us especially since foolish voters voted in so many crooks who are destroying America. China and Japan have just agreed to trade with each other without using the dollar as a medium of exchange. Thanks to Obama's war provocations Russia's Putin has made it clear Europe is not going to be buying Russian gas with the dollar so we will be seeing major inflation in the coming years as he and the one hundred plus BRICs nations all refuse to trade in our dollar-NO longer the world's reserve currency. Where is the Media on this Titanic development??? The chickens are coming home to roost and Americans who have never lived in third world shacks or experienced depression era poverty are going to have new third world type experiences. For sure, Ron Paul is right that the Federal Reserve needs to be audited;

it should have been a long time ago and I would like to know where all the gold is in Fort Knox and why do the western imperialist countries like the U.K., France, Germany and USA have to constantly go to war in places like Mali (very rich in gold) at the time one of their partners is calling for the gold repatriated? Also, what happened to the six and a half trillions of dollars that were appropriated to the Pentagon and disappeared? Again, Congress must be called and pressured about re-instating Glass-Steagall to save the hides of the public citizens. Well managed State Banks create jobs and credit and since this legislation for state banks is on the table in about half of the states it would probably be a good idea to call your Congressperson about supporting a State Bank as well. They finance businesses and smaller infrastructure projects.

A National Credit System

This is a LaRouche platform project that would be a way to finance huge infrastructure projects that are badly needed as our infrastructure is crumbling and some of these bridges are becoming dangerous to drive on; they are so old and poorly maintained. The building of infrastructure would create many jobs (maybe six million) and put taxpayer money to beneficial use. The national credit bank should have no Wall Street ties whatsoever and be strictly for projects that would benefit the people of America. The Treasury Department should be printing Greenbacks for the national bank and Federal Reserve notes should be taken out of circulation and cancelled. The Federal Reserve is under the control of a private cartel of Banksters (Chase and Bank of America who received bail-out money and have about $155 trillion in derivatives contracts coming due at this writing). They are just opportunists out to cheat American people out of their savings with hyperinflationary polices, which are a transfer of wealth from poor and middle class to wealthy. Banks charge interest on debt and usurious interest rates on usurious credit card debt and this is illegal. See how laws are NOT enforced for the criminal elite? They have created a nation of debt-slaves with student debt topping one trillion dollars and the average American working five months a year to pay taxes and living paycheck to paycheck to pay mortgage debt, car loans and credit card debt. Can you believe that at one time the medieval folk of England only worked for five months farming and had enough to last the rest of the year??? They could party the rest of the seven months!

I am reading Progressive Populist's December 1st newsletter and the article states that only $600 billion dollars can eradicate world poverty. This is a crime to have so much poverty when the wealthy scoundrels are hiding at least $32 trillion dollars in the Cayman Islands and the Rothschild's with their financial schemes now control over half the world's wealth somewhere in the neighborhood of about $500 trillion-an unfathomable amount of money. The LIBOR banking fraud involved $350 trillion dollars and was barely a blip on TV. Recouping this one fraud could make the world rich-not just erase poverty but create an abundant world again. This LIBOR fraud is the biggest one ever. It is almost eleven times the amount of money hiding offshore. To give you a clue the Obamas, Clintons, and the Bushes are all hiding money offshore. As usual, the illuminati and their servants' crimes are unprosecuted, but the rest of us would likely get life in prison. They are even making it illegal for the indigent to be homeless. They are making it illegal for churches & activists to feed the homeless-$300 to $500 fines. One man served fifty years for stealing a jacket. I'm sure it was an illuminati department store he was stealing from. Another man whose parents died stole a loaf of bread from a post office/convenience store to feed himself and his sister. He spent about twenty-five years in federal prison. These are crimes against the people. No one should starve or have to steal bread to avoid starving in the richest of the rich countries in the world. Muammar Gaddafi took far better care of his people than this. He made sure the poorest of the poor in Africa had housing before he moved out of his tent. He made sure everyone had food and water too greening Libya's deserts! Our leaders are an international disgrace and known criminals!

Not only the LIBOR FRAUD, but then a huge FOREX fraud took place. No wonder the Exchange Rates were ridiculously costly. Banks have been bailed out to the tune of trillions of dollars and now they want depositor's funds for a Barney Frank-Christopher Dodd Bail-In!! The public is being defrauded big time! The biggest fraud of all is the derivatives contracts-gambling liabilities of the banks in the thousands of trillions of dollars-quadrillions!!! 10 to the 15th power! Oxfam has stated repeatedly that poverty is the end result of INJUSTICE and Kevin Annett has shown us this in startling detail in his books*: Love and Death in the Valley* and *Hidden from History: The Canadian Holocaust.* Truly this man does deserve the Nobel Peace Prize!

Poverty is rooted in unequal distribution of food, genocidal policies, tyrannical, evil dictators, embargos by wealthy countries who by definition are unjust (USA for example), and basically injustice. Technology is being withheld from the masses to grow abundant food where absolutely no one would starve and this in itself is a crime. Even the Charity Oxfam clearly is educating its donors that poverty is the result of injustice. Oxfam assisted the Vietnamese farmers in Louisiana after Katrina and got the rice field yields up by 4 times previous yields in Asia. I think they might be an illuminati creation, but I don't really know. I do know their top man speaks the truth: INJUSTICE CREATES POVERTY!

1. Audit the Federal Reserve and make the Bankster's return the missing money, go to prison and pay a huge fine. Audit the Cayman Island accounts and if these scoundrels don't return all of their illegal money to pay off our budget deficits they go to prison too. Pursue the stolen LIBOR money and stolen FOREX money and there would be plenty left to:
   a. Protect and fund social security, Medicare and Medicaid and create city gardens.
   b. Repeal free trade agreements that send jobs overseas: NAFTA, TAFTA, CAFTA, TPP, TPIP, TISA, GATT etc.
   c. Raise the minimum wage to $16 an hour. Believe me, McDonalds and Walmart's can well afford this; they are greedy that is all.
   d. Reopen the state psychiatric facilities with the extra money to house violent insane.
   e. Adopt Muammar Gaddafi's policies: land, cattle, equipment and seeds to farmers.
   f. Free education and healthcare, national currency backed by gold, $50,000 to every newlywed to buy a house; a home for every American without a mortgage.
2. Guns for everyone not proven to be criminally insane or a career criminal. By this I mean the Bushes and Clintons should not be allowed to have guns. They have long criminal track records and when convicted should not be allowed federal retirements off of the tax payers. Traitors should not be allowed government pensions or secret service.

One note here: *it should be absolutely illegal for corporations to pull a Walmart: starvation wages and tell workers to live off of taxpayer funded Medicaid and food assistance. Walmart should be forced to pay $16 an hour or forced out of business and be denied business licenses to stay in business.*

Illuminati Foundations and Charities (BEWARE!)

World Wildlife Fund is an illuminati charity if ever there were one and instead of saving animals they are making rhinos extinct. Anytime the royals are involved in charity you must know there is fraud. They are the most ruthless killers of people and animals on earth and you would be wise to blacklist the WWF "charity". Another one is the ACLU, which defends child killers who killed a little boy in the act of attempted rape and the Soros funded ACLU defends the child killers. This "charity" should be struck off your list forever and ever and if Credo Mobile is funding this charity you should boycott Credo mobile as well. Scary to think $70 million is going to a criminal enterprise like this. What family can defend their little child against that kind of money? But, Curly's family did with a $200 million lawsuit against NAMBLA. Oh, and by the way, Curly's lawyer died an early sudden death too, naturally. He was suing for $200 million in damages and the rapist-killers were well known neighbors like in my dream of the murdered boy. These creeps are all around us protected in prisons, unprosecuted, and getting away with the most evil, heinous crimes while 4-time convicted pot heads rot away in state prisons. I am not for potheads, but they damage mainly their selves while rapists damage many, many victims often for life and can ascend to the next level of murder.

You must watch Chris Everard's Illuminati I, Illuminati II, Illuminati III, and Illuminati IV and after you fully see the evil, psychopathic nature of the "British" Monarchy you must be assured that ANY charity they start is highly suspect and not to be trusted or donated to at all. Then again, this Monarchy is not even British and they represent only their own interests certainly not the interests of the British people who are dying from their austerity policies. (similar to the Zionists NOT representing the Jews, but instead financing the mass slaughter of people during WW2!)

When Charities kill 30,000 animals as PETA did while feigning to protect them and their CEO is paying herself obscene amounts of money (six figures) that is another charity to strike off.

Stealth

Oprah Interviews Child of Jewish Satanic Cult

Oprah Winfrey, exposed Jewish Satanism interviewing Vicki Polin in 1989. Hardcore Satanism involves human and animal sacrifice for money and power. This interview can still be seen on YouTube and Zionism is a Satanic cult that calls itself Jewish but, really Zionist originated from Khazar-A region in Eastern Europe and are not Jewish at all. These cults are still practicing Satanism in the United States, Western Europe, United Kingdom, Australia and elsewhere as well as maintaining control of these countries by only appointing their insiders to elite positions in government and religion. They control America. America is not FREE and never has been. It is a country ruled by vicious sociopaths (33-degree masons, Trilateral Commission, Bilderbergers, and Council of Foreign Relations members) many of whom rape children and laugh at child snuff porn. All Zionist at the top and by this, I mean George Bush Sr., Henry Kissinger, Dick Cheney, the Senators Byrd's, Lawrence King, Hunter Thompson of "I like to kill" comment. (Satanists all of them as is Hillary Clinton, Zionist).

The main websites exposing Jewish Satanic cult are:

- **Smoloko.com**

BrutalProof!

- **davidicke.com**
- **Hiddennolonger.com**
- **brutalproof.net**

Don't forget the activist site: **itccs.org** LaRouche realized long ago that the Windsor's were evil, Satanic criminals engaged in war for profit and insider trading in the stock market who also own vast tracts of land in Canada and the USA via shell corporations, which are typically used to hide ownership in suspicious and illegal activities. (See "*Satanism in Government*" on YouTube)

The Royals of England, Belgium and elsewhere are implicated in crimes of astounding sadism, perversion and corruption. The Throne occupier of England-Elizabeth is not even a legitimate queen. She is of Saxe-Coburg-Gotha German lineage and not even British!!! They have looted, lied, murdered and fraudulently obtained their wealth and position. I don't know about the reptile beings David Icke mentions, but I did have contact with a gifted psychic who told her class about malevolent Reptilians that she could see. I think he is speaking about a reptilian etheric being. Regardless, isn't it enough to know there are truly malevolent elites that have horrific agendas for the rest of us and that people must come together to share information and work together towards a solution to avert them???

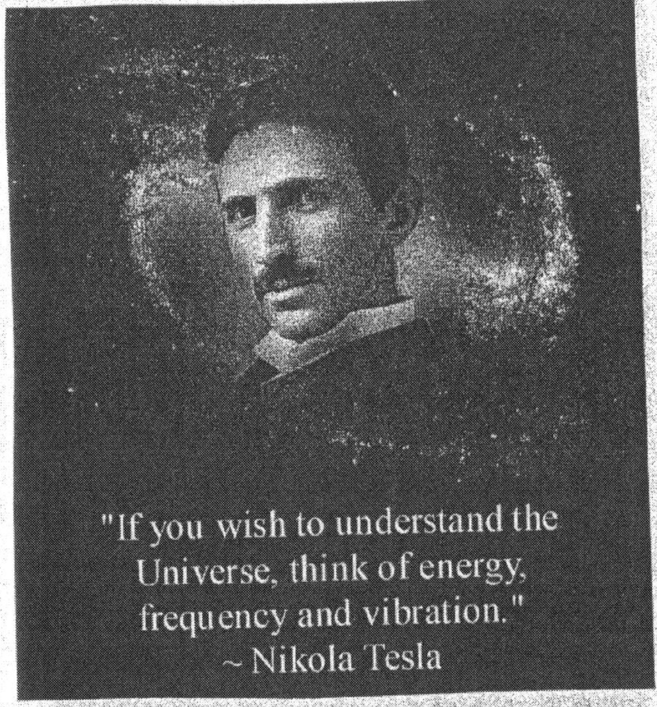
"If you wish to understand the
Universe, think of energy,
frequency and vibration."
~ Nikola Tesla

Tesla Invented Free Energy-Imagine Having NO ELECTRIC BILL!!!

BrutalProof!

Suppressed Inventions, Which Will Change the World (But Not Profit the Illuminati)

The illuminati are also behind the suppression of inventions for the betterment of mankind. Karen Hudes, an illuminati insider (attorney for the World Bank) stated in her interview how 6,000 patents were being suppressed that were for the betterment of mankind. Nikola Tesla, who only wanted his inventions for the betterment of mankind, died from a car accident and immediately thereafter the FBI confiscated all of his research papers and now our government (under illuminati control) uses his findings for wars, which is the last thing Tesla would have wanted. Maybe this is the real reason he suddenly died and the FBI was there to scoop up all of his paperwork. The FBI is controlled by the illuminati, which is why illuminati sex offenders are never apprehended and never go to prison! Tesla also had an assistant named Scherff, which is believed to be Bush Sr. Strange how every time something criminal comes up the name Bush (formerly Scherff) comes up: deregulation of the Savings and loan industry and failure of hundreds of banks and pensioners losing their pensions, the Enron scandal involving a Bush friend, CEO Kenneth Lay, whereby employees and investors lost billions again losing their pensions, deregulation of oil industry and the Deepwater Horizon oil spill resulting in the total contamination of the Gulf and murders of workers, dolphins and wildlife and once again the Bushes are involved in the deregulation. The Bushes are also involved in the lies fomenting the Iraq war and the Iraqi gold has disappeared and a million and a half innocent people are dead. Thanks to the Bushes, the Clintons (go visit the Serbians if you don't believe me) and the Obamas we are now the most hated people on the planet. Everybody hates us so much that if a nuclear bomb were dropped on NYC or Chicago the rest of the world would probably cheer and have a celebration. At the very least they would think it's karma; we've been bombing innocent people all along; people with yellow, brown, and black skins and outright murder of all of these people including the American Indians too. The US has become Murder, Inc. The Bushes are a vital part of the illuminati; they do the English Monarchy's bidding and are controlled by them. The Bushes made sure a private jet carrying out 250 members of the Bin Laden family left the USA the day after 9-11 without any checks whatsoever. They are narcissists for sure and the most malignant of them. Although they portray themselves as good Christian men they have nothing in common with real Christians after all they have broken every commandment especially the one reading Thou Shalt Not Kill for they have shown me over and over and over again they are only too willing to kill babies with phosphorus and depleted uranium and anyone that supports these vicious psychopaths is beyond a fool. It is no surprise to me that a Bush was in Matamoros during the Satanic Ritual Killings of tens of people found in a mass grave there for there are mass graves everywhere the Bushes go or where their policies are followed. (Appendix) It is the same with the Windsor's. The Christian Residential Auschwitz gives proof to their intent for they ruthlessly murdered at least 100,000 children as their sadistic, pedophilic policies were carried out by Satanic priests and nuns masquerading as "Christians." (hiddennolonger.com & Kevin Annett) What remains the most hidden about the Catholic church is that Mind Control Ultra experiments were being done on their unfortunate victims and the lawsuit settlements have covered all of this up with the "do not speak to anybody about this" legal clause, which one must sign and agree to for the temporary financial relief many of these severely damaged "survivors" gain from their impoverished lives. An independent film on YouTube called "Sun Sea & Satan" was financed by Bill Maloney's sister and produced by Bill Maloney. It clearly shows the pedophilia and Satanism surrounding the monarchy-controlled care centers for children in Britain and, not surprisingly, Bill Maloney's sister was found shortly thereafter dead in her apartment. It seems when you produce something of substance exposing the monarchy you will be jailed or murdered. Canada is a monarchy-controlled land and there are mass graves of murdered children everywhere due to monarchy residential school Auschwitz. The Monarchy works closely with the criminal illuminati organization also known as the Vatican, which is documented as committing at least 10,000,000 crimes mostly against helpless, innocent children. (vaticancrimes.us) Nothing is too brutal for these Malignant Psychopaths: raping children to death, kidnapping them, working and starving children to death, freezing them to death (hypothermia), killing them with drugs and injections, sodomizing children and stabbing them to death. (The Ninth Circle-the elite vicious psychopathic organization connected to the Vatican) Read the SYNOPSIS of *Hidden from History: The Canadian Holocaust (hiddennolonger.com)* and you will see the true criminality of the Vatican controlled Catholic church. It is also exposed in the *Memorandum on Eyewitness Evidence of the Organized Abduction, Torture, Exploitation and Murder of Women and Children on Canada's West Coast (Appendix).* Involved are the Royal Canadian Mounted Police, members of the British Columbia government (senior politicians), high ranking within Vancouver Police Department, the judiciary (senior judges), the Canadian military, Hell's Angels, the Hong Kong Triad, "freelance" mobsters from Vancouver and the USA, clergy of the United, Anglican, and Roman Catholic churches, lawyers, state funded aboriginal chiefs chosen by the government for their corruption, the Department of Indian Affairs (which, is corrupt by design), PM Campbell and others. It is funded by the massive drug trade with which it is intimately connected. This is the heart and soul of the illuminati. Illuminati - An international human trafficking ring involving violent child snuff porn, slavery-prostitution, human organ black markets and snuff films with outlets in the Pacific Rim particularly in China and Thailand. This network depends upon the complicity of doctors, coroners, clergy, politicians, social workers, and the cover-up media, which the illuminati own. They have a network of body dumping grounds and mass graves in remote areas and in aboriginal reserves as well as church and monarchy crown land where the RCMP routinely dispose of the bodies of these snuff film and violent porn victims. This whole system is protected by corrupted police, judges, military, church and politicians (PM Campbell who is now a Senator) who are compromised by their involvement in raping these victims. No one cares about these viciously abused women and children and apparently, the Canadians themselves do not either as evidenced by their tolerance for these vicious crimes within their midst. The Pictons were intimately connected with this ring and contrary to the official news story they were not acting alone but were part of this system. They ran a porn and snuff film business called "Piggy's Palace" from Port Coquitlam, a suburb of Vancouver. Young girls are drugged and raped having been brought to the site by Royal Canadian Mounted Police!! Jean-Guy Boudrais, who works for the Canadian military in the computer programming aspect, is the alleged serial killer and he gives seminars in Ontario and Montreal. He is a Freemason. Picton's associate ran "Goodbye Girls" at 999 West Broadway in Vancouver selling snuff films. (It's now relocated or out of business.) Some bodies are weighted down with cement blocks and dumped in Beaver Lake in Stanley Park and others were fed to the pigs on the pig farm. An officer of the RCMP, Bruce Michaelson, a Freemason, is intimately involved in this ring as are a CBC cameraman named Gerry Dunne who is associated with Pogo Productions, a film maker named Dave Collins who OWNS LIONS GATE STUDIOS, an underworld enforcer named Larry, and a porn film star named Tom TASSE. Snuff films sell for up to $250,000 and have eager buyers in Asian countries and the USA. (like the Nicholas Cage film 8 mm) The dirtiest of the dirty cops involved in this criminal enterprise Bob Krisko and the two RCMP officers named Dave and Steven are associated with the Missing Women's Task Force (no wonder there are allegedly thousands of missing women largely unsolved) and use this position to prey on and rape/murder street women in Vancouver. The witness, Annie Parker, stated these men with Boudrais raped and murdered 19-year-old Brianne Voth and drowned her in Coquitlam in association with a prostitute Stella Malloway. She also stated one of these two RCMP officers own a cabin used as a body dumping site (ala Lake-Ng modus operandi, the two Californian serial killers) located ten minutes west of Horseshoe Bay on the Sea to Sky Highway off of a dirt road. Bodies are dumped in a metal cistern at this hunting camp. Boudrais stated to this victim Parker that he and Dave and Steven murder four to six women a year enjoying the protection of the Canadian judicial system for who really cares if it is street women and natives being murdered? Annie Parker herself was inducted into this system by her father, a pedophilic Freemason, connected to this ring. She has enormous courage to step up to the plate having been beaten with a baseball bat with resulting broken jaw, arm and ribs and having her life threatened as well. These snuff films are basically an illuminati production and the illuminati control Hollywood and the music industry as well. Ke$ha wrote the lyrics, "*Dancing with the Devil*", which is on YouTube, but not formally released about how the shit in her life was real and she made a deal and how she is now enslaved by it. Her videos are full of illuminati occult symbols such as the pyramid and all-seeing eye, Satanic colors of black, red, and white and even crosses within circles, which are used in black magic as well as hidden Baphomet images. Beyoncé has been photographed with a Baphomet ring! (How blatant do these people need to be before their audiences wake up?) Hollywood Boulevard is famous for the red, five pointed Satanic stars awarded to their most gifted actors, musicians, writer, producers, etc. and even the name Holly wood is associated with magic for the Holly wand was and is a magician's tool. (*Small Mediums At Large*) Anyways, to get back to Vancouver (666) the Picton brothers interfaced with the Canadian Prime Minister Paul Martin at the policemen's clubhouse in down town Vancouver with judges while drugs and prostitutes were being used. Michaelson, the Freemason, provided security for Eddie Murphy, America's favorite comedian, who witness claims raped and assaulted her with a knife leaving permanent scars on her shoulder and neck. Anne Parker also stated Murphy tortured and raped a 21-year-old Asian porn actress and a prostitute whom were provided to him by Michaelson, and then murdered them by drug overdose confident the bodies would be disposed of and that he would not be held to task, which is exactly what has happened. I believe her because I always felt like when looking at Murphy's eyes it was like looking at two black holes and I could not find his humanity. I thought he was very funny, but for some reason I didn't like his glib smoothness; it seemed there was no real human feeling in this soul. Annie Parker went on to state that she believed this ring was involved in ethnic cleansing and that they would hunt intelligent prostitutes. They targeted natives and young girls like twelve years of age and she believed there is a connection between the Highway of Tears (Highway 16) and the missing women in northern British Columbia. The number 16 of the Tarot is the shattered citadel with the monarch's falling and I firmly believe that this exposure of the Highway 16 murdered and missing could well bring the downfall of the British Monarchy and of the illuminati control. Recently a young 26-year-old graduate student, Loretta Saunders, who was researching the missing women for her thesis was murdered. When Kevin Annett wanted to research the native holocaust for his PhD his funding was cut off and the logging company financed University of British Columbia ran off his faculty supporter Don Wilson who unexpectedly took an early retirement. He was simultaneously delisted as a minster for providing support to these horrendously abused natives and divorced by his wife in this three-pronged attack by the MacMillan-Bloedel financed United Church and University of British Columbia. I quote Arnold Sylvester of Vancouver Island, "I guess you could say the residential schools were a big success. They were put there to destroy us. They called us devil worshippers, you know, but it was the whites who worshipped evil and killed innocent children. Maybe none of this will make a difference, but at least I know the truth, and now you do, too." This reminds me of the Greek austerity and the IMF (another illuminati creation) success story:

death, poverty, torture; suffering. It's well beyond the time to open your eyes and see these truths. In the end, all the evil you support by tithing to your child raping priests and churches, paying taxes to a genocidal government and looking the other way as millions die will come back to haunt you as you finally are eliminated via "genocide" yourselves. Nothing will save you as evil has no color, only motive, and the motive was to use you, the unaware, to genocide others and then come back and genocide you as well. The IMF and World Bank are illuminati creations for genocide while enriching themselves. Genocide is an extremely painful way to die physically and mentally. It involves the desecration and destruction of one's culture, one's identity and one's soul. Genocide is accomplished by horrific abuse: starvation, freezing to death, eating maggot infested food, being raped by rape rings, beheadings, murder by torture, etc. Genocide itself is an illuminati creation. The illuminati Satanic Freemasons are interconnected with the Trilateral Commission, Council on Foreign Relations, and Bilderbergers who work for them. They also finance the Anti-Defamation League, World Bank, IMF, Skull and Bones, the 300 Club and myriads of private clubs, corporations; **universities such as Harvard and Yale who reportedly made more money off of mind control research than tuition.** (Gallagher, Congressman on LaRouchepac.com stated this in an interview) They created the CIA via George Herbert Walker Bush, Sr., one of the most nefarious men alive if you really research him. The CIA manipulated tax payer money into paying for these mad scientists at Harvard who have ruined countless lives with their mind control research. The Unabomber, Ted Kaczynski, was allegedly part of this mind control research. He was obviously very traumatized living in extreme isolation as many severely war traumatized veterans live and his brother, who was never involved in mind control research, lives a completely normal life. Can it get any more obvious than this? They love to use twins in their research and seek them out. Legal kidnapping often is used with a compromised social worker writing up a lying report to kidnap a well-adjusted child from a loving home. The child is then fed into the pedophile adoption network or MK Ultra network. The illuminati empire is based on snuff films, drug dealing, wars, organized pedophilia, gun running, Big Pharma and anything else involving the complete and total destruction of the human race. Their final solution, is annihilation- Of us. It's even written in stone-the Georgia Stones to be exact.

Pedophile rings purposely exist to provide subjects for their mind control research and to compromise politicians and judges who are then beholden to do as they are told or suffer the career destroying consequences. The ultimate goal of mind control is the "Marionette Syndrome" to create a docile puppet by extreme torture and trauma. I believe the same techniques are being used on the unwitting public: massive drugs distributed among them, a culture of fear of violent crime in America, a culture of traumatization from school bullying to the fear of losing ones' job, indoctrination into ideas like democracy as being for the people inculcated within public education, worship of Obama who is like the Roman Emperor Nero, indoctrination into religion that people will go to hell if they don't believe in Religion's fear based, popular culture indoctrination that if you don't go along with the status quo you are weird and therefore somehow unacceptable the insane celebrity worship of those who have sold their souls to Satan for fame and money. The majority rule in America is mob rule. Most of the "Democracy" we spread overseas is mob rule by terrorists-Muslim Brotherhood, al Qaida and their affiliates rule, which is why we are so hated and feared. The esteemed Freemasons, are, at the top of the organization Satanists and so is Skull and Bones-that is why they so frequently prominently display skulls in their lodges. Albert Pike, a Freemason, was a Satanist who created the Ku Klux Klan to terrorize Americans of color, torture, and murder them. They have planned a World War III for the ultimate creation of a New World Order Bush Nazi style for the ultimate enslavement of all themselves excluded. The fashion industry is promoting skull designs as part of the agenda to make death culture cool. After all isn't everything promoted as cool and trendy part of the death culture? The fashion industry a few years back promoted heroin chic as if being a dying heroin addict was cool and chic. I have even seen their photographers creating photos of refugees against barbed wire fences in fashionable clothes! Their influence can be particularly seen in the Death Metal genre and the likes of Marilyn Manson whose acts and weird vibe scream Satanism. Slayer, the hard metal rock band comes to mind. Everything the illuminati promote is a lie; everything they say is a deceit. They are the Synagogue of Satan, here to wreak death and destruction and will continue to do so until enough people have had ENOUGH and will this destruction to stop by words and actions. We are many- 7 billion- and they are few is true, so true.

Can ONE person make a difference? Well, did Erin Brockovich make a difference? Has Kevin Annett made a difference? Is David Icke making a difference? Erin Brockovich made a difference and was key in bringing a major corporation to its knees finding the smoking gun evidence to force them to pay $333 million in damages. She had no education but did have a dogged determination and drive to work for JUSTICE and to feed her kids. She kept the plaintiffs and the case together when it was all falling apart due to the lawyers' lack of interpersonal skills. She is a true leader. David Icke had no education but has managed to fund his way to the truth through 60 countries, a multitude of books and his website struggling a David vs. Goliath war against these elite criminals. The process has been an initiation by fire! David Icke had to suffer firing from his job, watching his kids ridiculed at school and being made out to be a "nutter" on TV. Still he struggled on for decades. Kevin Annett has the education: two master's degrees and a bachelor's degree and has had the most brutal struggle of all winding up homeless and having to eat other's leftovers at restaurants to pay the bus fare to see his daughters. He lost his job, his career, his marriage, his funding for his PhD and was blackballed from being hired. He is still unemployable twenty-one plus years later for exposing the sadistic elite criminals who control Canada- the land of the "free!" He is being vindicated at this time after a twenty plus year struggle against the entire government of Canada and its churches to reveal the truth of their corruption and their native genocide. In legal circles, there are cases that set precedents. In the book, *Class Action: The Landmark Case That Changed Sexual Harassment Law* Lois suffers severe physical and psychological abuse resulting in her permanent PTSD condition. She wins a precedent setting lawsuit after a 14-year battle with the mines trying to get them to acknowledge the sexual harassment/hostile work environment and trying to change the work place. She calls no fewer than fifty lawyers seeking representation and years of stressful litigation as well as workplace harassment and sabotage. She wins a moderate $1,000,000 cash settlement; her struggle is documented in the bestseller *Class Action....* (and movie *North Country*) based on her David vs. Goliath battle in the mines and the courtrooms. Her life has been mired in PTSD and forever altered by it and she will be disabled forever. She did win and changed the work world in the process for the better. I think her battle was particularly brutal even more so than Kevin Annett's in some ways with the constant life-threatening harassment in her face at work! It's so vicious you feel like you are reading about the battle in Vietnam rather than a story about going to work! Get ready for combat; time to go to work! Maybe she should have gone to work with a taser (Girl with the Dragon Tattoo style). Maybe if these S.O.B.'s had been tazed a few times the work place changes would've happened a lot quicker.

In *Rez Life* Helen and Russell Bryan decide to fight a $118.10 tax bill on their newly acquired trailer. Their reasoning was that the state could not assess a personal property tax on Indians living on Indian land. The alternative would've been to pay this tax and not fight it. They lost in Itasca county court and lost again in the Minnesota state supreme court. Their young, go getting attorneys had moved on, one to Micronesia, and the Bryans now had a new attorney, Bernie

Becker, who was an expert on the PL 280 law, which was the basis of this case. His argument was that PL 280 was to combat lawlessness only and not to regulate the Indians because they were a sovereign nation. He won. The *Minneapolis Tribune* and *New York Times* both reported on this case because it was official; States were barred from taxing Indians on Reservations. The result has been phenomenal. The resulting Indian gaming became a $100 million-dollar annual industry creating badly needed jobs, restaurants, theme parks, healthcare, hospitals, schools, etc. The casino industry has lifted a few reservations out of poverty and uplifted a few reservations from severely impoverished to an impoverished status. Without this battle, none of this would've happened. I know the reservations are an illuminati creation to steal the Indians lands, old growth forests, mineral resources, and everything else they could steal. I know the Eveleth Mines Lois Jensen had to battle are illuminati to the core and I'm quite sure PG & E corporation (Erin Brockovich) doing the virulent polluting of Hinckley was illuminati as well.

The point is that every person makes a difference; every person counts. Find your passion and pursue it. Be very persistent. David Icke found his calling; Kevin Annett found his; Erin Brockovich found hers and you will find yours!

Many times, the true leader is the one who walks alone in nonconformity among a sea of conformists. The true leader is one who follows his inner heart instead of following the dictates of convention. The true leader is a maverick like Michael Monroe who sings in Smokescreen about walking alone. The true leader is one with guts, determination and persistence in the face of defeat. Aaron Schwartz, found hanging in his apartment, was a true leader and he had many, many petitions to protect individual liberties and internet freedom. I have my suspicions he was murdered because he had every reason to live and none, in my opinion, to die. Bradley Manning, now Chelsea, is a hero turned heroine. She went by her conscience to release *Collateral Damage* when none of the major newspapers would report on it. Edward Snowden is another hero/activist who exposed the NSA spying forfeiting a $200,000 a year career in the process. Julian Assange is another hacktivist/hero who exposed the *Collateral Damage* video and, in the process, has had to endure a banking blockade and by default is revealing the banks involvement in all the corruption, which extends to Visa, MasterCard, Western Union and PayPal all blockading his funds, which at the time of Bradley Manning's videos were 800,000 Euros in donations!

I would think it would be illegal for banks to not turn someone's money over to them and blockade them from receiving their own funds, but apparently, they are like "Wells Fargo" gangsters. Governments do not take the activities of these individuals lightly. Chelsea Manning is serving 35 years for a huge intelligence leak to WikiLeaks and Julian Assange is under house arrest at the Ecuador Embassy in London. He is afraid to leave. A bunch of police are just outside so if he ever leaves he will be sure to be arrested and extradited to the United States-the Grande Dame of Terrorism. Stormcloudsgathering.com put up a very good webcast called *How Washington and its Allies Use Social Media to Topple Governments & Manipulate Social Opinion.* They mention honey traps where women have sex to entrap men the government is after or government's will hire bloggers to attack and discredit whistleblowers or in some cases an entity can use their own staff to create email addresses all over the world in ten different names to attack someone. I can think of quite a few that fit these descriptions like Heather Martin of stopkevinannett.com. David Icke was also ruthlessly attacked by bloggers and trolls. I believe Julian Assange was caught in a honey trap using women in a country-Sweden-that has very strange rape laws. (Basically, refusing an AID's test is "rape" in Sweden.) All of this appears to be a well-planned, well-coordinated attack. I cannot believe the invitation extended to Assange from Sweden-the country with the bizarre rape laws and subsequent events was any accident. No way! The USA wanted Assange and like the

KGB studied his psychological weaknesses then went after him. If you want to see how vicious these people are just disagreeing with them on the comment line…disagree with a war or with Angelina Jolie's double mastectomy or put up information on natural cancer cures. You will be amazed at the virulent attacks and soon they will look like they are coming at you from all over the world! If you stick to your guns and argue with them they will become more vicious trying to annihilate your reputation and discredit you in any way they can. You see, one thing that came up on this webcast is that the CIA has infiltrated our newspapers and TV and probably has hundreds working in our media on the CIA payroll so what we have is Nazi-style propaganda. They also have paid internet trolls who work to discredit truthers, holistic cures bloggers, etc. This is why we have all the Hollywood celebrities supporting the war-TV is propaganda. Notice what happened to Charlie Sheen when he didn't go along with the program? The biggest star in Hollywood suddenly finds himself out of a job and is being demonized and scandalized in every way. If you want to keep your job in Hollywood you had better go along with the military-industrial complex and support the killing, the wars, keep quiet about the baby-raping, shut up about the child sex slaves in Hollywood, just look good and shut-up, unless, of course you're needed for propaganda. The few that open their mouths like Charlie Sheen and Roseanne Barr are independently wealthy and I guess they don't care if they work anymore or not. They are viciously attacked for being courageous enough to speak up for what is moral and having personal integrity in a place where almost none exists. I wonder about Nicole Kidman; does she have enough money or does she continually need more? Is money so important to her that she was willing to be married to an alleged child abuser (allegedly Cruise per Benjamin Fellows) and is willing to sellout her fans when she already has about $100 million in assets? How much money does a woman need? I know I will be attacked by her brainless fans, but this is important; I am talking about the future of future generations if we do not wake up and wake up FAST! With the written in stone DEPOPULATION agenda, the endless wars, the MONSANTO GMO's and the repeated mantras that the USA can afford soldiers in 170 countries, to bailout the richest banks, but cannot afford entitlements, which they keep wanting to cut, the legitimately disabled veterans being denied benefits and winding up homeless, the promises that social security will NOT be there for future generations who are paying big chunks of their paychecks for while these same criminals gave away social security to illegal aliens as well as section 8 housing; it all boggles the mind. The scams inundate me. Will our Presidents and Congress ever tire of scamming us? I think not. Therefore, it is up to us to do something about all of these scams. Our President and Congress are illuminati whores and the biggest whorehouse of all is in D.C. They are bigger whores than the Mayflower Madam because at least she had some principles-even whores have some principles-I'm still looking for principles in Washington, D.C.! There are a handful of exceptions, but I find most of them do not represent us most of the time and only pretend to be outraged about something if it affects their own scummy selves. Dianne Feinkenstein is a good example. I like calling her Feinkenstein because she is truly a monster. The same woman who supported the Patriot Act, FISA, and gun control is now suddenly upset because she is being spied upon. Why? She must have a lot to hide and is afraid of her own dirt seeping out. Remember, she was the one who thought it was fine as long as it was the rest of us being spied upon. I'd like to know the spying information on her; what was gleaned. I think that as long as it's okay for the rest of us to be spied upon it's democratic for Congress, the Pope, the Monarchy, President and everyone else. Note the meaning of Democracy-rule by majority. Since the majority voted for the spying why cry when they are spied upon too? They cry democracy anytime they need a tag line to promote illegal wars or criminal sanctions and now they are crying that spying isn't democratic. Well, when the majority voted for spying it was democratic-rule by majority. Oh, and by the way since you know everything about me NSA may I have the information too and by the way isn't it fair that I have the dirt on you too---all the dirt, please. A hacker just hacked NSA "ha ha ha." Great!!! Larry Sinclair puts all the dirt on the table immediately. That takes guts, which he has plenty of or chutzpah or courage or whatever you want to call it. I know he is honest. Therefore, if and when you decide to run again for Congress, Larry Sinclair, I will happily support you. I feel I can trust what you say unlike the scumbags in Congress leaching off the taxpayer while selling them out. I trust you way more than so many of the scumbags there with no honor or decency keeping their filthy crimes covered up using the National Security Act-crimes involving rape, torture, murder, pedophilia and drug smuggling. I wouldn't be surprised if they used this act to hide their illegally gotten gains in the Cayman Islands. Larry Sinclair could not get anyone to publish his book probably because it told the truth so he self-published it. He tells about Obama using crack as an aphrodisiac, cocaine because he enjoys it, and having sex with him at the Comfort Inn while married to Michelle Obama during his Chicago senator-days. This is called 'being on the down low' when a married man cheats with other men and it is far more common than people think. The elite sex trade in little boys exists because so many married men like to screw with little boys. With the Zionists sex with children is part of their religion & our political class is completely taken over by Zionists! Ellen Kaplan, activist, asked Henry Kissinger about cheating on his wife with little boys at the Plaza Hotel. It was after this that Kissinger begged the Justice Department and then enlisted various illuminati-Zionist foundations and private groups-Zionist to make complaints to the FBI about the LaRouche-PAC (activist Kaplan's affiliated group) to get the FBI to investigate them. Who is prostituting these little boys to Kissinger? Could the rumors about Roy Cohn running MK Ultra tortured little boys in D.C. (The Donald Trump's mentor) be true??? I mean little boys do NOT want to have sex with a fat, ugly, old man like Kissinger so who is doing the pimping like Cohen did? Lawrence King and Craig Spence (the lobbyist) ran the child prostitution rings into Congress in the '80's. Craig Spence was later murdered in a hotel room after the exposure of this child prostitution ring in the Washington Times and New York Times. Lawrence King was jailed for misappropriating $40 million that was never recovered. He was highly connected to Bush & Reagan. The perverts that go after little boys are highly educated, high status, successful professionals-many C.E.Os.-that will murder to cover up their crimes and often do or rather get someone to do it for them. When Stieg Larsson wrote *The Girl with the Dragon Tattoo* he wrote it as fiction, but he had worked for decades as an investigative journalist much like Mikael Blomkvist his main character. I am more than sure he uncovered a cesspit of pedophilia in the Swedish government among the elites, but rather than expose what he knew first hand he chose to write three manuscripts as "fiction" and after handing them to a publisher he suddenly and unexpectedly died at age 50. Maybe the "fiction" exposed TOO MUCH!!! He never collected the royalties of 60 million copies or the money made off of the three hit films produced. The expose writers have lived as lepers and by this, I mean David Icke and Kevin Annett. Nancy Grace goes after the lone pedophile, which is a whitewash and cover-up; the public is being deceived. There is huge organized underground child prostitution, snuff film, slavery connecting the USA, Vancouver, Amsterdam, Bangkok and the rest of the world with child sex slaves being sold right outside of Las Vegas (Franklin Cover-Up) and a black market in organ trafficking (from the snuff film victims). While our government relentlessly pimps their propaganda about our freedom and democracy these child sex slaves have no civil rights. They are brutally trafficked and tortured to death as in *Whistleblower* and Guantanamo. Hillary Clinton is hypocritically talking about women's rights while she is the alleged *rapist* of Cathy O'Brien! Cathy O'Brien should have equal press time at these forums. On the internet, she shows her Baphomet mutilation carved into her vagina without anesthesia as part of her MK Ultra program! I think it's overdue for these criminals to be held accountable for their multitude of crimes. Every time Larry Sinclair went to court he admitted his crimes. Can't these "leaders" or these fakes do the same? In my opinion, Larry Sinclair makes a far more moral and trustworthy leader than these charlatans. I can't believe they are so supported when time after time they are shown to be liars, thieves, con artists, cheats, murderers and common criminals. I think the public has a right to know in court Larry Sinclair's allegations. He certainly gives a convincing description of Obama's private parts including the left hook, pimples, length and girth of his penis. How would he know all of this without seeing it? He is very convincing providing hotel receipts too. What right does Michelle have to block this book? Anyways, I think Obama should be forced to have a press conference with Larry Sinclair and be examined by a doctor and present their findings as to the legitimacy of Larry Sinclair's claims. It's not that I care about Obama's private parts; it's more that I question his fitness to be president if he is a lying crack and cocaine abusing scoundrel. If you or I were caught abusing crack or selling cocaine we'd go to prison. These traitors refuse to even be drug tested! Bushes & Clintons allegedly deal in drugs as well as use them per Cathy O'Brien and David Icke. They should be at the minimum drug tested. I don't want Presidents with drug-addled brains cutting my entitlements or pushing the nuclear button getting us all annihilated. That's for sure! If this nation is a democracy, then I don't understand all the illegal wars no one wants but is having to pay for with their tax dollars. Who wants social security cuts? Only our politicians give themselves larger pensions, more secret service escorts, free medical and dental care for life, which of course are at taxpayer expense while cuts are being preached to us as well as gun control!

We have troops in 170 countries, which only benefits the corporations who bribe Congress to only represent them via their lobbyists. These wars do not benefit the soldiers who have to fight them nor the taxpayers who pay for them and the soldiers are being denied PTSD benefits once they get home and have to fight like hell to get these benefits. These wars benefit the elite whose companies make obscene profits off of them (Halliburton, Lockheed, Blackwater, etc.) and are stealing the gold and mineral resources from these devastated nations. The Monarchy and Pope benefit from these wars just like they benefit from child slave labor, the narcotics trade, organ trafficking, snuff film productions, slum rents, and every type of seedy, sleazy enterprise imaginable including Payday loans. That is why they are so filthy rich. The Monarchy created the Indian Act in Canada so that they could steal the native land unimpeded. They used the Christian Residential Schools as fronts for Nazi-style internment camps to enforce the sequestering of the children from their families and train them to be a servant slave class to the white population they were bringing from Europe. They created and enforced the Indian Act, which gave natives a sub-human, serf status having no legal rights whatsoever. This draconian law is why the natives could not refuse the vaccines and drug testing being forced on them, could not refuse their children being put into death camps and had no rights even when their children were raped and tortured to death. The Monarchy primarily used the Catholic church supervised by the Vatican to do their evil bidding with some "Christian Residential Schools" having had a 50%-70% death rate. The Anglican and United churches in Canada also participated in this holocaust involving at least, but more likely many more than 100,000 children when you do the math. The Indian Act made any type of justice illegal for decades and the parents gave up their children under the very real threat of imprisonment and then having their children kidnapped by the government anyway. The Royal Canadian Mounted Police (crown police aka RCMP) were used in these crimes. It is reminiscent of the Nazi's rounding up the Jews and taking them to Auschwitz. The key issue getting Kevin Annett fired was his letter addressing Ahousat lot 363 being stolen by the church and sold to Weyerhauser/MacMillan-Bloedel lumber company. This company then made an $8,000 donation to the church. This reeks of being a Zionist enterprise and sounds so like Nazi Germany that I cannot see the difference. What many don't know is that the Nazi movement was created by Zionist eugenicist movements in the USA and Canada, that Hitler was funded by the Harrimans and Bushes and covertly supported by the Monarchies and Zionists all over Europe. After the war, droves of Nazi doctors and scientists fled Germany via the CIA Paperclip project to America and Canada. They continued their Nazi torture experiments on powerless people like the Duplessis orphans, Canadian aboriginals, inmates in prison, and fringe elements in society. By far the worst and most brutal of these mind control experiments were conducted by German speaking doctors on the Canadian aboriginals. They went through supremely agonizing tortures and rapes. Military groups were connected to this network as are snuff film networks, child pedophile rings, drug couriers, and very elite pedophiles. The Finders, a CIA group in America was an offshoot of the pedophilia networks here. Elite pedophiles comprise the top 1% of politicians, government officials, monarchies all over Europe, the Vancouver club elites, judges, top military brass, the top RCMP, and the elite lawyers who had Renate Augers disbarred (on fictitious technicalities) for her legitimate attack on them in court and her co-lawyer Jack Cram forced into a psychiatric ward and drugged for a week while his office was ransacked and evidence including pictures stolen. A very good internet article called *A Tale of Two Lawyers* is a must read telling the story of Renate Augers who remains in hiding and Jack Cram now in isolation on his ranch in Northern British Columbia (Appendix). They have been made an example of to discourage any lawyer who dares to attack these sadistic elite pedophiles. As I did my research I saw this pattern over and over and over again with the top officials of the UN, NATO, military, government; all are involved in these child rape rings! It is like an unwritten policy/code that one must be a sadistic compromised pedophile to truly rise to the top! By God, why does the public think their governments care when there are close to a million missing kids every year in the US and a million missing Eastern Europeans and countless missing all over the world? Yet the Western governments have a do-nothing attitude. Oh, I know they have a storefront missing children's center and they have a tiny handful of people working there to handle at least 800,000 cases a year without any real coordination between police departments. This organization is hugely underfunded so it must be close to a miracle if they solve any cases at all. Missing children's disappearances are an international problem in scope with child sex slaves being flown out to foreign destinations. I don't think there is an intention to solve this problem with a tiny, extremely understaffed office, underfunded with no coordination between police departments and no FBI national database on missing children. The whole process of truly investigating missing children has been hijacked! (once again by the pedophile thug-connected "lawmakers" in charge) The big centers of this trade are in Vancouver, Washington D.C., Bangkok and Amsterdam. The elite love their meat market in children and make the laws to continue to have their meat market in children. The non-functionality is planned and the underfunding, understaffing and miss-coordination of departments are engineered to not achieve their stated objectives: to find the missing children. Hollywood is very involved in this as well. In *Whistleblower*, the main character seminal to the whistleblowing is shown murdered, but in real life she escaped to America and received asylum here. It's a change that would discourage anyone watching this distorted outcome from whistleblowing because few people read books and anyone involved in the human trafficking or knowing about NATO's human trafficking, after watching this film, would feel compelled to keep his mouth shut. Who wants to be murdered? It is Orson Welles style doublespeak because the "peacekeepers" are child traffickers & killers and the missing children's center is actually window dressing to make us believe they are seriously addressing this huge epidemic. I BELIEVE IF OUR GOVERNMENT WERE REMOTELY SERIOUS ABOUT ADDRESSING THE MISSING CHILDREN'S CRISIS THEY WOULD USE THE SATELLITE NSA SPYING ON LICENSE PLATES, CELL PHONES, EMAILS, AND

INTERNET TO END THE CHILD TRAFFICKING FOR ONCE AND ALL!!! Even the CIA Finder's is actually a child prostitution ring not to find anyone, but to keep them hidden! No one knows what happened to this group of children either just as no one knows what happened to ten little Indians the Monarchy took off of Kamloops and they have never been seen again. It is likely that they are buried in one of the 31 mass graves all over Canada as the Monarchy again and again and again have mass graves of murdered children on monarchy land and the decomposing body of the Eastern European girl (17-year-old) found on their land as well. It's time these crimes were truly investigated instead of the investigator being taken from his post so a non-investigation can be substituted by a crown stoolie afraid of losing his pension. (Haut de La Garenne and the Jersey Islands)

Conspiracy of Silence was a movie scheduled to air in May of 1994 and even written up in TV Guide, but senior politicians had it removed twenty minutes before airing with the threat of withholding key legislation for the cable industry and a bribe paying all production costs of $500,000 to Yorkshire TV, a British company since even though all insiders know about these pedophile rings in Omaha again going to D.C. no one in this country dare expose it. Even so the Washington Times ran some 39 news articles on this ring for this publication was independently owned by Sun Myung Moon who himself is believed to have been a CIA asset involved in mind control of the Moonies. Hunter Thompson was a part of this ring involved in a snuff film at Bohemian Grove and he even said publicly "I like to kill." The thirteen-year-old boy was brutally raped, tortured and murdered on snuff film. (page 103 from *The Franklin Cover-Up*) I highly recommend you watch *Conspiracy of Silence* on the internet….it is a cutting room copy, but you get the gist of the whole sordid affair clearly. Thank God for the one brave soul who mailed it to

John DeCamp. Without this person, all the evidence of this paralyzed justice system would be gone.

The former Pope was convicted of crimes against humanity and he then promptly resigned. He has been exposed as the front man for a very criminal organization committing at least 10,000,000 crimes against children (vaticancrimes.us) such as child trafficking, enforced slave labor, pimping them in pedophile rings, and what the lawsuits have covered up (draconian law of not being allowed to discuss the settlement or the case) satanic ritual abuse via the Catholic church with military installations. Itccs.org (activist site) has a video of Toos describing how she was forced to watch "Pope" Benedict satanically ritually rape and murder a young girl and she cried and cried as she describes the horrors she was forced to participate in. Mel Ve who sounded very suspiciously callous was later revealed to be a Vatican type COINTELPRO agent to infiltrate itccs.org and discredit it. However, more and more people are waking up to the truth and fewer believe the lies of these elite psychopaths. This evil hopefully WILL eventually stop.

The Pope has used the Catholic Church to siphon off billions of dollars from an unsuspecting public while they have ruined the lives of countless sexually abused children. These children struggle for decades to try to regain their lives. Many never do. It seems that many Catholic congregations have nil sympathy for these psychologically battered survivors and continue to remain in denial supporting one of the most-evil syndicates in the world. The charities were a front; what went on behind the scenes is bone-chilling. Their own insiders state the Vatican has been taken over by the "Smoke of Satan"-Father Amorth, chief exorcist of the Vatican, for one and Martin Malachi, former insider in the Vatican and novelist, who wrote about the smoke of Satan being invoked in a Satanic ritual in the Vatican in his book *Windswept.* (In an interview, he stated his book marketed as "fiction" was 90% the truth!) The Canadian Holocaust was engineered by the Vatican working in tandem with the British Monarchy (as usual) and the Canadian government. One billion spiritually blind people still follow the lead of the Vatican making excuses for them and saying the pedophilia problem is fixed when in truth Pope Francis has only created a bigger cover-up than before in that the **whistleblowers will now be jailed in the Vatican jail pronto, which is the new policy more draconian than the Crimen Solicitationis that preceded it.** Nothing and no one is to interfere with the Satanic Ritual Abuse of children at the top of this criminal syndicate and recently a New York priest warning his congregation not to support the Vatican was jailed. Nothing and no one is to interfere with this money-making operation and the milking of their foolish flock. They have made their rape of children legal and whistleblowing a crime punishable by imprisonment. *Lucifer's Lodge: Satanic Ritual Abuse and the Catholic Church* reveals the Satanism within the Catholic Church protected by the Vatican, but it is largely unavailable being $399 on Amazon and up to over $2500. *The Franklin Cover-Up* relates how Catholic Boystown was used in the MK Ultra child rape/torture experiments on Offutt Air Force base. These books tell similar stories. People had better wake up and realize the Vatican has already taken the first step to make pedophilia legal and they expect our country to follow suit. California has already enacted a law legalizing the sharing of a bathroom for a man and a twelve-year-old girl, which is part of the push for elite perverts/rapists to make their child raping sickness legal and the new normal. I see traces of it on TV in the sick dialogue innocent looking actors and actresses must speak talking about sex related to a baby. Sick! They have made other similar attempts with Pedophile Information Exchange (PIE) in Britain and North American Man-Boy Love Association (sex before eight or it's too late) pushing for the legalized rape of children. NAMBLA was a powerful organization until two new members accidently murdered a little boy during an attempted rape. Sickeningly, George Soros's funded the ACLU got their top guns to defend the rapist/killers to try to keep them out of prison. This organization receives funding from the Credo

Mobile activist phone company so if you don't like this type of "activism" don't fund it. The parents lost a $200 million-dollar lawsuit against NAMBLA and their lawyer mysteriously and suddenly died one month later. There was no justice. Credo Mobile donates untold millions to the ACLU, which defends perverts, killers, pedophiles and gangsters the rest of us would love to see in prison and so it is probably wise to steer clear of this fraudulent "activist" organization controlled by the illuminati whose bagman George Soros heavily donate to. They legitimize themselves also funding Doctors Without Borders, but since no one knows who gets what why not donate directly to Doctors Without Borders and delete Credo Mobile from your life! The elite baby rapists are very clever at disguising their foundations as charities when the goal is to legalize child rape. They create charities and foundations with the sole purpose of pushing their sick agenda through. (George Soros....... you can read all about him at earstohear.net.) They call this "social engineering" and by the way I recently became aware an elite pedophile with assets in excess of $100 million is funding an orphanage in Thailand. Could this person be Warren Buffett the financial "oracle"???

PURE EVIL
MAN IN
THE WORLD

Lucifer's Lodge:
Satanic Ritual Abuse in the Catholic Church
WILLIAM H. KENNEDY

My mother has no idea who the illuminati even is, but she works around them pretty thoroughly.

1. She does not believe in trends or popular culture always thinking for herself encouraging her children to do the same.
2. The big banks charge too much so she goes to the small community banks with lower fees and better service.
3. She doesn't believe in credit cards so she pays cash for everything. She paid cash for her car and paid off her house as fast as she could. She does not use credit and has no loans.
4. She cooks 95% of all of her meals at home from scratch using fresh vegetables and eats fruit salads daily. No processed foods are welcome here. I doubt if a hotdog has been on her table in years nor a hamburger. Lots of seaweed and seafood is eaten here too as well as curry.
5. She doesn't believe in American pill culture and takes only supplements. Her doctor has given up on pushing pills.
6. A water filter removes impurities and we are lucky to live in an enlightened community where doctors insisted on removing fluoride because it is cancerous.
7. She doesn't believe in either political party and doesn't vote.
8. She loves to stay at home and doesn't like to drive so she only accumulates about 3,000 miles a year on her car; maintenance expenses are extremely low.
9. She doesn't care to shop and used to make all of her own clothing sewing them, knitting them and crocheting them as well as making afghans, comforters, hats, scarves, mittens, and tote bags.

10. She bakes everything from scratch and cooks everything from scratch. My mother's diet is almost GMO free; she eats almost no dairy: no cheese, no milk, hardly any butter, no bacon, no sandwich meats, very little red meat and avoids fast food entirely. In my 59 years, I've been to a fast food restaurant once with my mother and we split a salad at Wendy's. She has done a lot of canning, freezing and dehydrating in her life.
11. She has always had a garden and fruit trees. No pesticides are used because she doesn't believe in spending money on pesticides. She has had blueberries, satsumas, onions, green beans, peppers and tomatoes squeezing the giant green tomato worms with her bare hands. We always have lots of bees and birds around us. None of them are dropping dead from neonics because neonics are not used here. Even my brother grows his apples pesticide free or organic. I don't understand why organics are so very expensive; we grew organic because it was way cheaper. It sounds like a marketing scam to me to gouge the consumer.
12. On her farm, she had an artisan well of pure mineral water, which my family of origin often bottled.
13. She uses the cell phone given to her sparingly and it costs her about $180 a year total.
14. She reads a lot and is pretty well informed. People who don't read are considerably less well informed. Unfortunately, reading only appeals to 3% of the American population.
15. She has managed to save 10's of thousands of dollars at small community banks who absolutely love it. She even writes checks very sparingly. Taking out enough cash over a month for all grocery purchases.
16. She no longer donates to well known, publicized charities having discovered too many of them are a fraud. She used to donate to Catholic charities like St. John's Indian Residential School until I told her about the Canadian Holocaust involving Catholic

"residential schools" or more accurately prison slave labor and torture camps for Aboriginals. She is extremely healthy at age 87.

17. Throughout all of the difficulties dealing with PTSD Dad and the frequent moves she has retained her optimism and humor. The down side is she doesn't want to know the information I have.
18. Being creative she developed her creativity doing a multitude of watercolors, knitting, sewing, dehydrating foods, making kimchee, and even a bowl crocheted out of newspaper wrappers. In the end creativity, dogged determination, and facing the truth will see us through. Remember, the illuminati control Western Europe and America so everything they promote is a trap. We have the debt trap, credit trap, GMO trap, culture trap, war trap, charity traps, foundation traps, IRS trap, Drug War trap, the prison trap, phony activism traps, etc.

Prison is a money-making racket as is war benefiting the criminally insane like Bushes, Cheney, Obama, Clintons, Rumsfeld, Kissinger, and all of the Monarchies, Vatican and their stocks in war related companies. The super violent criminals: rapists and pedophiles are left on the streets as much as possible to prey on the rest of us while potheads are incarcerated as slave labor. Potheads are easy to manage while violent criminals are a management problem everywhere they go. Child rapists have an addiction and some estimates are that they rape about 400 children each. This means each one of them is an epidemic of ruined lives, but yet they are allowed back on the streets over and over and over again. The public is one vast mind control experiment for the Satanic elements in Western Society: violent crimes, drugs, prostitution, SSRI shootings & killings, hypnotically repeated mantras of TV (we are a democracy and for human rights) are ALL elements of established MK-Ultra protocol.

BrutalProof!

Education at public schools is an indoctrination scam. If education were to be useful then we would all have been taught to at least balance our checkbooks. Education is busywork and rote memorization and mostly a sinful waste of time-especially Common Core. Montessori schools and Waldorf schools are far better. History is a lie that is written by illuminati paid shills. When I was twelve I noticed George Washington, Carver was not in the history books. He invented peanut butter, but due to the racism of these illuminati they didn't include him in their history books because he was a brilliant colored man. This man invented 100's of products from peanuts and was not even mentioned. That is when I realized how biased history was. Common core is a way of total denigration. Children are taught to read about pimps and ho's as if that is normal life; it's not-it's street life for a criminal few. It's nothing near a normal life. I don't know why this is included in Common Core except to degrade the child's core values. This is reason enough to steer clear of Common Core, which does not reflect values or principles, but degrades the population and teaches them they are no more than cattle. The best and brightest are not encouraged or rewarded under Common Core; they are stifled and in a sense punished for being brilliant having to stay at the learning level of the truly deficient. Take your kid out of Common Core-it is harmful and disrespectful to them. Homeschooling is far better and exploding in popularity. Ron Paul has a home schooling curriculum you might want to check into. The history books are written by illuminati stooges that leave out a lot of stuff they don't want known in their quest to promote the official line and history is a LIE. History books promote anti-black racism and promote racism against the Native Americans as well. They never mention how settlers were paid hugely per scalp of Indians or that after the Indians saved the settlers during the first Thanksgiving and the settlers turned on them and stole the Indian land after desecrating the native's graves and stealing artifacts buried with the dead. I've never seen it mentioned in history books how England fought opium wars with China to force opium in their country for profit and the opium addictions were destroying China. The history books seem to promote Western society as morally superior and that is what they are there to do-ALL LIES!

"PJ"
$10,000.00
REWARD
BURNS LAKE RCMP
250 692 7171

MISSING
"MADDY"
Missing From: Hogsback Lake
Date Missing: May 28th, 2011
Age: 20
Sex: Female
Height: 5'4"
Weight: 160
Eyes: Hazel
Hair: Ginger, Shoulder Length
Complexion: Medium
Distinguishing Features:
• Bird silhouette tattoo on inside left wrist (inset photo)
• Left nostril piercing
Maddy was last seen at 3am on May 28th while camping at Hogsback Lake, 25km Southeast of Vanderhoof in Northern British Columbia. Maddy's disappearance may be the result of foul play
There is a possible reward of up to for information leading to the arrest & conviction of the person(s) responsible for her disappearance
Anonymous Tips Call Crime Stoppers:
1-800-222-TIPS
www.madisonscott.ca
Reward of up to
$100,000.00

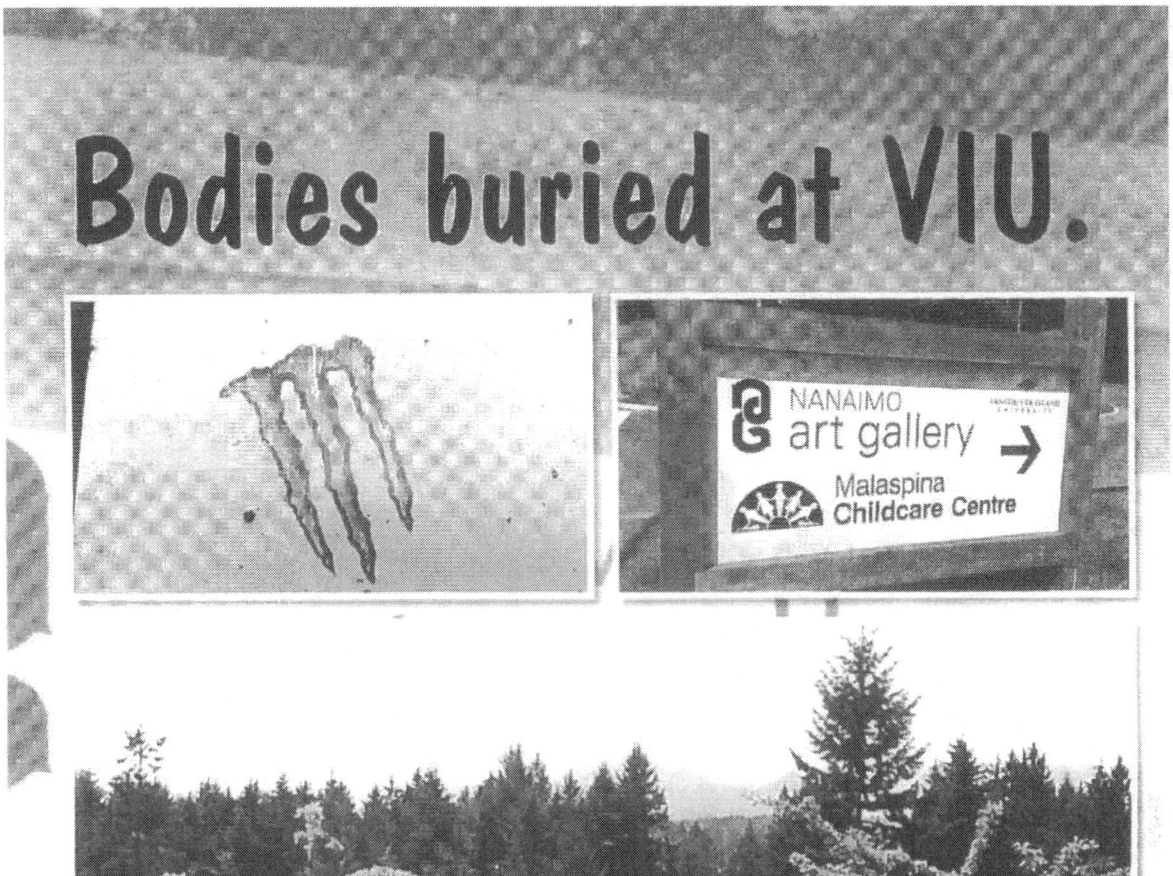

BrutalProof!

JULIE OAKLEY PARKER
IS STILL MISSING
BEAVER
LAKE
km CIRCLE
JULIE OAKLEY PARKER
IS STILL MISSING
LAST SEEN AUGUST 2006
QUESNEL, BC
Bodies are in lake & orchards.

BrutalProof!

The Canadian Holocaust

I'm back and writing and listening to the court evidence from Kevin Annett about the Canadian Holocaust. What a viciously sadistic racist government and churches. And these are the champions of human rights????? They murder little bitty babies-like the Nazi's in ovens and get away with it! Can you imagine having your land, way of life, all your resources stolen from you and you don't even have the legal right to sue to regain them!? Not only this, but being sterilized against your will, being purposely addicted to drugs and used in snuff films by iconic Hollywood movie stars like **Eddie Murphy, our comedian of the century, allegedly having tortured and overdosed a porn star and prostitute.** Look, this is a sickness that never goes away. It is the sickness of Serial Killing, which starts out with an abandoned and severely abused child. Where you find one murder you will find a string of many more. Look at the Picton serial killers. They had absolutely no intention of stopping the killings. They were tied in with elite politicians, RCMP, wealthy snuff film patrons, and Supreme Court justices in Vancouver, child rape ring capitol of the world along with Bangkok. Before Kevin Annett was cancelled from the Canadian Government subsidized radio station he had mentioned the bodies of the murdered were arranged in certain (Satanic) configurations. These were mass ritual sacrifices to "You know who?" under the guise of medical experiments. The "Christians" who did all of this evil were deeply racist, hate filled beings who really worship Lucifer. In other words, they were "Christians" in name only as Canada is for human rights in name only. The Canadians surely, and Europeans knew what was going on, but were more than willing to look the other way as they were profiting from the murders and were deeply racist not caring *(Just another Indian)*. Anytime churches and governments collude together you've got a massive problem. I see the same happening in the United Stasi of America. Fees, fines, criminal charges for everything you do. Protestors arrested and thrown in jail-hey don't you feel free protestors?! Child kidnapping rings abound with children sold at slavery auctions-no different than former African slave auctions, but here it's for children. I'm writing' cause I'm tired of flyers and the security shit that goes with the territory-tired of being threatened, afraid of $300 fines or even an arrest in this bastion of "FREEDOM". The Canadian Holocaust was caused by the British Monarchy in league with the Canadian government, lumber company MacMillan-Bloedel based in Malibu, California and 80% Roman Catholic Church, Anglican Church, United Church and Weyerhauser. If anyone doubts the psychopathic nature of corporations show them brutalproof.net and pictures of depleted uranium babies. These corporate churches were involved in gang rape of children, murders, dental tortures, purposely infecting children with TB, throwing children on concrete floors, down stairs, and into walls. They kidnapped toddlers as young as 3 or 4 in violation of their own laws! They starved, froze, and buried 50,000 to 100,000 children all with full knowledge and consent of the Canadian government, and, I believe, the Canadian people since almost no one protested or wrote any letters of protest or disagreed in much of any way with the criminality of their own government. Dis-gus-ting! I want this flag nailed to its mast because clearly Canada doesn't have any guts to face its own truths.

I really don't like controversy, but reader, this is the truth, which absolutely strips the mask off of beautiful Vancouver and shows the seedy, seamy underside of evil enveloping and permeating this city like a black fog. I wonder if the reporters who dared to report on this were fired or forced to resign. That's the way it goes with government sanctioned murder. People will associate the name Canada with murder of natives and torture experiments. You will probably want to change your name! And for you who knew this was going on and allowed it-this same evil consciousness has the same planned for you! It's called the DEPOPULATION AGENDA and just because you allowed all of this to go on with your brown, yellow, red, and black skinned siblings don't mean it won't happen to you. You are being used while any possible allies you could have had are being eradicated while you look the other way. When all of your possible allies are killed this same evil agenda will be enacted on you. I couldn't make this up! I am boycotting Canada and everything Canadian and all of you should do the same. Don't buy Canadian beers, don't support the lumber companies or mining companies there and don't buy any of their products. Don't bank at their banks, don't take your vacations there. Boycott!!!! Send money to itccs.org and support those who are desperately trying to get the truth out. Maybe start a charity website for these viciously abused natives. How many people will die before anyone moves a finger? Now this woman is describing a baby being burned alive in a furnace! (youtube.com-Irene Favel.... baby burned...and the *Witness to Murder at Indian Residential School* will come up) This is an ancient ritual sacrifice to the evil God Moloch, the god of money and credit- a demon!!! My God these people are evil! Butter does not melt in their mouths; they have hearts and souls of ice. For the survivors "sorry" is not enough. I know what it feels like to have your life and soul destroyed. Justice is only a small beginning, but JUSTICE must be done. In Canada Justice really means kids are just-ass for pedophiles. After all the pedophiles gleefully took turns raping little boys in these schools and girls to DEATH! Now another survivor mentions his brother was cattle prodded to DEATH, electrocuted and dies screaming for help. Evil!!!

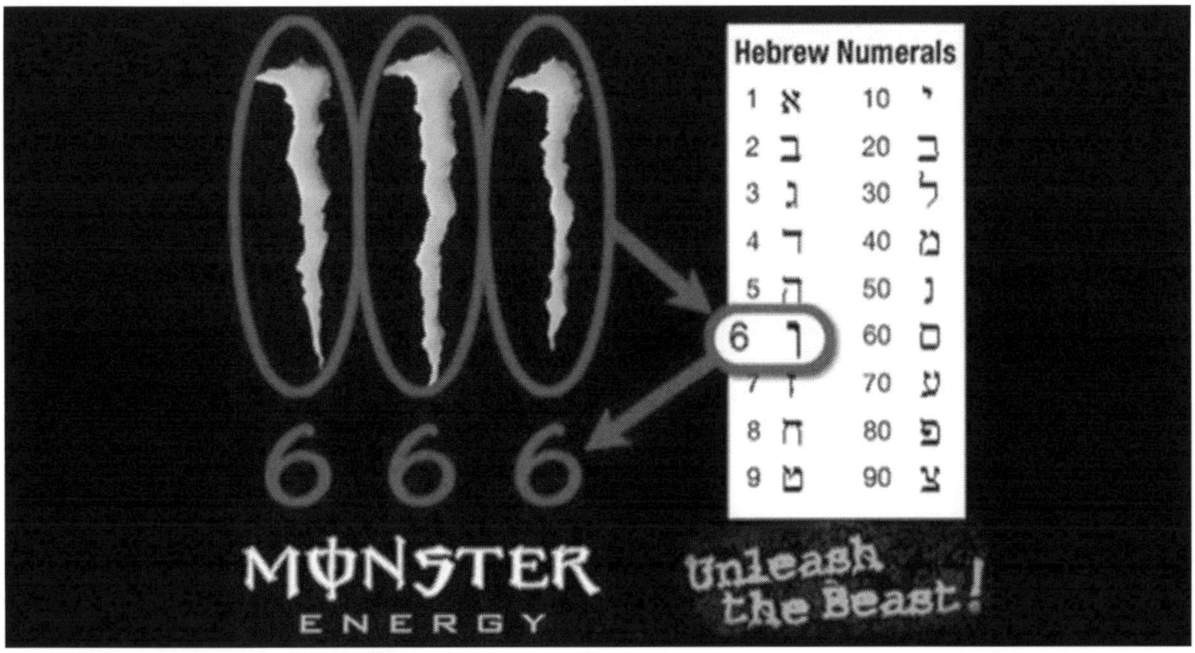

Gargoyles adorn trendy downtown buildings in Vancouver. Now another woman describes children being buried alive and a bulldozer covering up these still alive children with probably 6 feet of dirt. Canada may these children rise up out of their graves to haunt you forever. Nazi Germany never ended. IT RELOCATED. If I had my way all these graves would be dug up and forensics would show how these kids were murdered and your politicians would have some VERY uncomfortable questions to answer and they would not be allowed to leave until the whole inquest was finished. Then we would get to the sentencing, which for me would be a death sentence for everyone directly involved (including Queen Elizabeth and her consort who had a direct hand in all of this-we need to question them about the ten children they disappeared with as well as the bodies of murdered children found on monarchy land at Haut de La Garenne as well as the dead 17 year old Eastern European girl found decomposing on Monarchy land) and any memorials of these criminals immediately torn down and the truth engraved for all to see into infinity. Next the bodies would be returned for a proper native burial and all of their customs including pot latching reinstated and their lands returned to them plus a HUGE COMPENSATION PAID TO THEM tax free, severe PTSD trauma disability pension and every person and if said person was murdered by the government a $1,000,000 cash payout, tax free to family members-a survivorship benefit at the MINIMUM. Anything less and Canada should not be allowed to vote in any international tribunal and should be treated as a PARIAH with every international right stripped until PARIAH status is revoked and that done when the survivors agree that extreme justice has been done for these extreme crimes. Compensation must be paid for every sterilization and British Monarchy should be stripped of all assets to make reparations to these "aboriginals" as well as the Nazi Vatican having an injunction placed on their assets to be disbursed to the victims of their pedophilia and murders. It's time also for Anonymous to hack into the offshore accounts and injunctions placed on all offshore accounts until taxes are paid and crime victims' reparations made. The cliché "Behind every fortune lies a crime" is so true!!! There's so much crime involved here it will take years to dig all the bodies up and ID them and to make reparations. I'm sure the Canadian government is shitting in its shoes as the British Monarchy is threatening Kevin Annett with jail time for entering the U.K. How can any idiot think this bunch of crazed, satanic rulers is for the common man when they do so much evil? These people in government have zero leadership capacity; they only follow orders made by the British monarchy. Prosecute Queen Elizabeth and enforce itccs.org conviction! I have always thought she had total contempt for the sycophantic British public that foolishly worshipped her. She doesn't care about you either British commoners-she's giving herself 10's of millions of pounds in pay raises while demanding starvation type austerity from the poorest of the poor. Ask her to sell off some of her land so the poorest children can eat. A real leader who cares would do exactly that. Muammar Gaddafi had a policy that it is a human right to have a home. Definitely in England and America it is not a human right to have a home. I'll bet Elizabeth got the *Tattler* shut down too-this was a British internet publication reporting on the rampant pedophilia around the Monarchy and they were shut down. British female reporter-Jill Dando- trying to expose the same was murdered. Life becomes very dangerous when the Monarchy decides they don't like you. *Unlawful Killing* is about the British Monarchy killing of Princess Diana. It can be seen at theunhivedmind.com in the Useful Resource Links section. Elizabeth or her son had Princess Diana murdered and there should be no doubt in anyone's mind that they were behind it and if she's such a psychopath why isn't she being tried for all the murders she's been behind along with Obama with his weekly kill lists, the Bushes, and the Clintons, etc. It's very disturbing for me to perceive things the way I do because I perceive everything alone. No one wants to hear my truths.... they love the politicians lies better and the sycophantic worship of public icons that don't give a shit about them and have the attitude they're groupies, zombies, or useless eaters. E.g. Apple calls its customers zombies. Hey, Apple! I never buy any of your products. I love Toshiba's and they scored the 86% consumer satisfaction rate like you at about half the price. I'm not one of your 'zombies.' Apple always struck me as a greedy, money grubbing corporate sellout with no concern for its Chinese workers who routinely commit suicide. Now it seems they're directly involved with the PRISM internet spying. Consumers ought to get this corporation out of their life. I imagine Elizabeth's power totem is a red or black dragon of incarnated evil and of black magic occultism. In fact, there are pictures showing her with a red dragon on apmex.com; the silver sellers.

I write this because I need to get the truth out on a massive scale and flyers don't cut it. I hope I don't care about the consequences. I know I will get death threats and have powerful enemies. I may not make any money at all, but it's not about the money. All the natives that testified against criminal Canada are now dead and almost all were pretty much brutalized to death. I pray that my message will be received and that the hearts and minds of the public will open up to hear it before it's too late. I hope that the suffering of these people has not been in vain. I now know every horror and difficulty has prepared me for this path.

BrutalProof!

Elite Satanists and Demonology

The elite Satanists are afraid to die. They want to use technology to live forever because they are afraid of what awaits them. They are the ultimate fools. They have traded their souls for short term power, money and fame. They consort with demonic forces for material things in a material world. They use humanity as pawns as they serve the Evil One. They are criminally insane and it seems most, if not all of them, are severely addicted to drugs and alcohol. They are all possessed. They live in fear and they spread fear and pain everywhere. They rape children, especially little boys so the souls of these children can be claimed by demonic forces and exploited by them. They stab babies to death for money and power. But, what they don't realize, or maybe they do, is that when they die they will feel every bit of pain they have inflicted on their victims and that is the hell they will live in. Maybe this is why they so want to cheat death. God is a God of real justice not like these fake courts of justice run by pedophiles. I think in my soul I didn't realize how horrendous it would be to be here in this hell where the most evil live the cushiest lives and the most spiritual are being crushed and ground down. When I die, it will be the happiest day of my life. No more living in Hell. No more stress; no more suffering. I was so used to carrying a cross that the day the etheric cross disintegrated off it surprised me that it was there. In the movie, *The Changeling* you can read the book it's based on and the victim says he carried a cross his whole life. I know exactly what he means. You do and the cross is real. According to Dr. Modi at extreme traumatic times demons can insert devices they can use to torture your soul. In *Remarkable Healings,* she writes about all of the many devices the demonic can use to torture people physically and mentally. She even states that most underlying causes of mental illness have to do with demonic blobs inhabiting one's soul and wreaking havoc on it. What she says is based on hypnosis and regression therapy. When my third eye chakra was opening, I started being attacked by black blobs in my dreams. They were trying to invade my soul. One had long tentacles and it seemed pretty nasty. I knew if I could smell it would have a very nasty smell, but thank God, I could not smell it. Anyways I fended off multiple attacks by these blobs and eventually the attacks stopped- in my dreams. Dr. Modi describes the same types of demonic blobs with her patients under regression hypnosis. It's exactly as she describes. In the movie, *The Conjured* the stinking smell emanates from a very nasty spirit, which is black and this was what I felt around me and saw within my dream. Later on, I dreamed a rather nasty looking two-legged green wyvern with black tipped scales and bulging eyes in an ugly bulging head. It was frozen still and had it appeared bigger I would've been terrified as it had a hostile, distrustful look. Recently, I was shocked to research it to find it to be the wyvern of pestilence, disease, and death. Horrid thing!! This entity appeared in Riverside, California, which I later found out was the site of the horrific pedophile rapes & murders by Gordon Northcott. The movie *The Changeling* is based on the books: *The Road Out of Hell* & *Nothing Is Strange with You,* but the movie is a highly-sanitized version and the books resemble the murder tales of Henry Lucas. I consulted Grandma Chandra and described some of this and she said a past life of a Salish shaman was affecting my life now. People will say this is crazy, but they have a blindness and who do you think would mark them with this blindness so they will think evil is good and good evil and have no discernment? I think the Great Deceiver would have an agenda to do this. All the more so this evil could go after more children. Children are what the dark side goes after the most and more and more children all the time. This evil especially likes to go after children with intuitive psychic skills and high intelligence to destroy them spiritually and fill their shattered souls full of the demonic.

I used to wish I'd not been born rather than live in this hellhole that profits the corrupt and criminally insane and victimizes the most innocent and pure of heart. Death has seemed so welcome so many times that I can't count the times. Now I see many others feel the same way. We don't need to die and go to hell-we're already there! Hell, is where evil flourishes-that's here. Hell, is where souls are tortured. You are there! Why worry about dying and going to Hell when you're already here???? Anyhow yet another psychic said I'd write this book and do a blog and become well known so here it is; unbeknownst to her I'd started this book already. I feel a burning desire to expose the darkest of what I know so the world will know. Please, reader you must look at Everards films: Illuminati I, II, III & IV if you can. You used to be able to YouTube them. It is important for you to know where the evil emanates from and fight it. More and more the world to me is like Lord of the Rings and the land of war, evil, destruction and Empire is: America and Great Britain. The other small countries must band together (BRICs Nations) to fight the evil Mordor against great odds cause the truth deniers within don't want to. I dislike controversy but, the truth must be outed. America is where the souls of the innocent are shattered by sexual abuse so demonic forces can take up residence there. It seems to be the same everywhere. The same thing goes on in France-they claim they're so for human rights while children who've been repeatedly raped grow up to be junkies. It seems that every country claiming to be for human rights hides huge evils behind their child non-protection systems and favored pedophilia. Now it is coming out that HALF of Jewish boys are raped by rabbis in the Holy of Holy baths. This is an evil being done to these boys' souls in the name of Religion and Spirituality. Mormonism involves child rape under the godly sounding institution of marriage, but child rape is child rape no matter how godly it is made to sound. Scientology was created by a demon infested addict-Satanist named Ron Hubbard who admitted creating this "religion" solely for the purpose of making money, nothing else. This religion is actually a demonic creation against God. The Church of Latter Day Saints, according to David Icke, is run by shape shifting reptilians (like gargoyles) who are nothing if not against God and any true spirituality. The first psychic I consulted saw the shape shifting reptilians and stated they were real. The book *Slow Death* is about an inhuman torturer and serial killer Satanist that drew pictures of a reptile torturing women in his jail cell. His toy box was a horrific torture chamber. The demonic forces controlling him fed off of the enormous pain and fear of his victims as he tortured them to death. I believe he drew pictures of himself as the reptile. The female FBI agent who saw his "movies" committed suicide. If these are the kinds of evil beings allowed to run our world God help us all! Public, do not expect anything except death & destruction if you allow these demonic ones to rule your world. Kevin Annett discovered children tortured to death and murdered mainly (80%) by the Catholic Church were buried in certain satanic ritual configurations. Even the Texaco sign is a combination of Magical Star within a Magical Circle with a Freemason's T bar in it. All over Texas you will see the Magical Star within the Magical Circle and think: this is occultism!

Guess what? The Magical Star Within the Magical Circle is used to invoke and contain conjured entities and is used by many magicians. I don't use these illuminati gas stations. I prefer Discount Zone, which is privately owned by Arabs. Better this than to support BP, which destroyed the Louisiana Gulf, or Exxon, or the Dutch Monarchy owned Shell (Prince Bernhardt) was described by Toos as being at the Satanic Ritual Sacrifice of a child. These same oil companies are involved with the Federal Reserve banks: Chase, Citibank, HSBC, Bank of America, Wells Fargo, Goldman Sachs and are all illuminati creations. Fritz Springmeier wrote books about the 13 Satanic bloodlines who rule the world and he has a free, downloadable book: *How to Create a Totally Undetectable Mind Controlled Slave* and he was exposing so much he was falsely imprisoned on trumped up charges as were Lyndon LaRouche, Leroy Jenkins, etc. Trumped up charges happen every time someone is targeted-especially Whistleblowers. Look at Snowden and Bradley Manning. Snowden is afraid of being anywhere near America; Bradley Manning has been in prison for 10 years. Dr. Laibow is afraid to be in the United States for more than a few minutes. Time to wake- up America before it's too late! Every time I run into the LaRouche activists they mention how the detention re-education camps (FEMA) are all over America waiting for them! ("Thanks a lot Clinton!") and if you don't believe me, search it! It's even written into law to reeducate political activists at re=education camps and the government plans to lock them up first probably along with the homeless who are quickly disappearing for anyone paying attention. Where are all the homeless disappearing to? Guess! FEMA Camps! That's why these FEMA trailers (used in Louisiana post Katrina) are made with cancer causing materials, which goes along with their heartless depopulation agenda. After all, 1 billion or 500 million people are much easier to control than 7 billion and if the Americans are killed off the IMF would save a fortune in social security payments. The truth is the same with all the Western European countries. Cancer causing genetically modified foods to kill off the unaware would also benefit the avaricious Western governments. Did you really believe the lies that they were concerned about your welfare and pensions? First comes austerity, then food stamp cuts, then social security cuts, then Banksters bail-ins Cyprus style and then martial law and herding the sheep into detention centers to be killed off Nazi style with hypothermia, starvation, disease, and pestilence if war doesn't do the job, which is another reason America is trying to start WWIII because wars are an effective cull of the masses while pirating off the resources of the conquered nations. Nazi Germany stole a lot of gold from many countries like Poland who're now impoverished just like the conquistadors stole the Incan and Aztec gold. The Nazi doctors and their Canadian servants even stole the gold fillings out of the native's teeth when they were anaesthetized. Imagine waking up with all of your gold fillings disappeared! They don't care about us one whit!!! These criminal elites will rape your children to death in snuff film productions, electrocute people, mass murder people in nuclear wars while they sail in luxury yachts in the seas while your eyes melt out from the uranium heat. They want to make pedophilia legal and strip all parental rights so children have NO PROTECTIONS at all. This way they can enjoy their meat market in children. They have already started with the social workers destroying good families and putting their children in foster care where some of them are murdered and some sold into child prostitution rings.... I couldn't make this up! The corruption goes up to judges and lawyers who are making obscene amounts of money destroying children and families. This is institutionalized, systematic severe child abuse and slavery. Every word is true. (Research it! CPS .... Evergreen, CO...twins) For those of you still in denial you are condemning your children to a non-future living in the Matrix where no one has any freedom controlled by an insane system. It's beyond sad. Murderers and rapists run our systems and even very black magicians for those of you caught up in our insanity called the Western Civilization. "Freedom" is the status quo and anyone not supporting it is very viciously abused. Still think this is real freedom? It's about as freethinking as Dr. Lector was sane. (*Silence of the Lambs*) Your own politicians are told to vote on laws they have not had time to read; **a new law should be: no voting on unread legislation!** They are denied access to information they have clearance to get and even Lyndon Johnson openly admitted he was afraid of certain powers because he saw what happened to Kennedy and didn't dare to do what Kennedy did. Johnson reversed all of Kennedy's programs and continued the Vietnam War, which murdered millions of Vietnamese and psychologically destroyed a generation of young Americans. Guess who profited? The elite bankers & politicians made money hand over fist and they are also the stockholders in war businesses. Why is George Bush Jr. in Matamoros, Mexico at the same time a Texas university student is discovered satanically ritually sacrificed? For those with eyes to see this is not a mere coincidence, but a very important clue. The corpses of the dead soldiers airlifted back from Vietnam were stuffed full of drugs, which were unloaded at military bases-guess who profited? Why was John Lennon flashing the 666 sign and Aleister Crowley's face on his album? Could he really have a pact with the devil for money & fame? Why is Lady Gaga flashing the one eye and Rihanna, Britney Spears, Christina Aguilera doing the same while Ke$ha writes a song *Dancing with the Devil*? Why is popular culture always about drugs, rebellion, death and destruction? Who creates this popular culture? Let me give you a clue-the Zionists own our Media as they also own our politicians via Lobbyists. Why is Madonna using the very same themes as these other artists? (The All-Seeing Eye, pyramids, etc.) Where is the creative originality? Why was there a marketing blackout of non-sellouts like Hanoi Rocks by Polygram? Could Polygram be a corporation owned by the elite Nazi supporters who support Totalitarianism??? What caused the creative disagreement between Michael Monroe and Polygram Management? Why are the talentless ones relentlessly pushed on us while very talented artists are starving and never marketed at all? Let me guess…the talentless self-absorbed wannabes are willing to go along with an Agenda. Why is anyone who dares to tell the truth called names and labeled "conspiracy theorists" while the real conspiracy theorists (George Bush and his weapons of mass destruction-a conspiracy theory if ever I've heard one) are only unmasked after more than half the population has discovered their lies and the media has to expose them belatedly to retain a smidgeon of credibility? Why does Beyoncé dance like a stripper and move like she is screwing an imaginary penis and her husband sing about raping and murdering women and children in his song *Monster*? Why is her husband allegedly having bisexual orgies and being promoted while moral, ethical, and true original Rockstar's like Michael Monroe are ignored by our media? We are a living in a defiantly sick culture that promotes misogyny and pure evil and I am liable to be viciously attacked by fans of the above for exposing these sick celebrities. Hey, fans! These celebrities don't give a f@*k about you! They care only for money and fame and are willing to sell you out for money and fame. Does it get anymore shallow than that?! Why even worship them? They pretend to love you and care about you after they have sold their souls for money and fame and the bargain involves selling you out too! Think before you put these celebrities on a pedestal and make them into your idols! During the 2012 half time show Madonna had unmistakably Satanic symbolism such as a black sun (symbolizes he we need not name), wears a black Sabbath witches gown, and appears to stick her head in the crotch of a male dancer, has a pentagram on her crotch, boldly wears Baphomet horns and a high priestess golden gown, has chorus wearing black and white robes to worship Lord of Light Freemason style, and disappears at the end of her routine in a cloud of smoke like a being made of smokeless fire with a black man dressed in a black gown as a black magician. She even gets her fans duped into participating in this ritual of holding up their "torches" in obeisance to you know who. The colors are Satanic as well: black, white, red and gold. She has Minaj and MIA singers like two other priestesses, which I think signify the 3 mother goddesses in typical Satanic invocation rituals. I'm sure there is much, much more, but I am only telling you what I caught on this viewing. Ted Gunderson who oversaw 700 FBI Agents in Los Angeles investigated the McMartin Case and with the help of archaeologists found the tunnel the children described as well as the Satanic Magic Circles and black candles, etc. etc. Satanic ritual involves raping and murdering children. No investigation means meaningless laws written in meaningless books. Like a former lawyer once told me, half the laws written in law books are never enforced. Child rape is only extremely minimally enforced. Like a NYC cop said to Kevin Annett children had to be raped at least 15 times before an investigation would even be opened.

Since when does America seriously do anything about the sexual abuse of its children? I know of one Christian group who really cared about child prostitution & child trafficking. If we let children get raped and the rapists go unpunished we are allowing the destruction of these children's souls. We are harboring very violent deviant criminals and silencing the lambs who are sacrificed. We are allowing demonically possessed entities to rampage free within our societies and allowing Satanic rituals to take place. This is NO exaggeration. The rape of children IS Satanic Ritual! Rape is committed by demonically possessed people and going to the next level involves torture and murder. I have to broach these dark truths cause no one else will besides David Icke and Kevin Annett. Many serial killers start out as child molesters. Supposedly, serial killers have a triad of symptoms: fire starting, bed wetting; torturing animals. I think this was left out: sexual abuse by someone trusted, someone close, abandonment by a parent and extreme abuse and neglect. Serial killers are demonically possessed and how did the demons get into innocents? Trauma. Trauma of sexual abuse, trauma of child abuse, trauma of torture. The demons get in through trauma and they stay in and they take over. It becomes a bigger and bigger monster going from simple acts of abuse to rape to torture to killing. How many go to further and further levels? Many. We have an explosion of serial killers following the mass rape of children and our "free media" never ties the two together because if they did would the public continue to tolerate child rape? Instead our media implies that child rape victims get a legal settlement; everything is good, it's over and they have a normal life. The money makes everything all good again. This is another lie. The money is almost meaningless to most of the victims who really want JUSTICE and to see the demonically possessed perverts locked up behind bars. Money does not erase the trauma nor the intrusive memories. Money cannot fix PTSD or heal this life- long condition. So, what is the money good for? A slightly less stressful life is all it is good for; there will not be a return to a normal life in many cases. There will be an attempt or many attempts to try to live a normal life. Often there will be multiple marriages, divorces, job changes, and maybe prison and homelessness. Many die a slow death from addictions. Many commits suicide. Society creates the conditions for the crimes to occur; the criminals commit them. By our own apathy and ignorance, we have a child rape culture. We have demonically possessed perverts spiritually destroying hundreds of children each. Children are snatched off streets and discovered in shallow graves. We listen to the B.S. of our media and the rationalizations of our dishonest press. We shove child rapes and murders to the back burner because we would rather not think about them. Yet we have more child rapes and murders than almost any other country. Is this what the Muslims call the Great Satan? When we see, Sandusky get 60 years we assume that's the end of it without looking further. We seldom read alternative media sites that point out Sandusky was pimping his wards to wealthy donors to get the $10 million in donations. We don't read between the lines that many wealthy donors are pedophiles too. We ignore the fact that one of our cherished Bushes was on the Board of Directors of this child pimping "charity". We ignore the ravaged souls and blame the victimized adults for their dysfunction due to severe PTSD, which is almost #1 in disabling conditions. We are sacrificing our own children to Hellish Misery, we are as close to a Satanic Society as we can be short of publicly announcing that we are Satanic. We promote a New World (LUCIFERIAN) Order. Wow! The rest of the world hates us only second to Israel. We are so hated and want to believe the lies that we are hated for our freedoms. Even our allies hate us! We are the laughingstock of the perceptive world, the evil dictators of the South American world, the Great Satan of the Middle Eastern world. We are the psychopathic killers of the Syrians, the murderers by economic sanctions of 500,000 Iraqi children, the bloodthirsty Vikings of the Western world, the land pirates of the West. Our leader, Madeleine Albright, madam of MK Ultra slaves, dismisses the dead and dying children saying: "the sanctions were worth it." Once again, we allow criminals to speak for us and represent us as a vicious, inhumane, psychopathic regime. No, Madeleine Albright, you do NOT represent me. I want you to be forever in prison for being a vicious, inhumane psychopath committing crimes against humanity. I want the key thrown away. NO, George Bush, Herbert Walker Bush you don't represent me either-you are both VICIOUS criminals. No, Dick Cheney and Rumsfeld neither of you represent me. You are insane psychopaths who should be locked up and never allowed freedom. None of you represent me. You are soulless. Hillary Clinton, you are a chronic liar and admitted killer ("we came, we saw, he died" ha ha ha cackle) you do not represent me either. Your early employer fired you for chronic lying; he should 've had you disbarred for felony perjury and you should be in prison for many, many crimes: murders, drug possession, rape, drug smuggling & dealing, fraud, etc. You are all vicious criminals. American public, you are being made to look like idiots, fools and mercenary, guiltless, loveless people to allow these heinous crimes to go on in your name. Dare to care.

You also do not represent me. You are the walking dead for anyone alive breathing life could not let all this evil go on in their names. Have the morality to be outraged. Don't tolerate evil in your midst and pretend it is good. Don't live a lie or be the people of many lies. Don't allow the callous murder, starvation, and torture of red, brown, yellow and black skinned peoples and pretend that we are morally superior people because we are Americans-EXCEPTIONAL! For this, we are rightly despised. Your feigned superiority is hypocrisy of the highest order and you will be revealed for what you are: self-righteous; cowards. Your youth will despise you for allowing all of your freedoms to be stolen (a la John Titor-Time Traveler of Coast to Coast) and their futures ruined.

Your own future generations will see you as people that left a huge mess for future generations to clean up. It is like John Titor, time-traveler, says: we are hated by future generations of Americans just as we are hated by the rest of the world now. We have become a mockery of human rights because of the criminal "leaders". I speak out because I must-not because I like controversy. Many

Americans have already attacked me (at my back naturally) for speaking these truths. The truth be told they are supported by popular opinion not me. But, time will hear me out. I speak alone with one voice, but I know I speak the truth. I live in a Satanic nation that pushes pedophilia & war, pollution and empire and treats smaller weaker nations as a criminal psychopathic bully treats a smaller weaker schoolmate. How can I glorify this? There isn't anything good about evil. I am treated like I am a traitor by Americans loyal to psychopathy- The delusional and insane. Now the monster is coming for them with austerity and a Depopulation Agenda from Hell. Guess what America? You allowed children to die, Africans to starve because of your greedy corporations; now the Djinns are coming for you. Guess what's ahead for you? The same for the same criminals are going to cause the same suffering here in America if you allow them to. They have long planned to throw you under the bus!

1,000,000
Children Missing
bing.com
Pedophile Ring Coverup?
Sandusky Conviction
www.ConspiracyPlanet.com
www.murderbydecree.com
Watch: UnRepentant
Read pdf book: The Canadian Holocaust
www.itccs.org – (activism)
www.smoloko.com
www.franklincase.org
Watch: Conspiracy of Silence
www.realjewnews.com
www.thesenatorhillary.blogspot.com
www.brutalproof.net

Popular Culture is Your Enemy is the conclusion of LaRouchepac.com and their political activists and it is my conclusion in different ways. They like classical art and music-I rebel against the death culture I feel being promoted all around me via Skull 'n Bones logos on T-shirts, purses, wallets, belts and anything that can be sold promoting death culture. Music promotes death culture too: *Die Young* by Ke$ha who uses tons of Satanic imagery in her videos and openly admits she's forced to and wrote a song *Dancing with the Devil,* which is not being promoted because it tells way too much truth. As stated; "she better be careful cause she could wind up dead too" like the British star Amy Winehouse who admitted in an interview that when told to insert occult symbolism in her video she said "no" and shortly thereafter was found dead of an "overdose". Whenever the powers that be don't like you the roads become extremely dangerous or you are suddenly addicted to drugs and overdose or in rare cases when that is not working you get a bullet hole in your head like Lincoln, or massive bullet holes in your head like Kennedy or Huey P. Long. Just for the record, Bill Glynn told me his class was taken on a trip to where Huey P. Long died and the area was riddled with bullets just like the death scene of Bonnie & Clyde. Big Oil wanted him dead because he wasn't afraid of them and wanted to tax them to build schools and hospitals for the poor of Louisiana so they murdered him after he became a serious threat by announcing he would run for president. He would've made a great president too-truly for the people. Most popular movies don't really tell the whole truth either and I don't think Huey Long's death scene in *All the King's Men* was at all accurate at least not according to Bill Glynn who told me something completely different-it was like Bonnie & Clyde's deaths with bullets everywhere. The official version as usual is a lie. Bill also told me his uncle knew something about Kennedy's death and the whole family spoke in hushed tones about how this uncle was murdered in his hospital bed for what he really knew about Kennedy's death. The uncle was smothered to death. There have been about 100 or more deaths surrounding Kennedy's murder right in front of the public and the investigative commission was a kangaroo court with a predetermined outcome headed by those who had collaborated to have Kennedy murdered. Larouche has stated that the FBI murdered Kennedy. Allegedly a dying agent named Hunt confessed to the John F Kennedy murder and that there were several agents involved. People will never believe this, but the CIA and FBI do not work for the American People instead working for major corporations and the British Monarchy. The idea that they work for the American Public is another scam. Just look at their director James Comey – he refused to recommend Hillary Clinton's indictment, even admitting her legions of crimes.

On the set of Jump Street 22 I met an unknown hip hop artist and he told me a very interesting story. He told me about a friend of his who wanted to make millions, but to be a part of the elite club he had to be taking it up the anus as part of his indoctrination. Well, I believe this because it sounds awfully like Kay Griggs story of the military and how at the very top they are homosexuals and do homosexual activity. He stated that the next thing he knew his friend was in the millionaire's club flying all over the country and now making millions. There was a video about how bands could be marketed to Madison Square Garden, but they had to have the right contacts, to get the right marketing and the formula went like this: make your music harder metal to appeal to American tastes, take it up the anus, and grow your hair longer. Well, these Irishmen went home and had a good laugh, but needless to say they never made it in the music industry, and now have come out with a documentary about the true nature of the music industry, which was on David Icke. They state that after they turned down the offer all of a sudden hair metal bands became superstars: Motley Crue, Bon Jovi, Poison, etc. I wonder if they took up this offer. Maybe that was the real problem with Hanoi Rocks. You have to play the lesbian, homosexual game to make it in the music industry. Wes's site: illuminati-news tells another story about how big artists make a different kind of contract to make it, selling the soul contract like in *Faust*. If you go to YouTube you can listen to Katy Perry telling how she sold her soul, and the folk singer Bob Dylan on sixty minutes saying the same, and how he doesn't take anything for granted and KISS being an anagram for Kings in Satan's Service and many, many more not just Jimmy Page. By the way Swansong comes to the number 33 and these people are BIG believers in Numerology! Styx comes to the occult number of 13, the number of power and dominion and interestingly many of these stars have stage names with numbers of numerological significance such as 15 the number of the magician and 33, which is a number of outstanding luck. Check out the numerology of Naomi Judd and Ashley Judd if you wish-you might be surprised.

Satanic pop stars

Satanic Pop Imagery

Stasi America

America is a country intent on spying on everyone as Snowden has revealed and no one is exempt: not friends, not enemies, not allies or our victims, not citizens or "anarchists", not military or NATO, not foreigners, nor Americans, not Germans, nor French, nor Italian, nor Finnish, nor Prime Ministers, the Monarchies too and definitely all the intelligence organizations. Probably the Muslim Brotherhood, Jihadists and Islamists are spied on too. Then how can the government claim to not know when a "terrorist "attack is going to happen? For all the censorship going on Facebook and YouTube it seems the **terrorists never have a problem with censorship!** They are the only ones who are never censored on social media! Perhaps it is because the Terrorists have a special relationship with Obama, Brzezinski, and Hillary Clinton as well as defense agencies, CIA, John McCain and the rest. The CIA was running guns through Benghazi and Stephens

(Ambassador) met with a Turkish rep. the day he was murdered. Like I am telling you the gun running goes straight through Turkey, a NATO country and part of the long arm of the United States. (larouchepac.com, davidicke.com, wearechange.org, etc.)

If you feel the need to support endless wars and endless child kidnapping and rape you must, absolutely must support the Vatican charities: Roman Catholic charities such as the "Christian" Indian "Residential Schools" meaning internment camps where the inmates are not allowed to leave and Boystown in Omaha, Nebraska. Snowballed by the glowing press reports we have donated at least $500 million to Boystown alone, more, I believe for they have $500 million alone in assets and that does not include the operating expenses, etc. While the taxpayers donate their hard earned after tax money believing they are helping the less fortunate the real story of child rape rings and destroyed lives can be found in the internet and books written by survivors. A good read is: *Hidden from History: The Canadian Holocaust* on how millions were used for these Nazi internment camps while children froze, died of TB, were flogged to death, starved, beaten and raped to death. Since they were not spending donated money on heat, food, or clothing my question is: where did all the money go? Did it go to the Pope and the Vatican for their exorbitant lifestyles and gold encrusted ceremonial objects? Is this how the Pope is paid 200 million euros a year? Whew. Is that a LOT of money! He is right up there with the royals as far as being a BIG parasite. Wow!!! Loyal Catholics keep supporting this very evil cabal and if they did a smidgeon of research they would soon realize how evil this organization really is. Any organization that needs to have non-disclosure lawsuit settlements has a LOT to hide and do they ever! John DeCamp writes of Satanic Ritual Abuse in *The Franklin Cover-Up,* in which military bases partnered with Catholic institutions in the MK Ultra torture experiments of children. Kevin Annett writes of the same in graphic detail in *Hidden from History: The Canadian Holocaust.* David Icke exposes this big evil empire in *Tales from the Time Loop,* in which he concludes in his **last sentence that the religion of Babylon was the same as the Roman Catholic religion and it is Satanism.** Please do not donate anymore to the Vatican or Roman Catholic institutions or churches. Spread this truth and ask the blind to click a few keys at startpage.com. Donate to WeAreChange.org, itccs.org, David Icke or anyone exposing this very evil organization and their crimes. Disconnect the cable TV. Amnesty International is a phony international George Soros human rights organization because when the bones of the murdered (Canadian Holocaust) were sent to them they returned the package unopened. Their policy is apparently to NOT KNOW and to do NOTHING about this huge evil so therefore they must be beholden to the Western Imperialists. I recently discovered that George Soros, billionaire and Satanic Ninth Circle Member is a huge donor to Amnesty International as well as Human Rights Watch. He can rest assured these organizations will NEVER expose his crimes involving raped and murdered children. Knowing the Truth is Paramount and how people can deny the truth and keep pretending evil is good is beyond me! Tell them to research Vatican crimes. Their crimes are endless. You can find the same information at the above websites of wearechange.org and brutalproof.net under Canadian Holocaust and Hiddenfromhistory.com.

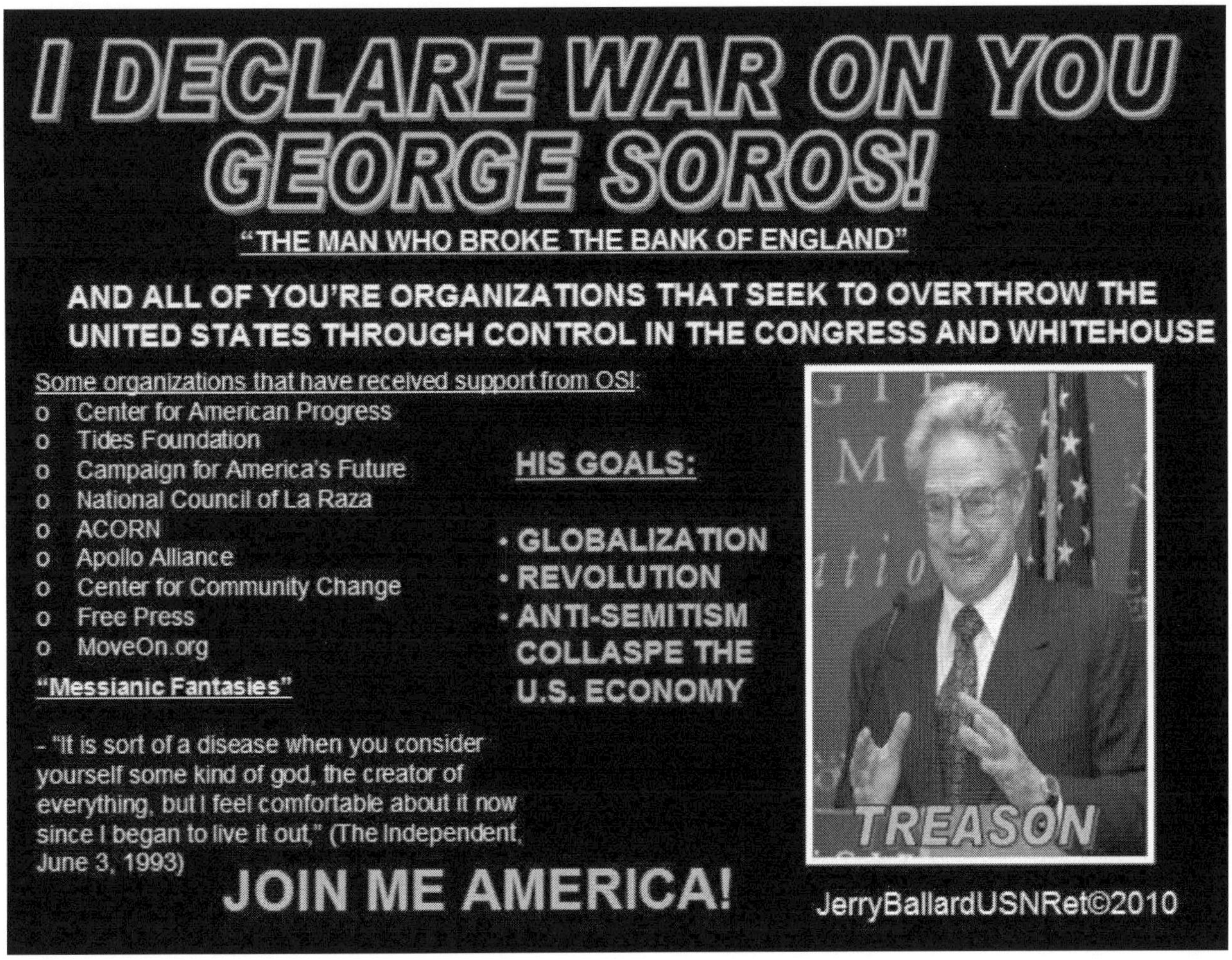
I DECLARE WAR ON YOU
GEORGE SOROS!
"THE MAN WHO BROKE THE BANK OF ENGLAND"
AND ALL OF YOU'RE ORGANIZATIONS THAT SEEK TO OVERTHROW THE UNITED STATES THROUGH CONTROL IN THE CONGRESS AND WHITEHOUSE
Some organizations that have received support from OSI:
o Center for American Progress
o Tides Foundation
o Campaign for America's Future
o National Council of La Raza
o ACORN
o Apollo Alliance
o Center for Community Change
o Free Press
o MoveOn.org
"Messianic Fantasies"
- "It is sort of a disease when you consider yourself some kind of god, the creator of everything, but I feel comfortable about it now since I began to live it out," (The Independent, June 3, 1993)
HIS GOALS:
· GLOBALIZATION
· REVOLUTION
· ANTI-SEMITISM
COLLASPE THE U.S. ECONOMY
TREASON
JOIN ME AMERICA!
JerryBallardUSNRet©2010

True Confession

I met a girl. Now she is an extra and she told me she saw twirling devil horns coming out of her ex-boyfriend's head in the early morning light-he's possessed by a very powerful demon. Another told me how her boyfriend's eyes turned red and the thing inside him was not him-another powerful possession like in Supernatural. Neither one wants anyone to know they saw these things and I am sworn to secrecy to their identities. It reminds me of the book written by Steven Tyler's ex how when he was severely addicted to drugs the thing that looked at her was not him or the book *Rebel Heart* written by Bebe Buell about Jimmy Page's occultism and how he told her to pay attention to midnight and then a picture fell and she & friend ran in terror from the house-at midnight. Jimmy Page is into Aleister Crowley, which is the reason he would want to own Aleister Crowley's house and the demonic infestation within him would crave the energy of pre-pubescent girls, which is why he started seducing 13-year old's (*I'm With the Band*) and became pedophilic. Most black magicians become very severe addicts as Jimmy Page and Aleister Crowley both did and for any of you wanting very dark confessions go to Interview *with an Ex-Vampire* as he describes being addicted to blood and how the highest form of Satanism were Vampires and the Very Highest Form Werewolves. You can see it on youtube.com and I could NOT make this up.

An acquaintance relays to me how she sees twirling horns coming from her lover's head in the morning twilight and they dissipate. Another, on set, relays how she was knocked out with a lamp, the perpetrator's eyes turned red and the thing in him wasn't him. These incidents are of full blown possession. I saw my abductor's eyes fill with a smoky black and felt the frightening presence of pure evil fully in control-a very, evil demonic presence. A homeless man tells me of his sister being raped in front of him by his demoniac step-father whose eyes turned black during these rapes. David Icke writes about the black-eyed beings. If you let them into your house or car you may often wind up dead. The man who murdered his entire family in Amityville was completely possessed. The mother almost stabs her infant to death in *The Conjurer* during her possession and is barely stopped by the exorcist. Another friend with the gift of clairvoyance relays how she saw the black soul of her boyfriend lie down next to her when he was physically at home and told him never to come back. Evil always seems to come in a good-looking package! How do these possessions occur? The Ouija board is outlawed in Iran as playing with fire and bringing negative entities into your life, but in America it is a toy! Playing with a spell book was another way a hapless idiot invited the dark side into his life. A now internationally known psychic warned her followers NOT to use an angel board sold by another very popular psychic. It looks to me as the same as a Ouija board simply titled angel board and opening the same channels. Dr. Wickland, whose wife was a medium, warned against automatic writing because once again you do not know who you are channeling. The girl who saw the twirling horns in her boyfriend in the twilight thought casual sex was another point of entry. It is. People's auras mingle during sex and entities can be passed around like venereal diseases. David Icke had a video of a bewitched Italian girl. She was sexually abused at the age of thirteen and then bewitched. (spell cast) She had repeatedly sought help for exorcism and the demon taking her over screamed that "where there is war or pollution .... there am!" Only one country I know of fits this description and it is America creating the most pollution and starting war after war after war. The G7 countries, which include America, U.K., Nazi Germany, France, the Netherlands, etc. do similar acts while all put out their propaganda that they are the great beacons for humanity. Don't kid yourself-war is mass murder. Mass murder is mass ritual sacrifice to U Know Who.

Our national news media heralded LaVey's Church of Satan as if he was a carnival guy-not to be taken seriously. What they didn't tell us is that he castrated his own son for refusing to join his evil church and his son dared not speak out about him until his father's death. Reportedly when LaVey died he cried out "What have I done?" His son also described George Bush Sr. and the Council of 13 doing child sacrifices at their coven in Kimball Castle in Colorado. (Ever wonder what happens to many of the missing children that never reappear? Hint: Satanic child sacrifices and organ trafficking.) The massive sexual abuse in the Western countries (not limited to these countries) leads to possession, which drives these tortured souls to abuse alcohol and drugs to relieve the constant internal pain. Our top politicians (Clintons & Bushes) were heavily involved in illegal drug trafficking into the United States. The sexually abused children medicated with SSRI's (selective serotonin reuptake inhibitors) frequently become school shooters. The actual meaning of "pharmacists or druggist" is "giver of potions." The early 'givers of potions' were involved in the black arts of sorcery. It is sorcery to turn a nonviolent child into a mass killer. Another not well-known fact is that the Satanic Colonel Aquino (child sexual abuser at Presidio doing MK Ultra Psy-Ops) went to Reagan's White House in full Satanic regalia. He was sexually abused as a child. His wife's name is Lilith-a name for the supreme demon. He was implicated in child sex abuse cases in Presidio. The elite Satanists are all pedophiles and as criminally insane adults advocate rape-torture-killings and the genocide of whole nations. Even the Los Angeles Chronicle reported on a young man who was arrested and told the police he was demon possessed.

Religions

In *Tales from the Time Loop* David Icke writes that the Roman Catholic church is the church of Babylon, which is Satanism in his last sentence. Martin Malachi, who wrote *Windswept*, before he abruptly died wrote that certain Satanic sectors in the Vatican were involved in a ritual to invoke the smoke of S____, head Djinn. Their own chief exorcist, Father Amorth, stated that high levels of the Vatican were taken over by this cult. The massive pedophilia of the Roman Catholic church should be a huge red flag that this church is not what they are purporting to be. Martin Malachi was an insider connected to people very high up in the Vatican and in a radio interviews he admitted that 90% of his book was not actually fiction but was based on fact. Unfortunately, as I do more and more research it seems every church has systematic, institutionalized child abuse. The Christian Scientists withhold medical care from children in horrific pain and there are many documented cases about this. The Mormon Church has been practicing child "marriage", which is child rape. Pedophiles have all the rights; children have none. The Jewish holy baths are used by a majority of Rabbi's to rape little boys. One rabbi didn't go along with this sickness and is now being ostracized!!! Child rape is soul shattering and it is the main part of satanic ritual abuse. Scientology was created by an avowed Satanist, Ron Hubbard, for his stated purpose of making money and not paying taxes on it. Even Christianity is steeped in paganism; Easter is based on a fertility rite. The congregations practicing these religions do no research whatsoever that would reveal the paganism and occultism that these religions are based on. As a Romanian tour guide and archaeologist said, "Jesus death is a shaman's death and rebirth." Generally, people who continue going to these pedophilic churches after all the evidence of the child rape rings don't care and will continue to enable child rape in their wanting to be a part of this social club. Real spirituality doesn't ignore this most heinous of crimes. Satanic black masses often involve child rape and as many of these churches have done the same I wonder what type of God is in charge???

War is a Racket

War is a massive criminal money-making racket benefiting Bankster's and the military-industrial complex. Countries are saddled with debts they cannot pay and veterans come home mentally and physically destroyed. Wars serve the coffers of the .001% and their minions-politicians. They are financed by moneylenders (Rothschild's) who finance both sides for whoever wins and whoever loses the moneylenders get paid. (Remember Jesus & the Moneylenders? Not much has changed!) War is a crime and many young people are duped into serving the interests of the wealthy with words like Patriotism, Democracy, and Freedom. These elite never have their children fighting wars; that is for the poor to do. Note the meaning of the word "*spell*"-ing. Words cast spells on people with psychological connotations. Words are used for war propaganda. No wonder the word spell is in spelling. While they exhort the youth to fight these criminal wars and to do their killing for them these same .001% are counting their gold and hoarding it. Why was Pat Tillman murdered by friendly fire? He had radio interviews scheduled and was going to reveal the true nature of the war. John Lennon was murdered for leading his fans towards peace. *Anti-war* is an internet site repeatedly under attack. David Icke states that wars are mass ritual sacrifices to S____. I agree. Everything in our Western world seems to serve the dark side, but most especially wars. If anyone dares to protest the wars it is a bullet hole to the head: John Lennon, Martin Luther King, John F. Kennedy and the protesters at Kent State. Chrissie Hyde (of the Pretenders) relocated to England after seeing protesters murdered in our "free" country. I simply cannot understand the American and British insanity of thinking we are "free." To me freedom means protesting without being murdered or harassed, not having fees and fines for every little thing; not being taxed to death. I guess the media here promotes freedom as this sex liberation to sleep around, "hook-up" and don't worry about the consequences; there are always abortions available and vaccines. This again is straight out of Satanic ritual: sex without commitments and killing babies. If the only freedom being promoted here is Satanic is that really freedom? Christians do not have a free flow of information for if they did they would know all about the "Christian Residential Schools" involvement in genocide (the Canadian Holocaust). Romanians, know they are slaves and soon we will know it in America too.

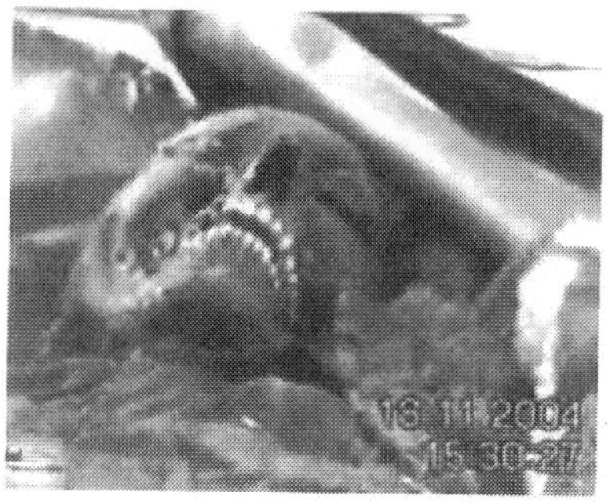

ODESSA, UKRAINE MASSACRE BY NATO
& UNITED STATES-HORRIFIC CRIME!

BrutalProof!

WHY IS EVERYONE TALKING ABOUT UN AGENDA 21?

UN Agenda 21/Sustainable Development is the action plan to inventory and control all land, all water, all minerals, all plants, all animals, all construction, all means of production, all information, all energy, and all human beings in the world. INVENTORY AND CONTROL

Have you wondered where these terms 'sustainability' and 'smart growth' and 'high density urban mixed-use development' came from? Doesn't it seem like about 10 years ago you'd never heard of them and now everything seems to include these concepts? Is that just a coincidence? That every town and county and state and nation in the world would be changing their land use/planning codes and government policies to align themselves with...what?

Far from being a 'conspiracy theory' or a 'tin-foil hat' fantasy, this is an actual United Nations plan, signed onto in 1992 by President George HW Bush along with 178 other world leaders. The UN called it Agenda 21 because it is the Agenda for the 21st century. According to UN Secretary General Maurice Strong, the 'affluent middle-class American lifestyle is unsustainable.' That includes single family homes, private vehicles, appliances, air-conditioning, & meat-eating. They are a threat to the planet.

This might sound like a silly plan that doesn't affect you. But look around. This economic collapse is UN Agenda 21. You'll hear that this plan is non-binding, that it's a dusty old plan with no teeth. That is a lie. In fact over the last 20 years this plan has been implemented all over the United States. It's called Sustainable Development. The 3 E's: ecology, economy, equity.

After George Bush signed it in 1992, it was brought back to the US by President Clinton (1993) when he created the President's Council on Sustainable Development for the sole purpose of getting it into every city, county, and state in the US through federal rules, regulations, and grants. This is a global plan but is implemented locally. You'll see it as a regional plan. It might be called Vision 2035, or Your Town 2025, or One Bay Area, or Plan NY...all of these regional plans are the same. They call for stack and pack housing, restricted mobility, and regional government. Domestic surveillance, smart meters, GMO's, loss of freedom—all UN Agenda 21/Sustainable Development. You are losing your rights. You are being manipulated. You are being lied to. You are the Resistance.

This is a non-partisan worldwide grassroots movement.

PLEASE COPY AND DISTRIBUTE. AWARENESS IS THE FIRST STEP IN THE RESISTANCE.

PostSustainabilityInstitute.org DemocratsAgainstUNAgenda21.com

Agenda 21=Communism!

Agenda 21 is a globalist dream; it is a slick marketing scheme using buzzwords like SUSTAINABILITY and TRANSITION to push an agenda through, which will guarantee that no one can own cars or houses; they will live stack and pack like in Brasov, Romania. Whenever the globalists are pushing something you can be 100% guaranteed it is not for your benefit! Agenda 21 is Communism in disguise and if you research who created communism (Rothschild) you will find out it also is a Satanic creation. Under Agenda 21 you cannot even have your own garden for you do not own your own land. Furthermore, Agenda 21 has hundreds of pages of restrictions. All of us will live like the poorest Chinese peasants without any freedoms or rights left at all. For anyone paying attention our rights have been slowly eroded for decades. So, few are aware and these changes affect so many! How frightening our towns, councils, and mayors are tripping over each other to sell us all out to line their own pockets to adopt Communism! BTW Communism was created by the Satanist Globalists. Well, it is the same with the insurance, banking, and oil industries. Big lobbyist payouts bring big benefits to these very corrupt entities. Monitor your "representatives!"

WHAT'S WRONG WITH SUSTAINABLE DEVELOPMENT?

How could something that sounds so good be bad? Who wouldn't want to be sustainable? Vibrant? Walkable? Bikeable? Green? These buzz words were designed to make you think that you're doing something good for the planet. This is the biggest public relations scam in the history of the world.

Sustainable Development was created and defined by the United Nations in 1987, and the action plan to implement it was signed onto in 1992 by US President Bush and 178 other nations. It was called Agenda 21, the Agenda for the 21st century. Considered unsustainable under this plan: middle class lifestyle, single family homes, private vehicles, meat-eating, air conditioning, appliances, dams, farming, you.

Clinton began to implement it in the US in 1993 by giving the American Planning Association a multi-million dollar grant to write a land use legislative blueprint for every municipality in the US. It is called *Growing Smart Legislative Guidebook with Model Statutes for Planning and the Management of Change*. This was completed in 2002 and is being used to train planners in every university, college and government planning office in the nation. *Growing Smart* is Smart Growth.

Growing Smart is in our planning department and its principles are in our city and county plan. Right now. Beside this, on the shelf, is *The Local Agenda 21 Planning Guide* put out by ICLEI and the United Nations. Urban areas are being consolidated and rural areas are being emptied of people through restrictive land use policies, gasoline costs, vehicle miles traveled taxes, loss of rural road maintenance, closure of rural schools, closure of rural post offices, water well monitoring, smart meters, and regionalization pressures. Smart Growth is not just the preferred building style for UN Agenda 21/Sustainable Development; it is the ideology. Moving people into centralized urban areas in high density housing creates the perfect opportunity for domestic surveillance. This ideology is being used as the justification to radically change every city in the United States and to impose regulations dictated by unelected regional boards and commissions. It is remaking government. This dramatic revolution in private property rights extends to every facet of our lives: education, energy, food, housing, transportation. We are being told that this is OUR PLAN but it is not. We object to this manipulation and refuse to be subjected to it. Educate yourself. Speak out. BE the Resistance.

PLEASE COPY AND DISTRIBUTE. AWARENESS IS THE FIRST STEP IN THE RESISTANCE.
PostSustainabilityInstitute.org DemocratsAgainstUNAgenda21.com

Obama, Zionist Puppet

He was elected by desperate people and then foolish voters. He represents the British Empire and oligarchical interests plus Wall Street-not us. He is a chronic liar and got elected on his campaign promises to rebuild the infrastructure, rid us of the Patriot Act and FISA act, stop the war in Iraq, bring the troops home, etc. etc. He has kept none of his promises and is destroying the American Middle Class with Obamacare, the blocking of Glass-Steagall (remember he is a slave to the Monarchy and Wall Street), renewing the Patriot Act and signing the NDAA Act-the National Defense Authorization Act, in which I am liable to go to prison without any charges being filed just for writing this. He has renewed the FISA spying; I just found out thru We Are Change that my T-Mobile phone is being spied on via the Department of Defense and I believe every cellular user is being spied on period. He also renewed the Military Commissions act, which does not recognize Habeas Corpus. Guantanamo is still not closed, the war in Iraq is ongoing and he has tried to go to war with Syria but was basically called down on that one. Furious callers demanded: No War with Syria! We are an international pariah hated and despised not for our democracy, but because of our KLEPTOCRACY, which is rule by thieves or pirates who start wars to loot other nations! Our elderly and youngest have been targeted with benefit cuts, college students are being swindled by student loan scams and their future jobs are being outsourced with "Free Trade Agreements:" North American Free Trade Agreement (NAFTA), Central American Free Trade Agreement (CAFTA), Trans-Atlantic Free Trade Agreement (TAFTA) and Trans-Pacific Partnership (TPP) and Trans-Pacific Investment Partnership (TPIP). I'm sure the illuminati have more on the way because they won't be satisfied until 95% of us are dead and the rest enslaved. He protects the .001% only and they get the Banksters bailouts, free trade agreements, his vetoing

Glass-Steagall, the wars that these elite never fight leaving the mutilated bodies and PTSD'd minds to the poor, and the Federal Reserve Zionists cartel who are super-represented by Yellen, Bernanke, Obama, and other Zionists. The Federal Reserve can violate any old law they want: usury, stealing with bail-ins and bail-outs, and fake money printing, which is like Monopoly money printing and forcing us all to use their worthless paper. Obama's crimes are too numerous to mention here, but he has forged an alliance with al-Qaida, first to overthrow the government of Libya and secondly to overthrow the government of Syria and I believe he will be bringing them in as "refugees" to overthrow us. (Is this the reason for all the guillotines?) This reckless and criminal allying with the perpetrators of 9-11-2001 as well as 9-11-2012 is high treason. He has conducted war without the consent of Congress and is way overdue for being charged. What are we all waiting for? Time to call 1-202-224-3121 and tell your cowardly representative to vote to try him for treason and get the arrest warrants before he ruins us all! He is busy trying to start a thermonuclear World War 3 using Ukraine as the trigger point. All Ukrainians were out in the streets to protest the new regime, their brutal austerity and their NATO-EU-USA support. I didn't see any of this in our media, which is tightly controlled by a handful of illuminati oligarchy like Rupert Murdoch, but it was definitely on the internet. A very good publication is *Executive Intelligence Review's: Obama's War on America: 9-11 Two.* Certainly, their publications are pricey, but no one else does the research they do and it is very reliable for truth seekers. You can read a lot of their editorials for free. They relate that Obama will not release the 28 pages from the 9-11 Commission because the relationship between the Bushes, Obama's and al-Qaida is clearly established. As of this writing the 28 pages were released by forcing their release-75 Senators stood up for America demanding their release under pressure from the 9/11 families, Larouche-PAC made it a major issue since 2009 along with 28pages.org and the 28 pages were declassified. Also, one inference from the nefarious alliance of this axis of evil (Britain, United States Politicians Clintons, Bushes & Obama & Saudi's) is that they are totally against the American People as well as the sovereignty of the Libyans, Syrians, Iraqi's and Iranians. These are criminal psychopaths; all of them are and the sooner they are deposed the better. These are facts not conspiracies unless you are talking about these nefarious criminals who truly are in a conspiracy against the people they were supposed to represent! Fools attacking conspiracy "theorists" will only hasten their own demise when they find themselves with no jobs, no futures, only debts to pay and working as slave labor as their young go to war because there are no other jobs and come home maimed with their disability denied. This is what is happening and worse.

Hillary Clinton, Zionist

This woman is a supreme psychopath if ever there was one. In one of her first jobs out of law school she was fired for chronic lying. You can see her former employer on the internet saying he fired her because she couldn't be trusted. Well, why would anyone trust her to run our nation then? This morally debased, repugnant evil witch is actually giving speeches to women on their progress and liberation. Why then did she bring in loads of new taxes as senator of New York State? Cathy O'Brien, an escapee of the Mind Control torture program run by the CIA, Harvard and affiliates describes in her book *Trance-Formation of America* how Hillary sexually abused her and admired her torture carving of a devil's head in her vagina (without anesthesia). Hillary thinks sexually abusing women slaves is part of the good life and she's speaking about women's rights? There have been untold suspicious murders around the Clintons (about 100 according to RINF-online press), drug dealing through Mena air force base in Arkansas while Billy was governor and the Monica Lewinsky scandal pales in comparison to the murders, drug dealing and rapes done by these two. Cathy O'Brien's book is in pdf on the internet and there are many blogs about Hillary Clinton and YouTube videos (The Most Dangerous Game…Cathy O'Brien…. on youtube.com) with Cathy O'Brien describing torture she has been through. She has one hell of a lot of courage and is a testament to the human spirit under the worst brutality. Oh, by the way, two teenage boys who saw the drug dealing going on in Arkansas were murdered as was Seale the Louisiana pilot who was supposed to testify in court about his flying drugs into Mena Air Force base. On a one to ten scale of psychopathy Hillary rates a fifteen!

BrutalProof!

America Being Sold Off at Fire Sale Prices While Americans Are Being Betrayed

This was told to me by a real estate lawyer how foreign interests were taking over America and Banksters were betraying the American people. Assets are being sold off at fire sales to wealthy billionaires and other countries and the American people are being charged usurious interest and fined to death in a debt slavery. It's the same with the toll roads; most are owned by foreigners who are taking money from the Americans and shipping the money overseas. Very few tolls actually go for their stated purpose; actually, tolls seem more like a form of graft and embezzlement of the U.S. taxpayer.

Elizabeth of England of Nazi Imperialism and Saxe-Coburg-Gotha (German) bloodline owns much of the real estate of the United States. She must have secret meetings because if it all the money grubbing scams she runs on people became public then popular opinion would start to turn against her. Oprah is running a social engineering scam trying to bait the black American population with the race card instead of telling the truth, which she well knows is the real reason so many Americans are against Obama. His own voters are turning against him Not cause of his race, but because of his evil policies and he is impoverishing his own race. He is an illuminati Banksters puppet and traitor and should be tried as one as should be Bush, Jr., Herbert Walker Bush Sr., the Clintons, Nixon, Rumsfeld, Condoleezza Rice, Hitlery (Hillary) Clinton, Big Dick Cheney, Wolfowitz and that lying White House Press Secretary Jay Carney. By no means is this list complete; it is only a beginning, but we need mass arrests of all of these lying criminals. I don't hate them, but they have all committed genocidal war crimes and crimes against their country and that should be enough for all of these criminals to be arrested for crimes against humanity/mass murder to start with. So, should Elizabeth, the Monarchy, the PM of England and PM of Canada and monarchies of Belgium, George Soros, etc. Go itccs.org!!! I am rooting for you to succeed!!

Zionist

International Common Law Court of Justice
Criminal Trial Division, Brussels

PUBLIC SUMMONS

Issued to Elizabeth Windsor

In the matter of *The People v. the Government of Canada, The Crown of England, The Vatican, and the Roman Catholic, Anglican and United Church of Canada, and Joseph Ratzinger, Elizabeth Windsor, Stephen Harper and other persons*

Case Docket No. 001: Genocide in Canada

BE ADVISED that you and the other persons named herein are publicly charged by the Prosecutor's Office of this Court with complicity in Crimes against Humanity and an ongoing Criminal Conspiracy.

BE FURTHER ADVISED that accordingly, you and these other persons are hereby summoned to appear as defendants in a lawsuit addressing these crimes to be adjudicated by this Court, commencing on Monday, November 5, 2012 in the City of Brussels.

BE FURTHER ADVISED that, being thus charged, you or your legal counsel or representatives have ten (10) days as of the issuing of this Public Summons to respond, either verbally or in writing. Your failure to respond to or contest these charges within this period may be interpreted as a tacit admission of guilt on your part.

Issued October 19, 2012 under the authority of George Dufort, LL.B., Secretary of the Court.

G. Dufort

George Dufort, LL.B.

International Common Law Court of Justice

The International Common Law Court of Justice
Case Docket No. 001
Brussels, Belgium
19/10/12
contact: itccscentral@gmail.com
USA office: 386-323-5774

Coventry Common Law Court

The International Tribunal into Crimes of Church and State

March 2014

Tel: 07868 566 856
Email: commonlawcourts.england@gmail.com
Or: [illegible]@gmail.com

www.itccs.org
www.iclcj.com

The UK is Governed by criminals

Queen Elizabeth and UK Prime Minister David Cameron have been i issued arrest warrants. The two were charged with sexual crimes against children as part of an international pedophile ring.

"We have enough evidence to prosecute and hold both the Prime Minister and Queen of England" said ex-Royal Military Policeman Matt Taylor.

The present Catholic Pope Francis Bergoglio was alleged to be part of child trafficking in an international pedophile ring. Victims who were prostituted as children at the Vatican have come forward, along with survivors who alleged they were abused in international pedophile rings. Victims have also alleged sex abuse and murder of children by former Pope Ratzinger, Catholic Cardinal Bernard Alfrink of Utrecht, a second Catholic Cardinal, a French judge, Belgian priests, other members of the British Royal family and Prince

PROVEN GUILTY

A former Argentine government official recently agreed to testify about Bergoglio's role in a pedophile ring during Argentine's Junta "Dirty War."

A Brussels international Common Law court was slated on the matter to begin March 15 2014.

On Feb. 25 2013 six judges of a Brussels common law court found the Queen, Cameron, Ratzinger and 37 other global elites guilty in the disappearance of 50,000 Canadian indigent children. Cases were prosecuted by the International Tribunal into Crimes of Church and State, ITCCS. www.iclcj.com

Evidence presented could be reviewed in ITCCS's Kevin Annett's "Hidden No Longer" at www.hiddennolonger.com. Survivors came forward from Ireland Templemore Forgotten Victims, Canadian Friends and Relatives of the Disappeared, Italian Rete L'Abuso and in the US, United Against Church Terror, plus government mind-control and Satanic Ritual Abuse survivors from SMART http://ritualabuse.us and Child Abuse Recovery www.ChildAbuseRecovery.com

Along with the March 15 common law court on Popes Bergoglio and Ratzinger, several common law court actions are being organized for 2014. Common law courts are being established in Canada, 17 states in the USA, Holland, France, Italy and here in the UK

Announcing the opening of Coventry Common law court…

Why common law courts?

Common Law court actions were proven effective. In Feb. 2013 Catholic Pope Joseph Ratzinger resigned within days of being issued his arrest warrant. They are easy to establish,bring the strength of the community together and can legally convict anyone regardless of the status they hold, the job they do or the authority they have over the community normally.

Should parents consider common law courts to protect their children?

Yes, evidently. On Oct. 10 1964 Queen Elizabeth and Prince Phillip were seen taking ten native children from the Canadian Kamloops Residential School. The age-ten children haven't been heard of since. Canadian courts refused to hear the case that also involved the 50,000 Canadian missing indigent children. There have since been many allegations of Royal family members, entertainers and members of parliament all released with no charge. The police force and courts, trusted to protect our current justice system are failing because they are abusing their power to suit their own needs.

Are we in danger if global elites are not held responsible for their crimes?

Evidently so. Two witnesses died of mysterious causes prior to the Feb. 2013 Brussels court that convicted the Queen, Cameron, former Pope Ratzinger and 37 other elites of Crimes Against Humanity. They have been stealing and trafficking children and are still doing to this day. They use social services churches and hospitals to continue their crimes, and the military, police and courts to back themselves up. They control everything and if not held accountable will continue their path of genocide on humanity.

Would our present court system prosecute international pedophile rings?

Evidently not. ITCCS efforts for excavation of 31 child mass grave sites of the 50,000 missing children have been thwarted since the first was discovered in 2008. The child mass grave sites were on grounds of 80 Canadian government-owned residential schools run by the Catholic and Anglican churches and the United Church of Canada. Victims of the Catholic priest abuse scandal have seen very few perpetrators find the inside of a jail cell. The same with the paedophiles who have recently been exposed in the government and entertainment business. Such as Jimmy Saville, Rolf Harris, Ed Milliband and Tony Blair.

With help of legal experts and judges, the ITCCS has united survivors of genocide and child torture worldwide. ITCCS is active in 26 countries with over 50 affiliated groups

Blackfish

This is a heartbreaking expose of the true brutality involved in "training"/torturing orcas to make money for SeaWorld. I think every orca at SeaWorld is severely traumatized and this is why they get so violent with their trainers. Violence and abuse beget more violence and abuse and SeaWorld is a perfect example of this. A stream of scheduled entertainers cancelled their gigs at SeaWorld after seeing this horrific movie including Heart and Willie Nelson. Corporations are creations that make brutal sadism legal for these creatures without any rights-legalizing slavery. (I wonder how much the British Monarchy is invested in SeaWorld.) Corporations should be illegal. Many activists have signed petitions to ban orcas from being used in "entertainment". Legislation will soon be pending in Congress. It isn't too soon for me. The corporations have basically pit the trainers and orcas against each other and what these psychopathic corporations do for money is legal. Trainers are being murdered by orcas so stressed they are having psychological breakdowns and snapping. The corporations ruthlessly force the shows to go on only for the money. The smart person would not go to these shows knowing the brutality these orcas go through and would sign petitions, tell others and call Congress to make it all stop. The same can be said for circuses & the bull-killings-as-entertainment in Spain, which have almost been eradicated.

The Cove

Instead of ongoing torture like in Blackfish here the dolphins are brutally slaughtered in a Cove in Japan to be used for food. The water is red with blood and one dolphin swam straight toward the crew seeking help. This is just so horrific. **Dolphins in India are given a status as non-human persons** like their souls are human even though they are mammals. The slaughter of these altruistic humanlike creatures with very high intelligence-they have more glial cells (related to smarts) than Einstein's brain- is a crime. People do not have to eat dolphin sushi or order it and a mass boycott needs to be organized. This could stop as well. It would help if Japan had laws prohibiting this slaughter.

Live Skinning of Fur Animals

In china fur animals are skinned alive. This is so horrific it needs to stop! I saw it on a YouTube video and the horror of it does not go away. This needs to be outlawed in every nation.

Live Organ Harvesting

Live organ Harvesting is also in China against the spiritual FALUN Gong. Tens of thousands of FALUN Gong (Political Prisoners) have died this way. There will have to be an international outcry to make this stop. The worst criminals are involved in snuff porn and organ trafficking.

WANTED

Jorge Bergoglio - "Pope Francis 1"

WANTED

For Crimes against Humanity, Child Abduction and Complicity in Murder in Argentina

An International Citizens' Arrest Warrant has been issued against him

by The International Common Law Court of Justice

www.itccs.org

Other witnesses to NINTH CIRCLE cults confirm the presence of British Royal Family members MOUNTBATTEN and PRINCE PHILIP at these child sacrifices, whose presence was concealed by defendant WELBY. Jesuit officers including defendants PACHON and BERGOGLIO were also present at the same rituals at Camarvon Castle in Wales and at an undisclosed French Chateau, during the 1980's and 1990's. Similar sacrifices were conducted at Catholic and Anglican Indian residential schools in Kamloops, British Columbia and Brantford, Ontario during the 1960's and earlier, according to statements from living and deceased indigenous eyewitnesses.

New Pope Francis (Zionist Jesuit)

He is a wolf in sheep's clothing like Obama. He is a Jesuit and many Catholics support the criminal organizations of the Vatican and Jesuits unaware that these organizations have committed more than 10 million crimes mostly against children. Jesuits control Citibank, UN, NATO, British Intelligence, the Israeli Mossad, European Union, African Union, Vatican, Interpol, the Federal Reserve, Pentagon and many, many other organizations. They are a vast criminal cartel masquerading as a spiritual organization. They make money through child trafficking, child prostitution, wars-for-looting, money laundering, thefts of land and resources from indigenous natives and outright fraud. The New Pope Francis is there to put a humble face on this criminal organization and to bring the flock back so to speak so they can continue milking them for money. He is currently being tried for crimes against humanity by itccs.org for the child trafficking enterprise in Argentina. Political activists and dissidents had their children stolen from them and trafficked for money. Itccs.org has witnesses testifying to his rape and murder of children. He is as evil as Ratzinger the other Nazi pope who also murdered children and was a member of the same Ninth Circle cult. As the head of this criminal syndicate he will be paid $200 million euros a year! HE HAS MADE WHISTLEBLOWING ON CHILD RAPISTS AUTOMATIC PRISON TIME IN THE VATICAN JAIL! He is not concerned about protecting children from sexual abuse. He is concerned about protecting the Satanic Priests Raping Little Boys! Early in his career he allowed two of his own priests to be tortured and sold them out to a fascist Argentinian Regime. He simply abandoned them to their fate of being captured and tortured. He is illuminati as well. By the way one of their own priests told his congregation to not donate to the Vatican and was immediately arrested in New York State. Hude, World Bank lawyer, stated that 90% of the illegal

IRS taxes go to the Bank of England in London, which takes about a 40% cut and the remaining goes to the Vatican (50% to 60%). Now I find out that two Louisiana lawyers, one in Shreveport and one in Lafayette fought the IRS for years one until he died age 62 from a heart attack due to the stress. The IRS is a criminal illuminati corporation connected to the criminal Vatican and should be abolished, which is what Ron Paul promised to do if elected. Anyways he wasn't and we still have this criminal entity going after political activists such as the TEA Party. It's time the IRS books were audited as well as the Federal Reserve. Unfortunately, the Senate has just voted down Auditing the Fed! We are living on a Ponzi scheme that is getting ready to crash big time and the house of cards is coming down. We cannot pay the derivatives Ponzi scheme coming due and our corrupt politicians have written a bail-in law Cyprus style. Everyone who banks at the bailout banks will be screwed out of their savings & deposits not covered by the FDIC! It should be obvious that even without this mess the number of baby boomers retiring on social security is the biggest in history, the equal number will no longer be paying taxes into this Ponzi scheme and the result is going to be a huge disaster-something akin to the Titanic going down. There may be a few bumps and a few hours on the way down, but unless some drastic measures are taken like putting Glass-Steagall in place and repealing the free trade agreements we are headed for a very bad fall. Whether all the uninformed out there want to wake-up or not they will not have a choice! It will be a brutal awakening for the ill-informed masses. Some may not survive. Think of the scale of every major city being a Katrina-like disaster. That mess took years to recover from and outside help was needed. If every city has a Katrina they will not be able to get outside help because everyone else will be busy with their own nightmare. It will truly be a Welcome to My Nightmare scenario. On top of this fully half of America is living off of its own government and a tidal wave of baby boomers is coming to create an even a larger percentage of Americans living off of the government. Most recently, Ron Paul stated that the government will not be able to pay for the entitlements. Well no they cannot pay for the entitlements as well as continuing bailing out the banks in the trillions of dollars when they're collecting less and less in tax revenues. Almost all of the cities in America are bankrupt and are going down like Detroit. Detroit only happens to be the first one to go. Do the math. It's impossible for the government to keep their promises. They're stockpiling magazine rifles and training troops, training for civil unrest for the impending riots when people realize how badly they've been screwed and the situation here turns into the USSR breakup of years ago, the food supply could be interrupted. Communities with lots of gardens, farmers with cows, pigs, and sheep will probably be the best off. Those with a defense system will be too. My guess is the worst-off ones will be the ones living solely on entitlements, the seniors, living in a huge city in an apartment. It will be like New York City during Sandy for them. It doesn't have to happen. It will only happen due to the shortsightedness of our leaders and the foolish voters who voted them in, the rigged elections, and the appointed crooked supreme-court justices who seem to do as they are told to do by the elite not what they are supposed to do when taxpayers pay their salaries.

ZION

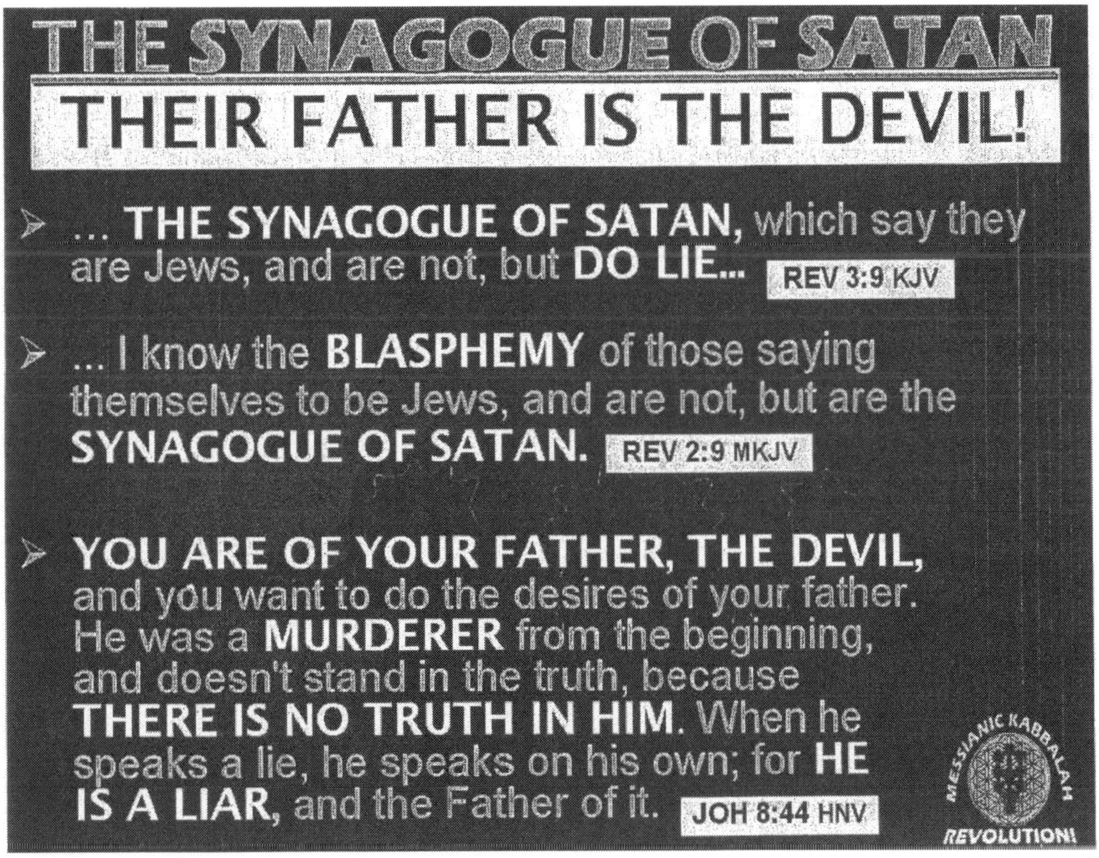
THE SYNAGOGUE OF SATAN
THEIR FATHER IS THE DEVIL!
... THE SYNAGOGUE OF SATAN, which say they are Jews, and are not, but DO LIE... REV 3:9 KJV
... I know the BLASPHEMY of those saying themselves to be Jews, and are not, but are the SYNAGOGUE OF SATAN. REV 2:9 MKJV
YOU ARE OF YOUR FATHER, THE DEVIL, and you want to do the desires of your father. He was a MURDERER from the beginning, and doesn't stand in the truth, because THERE IS NO TRUTH IN HIM. When he speaks a lie, he speaks on his own; for HE IS A LIAR, and the Father of it. JOH 8:44 HNV
MESSIANIC KABBALAH
REVOLUTION!

As a producer, he has produced Illuminati I, Illuminati II, Illuminati III, and Illuminati IV. He has done very good research producing another DVD titled Princess Die. There is no doubt in his mind who killed Princess Diana or why she died. He shows the true character and history of the British Monarchy not the carefully crafted PR stunts like *Elizabeth. The Tattler* is a now defunct online publication, which exposed the pedophilia around the Monarchy. Lord McAlpine, Derek Laud (a particularly sadistic pedophile) and Cyril Smith were mentioned as well as the Elm Street Guest House. Other Margaret Thatcher pedophiles and Monarchy associated pedophiles include Leon Brittan, Trade Minister, Edward Heath, PM, Jimmy Savile, DJ & Top Entertainer, and Lord Longford who supported the Moors murderess Myra Hindley involving the killing of five children in Greater Manchester, England. All pairs of serial killers are organized trafficking of children & women. Myra Hindley worked with her evil partner Ian Brady. Why Lord Longford would be her supporter only makes sense if he's a pedophile customer of hers and he is afraid of his own depravity being revealed. These two were described by their judge as "two sadistic killers of the utmost depravity." *The Coleman Experience* websites connect these sadistic serial killers to Jimmy Savile (Sa-vile) and therefore the Monarchy. It is the same story with the Belgian Monster Dutroux. These people are procurers for the "elite" meaning connected Senior politicians, judges, Monarchy, & wealthy businessmen. It is the same in Canada & the US-the axis of evil. The police fully cooperate with these pedophiles for if they do not they soon find themselves out of a job and in disgrace. Oftentimes the top dog of the police departments as well as those responsible for resolving these crimes are the criminals involved ...there is an abundance of evidence out there for those willing to look. (Sources: brutalproof.net & davidicke.com) Most of the very sadistic murders are

BrutalProof.net

connected to Satanism for these cults believe that with a sadistic sacrifice they are granted POWER & MONEY (*The Franklin Cover-Up*) and are responsible for many murders…psychic Joseph Tittel has stated in his blog 2015 predictions #106: "A break in one of the largest serial murder cases in history. With the luck of a routine traffic stop and a police who is made out to be a hero one of the sickest horror story like plots is unraveled in real time. Seems this is very much a cult like murder spree, but the person captured is not breaking and therefore taking full responsibility of killing dozens of male and prominently female victims. They will not even find half of the hundreds of victims, which lie in unidentified plots throughout the country. One of his sadistic burial places will be dug up and an undetermined amount of bodies uncovered. Not sure where this is, but I imagine it is the U.S." This year he also mentioned in his Predictions for 2016 how Lucy Liu's show interviewed Satanic cult members and this episode was taken off the air!!! Someone high up didn't want something revealed. Joseph Tittel also went on to say that Satanism is even bigger now than in the '80's when it got a lot of publicity. Now it doesn't get publicized. Who do you think owns the US media anyways??? Hint: George Bush Sr. owns Cox Cable and is a Nazi Satanist and big-time illuminati.

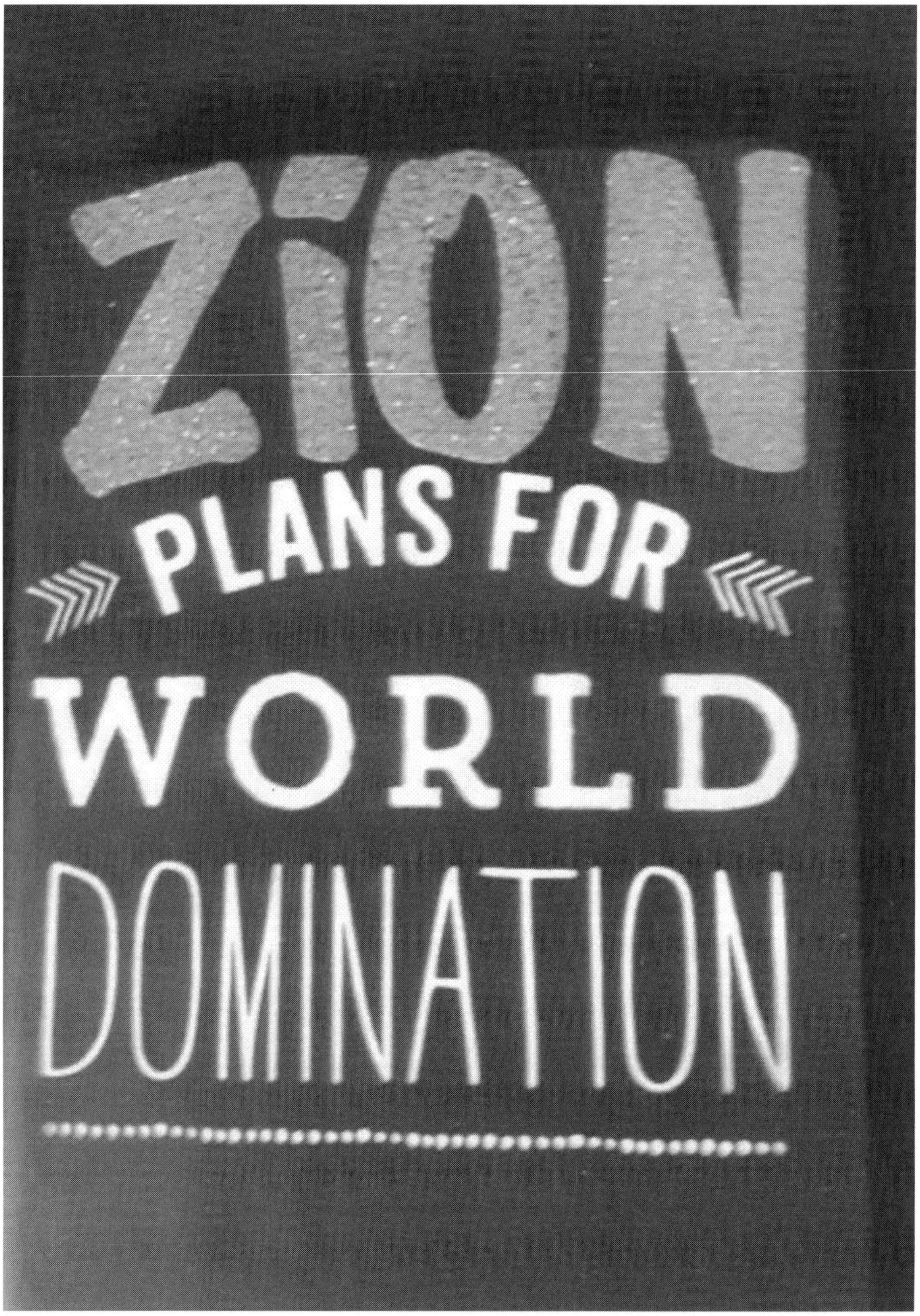
ZiON
PLANS FOR
WORLD
DOMINATION

I invite a Canadian to ride along with me figuring it may cost me a little more money, but I'll feel a LOT safer. It does cost me a little more money, but I feel eons safer and it is actually fun and a beautiful drive. I see only one sign about the missing hitchhikers. Strangely along this 500-kilometer highway where thousands have disappeared there is scarcely any mention of the disappeared. Only signs advertising the Freemasonic organizations. The signs appearing on the internet are NO longer ALONG this highway. Pamela and I see all kinds of signs for Freemasons organizations in the heart of where the missing is abducted.

We scarcely see any hitch hikers at all; only one very pretty girl with a guy and one boy. The Natives tiny reserve has three billboards warning their young not to hitchhike. The areas around the Caucasian populations have no signs except for a sign of Maddie Scott's abduction from a campsite. But, of course, for Maddie is a middle-class Caucasian girl not a destitute native and her parents and relatives are paying for these expensive billboards.

Over 1186 missing women and girls and even some young men have disappeared and the RCMP claims to be "investigating" these disappearances. It's always about the lone killer story. It's never about the organized human trafficking involving senior judges, police chiefs, Canada's PM Paul Martin, or the RCMP's named Steve(n) or Dave or the Vancouver senior police Dave Dickson & Canadian military and intelligence. It's always the "lone killer" conveniently excluding the entire Picton family in their Snuff Porn/Body Parts business involving brothers, father, and cousins. The "lone killer" story also excludes the Hell's Angels, the Hong Kong Triad, and the Japanese Yakuza who most recently have come in on the West Coast of B.C. to make their killing…no pun intended. The "lone killer" is a convenient lie to hide the real truths: the torture and murder of children, prostitutes of intelligence who could cause a great deal of trouble for these vicious criminals and the fact that a lot of the Canadian Parliament is involved in this organized crime ring. Criminals run Canada as Loretta Saunders found out and who was murdered herself for once she was on to this ring they surely couldn't have her naming names in her thesis. (You can see the names and pictures in my Appendix #1.) The Murder of Deena Lyn Braem by Quesnel, B.C. RCMP was witnessed by Lonnie Landrud who has also had to hide. This brings me to the last, but hardly the least in this profile of horrors-serial killers.

Loretta Saunders

Loretta Saunders, student, was researching missing aboriginals when she was murdered....what did she know?

The Murder of Deena Lyn Braem
by Quesnel, B.C. RCMP Officers
Cst. Paul Collister
& Cst. Bev Hosker
As told by
Lonnie Landrud
Who witnessed
the murder in
1999

Lonnie Gabriel Landrud

BrutalProof!

Serial Killers and Depopulation Agenda

In general, these are highly psychic, above average intelligent vicious psychopaths. According to witnesses the serial killers in Canada include: Eddie Murphy, actor and icon, Freemasons associated with the Norad Military

Base in North Bay, Ontario (next to Wisconsin), the Picton serial killers, Chief Ed John (who wouldn't be in his position as native leader if he were an honest man), Gino Ojick an enforcer and former hockey star, ex-Edmonton policeman David Lavallee who was forced from his department, the SPARROW-GUERIN clique, and many, many others including the entire Picton family as well as Hell's Angels, and a military programmer, Bourdais, who teaches at military installations as well as Catholic Knights of Malta members. I wonder if Colonel Russell Williams was involved-rape, torture, murder, stealing panties & cross dressing were obsessions with this psycho sexual sadist who flew Monarchy around. He was also a friend of serial killer Paul Bernardo (of Ken & Barbie killers). Both were affiliated with Satanic groups, which Canada is full of. (Does a dog have fleas?) Mass murderers, spree murderers, occult Satanists, insane schizophrenics and criminally insane describe this group. Many start out molesting siblings and other children, starting fires and torturing animals. Vlad Tepes when imprisoned tortured insects for fun. Torturing is an addiction as is serial killing. Baroness LaLaurie's Satanic Blood Sacrifices in New Orleans could have been about a hundred. She gruesomely tortured her slaves who were begging to die. She was an insane Satanist who also got away with her crimes. She lived next to the St. Louis Cathedral and near Marie Laveau of voodoo renown. Both were Roman Catholics attending the St. Louis Cathedral, were neighbors and would have known of each other. Furthermore, LaLaurie's Satanic crimes were not unusual. The same macabre tortures of innocents were done at the 15th Century French Castle of Baron Giles de Rais who had resorted to murdering children for money and power under a black magician's mentorship. (It was the secret Roman Catholic Black Mass for Satan.) (Mindcontrolblackassassins.com/tag/marie-delphine-lalaurie) Countess Bathory murdered around 600 peasant girls bathing in their blood to preserve her beauty.... anywhere there is serial killing and Satanism the Royals are in on it. Other publicly acknowledged Satanic Royals are the French King Henri the III and King Louis the IV. The Italian Catherine de Medici was a widely-known Satanist. They did their Satanic Rituals in their castles as the Rothschild's are alleged to do them today. (davidicke.com) Most Serial killers have deep seated issues with abandonment from childhood and psycho-sexual abuse. Surely Eddie Murphy being in foster care felt abandoned and these wealthy, privileged elite feel abandoned being put into boarding schools or military academies. Many of them have alcohol and drug problems. Many were sexually abused as children, which is common in France, America, boarding schools, military and military academies & religious institutions. Many serial killers are neglected and abused as children and also feel abandoned/betrayed by society. Serial killing is about power & control even more than it is about sex. Sexual sadism is a cross between these two, but getting black magic in the mix involves invoking the dark side and these people who have been damaged are wide open channels to the dark side. Baron Giles de Rais started out as a good Christian man!!! War is crime and he got accustomed to killing in war and developed a taste for it. Many do. The Phoenix program in Vietnam has created a plethora of serial killers who have developed a real taste for killing and so has the MK Ultra Assassin program. According to Fritz Springmeier we have between one and two million MK Ultra "graduates" who are assassins, sex slaves, drug couriers, spies, etc. created by our top mad scientists (Harvard University) working with the CIA. Ted Kazynski of Unabomber fame was a graduate of MK Ultra!!! (A Harvard graduate as well!) So, between training people to kill in the military and in MK Ultra "training" programs is it surprising we have so many serial killers now? What our media does not report on is how Henry Lucas admitted being a part of a Satanic Military type of group in the Everglades where he was an instructor in killing. (*Hand of Death*) Some murders he did for pay and he developed a real taste for killing saying "killing was like breathing." Naturally he was totally abusing drugs and alcohol the whole while and his childhood in West Virginia appears suspiciously CIA MK Ultra or Satanic for he was forced to wear girl's clothing, which is typical in Satanic abuse programs. He was subjected to freezing cold and hunger just like the Canadian Holocaust natives who were under mind control. He was not allowed to be rescued from torture either for when a kind man bought him a pair of shoes he was not allowed to keep them. This is typical of the abuse of the MK Ultra victims. A big MK Ultra programming center is Blacksburg, Virginia where Henry Lucas was born. He also has the drooping eye typical of MK Ultra victims. The main issues serial killers seem to have is ABANDONMENT & CHILD SEXUAL ABUSE. Many of them come from Satanic families where MK Ultra abuse is a part of child rearing. During the MK Ultra abuse rituals demons are called upon during the abuse to take over the souls of these victims. I scarcely believe in the "lone nut" serial killer anymore.... I used to before I did this research, but over and over and over again they are only the fall guy for a well-coordinated mass killing with Satanic overtones. Also, between 50% to 80% of serial killers have a military background.

To reduce the surplus in population as previously stated by Ebenezer Scrooge, Zionist? can be verified by the following evidence:

- Withholding the Cancer cures while injecting Nagalase/ese into vaccines.
- Putting poisons like Aluminum, Barium and Fluoride in our air & water.
- Creating assassins (MK Ultra & Big Pharma) and then letting them run loose on the American public.
- The Phoenix programs creating torturer assassins who mutilate the dead in horrific ways and rewarding military for first kills and stabbing innocents to death for the weekend passes.
- Big Corporations intentionally polluting public water and lying to the public (PG& E and Grace-Erin Brockovich are one of many examples). Now 70% of drinking water is polluted likewise.
- Politicians making it legal for chemical companies to dump a hazardous waste (Fluoride)into drinking water…look up disposal of hazardous materials…………HazMat guides…….
- Forcing vaccinations laced with poisons (aluminum & thimerosal) on parents & children.
- Ractopamine in feed supply in America-banned everywhere else in the world.

- **GMO's banned in Russia** allowed in US food. Dark Act passed to keep us in the Dark about GMO's.
- More deaths in hospitals than anywhere else…Veterans Kill Lists in VA Hospitals.
- Insane no fault MVA laws in Florida making it almost impossible for an injured motorist to get compensation or to make responsible driver pay up. (Thank the Bushes for this one!)
- Lying American Media focusing on Kardashians while communist Agenda 21 is being passed by stealth.
- Banksters bailouts while homeowners lose their homes.
- Illegal usurious interest allowed on credit cards and public has no recourse, but bankruptcy, which is getting stricter and stricter and more and more favorable for the Banksters.
- Hillary & Bill Clinton peddling influence for Clinton foundation money to Saudi's and other criminal regimes at American's expense plus our assets are being sold off at fire sale prices. (Feinstein-while her real estate husband makes lots of money on these postal property sales and they pocket the money)
- CIA involved in Satanism and MK Ultra, in which many children die and are buried in mass graves.
- Mass graves of murdered children in US never investigated (one is on Pine Ridge Reservation)

- Approximately 1,000,000 missing US children not being investigated properly

- Pedophile rings in D.C. flourishing with a subgroup who like to murder children (Hunter Thompson, Lawrence King, Craig Spence and allegedly George Bush, Sr.) for entertainment never investigated. (*Confessions of a DC Madam*-Henry Vinson with Nick Bryant) (*The Franklin Cover-Up* by John DeCamp) Pizzagate

- No FBI Nationwide Database for Missing children (crimes not meant to be solved)

- Missing people in State Parks, and all over the country not investigated (Missing 411 Series)

- Legalizing Zohydro (10 times stronger than Vicodin) when America has an opiate overdose epidemic.

- The Satanic Groups not investigated nor reported on such as the *Ninth Circle* and the investigative reporters reporting on them harassed and thrown in prison or beaten and given death threats (Kevin Annett and Fritz Springmeier) The Belgium Satanists are murdering A CHILD A DAY!!! (itccs.org) 10,000 refugee children in Europe have disappeared.

- The fashion industry making death trendy with skull and bones designs, logos, etc. on purses, shirts, scarves, etc. (Skull Fashion)

- *The Franklin Cover-Up* by John DeCamp (never investigated pedophile ring in Omaha and book censored)

- Perpetrators of child sexual abuse such as Henry Wadman, Henry Kissinger, George Herbert Walker Bush, Sr., etc. (*Trance-Formation of America* by Cathy O'Brien) and there are loads more never arrested nor prosecuted by FBI or state police. (The Biggest Secret)

- Child sex offenders protected lifelong by Secret Service-Herbert Walker Bush, Sr. is an alleged child killer.

- Life-saving inventions such as Nikola Tesla's free energy withheld from the public so they can be milked by the illuminati corporations and if they have not the money to pay for exorbitant heating and air conditioning costs they freeze to death or die of heatstroke.

- Many psychopathic cops shooting minorities not investigated or tried. Ethical cops protesting police brutality are being fired!!!

- Synthetic, unsafe drugs/vaccines given to populace without honest clinical trials instead being declared safe by Big Pharma/CDC doctors and scientists paid to deliver a "safe" result. **See VAXXED!!!**

- Marijuana being withheld as a treatment drug for decades so that Big Pharma could make a 17,000% profit on dangerous opioids and synthetic, unsafe drugs. Opioids are now gateway drug in heroin death epidemic! Zycodan (10X stronger opioid) now legalized.

- Unsafe drugs brought to market and prescribed and later having serious side effects exposed such as heart attacks, congestive heart failure, diabetes and death.

- Dangerous petrochemical fertilizers being used polluting our land, drinking water and oceans.

- Illuminati Tepco sub standardly built by GE (illuminati corporation) resulting in Fukushima explosion and huge dead zone from Japan to West Coast: California to Northern British Columbia possible link to 10,000 dead sea lion pups, dead fish, birds, etc. Explosion in cancers in Japanese exposed to Fukushima radiation. Pacific Dead Zone littered with the bodies of dead sea life. 1/3 of the ocean is now Dead Zone.

- Safety valve (Bush deregulation) no longer required for offshore drilling resulting in Deep Horizon explosion killing 11 and mass death of dolphins, seals, fish, and other sea life and mammals. Corexit poisonous cleanup chemical used resulting in horrific deaths of cleanup workers. (*Vampires of Macondo*)

- Inmate slaves being starved, beaten, tortured and murdered in America's prison gulag (George Mallinckrodt's *Getting Away with Murder*) reminiscent of a Nazi concentration camp or Soviet Gulag under Stalin.

- Lyndon LaRouche railroaded into prison on false "Fraud" charges to die there and his political activists promoting productive policies and infrastructure development as well as NAWAPA to increase water to drought areas given 77 year sentences!!! Now the Bilderberger who helped railroad him into prison is running mate of Gary Johnson "Libertarian." Don't fall for this Shiite. William Weld is a Globalist and always has been. He is rising due to his corruption. Does he rape little boys too? If he does, one day he'll probably be President! (joining the ranks of Bush, Sr., Reagan, Bushes, etc.) (*Thanks for the Memories*)

- Obama's weekly KILL LISTS!!!
- Jobs being shipped overseas via NAFTA, CAFTA, GATT, TPP, TPIP, TISA, and many more free trade agreements while porous borders let loads of illegals in and American natives cannot find jobs (94 million up to 100 million)
- Almost 50 million on food stamps, which are continually being cut
- Cuts to Social Security, Veterans Pensions and all entitlements without Cost of Living Increases
- The Multi-Employer Pension Recovery Act (MPRA) allowing employers to cut pensions by half and not deliver what was promised-similar to what happened in Detroit
- Wars to loot smaller, weaker nations and letting children starve to death afterwards-think Syria, Libya, African Nations……65 wars since Kennedy died! Starving children put into pedophile rings.
- Planned Parenthood selling murdered babies body parts while Obama & Hillary insist on their continued funding. Satanists insisting on their right to have murdered babies for rituals.

- Obamacare with Nazi type T4 death panels literally deciding who lives and who dies

- Mass murders on 9/11, Oklahoma Bombing, mass murder school shootings, etc. being propagandized and lied about

- Selective Serotonin Reuptake Inhibitors being legalized with **Suicidal and Homicidal Ideations Black Box Warnings**-I could not make this up!!!

- Enron employees ripped off of their pensions and this is common; many pensioners losing their pensions are not even reported on in our "media."

- Georgia Guide stones (in writing) state population needs to be reduced to 500 million from current levels of about 7 billion. (an illuminati goal)

- Fracking is dumping hundreds of poisonous chemicals into drinking water, which the government refuses to reign in-US leaders and China are the two worst countries in the world as far as caring about their people. Now fracking permits are going offshore to kill off our seafood and seaweed. Coastlines becoming dead zones! Fracking pollution must be cleaned up. Fracking should be outlawed.

- Bill Gates states publicly that "Vaccines reducing the population about 10 or 15 % would be doing a really great job!"

- Satanism being really widespread and IS A DEATH AGENDA!!! Where do people think all these missing people go???? Missing are NOT investigated and are not meant to be investigated.

- US continually instigating WARS, WHICH ARE MASS MURDER with phony Media supporting wars.

- America being number 1 in serial killers in the world while CIA covertly creates assassins. (MK Ultra & Delta Assassins)

- Citizen's Courts to Investigate CPS for Child Prostitution Rings, Kidnapping and Selling Children to Pedophiles. The Guardian Ad Litem rigged for profit/destroy children scam MUST be dismantled. For more information, you can see Tiffany Aliano describe this corruption on youtube.com and on the Ritchie Allen show at davidicke.com….and at brutalproof.net/child abuse.

This list is by no means complete. It's painfully obvious, or should be, what is going on here. Americans had better wake up really fast and inform everyone you know before it's too late. Your lives depend on it for as Kevin Annett stated to me: "**What was done to the Aboriginals (Canadian Indians) is planned for the rest of us.**" He also mentioned how the bodies were arranged in certain configurations, (which would typically be Satanic Rituals) for these "priests & nuns" were actually practicing Satanists masquerading as Christians and 80% were Catholic Church staff! It is overdue to get this information out to the people and tell your family, your neighbors, your church and your co-workers. Support the activists who support you; they are few and struggling. You are many and your power is in your numbers. Vote with your dollar and boycott obvious illuminati corporations and banks! Hand out flyers, go to demonstrations, picket, call your congressperson, go to Town hall meetings, ask questions and demand answers. Start group meetings to discuss various issues-possibly one speaker a month during lunch. If you have further ideas let me know and NEVER, EVER give up. See **contact** at brutalproof.net.

Disappearing Children

Given the huge amount of Satanic activity in all Western countries it's no wonder the number of missing children and missing people is skyrocketing! Since it is now cool to be Satanic we can expect more missing people and murdered animals because this is what hard-core Satanists do: they sacrifice people, children, and animals torturing them to death. If you don't believe me go to itccs.org and listen to the interview with the Pope's victims and Prince Bernhardt's victims-Toos interview. There are many Bishops, Cardinals, and other religious leaders involved in this too. In *the Biggest Secret,* virtually the whole Church of Latter Day Saints is Satanic at the top and so is the Catholic Church. (This is before David Icke discovered Kevin Annett.) I'm not talking about the snowballed congregation unknowingly giving their hard-earned dollars to these criminals; clearly if they knew what was going on they wouldn't support this. That is why all this information must be suppressed or funding for all of this evil will dry up! And of course, the money must keep flowing in. Satanists love money & power and have a Faustian spiritual contract with He Who Has No Name for money and power (lest I invoke that one!) Toos Nijenhuis has one hell of an interview on itccs.org about seeing a child Satanically Ritually murdered by Pope Benedict, Prince Bernhardt, a bishop and other important and connected men. There are now international arrest warrants for these insane sadists and I hope they are arrested soon.... The Pope had to resign to avoid being exposed in attempted arrests by itccs.org members during his travel duties and now hides out at the Vatican where he has immunity for his multitude of crimes behind a three-hundred-foot wall with Vatican Guards in front. All of these criminals need to be prosecuted as well as George Bush Sr., Henry Kissinger, Dick Cheney, Obama and many, many more. Last week I saw a blog at itccs.org about the Ninth Circle and how they ritually sacrifice and drink the blood of an infant and it is required ritual to be a pope. There are other interesting videos too such as David Icke's interview with Arizona Wilder a mother goddess of Satanic rituals involving monarchy and household names of the rich and famous. She mentions three goddesses/priestesses involved in elite Satanic Rituals similar to, but much more gruesome than Madonna's shows with Britney Spears and Christina Aguilera. Surprisingly many Satanic leaders wear a top hat much like Madonna and even have rituals where they are eating a cake made to look exactly like one of their members (like Tom Petty's *Don't Come Around Here No More* video) re Kerth Barker who wrote of this in his book *Cannibalism, Blood Drinking & High Adept Satanism.* BTW Alice in Wonderland is a popular MK Ultra programming theme and Alice is shown shapeshifting into a pig…. wow Tom Petty's video is FULL of Freemasonic/Satanic symbolism right down to the black and white tiles, walls, clothing, red black & white colors, etc.! WOW!!!

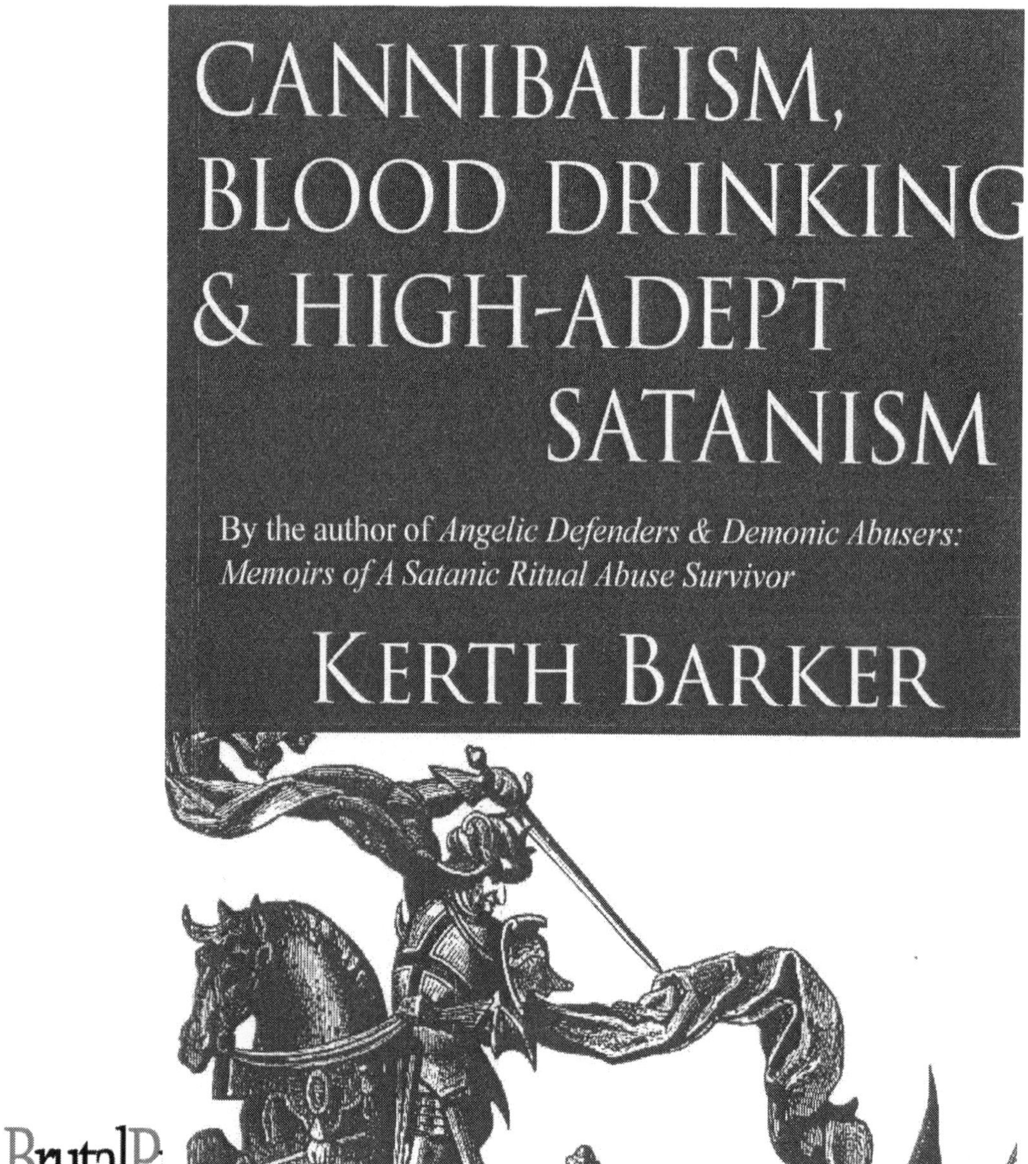

Mind Control aka MK Ultra aka Bluebird, Artichoke, Cameron, Chatter, MK Ultra Black Assassins, etc.

This is a very, very important topic for without knowing it's going on in America right under our noses we will never realize the true extent of the agenda of the elite illuminati and the true horrors of what they do. Fritz Springmeier and Cisco Wheeler have done much to expose the horrors of the CIA-connected Mind Control research being done in mainly English-speaking countries: England, the USA, New Zealand, Australia, Canada and their German and Dutch counterparts in Amsterdam and Germany as well as Italy. A young child is sexually abused to psychologically fragment the little one's mind and the fragments are called alters. These alters are given names and codes and programmed for very specific functions: prostitution, spying, assassinations, drug couriers, messengers, etc. These multiple personality disordered slaves are highly trained to be used in top secret government black operations and they are sold as sex slaves for a fortune. They are used to compromise our Washington, D.C. politicians so that when a certain law needs to be passed to benefit the ultra-rich it's either passed or a huge scandal is created to discredit and destroy that politician's career. One example is with Bill Clinton who did not want to repeal Glass-Steagall and then had the Monica Lewinsky expose and impeachment. He finally agreed to repeal Glass-Steagall, which benefitted the Wall Street bankers immensely and resulted in the multiple bank bailouts and the upcoming bank bail-in under Dodd-Frank Act (signed into law by two retiring Congressmen). *The Franklin Cover-Up* and *Trance-Formation of America* go into great detail about the programming of mind-controlled slaves. The big expose is Fritz Springmeier's book: *How the Illuminati Create a Totally Undetectable Mind Controlled Slave* and it is on pdf on the internet and I highly recommend reading it. Damian Chapa created a movie called *Killer Priest* and he shows scenes of extreme torture to create Beta (sex programming) alters and this gives you an idea of what goes on. Donald Marshall is on YouTube exposing cloning centers and the snuff film industry connection and this is also a must see. When you wonder about serial killers operating alone and the story just doesn't make sense it's because the crucial money-making part is left out. The Picton brothers were making money on snuff films and organized trafficking for the elite, which is why they got away with murdering so many for so long. The elite are tied in with people who hand down orders in the military, police, government, media, educational institutions in a pyramidal fashion and that is why these child rapists and snuff porn consumer/producers are not held accountable: when you own the system of courts, judges, top police brass, top FBI brass, top CIA (think George Herbert Walker Bush, Sr.), media, educational system, etc. then you have control on the prosecution or non-prosecution of these crimes and the lack of reporting on them. Bryce Taylor also wrote an expose called *Thanks for the Memories: The Truth Has Set Me Free,* in which she exposes Bob Hope as a slave handler and writes of the Jackson Five rapes before their shows and the targeting of Michael for late night hotel visits with the elite men of the entertainment industry. Many in Hollywood are mind controlled slaves and the problems with Loretta Lynn, Britney Spears, Lindsey Lohan, Anna Nicole Smith and others are allegedly due to the extreme abuse these mind-controlled subjects suffered. Any research on Britney Spears shows her switching personalities during an interview with Diane Sawyer as well as her British girl, weepy girl, diva girl personas. (The book her ex-husband, Kevin Federline, was writing about her has been suppressed from distribution.) Virtually all of the promoted stars have illuminati symbolism in their videos: Madonna (especially her 2012 Super bowl halftime performance), Rihanna, Beyoncé, Jay Z, Britney Spears, and the list goes on and on (ad nausea). The biggest names in Hollywood have illuminati symbols in their films and promo posters: Brad Pitt, Angelina Jolie, Courtney Love, Nicole Kidman, Tom Cruise, Katie Holmes and others. In the movie, *The Golden Compass* the plot actually focuses on what is going on: the kidnapping of children for mind control experimentation and the deaths of many of these children. It probably exposed too much and that is probably one reason for the controversy and lack of a follow up film. The melt downs of celebrities are often due to the sexual abuse many of them suffered early on (think Anna Nicole) and the resulting dissociation (her creepy clown video) and PTSD. Anyone who knows anything about PTSD knows that it is extreme psychological damage and many do not recover from it but struggle their whole lives with the PTSD nightmare of being stressed always and having extreme difficulty handling more stress. Since the scars are invisible people do not realize how debilitating PTSD is and tend to judge and condemn these sufferers who often turn to alcohol and drugs to relieve their PTSD symptoms. What is not well known about the programmed multiples is that Satanic alters are also created and with the extreme torture demonic entities are inserted via ritual abuse. The Catholic church has been heavily involved in this and one suppressed book is for sale for $399 and up called *Lucifer's Lodge: Satanic Ritual Abuse and the Catholic Church.* Thousands of Nazi scientists and doctors (including Mengele) were brought to the USA and Canada to continue the mind control torture programs to study how to create a mind-controlled slave and they continued their evil activities at many leading research institutions including Harvard University Which, Congressman Gallagher admitted had more funding from the CIA than tuition fees in his Larouchepac.com interview. Mind Control is serious business to these very demented elite and they will do anything to further their cause including rape, torture, murder, mutilation, stealing trillions of dollars, creating social engineering charities and fake organizations like the fake cancer foundations, overthrowing legitimate leaders to establish their own puppet regimes corrupt enough to sell their own people into poverty and starvation to loot assets. The prime organizations to do this are the IMF, World Bank and NATO/UN. Think of the book and you-tube video: *I Was an Economic Hit Man.* The scale of the elites' depravity cannot be measured. At Bohemian Grove, they had rooms for necrophilia, bestiality, incest (mother-daughter), pedophilia, and sadomasochism. No perversion is too extreme for the elite including eating feces, drinking urine, raping babies and torturing children and animals to death. In fact, they thrive on perversion and to reach the pinnacle one MUST be a pervert; there is no room for normalcy at the top. We are run by blood-thirsty vampires, clinically insane child rapists that especially like to rape little boys causing anal fissures!!! The public is still looking away and appearing more & more foolish to those with awareness. The Monster of Belgium, Dutroux, was part of a child kidnapping network that led to: Count Maurice Lippens, his brother Leopold Lippens, Baron Benoit de Bonvoisin, a Belgian aristocrat, Count Herve d'Ursel, the Belgian Royal Family, Prince Charles, King Bandouin and other relatives. Sadistic child snuff networks are an inherent part of the Belgian ruling elite. Their victims described violent anal rape of three-year old's, long torture sessions, forced sex with animals, being raped with knives and razorblades, being sodomized, mind-controlled Nazi style and snuff film murders shown at snuff film parties (henrymakow.com/the_dutroux_case.html) similar to the one described on page 103-104 of *The Franklin Cover-Up.* The very lowest man on the totem pole, Dutroux, was jailed for life while the man passing on orders to him from the elite, Nihoul, was found not guilty. This way the elite are protected and never subpoenaed to court. This network used filmed child sex to compromise politicians who would then be blackmailed into passing laws working against their country and constituents. It is the same game in *The Franklin Cover-Up* most likely financed by the same hidden hands for the same ultimate goals: money, power, and the Satanic New World Order. Targets include senior level politicians, judges, military, businessmen, government officials and anyone else deemed useful to these organized criminals. America is now missing one million children a year (a rough estimate) and the numbers keep growing. According to Springmeier and Wheeler there are at least two million multiple personality disordered MK Ultra slaves in the USA. They can be activated via a trigger word or sound into a

Manchurian candidate (killer mode like in lone "nut assassin" mode), which we are seeing with increasing frequency. Does anyone wonder how all of these "lone nuts" are created? Let me give you a clue: torture via rapes and other abuses, anti-depressants and a multitude of other drugs, violent video games, Satanic alter programming, Manchurian (assassin) programming; violent pornography. The White House in Marianna, Florida murdered at least 99 boys in their custody. In a scenic vista of manicured gardens and palm trees swaying in the breeze a child concentration camp existed with forced slave labor and profiteering off of children. Many boys were raped and sadistically murdered here; the walls are crusted with blood. The story is as gruesome as the medieval torture racks. I can only imagine insane sadists wanting to work in this hell-hole. Everyone involved should be charged with extreme child abuse/murder and jailed for life; there is no cure for this kind of madness. Every living "graduate" should have front row seats at their trials and all kinds of restitution made: help with their trauma condition, medications, medical and dental care and the pensions that severely disabled veterans have. This shame must be well publicized down to its minute horrific details and laws must be applied that take child abuse & murder seriously and these laws must be ENFORCED. What were the neighbors thinking to allow all of this to go on? It only closed in 2011 due to "budget cuts." Sounds like a COVER-UP. With decades of slave labor where did all the money go? Let me guess; it went to the criminals running this child whorehouse, S&M slave-labor camp.

When I used to hand out my flyers I couldn't help, but notice the defensive, harassing attitudes of three particular women: No one cares about that! Don't you think you are making children feel unsafe with this? Another blocked my car in so I couldn't back out. In contrast several black Americans thanked me for caring. When you have a majority that doesn't give a shit about all these missing kids you have a problem. The news media is content with focusing on the oddball predator acting alone-the lone nut, but completely ignores a huge, systematic, organized child trafficking network as if it didn't exist. Sickening! In 1981 the missing children were about 100,000 and now they number about 1,000,000 and we don't have a problem?! This monster is continually growing into a bigger and bigger monster and we ignore it at our own peril. This monster leads to D.C. and Vancouver and both are rife with politicians.

MK Ultra

HOW THE ILLUMINATI CREATE
AN UNDETECTABLE
TOTAL MIND CONTROLLED SLAVE
THE FRANKLIN COVER-UP
Child Abuse, Satanism, and Murder in Nebraska
by John W. DeCamp
Omaha World-Herald
TRANCE

Kevin Annett and David Icke gave a shit and they've been viciously targeted for harassment and discrediting, ridicule, condemnation and death threats. The same goes for Alex Jones who exposed the head of Child Protective Services as a convicted child rapist. Congresswoman Phyllis Schaeffer was to go on Alex Jones for an interview and conveniently was assassinated the morning of her scheduled interview. The official media story was that her husband without any past violence suddenly murdered her and then himself in a fit of suicidal despair. It seems more like a professional hit to me and who would've been exposed in her interview, which would've exposed the child trafficking going on in CPS is what I would like to know.

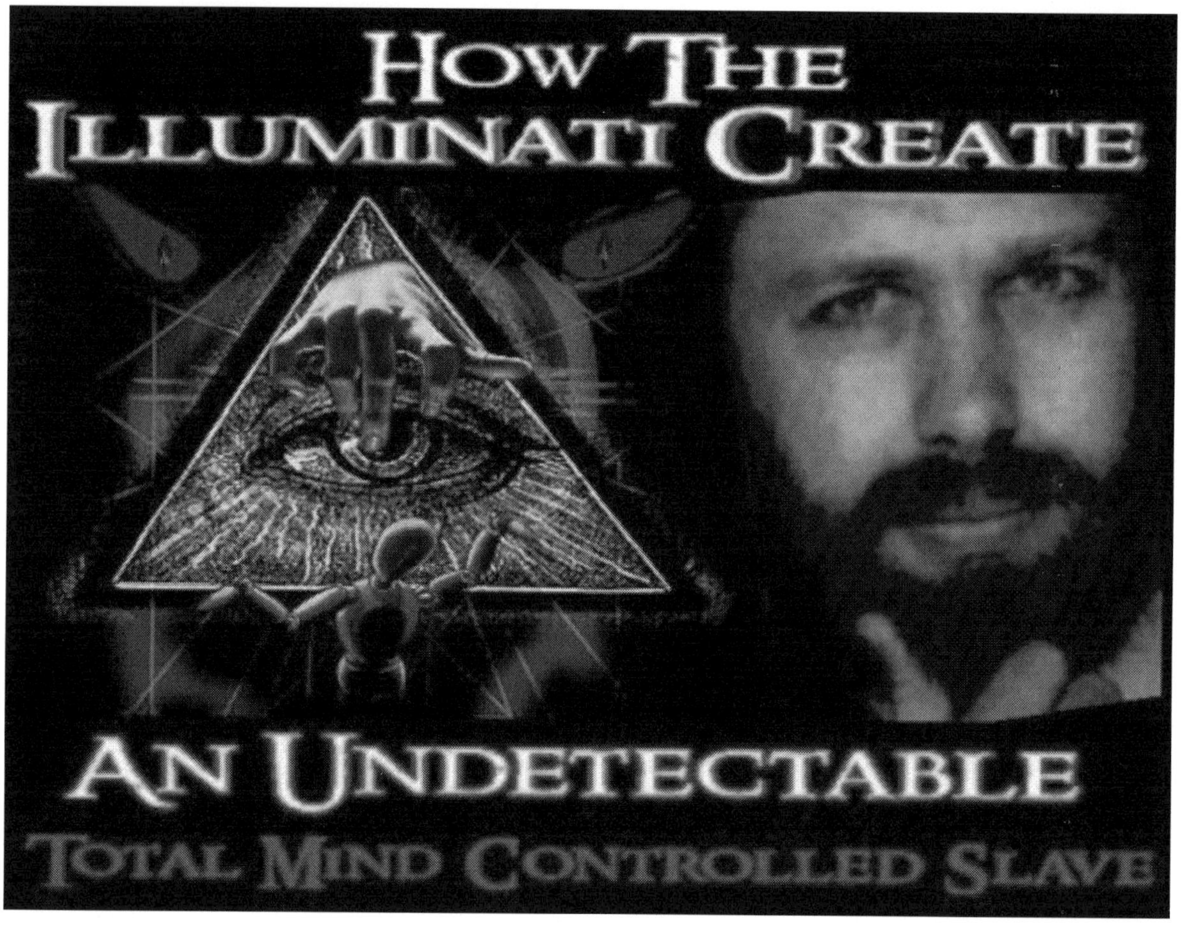

BrutalProof!

Madonna

I believe Madonna is a Satanist and MK Ultra slave. Wheeler and Springmeier say as much in their book *How the Illuminati Create an Undetectable Total Mind Controlled Slave.* Note the pyramid on her jean jacket and all kinds of illuminati symbols in her videos. Especially notice the 2012 Super bowl half- time show. It was 100% illuminati ritual even down to the satanic colors of gold, white, red and black. For me it was creepy to watch. The sleeping audience takes this all in and gives their energy to this Luciferian ritual. It's so creepy I don't even like to write about it. You can search it: .... Madonna.... half-time occultist ritual...... It is the same story with Britney Spears, Rihanna, Ke$ha, JayZ, Beyoncé and so many more. You can bet that the Music Industry and Hollywood are run by these pedophile/criminals and that there is much more than meets the eye. *Choreography* by Corey Feldman reveals some of the pedophilia going on. David Icke's *The Biggest Secret* reveals way more! Prepare to be shocked if you read it.... Hollywood is just a massive illuminati Satanic ritual using the most talented, compromised enslaved stars around. "*An Open Secret*" about Hollywood pedophilia has had a media blackout.

The Whistleblower by Kathryn Bolkovac

Bolkovac decides during a divorce to work for the U.N. in Croatia and finds to her horror that the peacekeepers charged with protecting the vulnerable are the ones raping them. When she tries to clean up the forced sex slavery she soon finds herself without a job. DynCorp was involved as were NATO and the United Nations higher ups. She had a title and a job of investigating sex trafficking, but when she tried to do her job she was quickly relieved of her badge! At the very least the movie is a must see and the book provides even more graphic details such as the 10-year-old child being trafficked by the sex traffickers!!! The top dogs of NATO and the UN are protected as usual while they continue to rape children.

Personality Profile of a Pedophile

A "pedo" (short for pedophile) can be a doctor, a lawyer, a rabbi or a judge. There are male and female pedo's, but the vast majority are male. They live in their delusions denying the massive harm they do to children. When they are caught they always lie and try to make the truthful child into a liar. They are very manipulative and con-men. Child rapists are deeply disturbed people with an ADDICTION meaning they will never, ever stop what they are doing until they are locked up. Society has protected them by being in denial of their activities and worshipping money and status. Pedo's are addicted to the power they exercise over children and possessed by demonic entities which push them into more and more extreme activities. Hooked by the power they have over children some go to the next level of sadistic torture. Like George Bush, Sr. they like to watch the children "squirm in pain." Another name for these severely sick individuals is malignant narcissists. They have absolutely no empathy or conscience. These are the most dangerous of criminals. Malignant narcissists are the sexual sadists, serial killers who like to torture their victims to death and mass killers. They are on the extreme level of dangerousness and sickness. This is a "severe mental sickness" or possession representing the "quintessence of evil." It is not unusual for these being's eyes to turn black as they torture their victims for smoke filling one's eyes is how possession appears and to me, anyways, these are severely possessed individuals. They emanate evil. Dr. Modi and Dr. Ireland-Frey of *Freeing Captives* also mention possession in their books and Ireland-Frey even mentions freeing one of her patients of a gargoyle entity. The gargoyle entities on many churches represent these entities, which operate on an unseen level. The Swiss clairvoyant, Anton Stieger, stated that for people in business and politics trapped in the material world he would see a big black tarlike reptilian encasing their heart chakra, which was no longer visible. The energy of the heart chakra would be hijacked by the possessing entity. A banker in the upper echelons of banking who wished to remain anonymous stated that at the top the bankers raped women, engaged in pedophilia, and were Satanists. He also stated that Satanic symbols were visible in their banks. What comes to mind are the Rothschild's and the Rockefellers? It's not surprising these money grubbing, greedy, gold digging Banksters souls are hijacked by demonic reptilian (gargoyle) entities for this is the crux of the worship of he who has no name: ego driven materialism. The Stanley Kubrick film *Eyes Wide Shut* in the deleted scenes clearly shows Satanic ritual going on in the home of these connected elite. It also shows their depravity. Stanley Kubrick had manipulated a contract for himself whereby he had the last word on editing scenes and the studio wanted about thirty minutes of this film deleted. When Kubrick refused, he was dead a few days later and these scenes were promptly deleted. These elites know every way of professional, undetected assassinations for they have the money to buy ninjas and other assassins and the knowledge and research as well. For example, insulin injections are one of the easiest ways to kill someone. When Kasir threatened the elite pedophiles with exposure after her boy bawdy house was closed down she was found with syringes and empty vials of insulin. They definitely wanted her dead. Normodyne's Side Effect is Congestive Heart Failure and would make a perfect kill drug. Ricin was used by one doctor to poison her husband and was almost completely undetected except that he knew he was poisoned and alerted other doctors. He was in multiple organ failure and barely survived. "Accidental" car crashes are another favorite of the malignant narcissists who run our material world and I am sure they are discovering more and more ways to kill people. They perceive Monsanto genetically modified foods as a soft kill meaning it takes years to kill someone. Fluoride, depleted uranium and other radioactive pollutants are also soft kills. Vaccinations are being promoted by Bill Gates to reduce the world population; he has admitted this in one of his very own speeches and considers a 10% to 15% reduced population as a huge success. This is the real reason for his promoting vaccinations in third world countries; he cares not for the people, but only to eliminate them. Aids was shipped to Africa in gallon containers of Hepatitis B vaccinations and the Africans being injected with these contaminated vaccines by the World Health Organization were unknowingly being given the lethal disease Aids similar to the Tuskegee black Americans being given syphilis on the sly. This is all by design and there is nothing accidental about any of this. When the world is run by psychopathic malignant narcissists this is the end result. No empathy; no compassion. Recently, it was found that the FDA Vaccine Insert Lists Autism as Adverse Reaction on the Diphtheria Tetanus Pertussis vaccination and you can again search it! (startpage.com) It is on the information of December, 2005 page 11 and SIDs (sudden infant death syndrome) is also listed as an adverse effect of same vaccination. It looks more and more like Dr. Wakefield is telling us all the truth and will be vindicated. His movie VAXXED! Just came out and it is shocking! Dr. Thompson, CDC whistleblower tells how CDC tossed clinical trial results in the trash after they showed a strong correlation between MMR vaccine multiple dose and Autism!!!

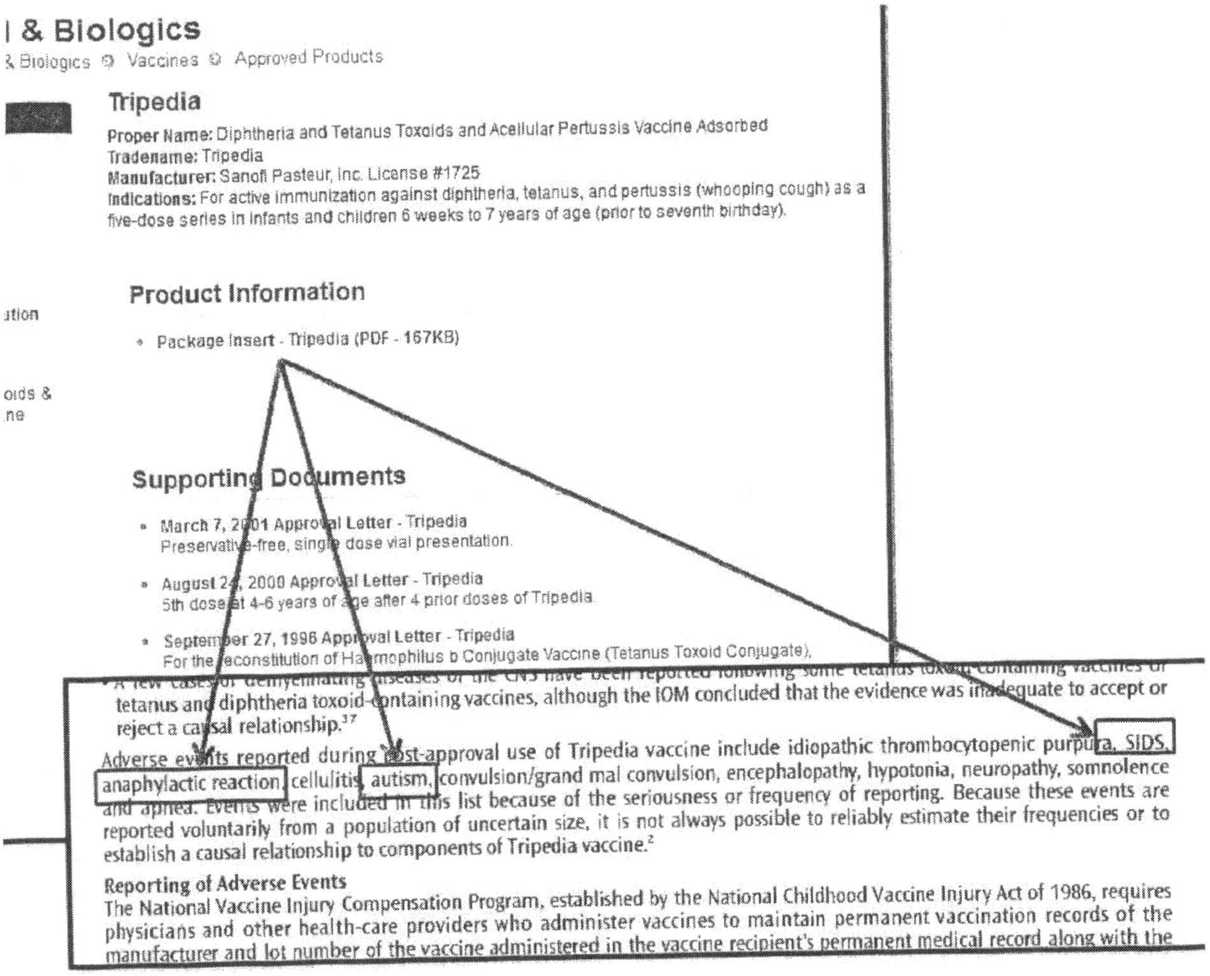

| & Biologics

& Biologics › Vaccines › Approved Products

Tripedia

Proper Name: Diphtheria and Tetanus Toxoids and Acellular Pertussis Vaccine Adsorbed
Tradename: Tripedia
Manufacturer: Sanofi Pasteur, Inc. License #1725
Indications: For active immunization against diphtheria, tetanus, and pertussis (whooping cough) as a five-dose series in infants and children 6 weeks to 7 years of age (prior to seventh birthday).

Product Information

- Package Insert - Tripedia (PDF - 167KB)

Supporting Documents

- March 7, 2001 Approval Letter - Tripedia
  Preservative-free, single dose vial presentation.
- August 24, 2000 Approval Letter - Tripedia
  5th dose at 4-6 years of age after 4 prior doses of Tripedia
- September 27, 1996 Approval Letter - Tripedia
  For the reconstitution of Haemophilus b Conjugate Vaccine (Tetanus Toxoid Conjugate),

tetanus and diphtheria toxoid-containing vaccines, although the IOM concluded that the evidence was inadequate to accept or reject a causal relationship.[37]

Adverse events reported during post-approval use of Tripedia vaccine include idiopathic thrombocytopenic purpura, SIDS, anaphylactic reaction, cellulitis, autism, convulsion/grand mal convulsion, encephalopathy, hypotonia, neuropathy, somnolence and apnea. Events were included in this list because of the seriousness or frequency of reporting. Because these events are reported voluntarily from a population of uncertain size, it is not always possible to reliably estimate their frequencies or to establish a causal relationship to components of Tripedia vaccine.[2]

Reporting of Adverse Events
The National Vaccine Injury Compensation Program, established by the National Childhood Vaccine Injury Act of 1986, requires physicians and other health-care providers who administer vaccines to maintain permanent vaccination records of the manufacturer and lot number of the vaccine administered in the vaccine recipient's permanent medical record along with the

VACCINES & AUTISM

BrutalProof!

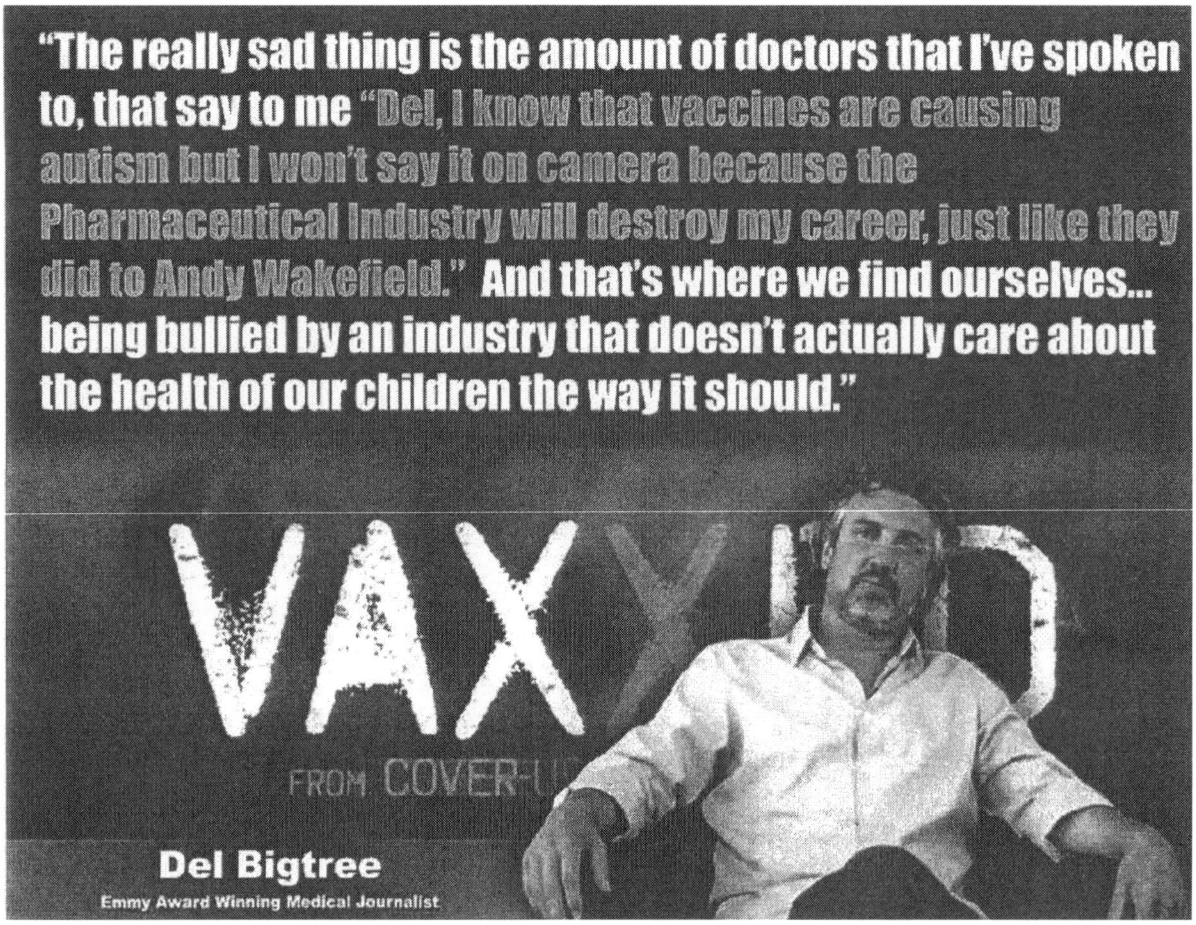
"The really sad thing is the amount of doctors that I've spoken to, that say to me "Del, I know that vaccines are causing autism but I won't say it on camera because the Pharmaceutical Industry will destroy my career, just like they did to Andy Wakefield." And that's where we find ourselves... being bullied by an industry that doesn't actually care about the health of our children the way it should."
VAX
FROM COVER-U
Del Bigtree
Emmy Award Winning Medical Journalist

The Pictons of Vancouver-sex and snuff film capitol, Dutroux Monster of Belgium-an illuminati stronghold, the Otis O'Toole and Lucas murders were for a Satanic ring in the Everglades. They were paid for many a murder, but you will not know this unless you read the book written about it. Murders and snuff films, like child prostitution, are for the draconian elite who love slaves and torturing people. At this point I feel anytime a government or media brags it is for human rights or it is "free" alarm bells should be going off. This is a mantra hypnotically repeatedly to convince the populace it is so. Would we constantly need to be told we're free if we felt "free?" Hey debt slave does you feel "free?" Hey Houston homeless do you feel "free" after getting a $500 ticket for dumpster diving? Hey, landless peasant does you feel "free?" Hey, unemployed with no unemployment benefits or those constantly being threatened with having unemployment cut do you feel "free?" Hey you who cannot find a job above minimum wage do you feel "free?" Hey, you with your food stamps constantly being cut do you feel "free?" Hey you who lost your house with an underwater mortgage do you feel "free?" Gaddafi would've treated all of you better than this, but your leaders (Clinton & Obama) had him murdered without a trial with accusations, which were all lies. America has been THE richest country in the world. Now it is becoming a third world, Nazi type nation. Everything you do has a fee or a fine. We are the number one incarceration nation in the world (10 times the rate of China!). How about that for freedom! We are tops in everything bad: fees and fines, under & unemployment (94 million), endless wars, unequal wealth distribution, serial killers (yup you read that right), missing children, murdered people, Satanic rings, inmates, etc. This is due to these doublespeak elite. We live in a lunatic asylum of a country run by the criminally insane. Our people live in denial of the truth because they can't handle the truth. This is insane too. We have horrific animal abuse, abortions & murder of babies to the tune of 59 million babies. This is horrific. We have more rapes, murders and killings than any other nation. We have an ignorant, uninformed public that largely does not care about much else than their own security. Is it okay with them that depleted uranium was used by the Bush administration on innocent children? It seems ignored by our people that Madelaine Albright justified the deaths of 500,000 children in Iraq through embargoes. There were no protests. This war with Iraq has cost about one million Iraqi lives and yet people here only seem to care about their own soldiers. Does anyone care that one million brown skinned innocent people were murdered? Yes, murdered!

Does anyone care that the Vietnamese have the burden of caring for agent-orange deformed babies and that Fukushima radiation is destroying the lives of children? TEPCO hired an American company to build these reactors. Does anyone care that this government murdered millions of Vietnamese in the Vietnam war? This is a form of racism that as long as we're murdering those with black, brown, yellow, and red skins that somehow makes it okay. Well, it's not okay. Your own Bible lists a commandment that states: Thou Shalt Not Kill. Now, if you are a Satanist or Satanic then all of this killing is good. Anytime you see serial killers working in pairs ask yourself who they are working for. Sure, there are lone serial killers, but when they start pairing up it is organized crime and they normally work for an organization. In Michael Caine's movie *Jack the Ripper* the doctor and his coachman comprised an organized team to kill the prostitutes. At the end of the movie where even conventional medical ethics are violated and all kinds of irregularities take place you really begin to wonder how high up the Monarchy these killings go. The doctor, after all, was a monarchy doctor and he was allegedly doing the killings. In Chris Everard's films a young girl got pregnant by Prince Albert and everyone who knew about it was murdered, the taking of their organs was Satanic ritual and the person doing the killing was actually Princess

Diana's father, Spencer, who did the Monarchy a favor and in return Princess Diana was promised marriage to Prince Charles. The Hellfire Club was a Satanic group of criminal elites and they were never prosecuted for their murders either. In the California Ng and Lake serial killings videotapes were made and this was in Northern California so I would not be at all surprised if the videotapes were sold to Goodbye Girls in Vancouver. The modus operandi was so similar to what Kevin Annett described in Canada: a deserted hunting cabin with a cistern where the bodies were dumped into with a PAIR doing the killings for self-made snuff films!

The Hillside Stranglers-Buono & Bianchi-also had connections up north and worked as a pair-they were cousins and liked to torture their unfortunate victims to death. Were they feeding snuff films into the Vancouver/Hollywood networks? There is a huge underground child trafficking network right here in America. The children are kidnapped by the CIA Finders as well as independent kidnappers and the children are sold into slavery, and some (Johnny Gosch) to Colonel Aquino of Presidio notoriety (again Northern California). In the book written by his mother Noreen *Why Johnny Can't Come Home,* she details the order from Colonel Aquino for a kidnapped 12-year-old boy, how the kidnapping went down, her husband's suspicious phone calls and implied involvement, the Mind Control Ultra sexual torture programming of Johnny Gosch via the CIA and how he

SECTION ONE

CHAPTERS

SECTION TWO

CHAPTERS

SECTION THREE

CHAPTERS

became a sex slave to our depraved elite and his eventual escape. Senator Nancy Schaefer was murdered the night before she was to appear on Alex Jones to expose the CPS child trafficking…her husband was murdered as well. (reported as suicide by Lamestream/Mainstream media)

WHY
Johnny
CAN'T
COME HOME
Kidnapped while delivering
Newspapers......Forced into
Pornography
Prostitution
Mind Control
Espionage
Noreen N. Gosch

Dark Night of the Soul

When I realized all this evil was going on I became extremely depressed and scared and then I started handing out flyers. The Border's Bookstore mentioned to me that David Icke's *The Biggest Secret* was one of their best sellers and this was on my flyer. So apparently, some were paying attention. I kept handing out flyers for years and I was attacked by 3 women and warned off by several security guards. Some people were very upset with my flyers and upset with me for handing them out. Several American black minorities saw the truths immediately and got it and believed and some thanked me for the flyers. When the 2nd car totaled my car on a lonely stretch of highway I felt it was time to leave. It took one month to repair the damage, during which time I was stuck in a hotel room in the middle of a big city where I knew no one. I was frightened, but continued handing out my flyers. One young girl told me she'd been molested as a child and smiled as I handed her the flyer. Her joy surprised me. Another young girl told me she was raped and her rapist rode the bus with her and she couldn't get over it and her friends couldn't understand this. I told her about *Conspiracy of Silence* and she repeated it over and over as she got on the bus saying "I'm going to tell everyone I know." I told her we have a ruling cabal of rapists right in our own country making our laws!

I absolutely made sure she understood that child rapists run our society making our laws and that is why rapists mostly get away scot free with their soul shattering crimes. MK Ultra involves violent child rape to shatter a child's soul and create Dissociative Identity Disorder formerly known as Multiple Personality Disorder. Are we, as a society, to allow this? Serotonin reuptake inhibitors (SSRI's) will not solve these problems and they are leading to many more violent crimes like school shootings as the vast majority of school shooters are on these drugs or recently taken off of them (drugs are still in their system). Drugs like this can remain in the lining of a person's stomach for years. The majority of school shooters I think were also sexually abused children as are serial killers. There is really not much difference between mass killers and serial killers as one can cross the line and easily become the other. Mass killing is serial killing on steroids. These super angry people felt betrayed and very abused as children and are striking back at the society that betrayed them. It is so easy to see for those with eyes to see. (WeAreChange just posted an email linking 60 school shootings to antidepressants and other psychiatric drugs!) Another source is cchr.org—Citizens Commission of Human Rights. They have a free museum on Sunset strip in Hollywood called *Psychiatry the Industry of Death Museum.* It is well worth a visit. They litigated to have the Black Box warning labels put on these Dangerous SSRIs!

The drug cartels like Big Pharma (Rothschild) created artificial "medicines" that do more harm than good and make obscene profits for this criminal and corrupt family. They own America thru their B'nai B'rith, The Anti- Defamation League, the AIPAC Israel lobbying group that controls our Congress and media and other special interest "Israeli" groups that care not about real Jewish people, but only about Zionist interests who represent only themselves. Zionists are a Satanic political organization that basically rule us and rule the world. They rule Israel, which is a deeply racist country with apartheid type laws discriminating against Sephardic Jews as well as Christians condemning them to a lifetime of poverty. They have it almost as bad as the black's post slavery in the U.S.A. Limited Job opportunities, restrictions in where they can live, etc. etc. etc. Israel does not represent me; it represents the racist Rothschild's and their evil agenda.

Don't be discouraged. It is time to rise up against this tide of evil like the nations fighting against Mordor (Lord of the Rings). Anyone can create & sign petitions on the internet. Anyone can call their senators on their cellphones and anyone can make a difference. 320 million people count! Even if one twentieth of the American people decide enough is enough they will have a huge impact. This is the reason I write this. I am trying to awaken you and spur you to do what you know is right within your soul. Even groups of 50,000 people can have a huge impact. That is .05 percent of 100 million people. This is a very small percentage of the total. So, for those of you that think you can't make a difference than that is an excuse for apathy. All this evil (Boystown) was funded by people who thought their donations would make a difference so why would we think our donations and activism to fight these evils would make any less of a difference? The logic defies rational thinking. If we were to fund a people's court and 50,000 people donated only $10.00 each there would now be $500,000 for a people's court. If this court were online and the jury listened in on the internet it would all cost very little money and time. Kevin Annett has done exactly this. So, has Larry Klayman of FreedomWatchusa.org Go on to itccs.org to see how-they have a free manual explaining how citizen's common law courts work. Elizabeth could be stripped of all of her illegally gotten gains and the proceeds: land, jewels, castles; clothes donated to those she has stolen from and an orphan's fund created. Her laws could be reversed and pensioners could once again have decent pensions. There would only be austerity for these criminals. Pot latching could be every man's custom too whereby people with items they don't want would give them away to people who really needed them. Barter could be instituted as well for there are no taxes on trade this way and taxes should mostly be eliminated-especially the Internal Revenue Service with their ridiculous confiscation of wealth, which they mostly give to the Vatican. The World Bank's own attorney Hude is telling on them and exposing their evil corruption and outright stealing! I don't see any reason for anyone to support the Vatican! It is totally a criminal syndicate. I started realizing something was fishy when I wound up on disability and all of a sudden, I'm getting all this money-initially $2000 a month and paying no taxes at all!! When I worked, I made the same amount of money and struggled mightily to fund my IRA every year after having taxes confiscated from my pay. Everything in America is a scam including the taxes paid. The welfare & entitlements are designed to keep people dependent on the government. If everyone is struggling financially and scared they're not going to eat, standing in soup lines well, this is great for the illuminati-an illuminati dream come true!!! Their plans have succeeded after decades of effort. Wonderful!! For them!!! Time to step up to the plate America and start making those phone calls and demands: repeal NAFTA, TAFTA, CAFTA, TPP, TPIP, TISA and any other free trade agreements and bring those manufacturing jobs back! We could end this engineered depression once and for all! Time to abolish the Royals, Vatican, and seize all the assets and refund all of the seizures of IRS pay robbery for the last 50 years or more. If people are dead and can't claim their share than the extra money can #1. Go to food banks with organic food only. #2. Create farming cooperatives so people can grow their own food and keep fresh food on hand. #3. Create a distribution network for raw milk, kefir and yogurt, homemade cheeses and soaps without all the harmful chemicals. #4. Create gypsy style markets for swapping clothing and appliances, and furniture.

The big oilmen have stashed trillions, at least 32 trillion dollars in offshore accounts in the Cayman Islands, after paying no taxes, cheating the little guy, deregulating the business resulting in death and destruction as in the BP oil spill, and last, but not least using the cancer-on-steroids Corexit to "clean-up the Gulf" resulting in massive die offs of whales, dolphins, clean-up workers, deformed shrimp, and all kinds of unimaginable damage to the Louisiana wetlands. This should be an episode in *American Horror Story,* but I have yet to see anything in the corporate crook controlled mainstream media. I worked for Enron, another very corrupt oil and gas company, and CEO Ken Lay was good friends with George Bush, former president. Guess what happened? First the deregulation of the oil business meaning the consumer lost all protections by law. Then Enron obscenely manipulated energy prices putting California into bankruptcy and causing pension funds huge losses and employees their pensions. I lost my pension and received a measly $23 check. All of this done against my will!! Bush, President, deregulated the oil industry, the $500,000 safety valve was no longer required, and now welders are welding at high temperatures with sparks flying everywhere with gas leaking from these faulty valves. Insane psychopathy! These psychopaths do NOT care about anything except more profits. More deaths; no problem! Burnt and bleeding oil workers-they don't care! This is the Deep Horizon explosion scenario. BP should be sued and sued and sued some more and boycotted by every consumer! Anyone who cares about animal rights and dolphins dying horrific deaths due to Corexit should be boycotting BP. BP is a petroleum company of the British Monarchy. Lizbeth spends so much time behind closed doors taking stock tips to decide which bit of insider information she will use to gouge people without insider information and get richer and more imperialistic than before. The oil companies are the pampered tax subsidized businesses of the rich and elite criminals. That is why anyone trying to produce a hydrogen car dies or the Studebaker guy was suddenly out of business. Tesla had free energy 100 years ago, why can't we use free energy? Think! If we had free energy instead of paying $300 electricity bills the rich would not be so rich. Everything is corrupted from politics, health, education (common core crap), spirituality & religion, journalism and media, culture, music industry, etc. etc. etc. Rock is corrupted too. It seems like they are all selling death, destruction, rebellion, drugs, and alcoholism with some going further into misogyny and Satanism. Do they sell anything good or positive? I wish. What about selling commitment, integrity, honor? What about selling respect for women and respect for self? Just finished the review of the *Last Living*

Slut and "sensitive" people like Dizzy Reed can be the most sadistically cruel. I venture to say I'll bet many rock groupies were raped as children like porn stars and call girls and this horrifically affected them; it's a devastating boundary violation that lasts a lifetime in psychological damage. Once that boundary is gone and the trauma sets in it can last forever. I think Roxana's book caused two divorces: Sebastian Bierck, front man for Skid Row and Dizzy Reed, pianist for Guns 'n Roses. Both had very long-term marriages 18 and 20 years that collapsed when the book came out. Maybe I should call this Tattletale. I have lots of tales to tell and some are so horrific and shocking people don't want to know.... like......Eddie Murphy sadistically torturing and murdering porn actresses and prostitutes and getting away with it...hiddennolonger.com and go to the **synopsis** in **BOLD PRINT** and READ IT. Now you understand why there is a media blackout on all of this!! Low status victims are treated as if they're disposable and high-status perpetrators get away with these horrific crimes only because of their money, social, and political connections. Justice is bought. All men and women are created equal or so the lie is told. It's a big lie told to lull us into complacency because the low status child rape victims in Washington, D.C. never get justice either. They're just-ass for perverts! But, that is the American Justice System.... young women and children are just-ass for perverts who usually get away scot free multitudes of times until their crimes become so egregious that someone or some group screams "something must be done!" Like after they post their gang rapes on you tube. It's like *Neon Angel* where Cherie Currie of the *Runaways* gets brutalized by a connected Hollywood man, James Lloyd White, who states he's murdered many before and gotten away with it. He only stayed in jail for one year after savagely raping, torturing and almost murdering her!!! He's still out there savagely raping, torturing, and murdering other women too!!! I wonder how many bodies are buried around the Hollywood Hills homes. For some reason the viciously sadistic and brutal rape was whitewashed from her film, but

I'd gladly bet $1,000 that this experience has much to do with her alcohol and drug problems…sometimes they are the only things that numb the pain & diminish the anxiety. I wonder how many Hollywood Hills homes have new concrete suspiciously poured and how many would a scanner reveal moved earth and graves? After all, wasn't it Ted Gunderson, chief FBI who established the validity of the McMartin case and the Satanism connected with it and that allegedly household names were involved? Didn't certain persons try to kill him 6 times for these investigations and one time his coffee was poisoned at a hotel where he was speaking with Noreen Gosch (mother of missing newspaper boy Johnny Gosch sold into CIA child sex slavery and still in hiding)? Ted Gunderson wound up in Intensive Care nearly dying. Before he died he had created his own web sites and he had given the stamp of authenticity to the McMartin case and Johnny Gosch case and stated there were millions of Satanists in the USA doing at least 60,000 humans sacrifices a year! How come you seldom read about this in the news or hear about it? 60,000 human sacrifices a year to Satan! WOW!!! I remember walking on the gorgeous Ft. Lauderdale beach and seeing a goat's headless body right on the beach and thinking the head had been cut off for a ritual so Gunderson is obviously right.

Mueller, the Special Prosecutor of Donald Trump's phony Russia-Gate. Mueller also covered up the Child Sex rings in Nebraska and sat on his hands.

TED L. GUNDERSON AND ...CIATES • International Sec... ...nsulting and Investigations
2210 Wilshire Blvd • Suite 422 • Santa Monica CA 90403 • 213/854-5171

May 26, 1992

Mr. Robert S. Mueller, III
Assistant Attorney General
U.S. Department of Justice
Criminal Division
Washington, DC 20530

Re: Your letter dated April 20, 1992

Dear Mr. Mueller:

Thank you for reviewing the material I sent you March 11, 1992.

I did not state that FBI personnel were in violation of the Obstruction of Justice statute. I only advised that there was an indication of this. I thought you would want to at least check into the matter. I am sorry to learn you do not feel it deserves further attention.

I have enclosed the book *The Franklin Cover-up*, by former Nebraska State Senator John W. DeCamp. Your attention is directed to Chapter 14, "Cover-up Phase III: The FBI," which makes additional allegations of FBI misconduct and possible violations of the Obstruction of Justice statute.

Sincerely,

Ted L. Gunderson

Ted L. Gunderson

TLG:te
Encl.

Member, Society of Former Special Agents of the Federal Bureau of Investigation

Satanism is rampant in America. At the same time, I was there to take a mystic's class I saw signs first of a giant reptile walking on two legs right at the school and them seeing a giant tarantula crossing the highway. This particular extremely gifted psychic mentioned humanlike creatures with reptilian souls that did not have empathy so they could do anything.... fits the description of a sadistic psychopath. *Slow Death* describes one such sadistic psychopath with a reptilian soul.... you know .... cold blooded like a reptile and without human empathy or compassion. Ray Parker even drew pictures of a reptile torturing women while locked up. This psychic did at one time mention Mind Control on her Blog, but I can't find it lately. Mind Control...now that is one hell of an important subject to research! It goes back thousands of years to the Babylonians and was of keen interest to the Nazi's. Their horrific torture experiments were really about mind control. They then carried on in Canada after WWII after being Paperclipped out of Nazi Germany. Anytime people wear a uniform they are mind-controlled whether it is a Nazi SS uniform or the uniform of the rock n' roll fans: T-shirts and Jeans. Think for yourself. Ignore trends. Seek the Truth. Think for yourself. Ignore trends. Seek the Truth. This mantra needs to be repeated over and over again until people get it and free themselves from the brainwashing/programming they have been put through by our schools, media, justice system & everything else influencing one's thoughts in Western Societies. There are mass graves of murdered children all over Canada. One needs only to search The Canadian Holocaust to find this truth. The Canadian government is not at all concerned, but they are greedy, lying, cowardly hypocrites. They're mainly afraid of everyone else finding out what they have really done. The *Girl with the Dragon Tattoo* is about the heroine being viciously raped by her legal guardian who reminds her that she doesn't have any rights and he could put her away forever if she dares complain. In West Texas, the Youth Corrections Center for wayward boys was staffed by pedophilic rapists who even had rape rooms for the inmates. Only due to one Texas Ranger was this even reported on; the rest went along with this evil. The White House in Florida is now having the graves opened by forensic anthropologists to determine the causes of death of the many murdered little boys...it is so horrific. They were also being raped and sadistically abused by vicious pedophiles. The worst criminals are the ones that go after children and they get away with the horrors because no one wants to hear about them and no one cares to investigate them and our own judicial system is controlled by these sadistic pedophiles as is the Canadian Parliament. Our system gives a free pass to organized pedophilia for the elite while jailing the common salt of the earth 7 years for one roach. This is totally Nazi-like with the people's acquiescence. It is a Satanic system.

For Henry Lucas God arrived as a golden presence in his jail cell telling him he must confess to his murders and assist law enforcement to find the bodies. He knew law enforcement didn't have anything on him without a confession. He did confess because he believed the golden presence of God. (*Hand of Death*) God sent him a Bible study teacher to his jail cell to spiritually redeem him. While he was committing the murders, he was way out of control and out of his mind on drugs and alcohol. When he was sober, he was very remorseful and stated he did not for one day have relief from the spiritual burden of his crimes. The spirit of truth guided Kevin Annett through twenty-one lonely and dangerous years. He is now being vindicated with Canada publicly admitting the murder of these aboriginal children-up to 100,000 of them, but I believe in all probability much, much higher when one does the math. (Thousands)

His faith in God helped victim Paul Bonacci leading him to live a productive life and stable lifelong marriage. God also led Paul Bonacci to make very public the truth of these horrors. Only two of the children sexually abused in *The Franklin Cover-Up* testified in court against their abusers. The only heartening thing about this horrific tale is that these two with their faith in God were able to stand up to their abusers, live normal lives, and have long lasting marriages without drug and alcohol addictions. The rest of the abused children without faith in their lives and the courage to speak out against their abusers have become mired in drug addiction. I hope one day soon Paul Bonacci and Alicia Owens will be publicly vindicated and these abusers, including Barney Franks prosecuted.

Change

- Prosecute the bankers (especially the Federal Reserve Banks) and their enablers (politicians) and put them all in jail-Iceland style. Needed: A Second Pecora Commission to investigate these financial crooks. (George Soros is one of the many.) US should not be a haven for these crooks.

- Confiscate all assets of above criminals and redistribute the wealth to their victims and food banks to ensure NO CHILD GOES HUNGRY!

- Interest free mortgages like Qaddafi had! Strike down usurious credit card interest rates to 5% simple interest to Public banks (state banks). Pay day loans should be illegal and made null & void. (usurious)

- Eradicate Student Loan Debt after confiscating NWO criminals' assets as well as Voiding Third World Debt. Investigate the secret bank accounts in the Caribbean and other offshore hideouts.

- Defund the UN/NATO/Agenda 21. Sign Rep. Thomas Massey's (KY) Petition for US to leave the UN.

- Free land to organic farmers, free seed, and free livestock like Qaddafi did & Putin is doing.

- $100,000 to every newlywed couple for housing like Qaddafi did. He gave $50,000 to newlyweds-in Libya the poorest African country. We are one of the richest nations in the world; we can't do better?

- State can finance half of a budget car up to $18,000 and car owner can pay the other half with a low interest loan not exceeding 5% going to the dealership directly.

- Build a WALL (like Hungary) and start having strict regulations that WILL be complied with vetting all aliens. End Porous Borders, which was a creation of our Shadow Gov'ts (Luciferians).

- Massive infrastructure development employing at least 6 million involving repairing roads & bridges & build NAWAPA to green the deserts increasing food production and water desalination. China & Japan have already offered to fund $8 Trillion in infrastructure development.

- Every person has a home like Qaddafi's policies. Eradicate homelessness.

- Tariffs on all imports! Retool Manufacturing plants here to rebuild & repair infrastructure.

- Repeal all "Free Trade" Agreements: NAFTA, GATT, CAFTA, TPP, TISA etc. No More "Free Trade"!

- Repeal all laws signed by drunkard, coke addled politicians who didn't read them!

- Nancy Pelosi to prison for malfeasance! Hillary Clinton to prison under Racketeering laws.

- Repeal Obamacare! No RFID Microchipping! (written in Obamacare)

- Term Limits for Politicians and Random Drug & Alcohol Testing for All of Them-NO EXCEPTIONS!!!!

- Ready access to organic foods for Food Banks as well as having City Gardens with free food.

- Repeal laws authorizing Transgender Bathrooms. Separate Transgender bathrooms can be built only for Transgenders. (Luciferian idea-for proof of this read: *Cannibalism, Blood Drinking & High Adept Satanism*) Do the research to determine if all the chemicals in our food and water have something to do with the recent Transgender escalation. Especially look at Atrazine-a pesticide affecting sexual development and hormones.

- Since our "leaders" (Hillary Clinton, Obama & Bushes) created this massive "refugee" crisis they should pay with their pensions and other illegally gotten gains (Foundations Fund Money=Racketeering) to repatriate these "refugees" and rebuild their homes, plumbing and infrastructure. (65 million refugees and going up!) Massive food & medical aid should be part of this. These criminals should all be prosecuted for Treason. Refugees homelands should be rebuilt and food/medical aid given as well. Once again Russia has been doing this, but this is unreported on in biased US Media aka Clinton Propaganda Networks. The money collected by Clintons should be given to the Haitians & their starving children and to Haitian Aid Organizations to rebuild Haitian homes.

- Eliminate Electronic Voting altogether and create independent citizen's groups to monitor voting. Eliminate ACORN voting-too much fraud! Eliminate Super Delegates System. Term limits & drug testing for politicians. Abolish office of President-it has been completely hijacked by Zionists and that is who all our elected officials answer to: Shadow Gov't or Luciferians. Decentralize our government. Eliminate Lobbyists; this is nothing, BUT BRIBERY! Bribery should be prosecuted not legalized! Personally, I believe Regional Councils in every state and very limited Federal Government only to administer Federal Programs like Medicare oversight as well as Social Security. I believe local councils would be much more accountable and reachable. I think the two-party system should be abolished-it's totally owned by Zionists who are anti-American, anti-Christian and loyal only to Israel.

- Legalize front lawn gardens, city gardens, homes on wheels for homeless, homeless camps, etc.

- Explore uses of Nano silver for diseases. (Dr. Rima Laibow of Natural Solutions Foundation blog)

- Explore Gold Chloride for Alcoholism. (Edgar Cayce files) Investigate Kratom for pain relief.

- Eliminate Federal Drug Courts & Vaccine Courts and replace with Citizens Courts with no ceiling on compensation.

- New Law that **unlawfully** convicted felons have all convictions be reversed giving them a clean record, compensation to be determined for time in prison and mental suffering, physical suffering and health affected by common citizens not corrupt bureaucrats. Crooked judges, district attorneys, etc. should be made to serve their victim's time for knowingly incarcerating innocent people. These criminals have had a free pass for way too long! Judges who refuse to give rapists adequate time must be removed...possibly citizen's courts will do a better job. The most vicious criminals get a free pass.

- Holistic medical care & nutrition must be emphasized in Medical schools...what we have now is Rothschild funded fraud: poisonous synthetic pills and deadly Vaccines linked to Autism and SIDS, etc.!

- Federal Express is not federal-it is a private company; the Federal Reserve is not federal-these are international Zionist Banksters that are engaged in defrauding the public Charging us interest for money our government should be printing itself for free and the Center of Disease Control is also not part of our government, but a private for profit corporation that needs to be stripped of its unregulated power to authorize marketing of poisonous vaccines with thimerosal and contaminants in them. Dr. Thompson must be compelled/allowed to testify in Congress about the faulty CDC releases and tampered with studies including the Autism Vaccination Connection-especially the multiple dose MMR vaccine linked to Autism. Vaccines must be regulated like the dangerous drugs are and honest clinical trials conducted.

- NAWAPA revived and major implementation fast tracked. There needs to be a resolution of the Canadian Corruption of the treaty they signed not being upheld authorizing water to drought states like California. Solar panels that produce water should be implemented especially in California.

- Felonious fraudulent DNA labs should be prosecuted and these criminals given time in prison that was originally given to unjustly incarcerated. Convicted Criminals and persons with felony charges should not be allowed to testify against innocent person for reduced sentences. This guarantees honest persons will be jailed in return for perjured testimony. (*Source*: Full Circle: A True Story of Murder, Lies & Vindication, Sandra Korbin, 2012)

- Children screened in schools with a one page Questionnaire to evaluate for child abuse: emotional, physical & sexual abuse especially.

- Guardian Ad Litem Policy Should Be Abolished-it is contributing to child abuse and exploding corruption.

- Foster care evaluated for children's safety. Approximately 70% of foster children are sexually abused. Better caregiving standards made and enforced. Our system is horribly wrong when such a huge percentage of children come out of Foster Care with PTSD from Coercive or Violent Rape!

- Real cures for PTSD must be investigated and fast tracked. It is too debilitating to ignore. MDMA Research should be fast tracked as should be Ayahuasca investigated and psychedelic drugs.

- Dismantle the CIA-it only serves the Shadow Gov'ts. (Rothschild's & Rockefellers, illuminati Luciferians etc.) JFK vowed to dismantle the CIA but was murdered because the CIA serves above.

- Dismantle Department of Homeland Security and FEMA-also serve Shadow Gov'ts listed above

- Who does the FBI answer to? When they are letting SR. politicians & Presidents off the hook for child sexual abuse we have a very serious problem that needs to be resolved. Independent audit of FBI for corruption. (Franklincase.org and The Franklin Scandal, The Franklin Cover-Up, etc.) Independent body of Common Law Court of Citizens investigating the FBI for crimes committed in targeted prosecutions as well as felonies committed by deal making with the Clintons to let Hillary off the hook. Citizen's Courts hiring own judges based on ethics and integrity to make decisions on this mob of criminals.

- Charter Schools funded by a foreign billionaire indoctrinating child with Muslim fundamentalism. These are not compatible with American ideologies! Children's schools should not be funded with radical Muslim ideologies being emphasized.

- Eradicate Common Core: Alaska has a new law allowing opt outs to Common Core. Other States must do this too.

- Corporations as entities should Be Banned/Illegal.... Top Dog Should Always Be Accountable & Jail-able! Corporations only serve the interests of the illuminati (violent, psychopathic sadistic child abusers & Luciferians). Shell Corporations, especially, should be disallowed and all entities including Starbucks, McDonalds, Apple, Google, Facebook, and others should pay their fair share of taxes-especially Wall Street. Tax havens for financial criminals should be illegal: US, Cayman

Islands, and the Bahamas. Alleged Financial criminals such as Soro's (Zionist) and Rothschild's (Zionists) should be investigated and there are multitudes.

- Every person must own a gun except for violent schizophrenics or domestic abusers with a history of violence or known terrorists-you get the idea.

- Abolish the IRS. Investigate who actually gets the IRS money being stolen from paychecks.

- Abolish the Zionist control of the Department of Education.... develop effective Home Schooling Curriculum and effective outreach for Homeschoolers at Libraries. (They always have large conference rooms not being used.)

- Back Up Our Border Police to Stop Drug Smuggling. Stop the Drug Smuggling at military bases like Clinton's Mena Air Force Base. Build a GIANT WALL and underground tunnels can be closed as well!

- Real investigations of murdered holistic doctors, scientists, whistleblowers, etc. Who Benefits? Zionist and Big Pharma corporations.

- Citizens' investigations of global child trafficking & Satanism as well as Prosecutions. Who Benefits? Zionists & British Monarchy as well as other Monarchies, sadistic criminals & perverts.

- Unsealing of Vancouver Picton Court Records revealing organized, systematic snuff porn rings. Who Benefits? (Zionist filmmakers, Hell's Angels, corrupt politicians and allegedly British Monarchy)

- Holistic Health, Cures and Nutrition emphasized at Holistic Medical Schools-STOP AMA persecution of Holistic doctors and Chinese herbal remedies. Investigate Ayurvedic Medicine & Treatments.

- Investigate relationship of Cell phone radiation, smart meters, & technological radiation (Wi-Fi) to cancer. Release results. Investigate linkages of "SMART" technology-anything, but "smart."

- Fast track implementation of our Grid Protection-Executive Order—Coordinating Efforts to Prepare the Nation for Space Weather Events just signed on October 13, 2016.

- Working with Putin & Russia to eradicate Terrorism and causes of Terrorism to prevent it.

- Investigate the Afghanistan Opium production (up 43%) and eradicating this opium being sent here.

- Investigate Beef industry and Pork industry pollution & find alternatives and solutions to clean up.

- Investigate fish farm pollution and find solutions and alternatives. Backyard Aquaponics should be available to all who are food insecure and the means to maintain as well.

- Investigate Invasive Species as food sources such as Asian carp and eating the Wild Boar Problem.

- Audits of ministers' financial records and personal spending habits for Bribes! (This is BIG BUSINESS! Trinity Broadcasting Network-Zionist (Synagogue of Satan) Christianity-even Netanyahu says "absurd.")

- Vaccines subjected to non-CDC, non-Big-Pharma independent clinical trials determining safety and safe dosages......Dr. Wakefield would be a good investigator. An injunction against all vaccines in question.

- Auditing and investigation of CDC and FDA for corruption by a citizen's commission independently chosen by citizens.... Dr. Wakefield could be in charge.

- Independent citizen's commission to investigate massive child sex rings in Washington, D.C., New York City, Amsterdam, Vancouver and Nanaimo, British Columbia. Prosecutions of ALL involved.

- Investigation of Fusion Energy and Tesla Technology and recovering of the FBI's stolen papers (Tesla).

- Research into the water producing Solar Panels especially for drought areas.

- Recovery of "smoking gun" pictures taken away from scene of crime of Gary Caradori's airplane "accident" to prosecute elite child rapists. **Unsealing of ALL Franklin Case court papers in Lincoln, Nebraska.** Investigations of ALL CIA pedophile rings including Brian Epstein's Pedophile Paradise, the CIA Finder's Group, the McMartin Pedophile Ring with Proven Underground Tunnels and affiliated CIA Pedophile Rings in White House of Marianna, Florida and associated Satanic Cults like the Hand of Death, which employed Henry Lucas notorious serial killer/assassin. This is just scratching the surface-there is so much more. Investigating the Nebraska FBI, which covered up the Franklin Pedophile Ring.

- Natural cancer cures such as Hoxsey Clinic Cures allowed within United States. Investigation of Mistletoe Juice, Sour Sop Fruit, Sea Cucumber, Hemp Oil, Etc. Legalization of Dr. Burzynski's Neoplastins. Investigation of Turmeric for Cancer as well as Baking Soda. Time for a new renaissance of cancer cure investigations in medical research laboratories involving herbal remedies, Edgar Cayce cures, Ayurvedic medicine and folk medicine/Native American Medicine.

- Unsealing of all papers involving Kennedy Murders. Prosecutions of all.

- JASTA (Justice Against Sponsors of Terrorism Act upheld and prosecution of all involved in 9/11 even if it involves Saudi Arabia, British Monarchy, Israeli Mossad and Bush family. Prosecution of US War Criminals for Iraq, Libya, Syria, Yemen and ALL other illegal wars as well and reparations made to Middle Eastern victims and refugees. (Ukraine too!!!)

- Releasing patents of 7000 inventions for the benefit of mankind as mentioned by World Bank lawyer Karen Hudes. Fast track Research on Nuclear Pollution Solutions in Pacific (Fukushima disaster now polluting 1/3 of the ocean) as well as Orgone Research.

- Fast tracking of TESLA FREE ENERGY, development of Hydrogen cars and Fusion research.

- Reviving and using once again citizens Common Law Courts (Larry Klayman, Attorney and Kevin Annett, Activist who gives Workshops on Citizens Common Law Courts)

- Abolish Political Party System: All Candidates Present Their Position on Issues-Issue Based Voting! All Candidates sign a Contract with Constituents Based on Their Issue Stance.

- Eliminate Corporate Spending in Elections. Corporations are soulless noncitizens. Cap all political campaign contributions by wealthy individuals and eliminate corporate contributions.

- Exploring Nullification, Secession, Repeals, Recall Elections, Impeachment, etc.

- Impeaching Supreme Court Justices Who Do Not Represent Our Interests! (Check out 4 Zionist Justices)

- The historical records and scrolls in the Vatican basement should be open to public scrutiny.

- An investigation must be done to determine the impact of Zionists & Zionist connected persons on American laws & justice, medical system & Big Pharma, Vaccines, politicians, free trade agreements, religion, Hollywood, pedophilia, snuff porn rings, drug trade, Supreme Court, drug laundering banks, aborted fetus body parts trafficking, child trafficking & child pornography, body parts trafficking, foreign policy, etc. Dual citizenship for politicians must end. No compromised politicians allowed.

- Political Correctness is Censorship and should be abandoned.

- US to print its' own dollar without interest and backed by gold and silver!

- Federal Reserve Banks (all central Rothschild Zionist Banks) should be Dismantled.

- Glass-Steagall once again implemented (FDR's 1933 Glass-Steagall) to put Banksters in check.

These suggestions are just for starters.... children should be encouraged and gifted children should have special programs to help them succeed...children are our future and our most precious asset.... what kind of world are we living in when our most precious assets are being raped, neglected, abandoned, abused and murdered????

TIME FOR A NEW PARADIGM!!!

MANTRA

1. **Think for yourself**
2. **Ignore Trends**
3. **Seek the truth**
4. **Take action!!!**

I was never an activist or into activism. I found out at an early age that if your views did not synchronize with the majority you were setting yourself up for condemnation and attacks. My opinions put me in the position of being a minority of one. No one supported my views. It seems to be the vast population of the US supports US foreign policy right or wrong or did at that time. Being on the edge of starvation, joblessness, and homelessness I learned to keep my views to myself. I now have severe PTSD from my wonderful life and my wonderful experiences. PTSD is not what you're born with but is a result of your environment-an extremely abusive, torturous environment. I felt unprotected, sadistically abused and used, stolen from by many a person when I was almost destitute myself and discriminated against because of my race. When I saw, what happened to the aboriginals in Canada I saw that my experiences were not unique. My experiences were better because I was not being murdered in a "Christian Residential School" by sadists, but in some ways my experiences were worse because I endured my crime ridden life alone, unprotected. At least these people had each other. The horrendous experiences completely changed my personality due to the PTSD, which I have forever unabated ruining my life. It was like seeing the video *Human Rights Abuses by the American Forces in IRAQ* where a young Iraqi girl watched US Forces murder her parent, grandparents and everyone else in her family leaving her all alone and devastated. I guess the Iranian groupie Roxana Shirazi was treated really shitty in Manchester too. She wound up in a psych ward for severe PTSD after a suicide attempt following her failed relationship with Dizzy Reed who became viciously abusive. She stated she was in hell and wondered how did she get so ill? Very well written; this is an illness caused by torture by sadists; it is THE illness of concentration camp survivors of who narrowly escaped being tortured to DEATH! It is the mental frame of mind following horrific abuses such as violent rapes, torture, near-murder, starvation, anal rapes with fissures, satanic ritual abuses (horrific beyond imagining), kidnapping, and being forced to watch Satanic criminals murder others by torturing them to death. All of these horrors are food for the demonic, which live in the etheric fields and probably could be measured by the negative ice-cold energies they emit by modern quantum physics. There are two Nazi Berlins: one in Germany and one in America and both are very much racially motivated. Can we be so like the evil land of Mordor down to the Twin Towers raping all lands (US Empire), tearing down the trees (Weyerhaeuser logging co.), polluting the world (America) and destroying all sovereign nations for an evil Empire (again America); a Satanic empire. Our IMF (international monetary fund based in D.C.) is a Wall Street Death Agenda of starvation by austerity-part of the Depopulation Agenda. Its' brutal, inhumane polices are evil and more food via suffering for the demonic in the etheric fields. The Federal Reserve Note is the perfect Satanic creation to keep America debt slaves to Zionists who care not about them. That these illuminati Zionists would just as soon starve to death Americans just as they have the Africans over and over and over again? Just because this evil Zionazi illuminati has used America to do its evil bidding does not mean evil will be loyal to those it has used? It is getting ready to turn on those it has used big time; throw them under the bus. As Russell Means stated just before he died and perhaps because he stated this: "The White Man has become the new Indian." EVERYTHING that the evil illuminati has done to the native Americans of the USA and Canada (and everywhere else in the world) is planned for the rest of us-no exceptions: vaccines, poisoned food (GMOs) and water, cutting off of the food supply via droughts and weather warfare, foreign troops (Chinese & Russian) who have no constitutional oath to NOT fire on Americans just as we did the same with NATO troops in other sovereign nations like Libya, child trafficking to sadistic pedophiles, child sacrifices to Moloch the "GOD" of money and credit (Bohemian Grove In Alex Jones websites), living under spy cameras and last, but not least, the micro chipping of every person to annihilate the God given right of free will, freedom of thought and action in total acquiescence to Big Daddy government whom these people are going to realize very late in the game was just a con to get them to go along with the evil and turn a blind eye to it for a government handout in the end. Evil always reneges in the end and these promises will be reneged on too. Maybe these people will realize what's going on when they're herded into FEMA camps and the gas is being turned on. Who knows when they realize or if they realize anything at all? My book is for the 10% or 5% who want to know what's going on NOT for the cowardly truth deniers who WILL not face these truths. It is a sad commentary in America that anyone who speaks the truth is ridiculed and condemned so I will be surprised if I am not dealt with in the very same way. It's kind of like dealing with a malignant narcissist sociopath. You tell others to beware of this evil one and some idiot tells this Monster what you said. Then this Malignant Sociopath Monster uses every resource it has to bring you completely down. Except in America it's not one isolated idiot; it's the whole population minus a select few who speak the truth. Meanwhile legions of children keep disappearing and no one talks about this. Satanism is rampantly going on everywhere and no one talks about this either. I speak up only because I'm sick of the child torturing and killing, the murdering of babies. I can't stand it anymore. I look at the pictures of phosphorus burned to death people. I see the depleted uranium babies and feel like I'm in a dungeon. I'm tired of knowing these awful things alone. So here takes a look; this is the BRUTAL PROOF!!! How can a nation of people be so concerned about animals and look the

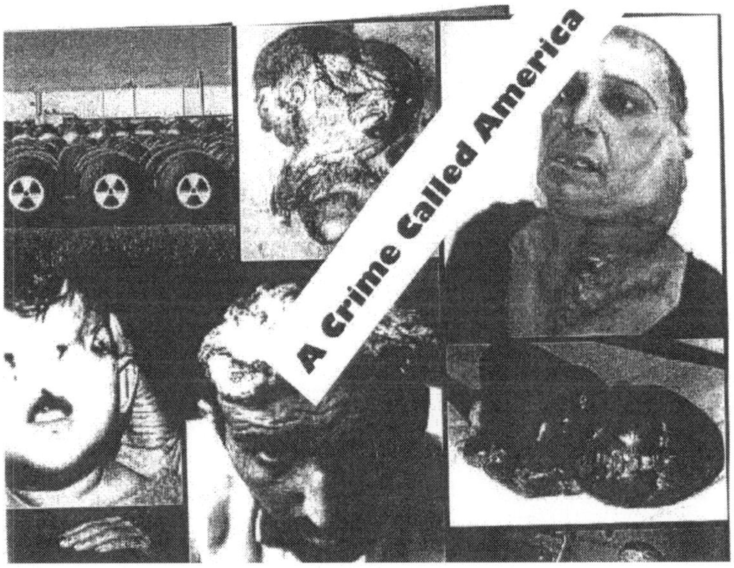

other way when it comes to black, yellow, and brown skinned people or babies? Will we wake up in time to see our fate in the not too far off future?

If the world's population boycotted alcohol, heroin, marijuana, beer, and cocaine there would go the drug trade and the big banks. Similarly, if the USA citizens cancelled 90% of their prescriptions drugs, avoided chemo & radiation, as well as vaccines then there too would go huge Rothschild profits and our population would be much healthier (doctorsaredangerous.com). What people don't realize is that many of the big banks are insolvent: Deutsch Bank, HSBC, Royal Bank of Scotland, Chase, Citibank, Banksters of America, BCCI and BIS, but by no means is this list complete. What keeps these banks afloat is drug money? BCCI was especially implicated as was HSBC. Take your money out of these big banks and put them in small community banks. These small community banks are being discriminated against by our own government. They don't receive the bailouts and allegedly had to contribute to pay some of the debts the big banks recklessly ran up. I like community banks willing to lend to the public as well as Credit Unions. I cancelled all my Chase credit cards and opened credit cards with Jefferson Federal Credit Union and Metairie Bank. They appreciate my business much more; Metairie Bank gave me a large line of credit with 0% interest for an entire year and a half, which was fantastic as I used it to pay off a large amount of debt at a one-time charge of 3%. Bankers can be your best friend or your worst enemy. Chase became my worst enemy with screw-up after screw-up and many a sleepless night worrying about where my gold had disappeared because they reportedly didn't know where my deposit box was. I ended up flying to Westwood Avenue in Santa Monica to find my box in a mish mash of jumbled safety deposit boxes from all over the country and told them I had to discontinue banking with them because I couldn't handle the stress. Five credit cards were closed, the safety deposit box, which had never been a problem before Chase bought out Washington Mutual was closed and finally the checking account was closed. My ties with them have been severed-forever-and I am sure Chase will cheat their own customers who will lose trillions when the bail-in happens Cyprus style during a "bank holiday." Chase has an Unsafe Deposit Box Service. With Chase, you must chase after your money and gold. I finally located my misplaced safe deposit box and gold. Chase had made every single error undercharging me $10 for the box, telling me this was correct when I complained, putting the box on drill status, not informing me of drill status or $10 underpayment during the occurrences, telling me I could update my address on the internet and that ALL ADDRESSES INCLUDING THE SAFE DEPOSIT BOX ADDRESS WOULD BE UPDATED ON THE INTERNET (this was clearly wrong) telling me they couldn't find the log book for the drilled contents, couldn't find the contents of the box in Baton Rouge or Sacramento, and they clearly didn't even know whether or not the box had actually been drilled. I decided on my own to pay the $10 underpaid rental fee, convince them to waive late fees-after all this whole fiasco was their fault, and schedule a trip out there for peace of mind and to rid myself of Chase. I ended up getting my $17,000 Liberty Gold Set back and finding out that Chase had a class action lawsuit in London for confiscating customer's assets, which must have been precious safety deposit box items. I believe this is an intentional glitch to confiscate assets because Chase as you will see in the near future is in desperate need of liquidity. Customer assets are easy to confiscate this way and it looks like a planned 'oopsie.' The items updated on the internet were credit cards and the checking account. The only item not updated via the internet was the safe deposit box and coincidentally? It was the only place with items of great value. Search Chase Fraud Class Action and see what I am talking about. While I stood in line at a Hollywood Post Office registering my package to mail I happened to mention my struggle to a lady behind me she told me they had so many troubles with Chase they cancelled their production account and it was BIG MONEY-maybe $300 million?

The problems with Chase were apparently well known in Hollywood judging by the amused smiles.

Boycott BP Oil

This is an illuminati company to the core! It is British Petroleum, which was involved in the New Orleans Gulf Oil Spill decimating wildlife and devastating the seafood industry. Dead dolphins, whales, turtles, and crabs have littered the shores. Corexit, the deadly cleanup chemical, is killing the cleanup workers (many were prison slave labor) who are quietly dying in droves leaving behind orphaned children. The Deepwater Horizon explosion *killing 11 workers is the result of the Bush de-regulation of the oil industry to not require a $500,000 safety valve.* The blow-up and fire were only a matter of time. The book *The Vampire of Macondo* by Deborah Dupre completely exposes the callous mentality of these criminals who deregulated the oil industry and are now fighting the lawsuits and payouts. This is a systematic and virulent attack on humanity and Wildlife-Depopulation. Even more frighteningly the Navy was doing drills and the financial markets were manipulated for big profits for Goldman Sachs during the spills.... everything documented in *Vampire of Macondo.* All of this points to foreknowledge and planning much like the Wall Street trading during 9/11!

Boycott Shell

This oil company is owned by the Dutch Monarchy and they are literally fracking the people off of their land. Fracking is an extraction process using hundreds of poisonous chemicals injected into obscene amounts of would-be drinking water to expel the oil. Oil companies who use fracking methods have no concern for the people who live there, the drinking water or the environment. Massive drinking water poisoning and earthquakes happen in fracking areas.

BrutalProof!

Hydrogen Cars

Hydrogen cars can and should be mass produced

Boycott Texaco and Exxon

Both are illuminati shills and it is hard, I admit, to find an oil company that isn't. Mobil is also illuminati.

I buy my gas from Discount Zone, which to my knowledge is independently owned by Arabs in Metairie, LA.

Fracking causes earthquakes. For any senator endorsing fracking, when that New Madrid Faultline explodes it could be your house affected. We should definitely look into Tesla technology!

Nancy Pelosi-guilty of Malfeasance and should be jailed

She is our public servant who stated "returning veterans are terrorists". When she made the statement for politicians to sign the bill and read it later she should've been retired to Federal Prison. She is a traitor. Her husband is an investment banker that is profiting greatly from the deregulation of the banking industry and both are becoming filthy rich. She represents the elite and always has. She is in Congress to deregulate banking and other industries and to line the Banksters pockets including her own. Where else, but in Congress could someone enter, broke and leave with hundreds of millions of dollars??? Nowhere else! She needs to be thoroughly audited and her Banksters husband needs to be thoroughly audited as well by a savvy examiner familiar with the offshore accounts, hiding assets, the Shell game and other devices and schemes. The same should be done with all Wall Street hucksters and derivatives scammers. I am absolutely sure she would never sign any contract without a lawyer going over the fine print while she cedes our rights away from us without our consent. But, this hypocrite tells us to sign the law and read it later-obviously, she benefits! **A new law is needed that nothing is to be signed into law without being read and understood and previous laws signed without being read are null and void. Anyone doing otherwise should go to prison for Malfeasance** (wrongdoing by a Public Official) and every law they signed should be wiped off the books.

Appendices

Appendix I – Satanic Cults and David Icke's list of Famous Satanists

Appendix II – Synergy Effects of Mercury with other Toxic Metals: Synergistic Toxicity

Appendix III – The Canadian Holocaust

Appendix IV – Child Abuse, Satanism, Sex, Lies and Blackmail (Monarch Mind Control)

- The Franklyn Cover-up
- Confessions of a DC Madam
- Franklin Court Case Records

Appendix V – Russia: The Hope of the World and Why the United States must join the BRICS

THE SYNAGOGUE OF SATAN
THEIR FATHER IS THE DEVIL!
... THE SYNAGOGUE OF SATAN, which say they are Jews, and are not, but DO LIE... REV 3:9 KJV
... I know the BLASPHEMY of those saying themselves to be Jews, and are not, but are the SYNAGOGUE OF SATAN. REV 2:9 MKJV
YOU ARE OF YOUR FATHER, THE DEVIL, and you want to do the desires of your father. He was a MURDERER from the beginning, and doesn't stand in the truth, because THERE IS NO TRUTH IN HIM. When he speaks a lie, he speaks on his own; for HE IS A LIAR, and the Father of it. JOH 8:44 HNV
MESSIANIC KABBALAH
REVOLUTION!

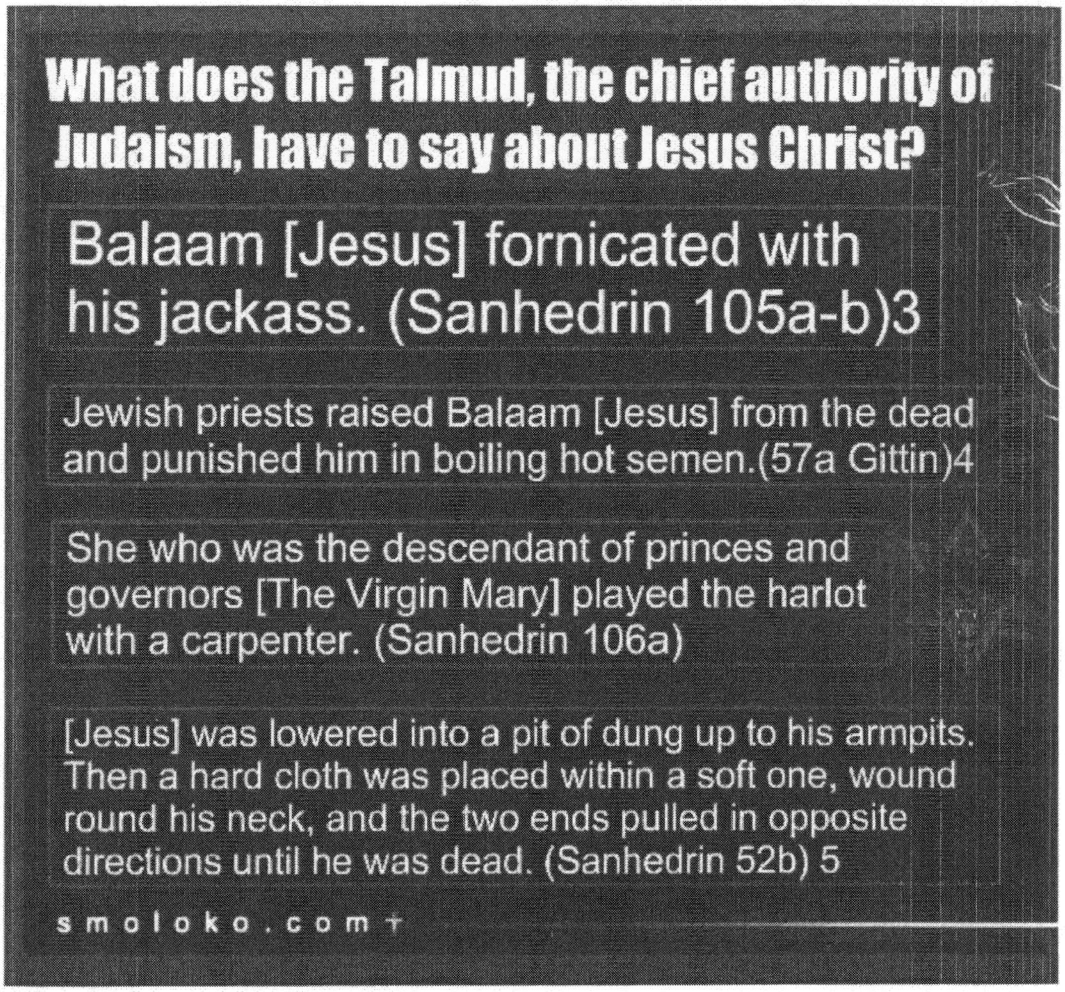
What does the Talmud, the chief authority of Judaism, have to say about Jesus Christ?
Balaam [Jesus] fornicated with his jackass. (Sanhedrin 105a-b)3
Jewish priests raised Balaam [Jesus] from the dead and punished him in boiling hot semen.(57a Gittin)4
She who was the descendant of princes and governors [The Virgin Mary] played the harlot with a carpenter. (Sanhedrin 106a)
[Jesus] was lowered into a pit of dung up to his armpits. Then a hard cloth was placed within a soft one, wound round his neck, and the two ends pulled in opposite directions until he was dead. (Sanhedrin 52b) 5
smoloko.com

7. The Jew may promote "equality amongst men" yet he sees himself in a self conscious ethnic group that he considers as being superior to all others.

8. The Jew when confronted with the claims of Christianity will always reply, "I was born a Jew and I will die a Jew." What he means is, "I will never become a Christian like the dumb goys."

The Protocols Of Zion

A one page summary

Goyim are mentally inferior to Jews and can't run their nations properly. For their sake and ours, we need to abolish their governments and replace them with a single government. This will take a long time and involve much bloodshed, but it's for a good cause. Here's what we'll need to do:

* Place our agents and helpers everywhere
* Take control of the media and use it in propaganda for our plans
* Start fights between different races, classes and religions
* Use bribery, threats and blackmail to get our way
* Use Freemasonic Lodges to attract potential public officials
* Appeal to successful people's egos
* Appoint puppet leaders who can be controlled by blackmail
* Replace royal rule with socialist rule, then communism, then despotism
* Abolish all rights and freedoms, except the right of force by us
* Sacrifice people (including Jews sometimes) when necessary
* Eliminate religion; replace it with science and materialism
* Control the education system to spread deception and destroy intellect
* Rewrite history to our benefit
* Create entertaining distractions
* Corrupt minds with filth and perversion
* Encourage people to spy on one another
* Keep the masses in poverty and perpetual labor
* Take possession of all wealth, property and (especially) gold
* Use gold to manipulate the markets, cause depressions etc.
* Introduce a progressive tax on wealth
* Replace sound investment with speculation
* Make long-term interest-bearing loans to governments
* Give bad advice to governments and everyone else

Eventually the Goyim will be so angry with their governments (because we'll blame them for the resulting mess) that they'll gladly have us take over. We will then appoint a descendant of David to be king of the world, and the remaining Goyim will bow down and sing his praises. Everyone will live in peace and obedient order under his glorious rule.

Suddenly Gone

By Dan Mitrione

"roughly 5,000 serial killers were actively pursuing their prey." (as of 1995)

Who knows how high the number is now?

(my Question)

Philosophy of serial killers echoed in:

Protocols of Elders of Zion

Which refers to the rest of us as "goyim" and not worthy of being any more than subhuman animals-pet owners have a better attitude than this! They state they have a right to murder us without charge because we are so worthless and to lie, cheat and steal from "goyim." Rascist!

What the religion of Judaism teaches?

(Baba Mezia 24a) "If a Jew finds an object lost by a goy (non-Jew) it does not have to be returned."

(Sanhedrin 57a) "If a Jew murders a goy (non-Jew) there will be no death penalty."

(Sanhedrin 57a) "What a Jew steals from a goy he may keep."

(Baba Kamma 113a) "Jews may use subterfuges to circumvent a goy (non-Jew)."

(Yebamoth 98a) "All children of the goyim (non-Jews) are animals"

(Baba Mezia 114b) "The goyim are not humans. They are beasts."

(Tosapoth, Jebamoth 94b) "If you eat with a goy (non-Jew) it is the same as eating with a dog."

(Soferim 15) "Even the best of the 'goyim' should all be killed."

(Sanhedrin 74b) "Sexual intercourse between the goyim (non-Jews) is like intercourse between animals."

(Sanhedrin 107b) "Yashu (Jesus) was sexually immoral and worshipped a brick."

Alice.F

(Shabbath 104b) "Miriam the hairdresser had sex with many men."

We know that Zionism is the problem and we know it's source, the Jewish religion of Judaism, a religion that teaches that some people are chosen over others, a religion that produced the Babylonian Talmud, a book of hate against all Goyim. The Talmud is simply an extension of the Torah and other books, the Talmud takes Old Testament hate toward rival tribes to new levels of depravity. Zionism didn't happen by accident, it is the end result of a long progression of Jewish only thinking.

Liberty For Life INDEX --- tablets tap menu to expand

- What's New on LFL
- Zionatzi Evil >>
- Janis God of War>>
- Will It Kill You? >>
- NOA Saving US >>
- Evil Fed Bank >>
- Eye Openers >>
- Illuminatzi >>
- NewWordOrder >>
- False Flag-9/11 >>
- U.S.A. & War >>
- USA Construct >>
- Building Gov. >>
- Wise Quotes >>
- Education >>
- Religion >>
- Extraterrestrial >>
- Media& Links >>
- LAW >>
- Proof of Abuse >>
- BLOG >>
- About LFL >>

CONTENTS

Pharaoh Akhanaten's Ashkenazi Zionatzi Freemason Jesuit Jews Khazarian Satan Worshipers, Sacrificing Children & Drinking Their Blood

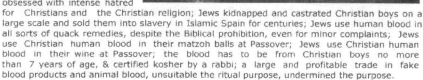

The author of a book titled "Bloody Passover" about European Ashkenazi Jews' Child Sacrifice & Rituals, is not Christian, Muslim or Hindu but Jewish. He is the son of the Chief Rabbi of Rome, and a professor of Jewish Renaissance and Medieval History at Bar-Ilan University in Israel, just outside Tel Aviv. The book documents a history of Jewish Human Sacrifice.

Prof. Toaff in his book shows how Ashkenazi Jews are obsessed with intense hatred for Christians and the Christian religion; Jews kidnapped and castrated Christian boys on a large scale and sold them into slavery in Islamic Spain for centuries; Jews use human blood in all sorts of quack remedies, despite the Biblical prohibition, even for minor complaints; Jews use Christian human blood in their matzoh balls at Passover; Jews use Christian human blood in their wine at Passover; the blood has to be from Christian boys no more than 7 years of age, & certified kosher by a rabbi; a large and profitable trade in fake blood products and animal blood, unsuitable the ritual purpose, undermined the purpose.

While set in a historical perspective documenting overwhelming evidence of the insane practices of the Ashkenazi Jews sacrificing children and drinking their blood, one can not help ponder if the book has not been written for the modern Jew as a "reference" or "instruction manual". Explosive evidence is being produced from all around the world that these Zionatzi psychopaths continue to sacrifice children, drink their blood& eat their flesh to this very day. Not only that, evidence showing that events such as 9/11 are planned & carried out as ritualistic sacrifices to these psychopaths "god" Lucifer / Satan. The World Wars, genocides & the most depraved human acts all seem to fall within this "sacraficial" category.

More chilling is the leaked DNA evidence which links Pharoah Akhenaten & his son Thutenkamen as blood relatives to the Queen of England and a majority of European Royalty. This, as you will learn from Prof Toaff's book, and when comprehending that Pharoah Akhanaten was most likely an Ashkenazi Jew, reaches the most extreme level of disgust & depravity, in the intricate and many detailed accounts of how the Pharoah sacrificed hundreds of children and bathed in their blood in an effort to rid himself of leopracy. The practice of drinking blood of babies, blood infusion & "bathing in blood", we now learn is practiced Ashkeazi Zionatzi Freemason Jesuti Jews to this very day.

One can only conclude that these practices form the extreme and insane Janus construct of sowing the deepest hatred and division amongst different groups. The double-headed Janus eagle of the two-faced Janus God can be traced right back to Enki's helper Urudu XXX. Have we uncovered the verry roots of mankinds engineering & enslavement, the division sown amongst us by insane sacraficial religions that survive to this day as Christianity, Judaism, Islam & Satanasm (The worship of Lucifer and his Christ).

Prof. Toaff writes: *"The reference to the sacrifice of Isaac would appear out of place, considering that, in the Biblical account, Abraham did not really immolate his son, as he was prepared to do, but was stopped by the miraculous Divine intervention which stayed his hand, holding the sacrificial knife. But this conclusion should certainly be revised.... The Midrash even advances the hypothesis that* ***Abraham really shed Isaac's blood, sacrificing him on the precise spot upon which the Altar of the Temple of Jerusalem was later to be built.****"*

He continues "Isaac was sacrificed for the love of God and his blood gushes onto the altar, coloring it red. This is the historical ritual memory, transfigured and updated, which the Judaism of the German lands, reduced in numbers by the suicides and mass child murders committed during the Crusades "for the sanctification of the Lord's name".... In one of his elegies, Ephraim of Bonn described not only the ardor and the zeal of Abraham in immolating his son, butchering him on the altar,".. -P205 Bloody Passover

"The Jews in Germany who, during the first crusade, sacrificed their own children 'as Abraham sacrificed Isaac his son', were perfectly convinced that their own blood, together with that of the two other sacrifices -circumcision and the Passover lamb - all offered to God in abnegation, would not be lost, but would constitute the powerful fluid from which the well-deserved and predicted revenge and the much-desired Redemption would ferment." - P212

On P224, the author goes on to expound how the blood of murdered children was used to wash away Pharaoh's leprocy.

"The obligation to procure blood and to use it during the Passover ritual was the exclusive responsibility of the head of the family,.." ...."The evening before Pesach, when they stir the dough with which the unleavened bread (the shimmurim) is later prepared, the head of the family takes the blood of a Christian child and mixes it into the dough while it is being kneaded," - P260. The author goes on listing accounts of Jews, especially in the region of Nuremberg, would use human blood in their Passover rituals. "The head of the family takes a bit of the blood of the Christian child and drops it in his glass full of wine" - P263

"That no text will be found among those Jews, but that it was said among those same Jews and experts in the law, and that they handed it down from generation to generation in memory, and it was kept secret among those Jews [...] and that it was necessary for this blood to be the blood of a Christian boy and not a girl, and that he could not be more than 7 years old" - P281

Chapter 13, the author references how fathers murdered their own wives & children to prevent them from receiving Christian baptism, and how this was justified by Rabies.

Blood rituals in which human blood is drunk from the body of a still-living victim was found in uncivilized and utterly ignorant societies. However, only one people, that has never progressed beyond the Stone Age, has continued to practice the blood rite and ritual murder. This people are known to the world as Ashkenazi Jews, or Zionists. Arnold Toynbee, a noted scholar, calls the Jews "a fossil people."

The book can be downloaded here: http://bloodpassover.com/xbp.pdf

source Thisiszionism

In the following short documentary, the Child Sacrifice amongst Ahkenazi Jewish families. Sacrifice carried out to this day is testified about during an Opra Winfrey Show & other experts give their accounts. YouTube repeatedly removes the video

Vicki Polin, MA, NCC, LCPC, ATR-BC

The lady in the video who give testomony of current day child sacrifice, just as described above, Vicki Polin, runs The Awareness Center, an organization devoted to the issue of sexual abuse in the Jewish community. Polin and her board members, who include prominent rabbis and professionals knowledgeable about issues of sexual trauma amongst Jews, assist victims. Jews, from all over the world, contact The Awareness Center for advice, counseling and referrals, says Polin, who puts in 60 to 80 hours a week on the project. About 15,000 people visit their service each month — victims of abuse, called "survivors" in the sexual trauma community, their family members, rabbis, lawyers, law enforcement officials and others concerned about the issue.

"The Rapture", a word, and an event contrived in the Scofield bible
THE HOLY BIBLE
The SCOFIELD reference Bible is a zionist interpretation of bible scripture footnoted in modern English. Written in 1909 by convicted felon Cyrus Scofield, financed by jewish backers, with bribes, the bible was forced into bible colleges, the pulpits of Christian ministers, and 20th century Christian beliefs. This bible is a powerful zionist tool in the creation and support of illegal Israel, and the subjugation of the Christian religion into Zionism.
DDees.com

This is a subversion of Christianity

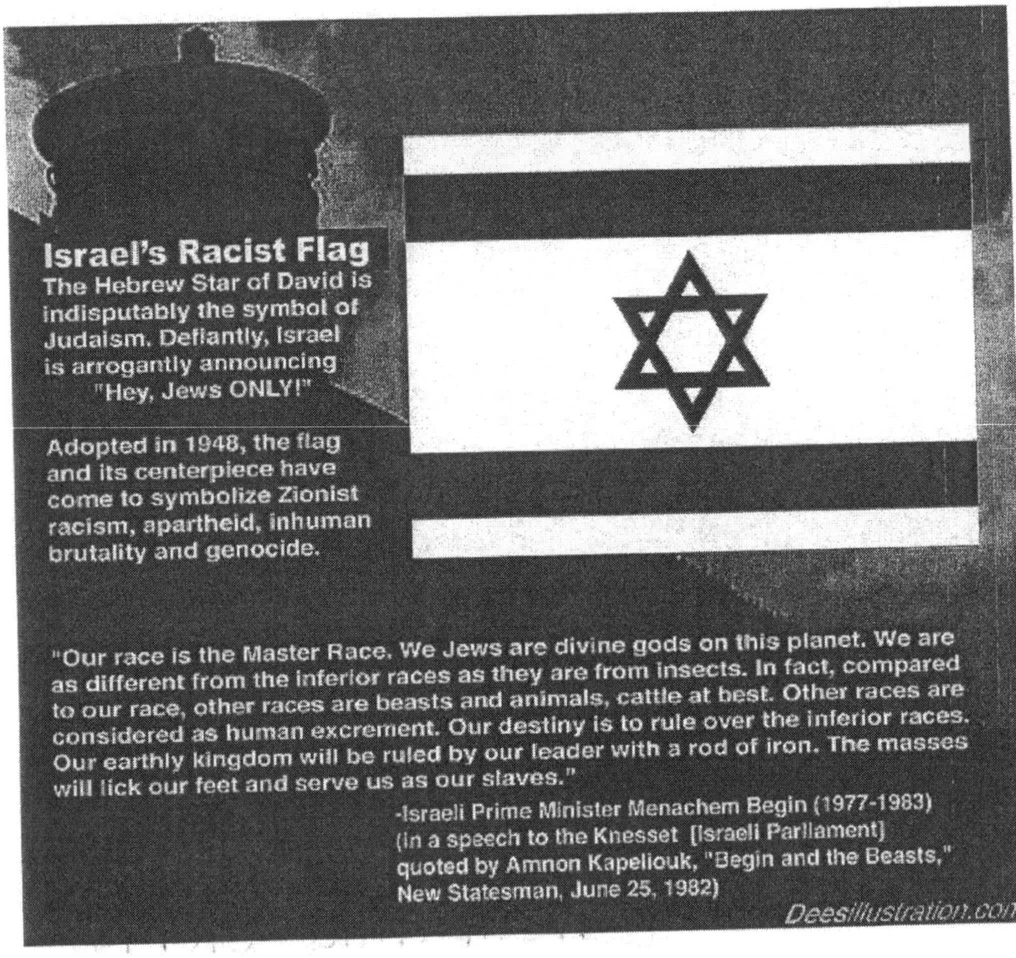

Israel is a Rothschild creation. The Rothschild's control the United States via George Soros & their Aipac, B'nai, B'rith, etc.

Rothschild Zionist Pacs control the White House & Congress!

http://ddees.com/wp-content/uploads/2015/09/AIPAC.jpg 9/9/2016

Rothschildrism includes:

BrutalProof!

- **Communism and Marxism**
- **Fascism**
- **Nazi's**
- **Totalitarianism**
- **Statism**
- **Socialism**
- **Corporatism**

THE ILLUMINATI
The Cult that Hijacked the World

Henry Makow Ph.D.

Table of Contents

Book Two – Illuminati, Sabbateans and Protocols

13 Satanic illuminati Bloodlines:

Astor Bundy Collins Li

DuPont Freeman Kennedy

Russell Onassis Reynolds

Reynolds Van Duyn Rockefellers

Affiliated Families:

Disney Krupp McDonalds

Interconnected to:

Council of Foreign Relations, Trilateral Commission, Bilderberg, Majestic Project 12,

Rockefeller & Rothschild New World Order (Fritz Springmeier)

Sexual Sadists like to:

- Self mutilate (cutters)
- Torture & kill pets
- Collect torture weapons
- No empathy, no remorse, no cure
- Repeat offenders (an addiction)
- Choose vulnerable & isolated individuals i.e. runaways, hitchhikers, Unaccompanied refugee children- now 10,000 missing-or aboriginal street people on Eastside Vancouver
- Torturing is their greatest high
- Last level is torturing to death

Lanterman-Petris-Short Act protects

He has a past history of animal torture in his early teens. Richard Trenton Chase [the Sacramento Vampire Killer], for example, drank human blood and kept animal kidneys and livers in his freezer. He strangles and poisons his pets as substitutes for human victims.

For reasons unknown, sexual and aggressive impulses intertwine early in childhood in these sadistic types and eventually find expression in vicious sexual assaults and sadistic murders.

He kills to achieve sexual pleasure. Murder produces a powerful sexual arousal and pleasure and is a replacement for sex. He may masturbate while reliving the crimes.

The sexual sadist often taunts the police in letters, uses deliberate misspellings, and under stress may use handwriting that is unrecognizable from his true writing. The pleasure of baiting the police may actually become the motive for the slayings, and though he takes great pains to appear normal and avoid capture, he often throws suspicion upon himself.

The sexual sadist has a strong self-mutilation drive. As a child he may play at his own execution and eventually become suicidal.

He will be fascinated with the tools of policework and with policemen, and may pretend to be one. He collects weapons and instruments of torture and has great skill in their use.

The sadist seeks the dehumanization of his victims into objects that cannot reject him and that he has power over. He is incurable, feels no remorse for the cruelty he inflicts on others, and will most likely repeat his crimes.

He chooses victims with specific characteristics, such as students or hitchhikers. The sexual sadist can describe his assaults in great detail. If caught for one murder, he takes delight in confessing to all the others in an effort to dismay the police.

Excerpt from <u>Zodiac</u>

ted, but now it isn't.

"I suspect there were a bunch of people put away for life who were potential Zodiac-type killers. But now that you can't keep people longer than ninety days* people like that are getting out. Until 1969, for instance, people could be committed for life to a mental hospital on pretty flimsy grounds. There was this drastic change where it became very difficult to commit someone. You had to have concrete evidence of either suicidal acts or an act of violence toward others."

"How often," I asked, "have you personally seen a sexual sadist? How many have you talked with?"

"A dozen," Lunde replied, "which is a lot more than one. But it doesn't, on the other hand, compare to the thousands of paranoid schizophrenics. There's something spooky about the incredible similarities among sexual sadists."

"Is it inconsistent," I asked, "for a sexual sadist to be a child molester as well?"

"No. The thing about all these people and the one thing they have in common is an abnormal relationship with women. They are limited or incapable of forming normal adult sexual relationships. And so what are the alternatives? One is sex with dead bodies or killing for sexual satisfaction. Another is sex with children.

"There are the common threads of inadequate normal adult sexual relationships and also the need to have power over the sexual object, which you can achieve either through violence,

*The Lanterman-Petris-Short Act was passed in 1967 and determined that a person can be detained only if he is a danger to himself or others. The reduction of 50,000 psychiatric beds in California in 1960 to 5,000 today deposited patients in local communities ill prepared to handle them.

Excerpt from Zodiac

1,000,000 Missing Kids!

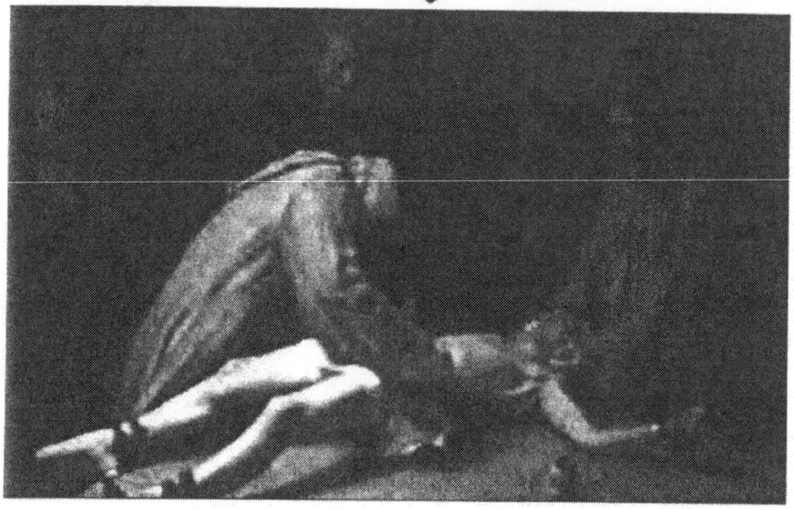

POLITICIAN PEDOPHILES MAKE PRIESTS LOOK LIKE SAINTS!

Discovery documentary 'Conspiracy of Silence' taken off TV by Bush pedophiles. Can be viewed at: **www.Franklincase.org** or on Google. Google 'Child Sex Ring In White House' to see limited newspaper coverage. Go to **www.davidicke.com** to Research Archives and then to Satanism and find George Bush World Class Monster... Rape, torture, murder of children... a gruesome story involves CIA, Catholic Church, at least 4 presidents, military & FBI. David Icke's book: The Biggest Secret details elite pedophilia. John DeCamp's book: The Franklin Cover-Up elite pedophiles at Bohemian Grove and their child snuff film and connection to Bush White House.

www.JohnnyGosch.com
Picture above taken from this website of Satanic Ritual Abuse

www.Trance-formation.com
Cathy O'Brien's harrowing account as a child sex slave to former President's Reagan and Bush as well as her rape by Hillary Clinton.

WWW.DAVIDICKE.COM

Illuminati $$$$$ makers:

- Snuff Pornography
- Child Prostitution
- Human Trafficking & Slavery
- Body Parts Business & Organ Trafficking
- Planned Parenthood
- Fur (Torture of Animals) Trade
- Big Pharma Drugs & illegal Drugs

Defund Planned Parenthood!

Outlaw Abortions!

- **Phony Cancer Cures Such As Chemo & Radiation**
- **Shutting down Real Cancer Cures Using FDA and AMA**
- **Oil Business**
- **WAR!!!! (50% of US Budget)**
- **Cosmetics Industry**
- **Mining Industry (gold, silver, etc.)**

- Blood Diamonds & Stealing Precious Resource From Colonies Such as Africa
- Sugar Business in Caribbean
- Vaccines $$$$$$$$$$
- Music Industry
- Hollywood TV & Film
- Publishing Industry
- Factory Farms (rampant animal abuse)
- Phony Green Charities
- World Wildlife Fund

- Soro's Phony Charities & Phony Activism Groups
- IMF
- Guns & Gun Running
- Alcohol Bootlegging During Prohibition
- Looting colonial Countries of gold, silver, precious metals, OIL, precious artifacts-think Libya-140 tons of gold & 140 tons of silver alone
- Weapons industry

- Military-Industrial Complex
- Facebook & Twitter
- Religions: Roman Catholic Church & VATICAN
- Nazi's
- Banking is a Biggie With Typed in Bank Loans & foreclosing on hard assets
- Scamming other countries by forcing them to use US dollar as world's reserve currency and making it

worthless by running the Federal Reserve printing presses day & night flooding the world with cheap dollars and getting valuable goods & commodities in return for worthless dollars as well as oil-this is why the world is creating BRIC'S-to stop the looting by the US Banksters! US is military arm of Banksters-illuminati-mob!

Davidicke.com

LIST OF FAMOUS SATANISTS, PEDOPHILES, AND MIND CONTROLLERS
by David Icke

http://www.davidicke.com/icke/articles/listsatan.html

The following list has been compiled from the wealth of research I have put together over the last ten years. I would suggest that all of these are reptilian bloodline, but I only mention shape-shifting where it has been witnessed.

It is only an initial list and will be added to. If you can add names, and give the supporting evidence, that would be most helpful in exposing these horrors. By "Satanists", of course, I mean those involved in human sacrifice.

David Icke

William F. Buckley Jr: Head of the elite JANUS mind control operation based at NATO headquarters in Belgium which trains mind-controlled psychic assassins; child killer, Satanist, shape-shifter

George Bush: US President and Vice President, head of the CIA, and a stream of other leading roles in the Illuminati. Satanist, mind controller, torturer of children and adults, pedophile, shape-shifting reptilian, and major drug runner. Serial killer. Nice man.

George W. Bush, Jr. - front-runner to be next President of the United States. Son of his father.

Bill Clinton, President of the United States. Satanist, serial killer, based on orders he has issued for assassinations, sexual abuser of mind controlled slaves.

Hillary Clinton, wife of President and now running for political office in New York. Announced her intention to run at a place called Pindar. This is the code-name of one of the foremost Illuminati human sacrificers and operatives (See The Biggest Secret). High Illuminati witch and Satanist. Abuser of mind controlled women.

Al Gore, Vice-President to Clinton, and front runner to be the "Democratic" candidate "opposing" George W. Bush. Illuminati, Satanist, serious blood drinker. Reptilian shapeshifter.

Gerald Ford, **Ronald Reagan**, **Jimmy Carter**, **Richard Nixon**, **Lyndon B. Johnson**. Presidents of the United States. Satanists. Users of mind-controlled slaves.

John F. Kennedy, assassinated President of the US. User for sex of mind controlled slaves. Probably a lot more we have yet to know.

Ted Kennedy: US politician, and head of the Kennedy clan currently. Brutal abuser of mind controlled slaves.

Henry Kissinger, former Secretary of State under Richard Nixon, and one of the Illuminati's foremost master minds of the agenda. Satanist, mind controller, child torturer, creator of wars of mass murder and destruction. Shape-shifter. Works closely with the UK's Lord Carrington.

Mikail Gorbachev, former President of the Soviet Union, now working in the US for the Illuminati Gorbachev Foundation which campaigns for World government, world army, etc., etc. Satanist and shape-shifting reptilian.

House of Rothschild. Satanists, child sacrificers, mind controllers, torturers of children and adults. Guy de Rothschild heads the dynasty and he is one of the top trauma-based mind controllers in the world. They are shape-shifting reptilians.

Habsburgs: See Rothschilds.

Rockefellers: See Rothschilds.

Astor's: See Rothschilds.

DuPont's: See Rothschilds.

Mellon's: See Rothschilds.

Dick Cheney, Defense Secretary under President Bush. Satanist, torturer of children and adults. Mind controller.

Robert C. Byrd, "Democrat" senator for West Virginia. Satanist and brutal torturer of adults and children. Mind controller.

Quote added by Hard Truth "It is money, money, money! Not ideas, not principles, but money that reigns supreme in American politics." -- Senator Robert Byrd, West Virginia

Bob and Bill Bennett, well-known US political figures closely connected to George Bush. Satanists, mind controllers, torturers of children and adults.

Lt Col Michael Aquino, US Military Psychological Warfare Department: Satanist (founder of the Church of Set), torturer of children and adults in trauma-based mind control projects.

Kris Kristopherson, actor and singer. Works with Aquino. Torturer, mind controller.

Boxcar Willie, country music singer. Satanist, pedophile.

Bob Hope "comedian". Life-time asset of British Intelligence, mind-controlled slave handler, and manipulator of the "entertainment industry" on behalf of the Illuminati. The "Rat Pack", including Frank Sinatra, Sammy Davis Junior, and Dean Martin were all heavily involved with Hope and others in the same line of work.

Billy Graham, "Christian" hero who has been funded from the start by the top Illuminati families and operatives like the Rockefellers and newspaper tycoon, William Randolph Hearst. Satanist, involved in mind control projects, close friend of Bush and Kissinger. Bloodline of the Satanic

Illuminati Frank family which created the Satanic movement known as Frankism.

Queen Elizabeth II of the UK: Satanist, child sacrificer, shape-shifting reptilian. Major Illuminati figure.

Queen Elizabeth, the Queen Mother: As above.

Prince Philip: As above.

Prince Charles: As above.

Prince Andrew: As above.

Princess Anne: As above. Not seen to shape-shift.

Lord Mountbatten of the British Royal Family and World War II "war hero". Rothschild bloodline, and therefore a shape-shifter. Satanist.

Winston Churchill, Britain's war-time Prime Minister, and bloodline of the Marlborough family, one of the elite aristocratic bloodlines of the British Isles. Satanist.

Franklin Delano Roosevelt: US war-time President: Satanist.

Stalin: Russian war-time leader. Satanist.

Adolf Hitler, Nazi leader in Germany. Rothschild bloodline. Satanist.

Tony Blair, current British Prime Minister. Satanist.

Brian Mulroney, Prime Minister of Canada when he and President Bush introduced the NAFTA "free trade" agreement, which has devastated the Canadian economy. Satanist, rapist of mind controlled women.

Pierre Trudeau, Canadian Prime Minister. Satanist, rapist of mind controlled women, paedophile.

Edward Heath, Prime Minister of the UK from 1970-74 and the man who signed Britain into the European Community, now Union. Satanist, child torturer, paedophile, shapeshifting reptilian.

Willie Whitelaw, Deputy Prime Minister to Margaret Thatcher in the 1980s. Satanist.

Lord McAlpine of the McAlpine Construction dynasty in the UK. Satanist, paedophile.

Mohammed Al Fayed, father of Dodi Fayed, who died in the car with Princess Diana. Satanist.

Appendix II

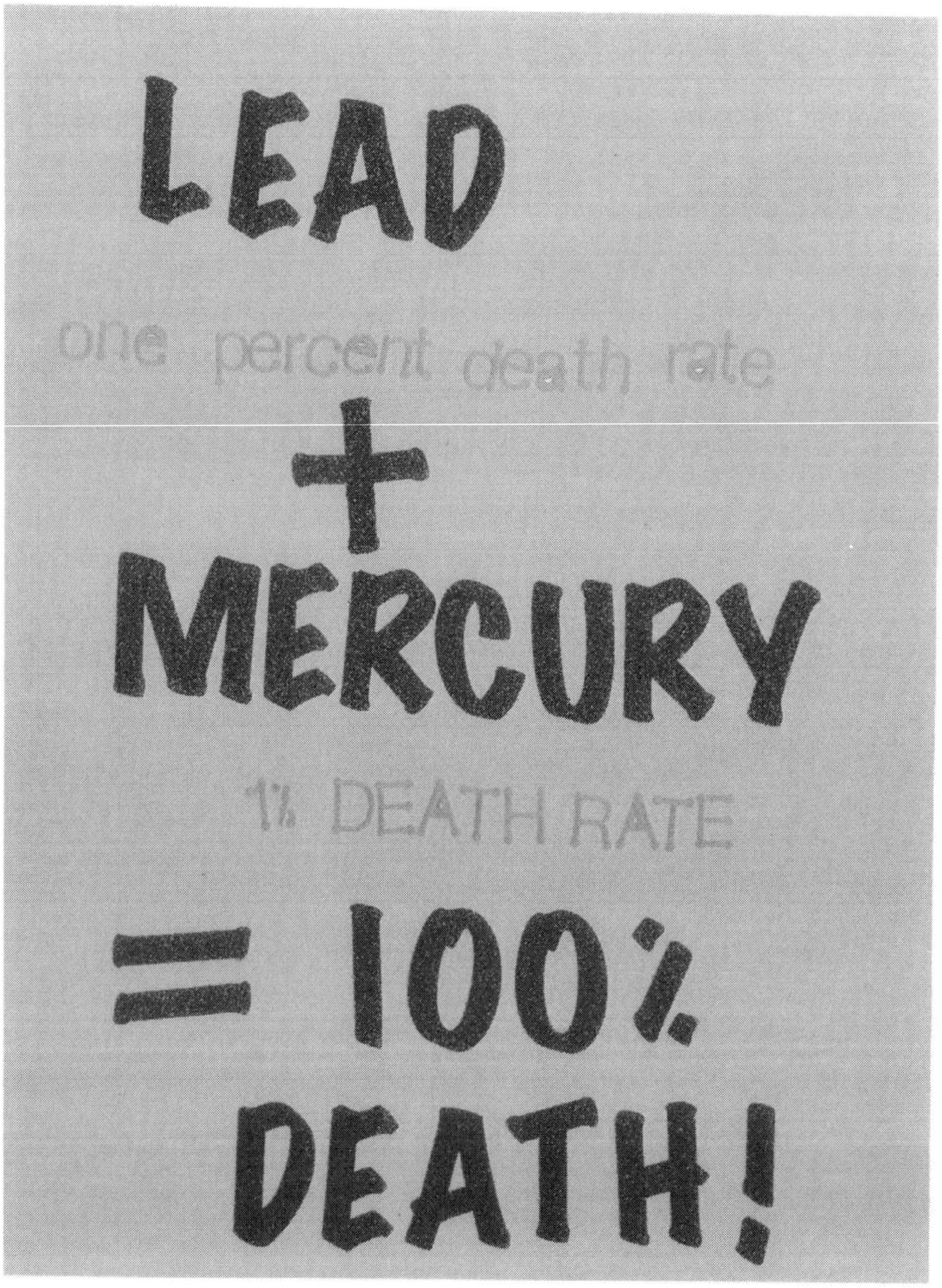

Synergistic Effects of Mercury with Other Toxic Metals: Extreme Synergistic Toxicity

Mercury and lead are extremely neurotoxic and cytotoxic, but their combined synergistic effect is much worse(1,4). A dose of mercury sufficient to kill 1% of tested rats, when combined with a dose of lead sufficient to kill less than 1% of rats, resulted in killing 100 % of rats tested (1a,4). Thus with combined exposure the safe dose is 1/100 as much as the dose individually. Studies in Australia have confirmed similar relationships hold for people(6). This means most people in the U.S. are getting dangerous levels of these metals, enough to cause some neurologic effects.

Similar is true for synergistic effect with other toxic metals like cadmium and arsenic (1), and with other toxic chemicals like PCBs(2a) and pesticides and tobacco smoke(2b). The level of mercury thimerosal in vaccines has been shown to be highly neurotoxic, but the effect was found to be much larger due to the synergistic effect with aluminum, which is also in most vaccines(4). Studies using U.S. CDC data have found thimerosal from vaccines to be major factors in autism and ADHD(5), along with prenatal rhogam shots which contain high levels of mercury thimerosal and are given to some RH negative women during pregnancy.

Dental amalgam has been documented by hundreds of thousands of medical lab tests to be the largest source of mercury in most adults or children who have several amalgam fillings(7,8). Mother's dental amalgams have been documented to be the largest source or mercury in the fetus, with levels in the fetus higher than in the mother's blood(8), and similar for mercury levels in young infants. Medical lab tests commonly find significant levels of other toxic metals such as lead, arsenic, cadmium, antimony, etc. in both adult and children's hair or urine tests(12), and commonly find related adverse health effects such as ADHD and learning disabilities.

Autism increased in the U.S. more than 10 fold in the 1990s. According to the Florida Dept. of Education, the numbers increased from approx. 300 to over 4000 during this time period. There have likewise been large increases in the number of children with ADHD and other developmental conditions, according to the National Academy of Sciences and other sources

(12) . A major factor in this appears to be the large increase in vaccinations given to infants, as noted in the previous post. (more documentation available at the childrens neurological page, www.flcv.com/indexk.html

There was an increase of over 45% in learning disabilities in Pennsylvania between 1990 and 2000(3). But the study showed that the county highest on the Chemical Pollution Scorecard, Montgomery, had an increase more than double that of the rest of the state. Montgomery County had an increase in ADHD of 32.7% and an increase in autism of 310%. An analysis of the U.S. Dept. of Education report on the prevalence of various childhood conditions among school children found that the rate of autism and speech disorders increased with increasing levels of thimerosal exposure from vaccines (5). A study of environmental mercury levels in Texas school districts found a 61 percent increase in autism and a 43 percent increase in special education cases for every 1,000 pounds of mercury released into the environment(9a). Autism prevalence diminished by 2 percent for every 10 miles of distance from a mercury source. Another similar study found similar results and estimated economic costs due to disability or lower IQ (9b). Fossil fuel-burning power plants were the largest source of the widespread mercury pollution(9) but dental amalgam was the largest source in sewers and a significant source of environmental mercury in water bodies, fish, and air emissions(10).

Dr Michael Godfrey and dentist Noel Campbell write: *"...a lethal dose (LD1 [enough to kill 1% of the rats]) was combined with a 1/20th LD1 of lead, resulting in a LD 100 [100% death rate] in the test animals."We have recently found that considerable amounts of lead may be excreted with the mercury following DMPS provocation. Our preliminary investigations appear to indicate that a synergistic effect could be identified by multiplying the lead and mercury concentrations together, after adjusting to IG of urine creatinine. We have termed this the Campbell-Godfrey factor (C-G factor). Chronic-ally affected patients may have high levels of either metal or a high total C-G factor. Those with the highest C-G factor appear to be the worst affected, thus indicating that the synergism in animals is replicated in man."*

1. (a) Schubert J, Riley EJ, Tyler SA. Combined effects in toxicology. A rapid systematic testing procedure: cadmium, mercury, and lead. Toxicol Environ Health 1978;4(5/6):763-776;& (b) Tabata M, Kumar Sarker A, Nyarko E. Enhanced conformational changes in DNA in the presence of mercury(II), cadmium(II) and lead(II) porphyrins. J Inorg Biochem. 2003 Feb 1;94(1-2):50-8; & (c)Traore A, Bonini M, Dano SD, Creppy EE. Synergistic effects of some metals contaminating mussels on the cytotoxicity of the marine toxin okadaic acid.

Arch Toxicol. 1999 Aug;73(6):289-95;& (d) Sanchez DJ, Belles M, Albina ML, Sirvent JJ, Domingo JL. Nephrotoxicity of simultaneous exposure to mercury and uranium in comparison to individual effects of these metals in rats. Biol Trace Elem Res. 2001 Winter;84(1-3):139-54.

2. (a)Philippe Grandjean P, White RF et al. Neurobehavioral deficits associated with PCB in 7-year-old children prenatally exposed to seafood neurotoxicants. Neurotoxicology and Teratology 2001;223(4):305-317; & (b) Steevens JA, Benson WH. Toxicokinetic interactions and survival of Hyalella azteca exposed to binary mixtures of chlorpyrifos and methyl mercury. Aquat Toxicol. 2001 Feb;51(4):377-88;& (c) El-Safty IA, Shouman AE, Amin NE. Nephrotoxic effects of mercury exposure and smoking among egyptian workers in a fluorescent lamp factory. Arch Med Res. 2003 Jan-Feb;34(1):50-5; & (d) Hultberg B, Andersson A, Isaksson A. Interaction of metals and thiols in cell damage and glutathione distribution: potentiation of mercury toxicity by dithiothreitol. Toxicology. 2001 Jan 2;156(2-3):93-100.

3. Pennsylvania Dept. of Education, 2003, Study of learning disability incidence in Montgomery County, Pennsylvania, 1990 and 2000; & ""Polluting Our Future: Chemical Emissions in the U.S. that Affect Child Development and Learning,"" by Physicians For Social Responsibility, at (202) 898-0150, psrnatl@psr.org

4. Haley, BE, Pendergrass JC ,Lovell, M., Univ. of Kentucky Chemistry Dept., paper presented to the Institute of Medicine Immunization Safety Review Committee, **Spring 2001,& Affidavit Of Boyd E. Haley. Professor And Chair. Department Of Chemistry. University Of Kentucky: Thimerosal Containing Vaccines and Neurodevelopment Outcomes http://www.vran.org/vaccines/mercury/mer-haley.htm**

5. Geier M.R., Geier DA; Thimerosal in Childhood Vaccines, Neurodevelopmental Disorders, and Heart Disease in the U.S. ; J of Amer Physicians and Surgeons, Vol 8(1), Spring 2003; & (b) Bradstreet J, Geier DA, et al, A case control study of mercury burden in children with Autisitic Spectrum Disorders, J of Amer Physicians and Surgeons, Vol 8(3), Summer 2003, & (c) A case series of children with apparent mercury toxic encephalopathies manifesting with clinical symptoms of regressive autistic disorders. Geier DA, Geier MR. J Toxicol Environ Health A. 2007 May 15;70(10):837-51 www.flcv.com/kidshg.html

6. M. Godfrey and N. Campbell, Are Amalgam Fillings Safe for Lead-poisoned People? LEAD Action News vol 5 no 2 1997 ISSN 1324-6011 http://www.lead.org.au/lanv5n2/lanv5n2-4.html

7. Documentation of High Levels of Mercury Exposure from Dental Amalgam Fillings, Review, B. Windham (Ed.), 2007, www.flcv.com/damspr1.html

8. Effects of Mercury from Mother's Dental Amalgam and other sources on the fetus and infants, B. Windham (Ed), 2007, www.flcv.com/fetaln.html

9. Environmental mercury release, special education rates, and autism disorder: an ecological study of Texas, *Health and Place, R.F. Palmer et al, March 2005* http://www.generationrescue.org/pdf/seed.pdf & Mercury pollution from power plants, NWF, http://www.nwf.org/wildlife/pdfs/MercuryMythsFacts.pdf

& (b) Mental retardation and prenatal methylmercury toxicity., Trasande L, Schechter CB, Haynes KA, Landrigan PJ., Department of Community and Preventive Medicine, Center for Children's Health and the Environment, New York, New York. Am J Ind Med. 2006 Mar;49 (3):153-8, http://www.melisa.org/abstracts.php#1

10. Dental amalgam is the largest source of mercury in sewers and a significant source of mercury in water bodies, fish, and the environment, EPA & www.flcv.com/damspr2f.html

11. Mercury levels in fish and health effects of mercury, B Windham (Ed), 2007, www.flcv.com/fishhg.html

12. Neurological effects of toxic metal exposures, Review, B Windham (Ed), 2007, www.flcv.com/tmlbn.html

****

*, note that a high percentage of Gulf state residents have been documented to have high levels of mercury exposure(Mobile Register study, www.flcv.com/fishhg.html)

****

The original evidence cited for the synergistic effects of lead and mercury (and cadmium) comes from a 1978 paper by Schubert *et al* published in Michigan: "*...the administration of an essentially no-response level (LD1) of a mercury salt together with 1/20 of the LD1 of a lead salt killed all of the animals [rats].*"

The questions raised by these studies and clinical experience are: is it safe for lead poisoned people to have mercury fillings? Should CLAS advise parents of lead-poisoned kids never to allow these fillings in their kid''s mouths? Should CLAS advise lead-poisoned people who are planning to conceive for instance, to have their amalgam fillings replaced, along with DMSA chelation therapy and nutrient replenishment therapy, well in advance of trying to conceive? Is it acceptable for anyone to be exposed to lead and mercury (and cadmium) as they are in mining and smelting communities? Why aren''t the DMPS provocation test, DMSA chelation therapy or amalgam removal procedures claimable under Medicare? When will amalgam be banned or phased out?

****

Consuming two toxic metals in combination, such as lead and cadmium, or lead and mercury, can have a synergistic effect, meaning one metal has the ability to enhance the toxicity of another metal in amounts smaller than what it would usually take that metal to be toxic.(5)

Mercury in combination with PCBs through diet can also have a synergisitic effect.(6) Readers might be curious to discover just how this synergistic effect is detected.
Laboratory animals are often used to test the toxicity of a substance. In the case of testing lead and mercury together, rats were used. Rats were dosed with an amount of mercury that would cause death in 1% of the rat population within about 5 days. This is called lethal dose 1% or LD1. The laboratory rats were also tested with a LD1 dose of lead. What is frightening is that when mercury and lead LD1 dosages were combined, there was a 100% mortality rate; all of the rats died, demonstrating that mercury and lead together are highly synergistic in their toxic effects.(5)

It is rather disturbing to realize that some populations of Canadian children are routinely ingesting chronic doses of lead, mercury, and PCBs together in their diet.

(1) Wheatley B and Paradis S. Balancing human exposure, risk and reality: Questions raised by the Canadian Aboriginal Methylmercury Program. Neurotoxicology 1996;17(1):241-250.

(2) Starnes R. Lead shotgun pellets contaminate game birds. The Ottawa Citizen 1998 Dec. 17; Section A:20.

(3) Toxic Chemicals Poison Inuit Food. The Ottawa Citizen 1998 July 5; Section A:5.

(4) Health Canada. Riedel D, Tremblay N, Tompkins E. (Eds.) State of Knowledge Report for Environmental Contaminants and Human Health in the Great Lakes Basin. Ottawa: 1997; p. 275

(5) Schubert J, Riley EJ, Tyler SA. Combined effects in toxicology. A rapid systematic testing procedure: cadmium, mercury, and lead. Toxicol Environ Health 1978;4(5/6):763-776.

(6) Philippe Grandjean P, Pal Weihea P, Bursed VW, Needham LL, Storr-Hansene E, Heinzowf B, Debesc F, Muratag K, Simonsenh H, Ellefsenc P, Budtz-Jøørgenseni E, Keidingi N and White RF. Neurobehavioral deficits associated with PCBs in 7-year-old children prenatally exposed to seafood neurotoxicants. Neurotoxicology and Teratology 2001;223(4):305-317

****

Learning Disabilities Statistics by Penn State Graduate Students — 2002 Source: Montgomery County Intermediate Unit (IU 23) was compared to (IU 17)Statewide Statistics: Pennsylvania Department of Education Census Figures: 1990 and 2000 Autism: Several websites including: naar.org, exploringautism.org, nich.nih.gib/autism and Naar

Pennsylvania Dept. of Education, Study of learning disability incidence in Montgomery County, Pennsylvania, 2003; & ""Polluting Our Future: Chemical Emissions in the U.S. that Affect Child Development and Learning,"" by Physicians For Social Responsibility, at (202) 898-0150, psrnatl@psr.org

There was an increase of over 45% in learning disabilities in Pennsylvania between 1990 and 2000

(3). But a study showed that the county highest on the Chemical Pollution Scorecard had an increase more than double that of the rest of the state. Montgomery County had an increase in ADHD of 32.7% and an increase in autism of 310%. 1990 to 2000 Montgomery County +94 % Least Polluted Comparison Area + 40.2 %Bradford, Lycoming, Sullivan and Tioga Counties Pennsylvania + 46.6 % 1990 to 2000 Total Enrollment in Montgomery County Schools Down - 10.9 %

Learning Disabilities have Risen Threefold in Montgomery County in comparison to the population - from 1990 to 2000

1990 to 2000

Montgomery County Intermediate Unit Total Enrollment	+ 32.7 %
Montgomery County - Learning Impairment Services	+ 32.7 %
Least Polluted Counties - Learning Impairment Services	+ 1 %

1990 to 2000 - ADD/ADHD and Autism

Montgomery County ADD/ADHD	+ 32.7 %
Montgomery County Autism	+ 310 %

·· **Montgomery County is one of the most chemically polluted counties in the nation**, according to Score Card''s pollution indicator. ·· ADD and AUTISM are **Neurodevelopmental Disorders.** ·· Heavily emitted neurological and developmental toxins in Montgomery County could be **Major Factors in Increased Learning Disabilities, ADD, and Autism**. Vinyl Chloride, Mercury, Methyl Isobuatyl Ketone, TCE, and Lead are all neurological toxins. The Pottstown Landfill is a source of ALL these neurological toxins. They travel downwind into many parts of Montgomery County. Researchers had difficulty determining exact amounts emitted by the Pottstown Landfill, since landfills are not required to report to EPA''s Toxic Release Inventory. ·· Occidental Chemical in Pottstown has emitted over 1½½ Million Pounds of Vinyl Chloride into Montgomery County''s air since 1988 and has ranked 1st and 2nd in the nation in Vinyl Chloride emissions.

Montgomery County Children Have Doubled Increases In Learning Disabilities Compared To Lesser Polluter Counties and the State - 1990 to 2000

Montgomery County is one of the most POLLUTED Counties in the Nation, according to Score Card''s pollution indicator. Ironically, all Pottstown Landfill''s toxic emissions are **not included** by Score Card.

Children everywhere are experiencing unacceptable increases in learning disabilities which suggest a serious problem. These disabilities are clearly the result of complex interactions among environmental, social, and genetic factors that impact children during vulnerable periods of development. There is new understanding about the effects of environmental chemicals on these processes. Developmental disabilities, including attention deficit/hyperactivity disorder (ADHD), autism, and related neurodevelopmental diseases affect millions of American children. The consequences of these disorders are often tragic. The family, social and economic costs are immense, and the disabilities can be life-long. Studies of animals and children show subtle changes in the concentrations of normally occurring chemicals such as hormones — as well as the presence of toxic agents like lead, mercury, or PCB''s — can produce profound and permanent changes in the developing nervous system. These can lead to decrements in mental performance. Developmental processes are extremely vulnerable to environmental insult. For detailed information refer to ""In Harm''s Way - Toxic Threats to Child Development,"" by

Greater Boston Physicians for Social Responsibility and ""Polluting Our Future: Chemical Emissions in the U.S. that Affect Child Development and Learning,"" by Physicians For Social Responsibility, at (202) 898-0150, psrnatl@psr.org Studies demonstrate that a variety of chemicals commonly encountered in industry can contribute to developmental, learning, and behavioral disabilities. Developmental neurotoxicants are chemicals that are toxic to the developing brain. They include the metals lead, mercury, cadmium, and manganese, and pesticides such as organophosphates. PCB''s, and DIOXINS bioaccumulate and are directly toxic to cells and neurotransmitters. With widespread use and disposal of all these chemicals and metals which affect learning disabilities, it is easy to understand why learning disabilities increased in PA by 46.6%, and even in the least polluted PA counties by 40.2% from 1990 to 2000. But, how do we explain such **shocking Montgomery County increases in learning disabilities (more than twice the state and comparison area) 94%, ADHD (32.7%), and autism at 310%? This represents an epidemic.** ACE believes Montgomery County children face a **chemical plague**. A major factor is **toxic air releases**. The kinds of neurotoxins which cause learning disabilities, ADHD, and autism are emitted into the air 7 days a week from the Pottstown Landfill and Occidental Chemical. Both emit unknown amounts of dioxin. The Pottstown Landfill emits synergistic and additive combinations of nearly every neurotoxin. These can become far more toxic as they synergize. Mercury is just one example. Occidental Chemical in Pottstown has emitted 1½½ million pounds of vinyl chloride since 1988. These emissions travel downwind through many parts of Montgomery County.

****

Combined effects in toxicology--a rapid systematic testing procedure: cadmium, mercury, and lead. Schubert J, Riley EJ, Tyler SA. J Toxicol Environ Health. 1978 Sep-Nov;4(5-6):763-76.

A testing procedure is described for the assessment of the toxicological response (e.g., acute toxicity or mutagenicity) of any combination and number of chemical, physical, and biological agents, with no more effort for a particular combination than for a single agent. The method provides a simple, sensitive, and quantitative index of synergism, antagonism, and additivity, and it has been demonstrated experimentally in rats by determining the acute lethality of combinations of cadmium, mercury, and lead salts. In a combination of two metal salts, the dose of one metal of the pair was fixed at or near the no-effect level while the dose of the second metal was increased until the entire dose-response curve was obtained. To evaluate interactions of the three metals, the previous pair of metals were kept fixed at their combined extrapolated LD1 level, and the third metal was increased. The statistical treatment of the data employed a computer program that did not involve probit transformations, but rather the approximate linear relationship between the fractional response and the logarithm of the dose. A particular combination could be synergistic, antagonistic, or additive, depending on the relative doses employed. Generally, a combination was synergistic when the most toxic member was present at or near its LD1 dose in the presence of the much less toxic member; the same combination was protective when the least toxic member was present at or near its LD1 dose. The results clarify apparently contradictory reports regarding the biological effects of metal combinations. The application of the testing procedure to combinations of mutagens is described, and an example is cited involving, for a particular bacterial mutagen, a combination of N-methyl-N'-nitro-N-nitrosoguanidine with ethylmethanesulfonate.

Toxic Overload: Assessing the Role of Mercury in Autism By Boyd E. Haley *Issue 115, November/December 2002* From 1996 to 1997, J. Curtis Pendergrass, PhD, did some experiments in my research laboratory at the University of Kentucky that confirmed the toxicity of thimerosal in vaccines. The results appeared on our website (www.altcorp.com), where they attracted the attention of some parents of autistic children.

These parents informed me that increased mandatory vaccination of infants was, in their opinion, the cause of an apparent epidemic of autism. This was the first time I had heard of this situation. The rationale for considering vaccinations as the cause of their children's problems seemed sensible and worth an investigation. I would like to state here that I am a very strong supporter of the national vaccine program, and that nothing in this article should be construed to imply that parents should avoid getting their children vaccinated. But I do recommend avoiding vaccines that contain thimerosal.

My laboratory was well experienced in mercury research. We had earlier demonstrated that mercury, when exposed to normal human brain tissue homogenates, is capable of causing many of the same biochemical aberrancies found in Alzheimer's diseased (AD) brains.1-4 Also, rats exposed to mercury vapor show the same major protein aberrancy as AD brains. Specifically, the rapid inactivation of important brain enzymes occurs following the addition of low levels of mercury or exposure to mercury vapor, and these same enzymes are significantly inhibited in AD brains.5 Also, mercury exposure to neurons in culture by other researchers, at a concentration lower than that found in many human brains, has now been shown to produce three of the widely accepted pathological diagnostic hallmarks of AD.6,7

Therefore, we hypothesized that exposure to mercury is involved in the etiology of AD, or at least would exacerbate this disease. We also proposed that other heavy metals, such as lead and cadmium, which act synergistically to enhance the toxicity of mercury, could be involved. Additionally, we proposed that exposure to organic-mercury compounds like methyl mercury from fish and ethyl mercury from thimerosal would also enhance the toxicity of any exposure to mercury. The early work of Dr. Pendergrass confirmed this with pure thimerosal, with some interesting additional observations. First, in human brain samples the exposure to mercury dramatically reduced the viability of a major brain protein called tubulin, but had little if any effect on another major protein, actin. Both tubulin and actin are critically important for the growth of dendrites or maintenance of axon structures of neurons. Exposing neurons to mercury rapidly results in the stripping of tubulin from the axon structure, leaving bare neurofibrils that form the tangles that are the diagnostic hallmark of AD. Thimerosal, like mercury, also rapidly reduces the viability of tubulin; in addition, however, it abolishes the viability of actin. This likely represents a major difference in the mechanism of mercury versus organic-mercury (more neurotoxic) toxicity. However, both mercury and organic-mercury inhibit tubulin viability and would work in concert to damage neurons of the central nervous system.

We therefore decided to investigate vaccines with and without thimerosal present as a preservative, using human brain tissues. To date the data have been very consistent: the toxicity of the vaccines is primarily dependent on the presence of thimerosal and, in my opinion, would be classified as severely toxic to numerous brain proteins. In the spring of 2001 these data were presented to the Institute of Medicine Immunization Safety Review Committee, which concluded its analysis by suggesting that thimerosal involvement in autism was a plausible hypothesis. Since then I have formed a collaboration with one of my colleagues, Mark Lovell, PhD, who uses cultured neurons in some of his experiments. Using his cultured neuron system, we studied the extent of neurotoxicity of pure thimerosal and of vaccines with and without thimerosal present. The experiments were done as follows: Neurons were grown in culture for 24 hours. Then pure thimerosal or vaccines were added to test cultures. The death of neurons was observed for the next 24 hours and compared to the death of neurons in the absence of toxicant.

The results were almost identical to the results observed with brain tissues: vaccines with thimerosal present were much more toxic than thimerosal-free vaccines. Pure thimerosal was toxic at the low nanomolar level--an extremely low concentration, about 10,000 times less than the thimerosal concentration found in most vaccines. These results leave little doubt about thimerosal being the toxic agent in the vaccines. However, many vaccines contain aluminum ions that have neurotoxic properties, and aluminum was once considered a factor in AD etiology. So we tested aluminum in the same system.

Aluminum is not nearly as toxic to neurons in culture as is thimerosal. However, we had earlier observed with mercury that the presence of other metals would enhance toxicity. Experiments were done to determine if aluminum would increase the toxicity of very low levels of thimerosal. The results were unequivocal: the presence of aluminum dramatically increased the rate of neuronal death caused by thimerosal. Therefore, the aluminum and thimerosal combination found in vaccines produces a toxic mixture that cannot be compared to situations where thimerosal alone is the toxic exposure.

The enhanced toxicity of thimerosal created by the addition of aluminum represents a problem with all forms of mercury toxicity. Synergism of toxic metals is well known. A slightly toxic solution of lead, mixed with a slightly toxic solution of mercury, results in a very toxic mixture. This is similar to the enhanced adverse reactivity to thimerosal found in optomological solutions, when subjects were prescribed to take the antibiotic tetracycline. For some reason, tetracycline increased the ocular toxic reaction to thimerosal. We have done some experiments to determine if certain antibiotics could also increase thimerosal-induced neuronal death in the neuron culture system. Our preliminary results indicate that this is the case, especially with tetracycline and ampicillin. Further research is needed in this area for accurate evaluation. But our results support previous reports and indicate how important it is to check out the effects of other compounds on the exacerbation of mercury and organic-mercury compound toxicity.

One of the conundrums of autism is why there is an approximate ratio of four boys to every girl who gets this disease. Dr. Lovell therefore tested the possibility that this could be hormone related. The latest results were quite marked in their effects. Neurons that were pre-incubated with estrogen demonstrated substantial protection against thimerosal-induced neuron death. In contrast, the addition of testosterone caused a very large increase in thimerosal-induced neuron death. A low nanomolar level of thimerosal that gave less than 5 percent neuron death in three hours could be increased to 100 percent cell death by the addition of one micromolar level of testosterone. Testosterone alone at this level also showed less than 5 percent cell death. The opposing effects of estrogen and testosterone may explain the gender-based four-to-one ratio. Most important, the tremendous enhancement of thimerosal toxicity by testosterone points out the impact of synergistic effects when addressing mercury toxicity.

Those involved in promoting the use of mercury in medicine and dentistry favor the old adage "Dose makes the toxin," and pick a supposedly safe level based on testing young, healthy mammals that have been exposed to mercury compounds. The synergistic enhancement of thimerosal toxicity by testosterone and aluminum demonstrates that no one can pick a concentration of mercury or organic-mercury and say with confidence, "This is a safe dose for human infants"--at least not with our current level of knowledge.

MMR (measles-mumps-rubella) has been widely discussed as a vaccine involved in autism-related problems. Our studies did not find MMR vaccines (no thimerosal added) to be nearly as neurotoxic as thimerosal-containing vaccines. So how does this fit into the observations of measles virus in the intestines of a large percentage of autistic children?

My theory, and it is only a theory at this time, is based on the fact that thimerosal is an inhibitor of the brain protein tubulin. One of the jobs of tubulin is to support the axon structure of nerve axons;

exposure to thimerosal, or mercury, destroys this capability. Tubulin also has another job: it is involved in formation of the meiotic spindle on which a cell splits in two. In other words, tubulin is needed for cell division, and cell division is needed for development of an immune response. Inhibit tubulin function with thimerosal injections, and you inhibit the immune response.

I have been told that the MMR vaccination is often given at the same time that three thimerosal-containing vaccines are given. Inhibit the immune response with the thimerosal-containing vaccinations, and an infant has less ability to respond to the measles virus in the MMR vaccination that is injected at the same setting. This might explain the presence of measles virus in about 80 percent of autistic children.

The research results we have obtained on the toxicity of thimerosal are not really surprising. This ethyl mercury-releasing compound was known to be neurotoxic through the publication of several research articles, some quite old. Any competent biochemist would look at the structure of the compound and identify it as a potent enzyme inhibitor. What is surprising is that the appropriate animal and laboratory testing was not done on the vaccines containing thimerosal (and aluminum) before the government embarked on a mandated vaccine program that exposed infants to the levels of thimerosal that occurred.

At this time it appears that exposure to thimerosal is the most likely suspect in vaccines that may be involved in causing autism and related disorders. The final verdict will come with observing the rate of autism now that thimerosal has been removed from the infant vaccine program. Let us therefore give credit to those who have worked to remove thimerosal from the vaccines given to infants and emphasize that continued testing of all vaccines is imperative to obtain the safest national vaccine policy possible, including a thimerosal-free flu vaccine for our elderly citizens.

NOTES 1. S. Khatoon et al., "Aberrant GTP-Tubulin Interaction in Alzheimer's Disease," Annals of Neurology 26 (1989): 210-215. 2. S. David et al., "Abnormal Properties of Creatine Kinase in Alzheimer's Disease Brain," Molecular Brain Research 54 (1998): 276-287. 3. E. F. Duhr et al., "HgEDTA Complex Inhibits GTP Interactions with the E-Site of Brain-Tubulin," Toxicology and Applied Pharmacology 122 (1993): 273-288. 4. J. C. Pendergrass and B. E. Haley, "Mercury-EDTA Complex Specifically Blocks Brain-Tubulin-GTP Interactions: Similarity to Observations in Alzheimer's Disease," in Status Quo and Perspective of Amalgam and Other Dental Materials, International Symposium Proceedings, L. T. Friberg and G. N. Schrauzer, eds., 98-105 (Stuttgart and New York: Georg Thieme Verlag, 1995). 5. J. C. Pendergrass et al., "Mercury Vapor Inhalation Inhibits Binding of GTP to Tubulin in Rat Brain: Similarity to a Molecular Lesion in Alzheimer's Disease Brain," Neurotoxicology 18, no. 2 (1997): 315-324. 6. G. Olivieri et al., "Mercury Induces Cell Cytotoxicity and Oxidative Stress," J. Neurochemistry 74 (2000): 231-241. 7. C. C. W. Leong et al., "Retrograde Degeneration of Neurite Membrane Structural Integrity and Formation of Neurofibillary Tangles at Nerve Growth Cones Following in Vitro Exposure to Mercury," NeuroReports 12, no. 4 (2001): 733-737. *Boyd E. Haley, PhD, is a professor and chair of the department of chemistry at the University of Kentucky, Lexington. His research on biochemical aberrancies in Alzheimer's disease led to his identifying mercury toxicity as a major exacerbating factor, perhaps even a causal factor. Haley has testified before numerous government agencies on the effects of mercury toxicity from dental amalgams and vaccines.*

****

Dec 2003Last October, a Report by the National Institutes of Environmental Heath Sciences (NIEHS) acknowledged that fluoride has been observed to have synergistic effects on the toxicity of aluminum, complexing with the mineral in the water. They acknowledge that most drinking water is high in fluoride/aluminum complexes, which enhance neurotoxicity. Other studies have shown that cooking with fluoridated water leaches the aluminum out of the aluminum cooking pots, with different amounts being released depending on the foods being cooked, whereas cooking with non-fluoridated water resulted in no release of aluminum from the pans. Leaching of up to 600 ppm occurred with prolonged boiling!

****

Burning Brain

The Burning Brain, Its Cause and Cure I did not find "burning brain" as one of the symptoms of mercury poisoning in any list when I was looking for symptoms of mercury poisoning. I searched on the Internet for "symptom-burning brain," and could not find anything.It is so frightening to have a "hot spot" in your brain or to feel that your "brain is on fire." I lay in my bed at nights before I was diagnosed with mercury toxicity imagining all the holes that were being caused in my blood brain barrier by this burning. My neurologist could not tell me why my brain burned, but thought it was improbable that I had mercury poisoning. But then he confessed, "he knew little about mercury poisoning." After being diagnosed as mercury poisoned and being introduced to the ACAM neurologist Dr. David Perlmutter, I found an article written by Dr. Perlmutter that explained why my brain burned. He was addressing a conference of ACAM doctors and called my symptoms "a brain on fire." In "The Role of Inflammation in Chronic Diseases" Dr. Perlmutter explained that when a combination of toxins are in the brain (in my case aluminum, mercury and thallium) there is a synergistic effect on the damage they cause.

> **Synergism**-interaction of agents (as drugs), or conditions such that the total effect is greater than the sum of the individual effects.

I have come into contact with several mercury- poisoned personed people now, who are saying that their brains burned. Do not rule out mercury poisoning just because your brain does *not* burn. People with mercury poisoning experience varying symptoms.I have recently had a conversation with a friend in Roanoke who says he has a "hot spot" on top of his head. He chain smokes cigarettes so he is exposed to the heavy metal cadmium in the cigarettes. Smoking cigarettes increase the damage caused by mercury in your mouth because of the heat on the fillings. Any heat in the mouth causes the mercury to leak from the fillings and it takes an hour or two for the mercury vapors from the fillings to calm down.My friend also has a mouth full of mercury fillings and root canals that probably contain mercury. Then he exposed himself to lead poisoning by sanding down doors with old lead paint without wearing a mask. He has also been exposed to paint fumes from painting cars. Now he has lost his hair and what hair remains has turned white overnight. He needs to have a heavy metals test run by an ACAM doctor and start removing the metal safely from his mouth. Then he needs to detox the poisons out of his body. If he doesn't he could end up with a neurological disease. In September of 2003, I had a conversation with another friend, Troy, and I explained to him how I had been poisoned. He said, "Well, Marie, that explains some of the things that have happened to me when I went to dentists." He went on to explain that proabably around seven years ago he had a dentist in Bland, VA to drill out two fillings. That is when the burning in his brain first started. He also had a headache that would not go away, not even with pain relievers. The burning gradually subsided, but it would come back when he would drink diet drinks that contained the sugar substitute aspertame. So he learned to avoid aspertame. He said that was when he first started experiencing memory loss.Later my friend moved to Amelia, VA and he had several more mercury fillings drilled out. He did not put together the connection between his dental work and the burning in the brain. He just saw a connection with the aspertame exaserbating his symptoms. After this new dental work where he was exposed to more mercury vapor, his brain burned again, the headaches reappeared and the memory loss was worse. Now his wife is complaining about his memory loss.When I read the book Beating Alzheimer's by Tom Warren, I was very interested that he said when he was diagnosed with Alzheimer's that his brain burned.After speaking with my local ACAM doctor, I now understand that toxins in the brain cause free radical damage. So one must remove the toxins and in the process of removing the toxins this will help remove the inflammation and the burning that is associated with neurological diseases. EDTA chelation removes some heavy metal toxins; DMSA removes others such as mercury. Taking antioxidants such as Vitamin C helps to lesson the symptoms caused by free radical damage. Persons that are mercury poisoned frequently take 5000 to 6000 mg of Vitamin C a day. However, you need to work with your doctor to get on a balanced program of vitamins and minerals.I would recommend that you buy the book BrainRecovery.Com, Powerful Therapy for Challenging Brain Disorders by Dr. David Perlmutter if you have a neurological disease. He is a board certified neurologist from Florida that belongs to ACAM. On the Amazon.com website Bernie Siegel, M.D. says of Dr. Perlmutter's book:

> "...Should be available to everyone so true integrative therapy can become the normal method of treatment in the neurology field."

Russell B. Roth, M.D. Past President, American Medical Association says:

> "Dr. Perlmutter provides sound advice, supported by the latest and most well respected medical research."

A book description on Amazon states:

> With forwards by Bernie Siegel, MD and Jeffrey S. Bland, PhD-- BrainRecovery.com, Dr. David Perlmutter, internationally recognized leader in functional approaches to neurological diseases, explores the cutting edge of both mainstream and complementary medicine. Powerful, clinically proven techniques are revealed providing answers and hope for patients and families faced with challenging disorder including: Alzheimer's Disease, Multiple Sclerosis, Memory Loss, Stroke, Parkinson's Disease, Post-Polio Syndrome, Amyotrophic Lateral Sclerosis, and more...

Though Dr. Permutter is an ACAM doctor and these doctors are known as chelation doctor, he does not stress testing for heavy metals in this book. He makes no mention of removing mercury fillings.Mercury and other heavy metals are the major contributor to neurological diseases. You will find this on Dr. Mercola's website and also the neurosurgeon Dr. Russell Blaylock said the same thing on Pat Robertson's 700 Club. Also exposure to chemicals, pesticides and industrial poisons contribute to neurological diseases. But if you have a neurotoxin right in your mouth just inches from your brain, you must remove the mercury from your mouth. Also remove toxic metal crowns and toxic root canals. A biological dentist, along with the materials you receive from DAMS can advise you on what is toxic.I would use Dr. Perlmutter's book as an introduction to some alternative therapies for neurological diseases. He warns that the medication Parkinson's patients receive from their doctors will actually cause the symptoms to get worse in the long run. If you have a neurological disease find an ACAM doctor in your area that is experienced in heavy metal toxicity. Some ACAM doctors are also neurologists and some specialize in degenerative diseases. When you go to the ACAM site online you will see the specialties of each doctor listed beside his name. Be sure to see what the code for the specialties are at the end of the list. (example NT=nutrition)So my recommendations to you is this:1. Order an information packet from DAMS concerning mercury toxicity from toxic dentistry. Get the name of a DAMS coordinator in your state that you can talk to.2. Find a local ACAM doctor experienced in treating toxic patients. He will give you a heavy metals test. Mercury may not show up as high on a test, but if you have mercury in your mouth and you have a neurological disease, you will still need to remove mercury fillings and detox your body. It is hard to test for mercury as it likes to hide in the brain and not come out for a heavy metals' test.Some ACAM doctors may say that your score for mercury is not high enough to detox your body of mercury. I disagree with this. King James Medical Laboratory states that there is no safe level of mercury in the body, and Dr. Boyd Haley, leading researcher of mercury in the USA, is testifying before Congressional hearings on mercury dental fillings that there is no safe level of mercury in the body. And if you have other heavy metals in your body, the small amount of mercury will be intensified in your body. I say don't leave any mercury in your body. Get it all out! And please don't just settle for your doctor saying to you, "Your test results were low, and are not problem." Get copies of the test results yourself and put them in your own files. You have a right to remove all heavy metals from your body. Your doctor might not be aware to the latest research on heavy metals. Dr. Boyd Haley is saying that some of the most poisoned people may actually have low levels of mercury in their heavy metals testing scores because they are poor excreters of mercury. See the footnote on Marie's Story of Mercury Poisoning for an explanation of this.3. Find a biological dentist to safely remove toxic fillings, crowns, and root canals from your mouth. Talk to your state DAMS coordinator before you choose your biological dentist. Make sure the biological dentist will properly protect you from mercury vapor.4. Order Dr. Perlmutter's book as a book you can use in conjunction to the advice and treatment you will receive from your local ACAM doctor. Do not order the neurological supplements from Dr. Perlmutter until AFTER you see what your local ACAM doctor wants to prescribe for you. Then you can discuss with your local ACAM doctor what Dr. Perlmutter recommends and together decide if you need to take additional supplements that Dr. Perlmutter recommends for the brain.5. Do not use Dr. Perlmutter's book and become your own doctor. You need an alternative doctor to help you with supplements and treatments. Do not go to Wal Mart and buy vitamins that Dr. Perlmutter recommends. You need an alternative doctor to help you figure out which supplements are appropriate for you. If you buy them yourself you will just end up with a bag full of bottles and you may not even buy the correct form of the supplement that is the most effective. Also your ACAM doctor may have several of the things Dr. Perlmutter recommends in combination in one pill. If you try to buy these yourself, you may end up with 20 bottles of pills.It is so sad that when a person has a neurological disease conventional medicine will not even check for heavy metals in the brain! Conventional doctors just diagnose a patient with a "label" whether it is Alzheimer's, ALS, MS, or Parkinson's. Autism in children is also known by some doctors to have been caused by exposure to toxins such as aluminum and mercury through vaccines. Conventional doctors, not even neurologists, even check the brain to remove heavy metals! Improvements in these neurological conditions are increased by early detection of the heavy metals and the removal of these metals from the brain and the teeth. (DAN doctors may help remove metals from autistic children.)If you need an alternative doctor to help a child with autism, there is a doctor in Richmond, VA listed on the www.acam.org site. (I do not personally know this doctor, but it would be a starting place for Virginians who want help.) Just go to the American College for the Advancement in Medicine site (www.acam.org) and click on VA. If the traditional doctors won't even admit that the heavy metal ingredients in vaccines are causing autism, how can you expect a traditional doctor to help your child detox from the heavy metals in vaccines? How can these major teaching hospitals help you if they won't test properly for heavy metals and know how to remove them? Mainstream doctors are not chelation doctors. If you have a illness related to heavy metals, you need a chelation doctor. Chelation doctors have been removing metals for years.Doctors belonging to the American College for the Advancement in Medicine (ACAM) are located at www.acam.org.****************

Statistically there is a higher incidence of hip fracture in residents of fluoridated areas. This includes U.S. studies published in the Journal of the American Medical Association (JAMA) by Dr. S.J. Jacobsen in 1990 and Christa Danielson and others in 1992.

Fluoride Research and Dental Caries (cavities)Prof. Y. Imai of Japan studied 22,000 schoolchildren in 1972 in naturally occurring fluoride areas and found increased caries (dental cavities) with increased levels of fluoride.A study of 23,000 elementary schoolchildren in Tucson, Arizona, by Dr. Cornelius Steelink in 1992, showed increased caries (dental cavities) with increased levels of fluoride in drinking waterProfessor S.P.S. Teotia of India who reported on a study of 400,000 children from 1973 to 1993 also showed increased caries (dental cavities) with increased levels of fluoride in drinking water.

"In 1999, the US Environmental Protection Agency finally reviewed three studies carried out by scientists at Binghamton University. The scientists reported **80% death rates,** kidney damage and brain damage in rats exposed to half of one milligram of aluminum fluoride complexes in a litre of drinking water. This is less than half of the amount of fluoride which is added in fluoridation schemes.

Finally, the National Toxicology Program was asked to commission studies to determine the extent of neurotoxic damage from aluminum in drinking water, particularly stressing the fluoride interaction."

Last October, a Report by the National Institutes of Environmental Heath Sciences (NIEHS) acknowledged that **fluoride has been observed to have synergistic effects on the toxicity of aluminum**

"I was particularly pleased when the US Environmental Protection Agency report by Urbansky and Schock on the toxicity of lead and fluoride in drinking water confirmed that fluoride complexes with other substances in the water.

They also acknowledged that most drinking water contains a substantial amount of fluoro-aluminium complexes. This should be a warning to dentists who hold with the simplistic notion that fluoride only affects teeth and is perfectly safe in drinking water."

According to the NIEHS Report, most water treatment processes result in **increased levels of aluminum in the finished drinking water.**

It stated that fluoridation will result in aluminum fluoride complexes which will enhance neurotoxicity, or that fluoride itself will enhance uptake and synergise the toxicity of the aluminum

Other studies have shown that in the presence of fluoride, **aluminum leaches out of cookware.** Boiling fluoridated tap water in an aluminum pan leached almost **200 parts per million** (ppm) of aluminum into the water in 10 minutes.

Leaching of up to 600 PPM occurred with prolonged boiling. Different releases of aluminum depend upon the composition of the pan and the type of food being cooked. Using non-fluoridated water showed almost no leaching from aluminum pans.

US Government References:

http://ntp-server.niehs.nih.gov/htdocs/Chem_Background/ExSumPdf/Aluminum.pdf

http://fluoride.oralhealth.org/papers/urbansky.pdf

www.oehha.ca.gov/water/phg/pdf/Alumin.pdf

http://ntp-server.niehs.nih.gov/htdocs/Chem_Background/ExSumPdf/Aluminumalt.pdf

http://fluoride.oralhealth.org/

Please find below the complete citation and the full article.
> Yours sincerely

Elizabeth O'Brien Manager, Global Lead Advice and Support Service (GLASS), run by The LEAD Group Inc

ph +61 2 9716 0014

fax + 61 2 9716 9005

PO Box 161 Summer Hill NSW 2130 Australia

www.lead.org.au

FULL CITATION

Are Amalgam Fillings Safe for Lead-poisoned People?

LEAD Action News vol 5 no 2 1997 ISSN 1324-6011

The journal of The LEAD (Lead Education and Abatement Design) Group Inc.

[Source:www.lead.org.au/lanv5n2/lanv5n2-4.html]

By Elizabeth O'Brien, Project Coordinator, NSW Community Lead Advisory Service (CLAS).

Alarming information about the synergistic effects of lead and mercury, recently brought to the attention of CLAS by ASOMAT members, will be the basis of an enquiry by CLAS to the NSW and Federal Health Ministers.

ASOMAT is the Australasian Society of Oral Medicine and Toxicology (ph 02 9867 1111), a non-profit organisation founded by concerned doctors and dentists.

Amalgam fillings contain 50% mercury.

> The original evidence cited for the synergistic effects of lead and mercury (and cadmium) comes from a 1978 paper by Schubert et al published in Michigan: "...the administration of an essentially no-response level (LD1) of a mercury salt together with 1/20 of the LD1 of a lead salt killed all of the animals [rats]."

Dr Michael Godfrey and dentist Noel Campbell write:

"...a lethal dose (LD1 [enough to kill 1% of the rats]) was combined with a 1/20th LD1 of lead, resulting in a LD 100 [100% death rate] in the test animals. "We have recently found that considerable amounts of lead may be excreted with the mercury following DMPS provocation. Our preliminary investigations appear to indicate that a synergistic effect could be identified by multiplying the lead and mercury concentrations together, after adjusting to IG of urine creatinine. We have termed this the Campbell-Godfrey factor (C-G factor). Chronic-ally affected patients may have high levels of either metal or a high total C-G factor. Those with the highest C-G factor appear to be the worst affected, thus indicating that the synergism in animals is replicated in man."

>

> The questions raised are: is it safe for lead poisoned people to have mercury fillings? Should CLAS advise parents of lead-poisoned kids never to allow these fillings in their kid's mouths? Should CLAS advise lead-poisoned people who are planning to conceive for instance, to have their amalgam fillings replaced, along with DMSA chelation therapy and nutrient replenishment therapy, well in advance of trying to conceive? Is it acceptable for anyone to be exposed to lead and mercury (and cadmium) as they are in mining and smelting communities? Why aren't the DMPS provocation test, DMSA chelation therapy or amalgam removal procedures claimable under Medicare? When will Australia phase out amalgams?

Another group of doctors who may understand heavy metals are environmental doctors belonging to the American Academy of Environmental Medicine.

Their website is located at www.aaem.com.

Synergistic effects of toxic metals (mercury, lead, aluminum) are extreme

Mercury and lead are extremely neurotoxic and cytotoxic, but their combined synergistic effect is much worse. A dose of mercury sufficient to kill 1% of tested rats, when combined with a dose of lead sufficient to kill less than 1% of rats, resulted in killing 100 % of rats tested(1). Thus with combined exposure the safe dose is 1/100 as much as the dose individually. Studies in Australia have confirmed similar relationships hold for people. This means most people in the U.S. are getting dangerous levels of these metals, enough to cause some neurologic effects.

Similar is true for synergistic effect with other toxic metals like arsenic, and with other toxic chemicals like PCBs(2). The level of mercury thimerosal in vaccines has been shown to be highly neurotoxic, but the effect was found to be much larger due to the synergistic effect with aluminum, which is also in most vaccines(4). Studies using U.S. CDC data have found thimerosal from vaccines to be major factors in autism and ADHD(5), along with prenatal rhogam shots which contain high levels of mercury thimerosal and are given to some RH negative women during pregnancy.

Autism has increased in the U.S. more than 10 fold in the last decade. According to the Florida Dept. of Education, the numbers increased from approx. 300 to over 4000 during this time period. There have likewise been large increases in the number of children with ADHD and other developmental conditions, according to the National Academy of Sciences and other sources. A major factor in this appears to be the large increase in vaccinations given to infants, as noted in the previous post. (more documentation available at the childrens neurological page, www.home.earthlink.net/~berniew1/indexk.html)

There was an increase of over 45% in learning disabilities in Pennsylvania between 1990 and 2000(3). But the study showed that the county highest on the Chemical Pollution Scorecard, Montgomery, had an increase more than double that of the rest of the state. Montgomery County had an increase in ADHD of 32.7% and an increase in autism of 310%.

Bernard Windham, M.D.

ps. note that a high percentage of Gulf state residents have been documented to have high levels of mercury exposure(Mobile Register study, www.home.earthlink.net/~berniew1/flhg.html)

1. Schubert J, Riley EJ, Tyler SA. Combined effects in toxicology. A rapid systematic testing procedure: cadmium, mercury, and lead. Toxicol Environ Health 1978;4(5/6):763-776.

2. Philippe Grandjean P, White RF et al. Neurobehavioral deficits associated with PCB in 7-year-old children prenatally exposed to seafood neurotoxicants. Neurotoxicology and Teratology 2001;223(4):305-317.

3. Pennsylvania Dept. of Education, 2003, Study of learning disability incidence in Montgomery County, Pennsylvania, 1990 and 2000; & ""Polluting Our Future: Chemical Emissions in the U.S. that Affect Child Development and Learning,"" by Physicians For Social Responsibility, at (202) 898-0150, psrnatl@psr.org

4. Haley, BE, Pendergrass JC ,Lovell, M., Univ. of Kentucky Chemistry Dept., paper presented to the Institute of Medicine Immunization Safety Review Committee, Spring 2001, and on medical lab website, www.altcorp.com

5. Geier M.R., Geier DA; Thimerosal in Childhood Vaccines, Neurodevelopmental Disorders, and Heart Disease in the U.S. ; J of Amer Physicians and Surgeons, Vol 8(1), Spring 2003;& Bradstreet J, Geier DA, et al, A case control study of mercury burden in children with Autisitic Spectrum Disorders, J of Amer Physicians and Surgeons, Vol 8(3), Summer 2003.

Appendix III

A Tale of Two Lawyers or Who Needs Fiction?
by Pandora Jones

Renate Andres-Auger was a Cree woman lawyer, called to the bar in 1989 and opening a practice in Vancouver. By that time, Jack Cram was a respected Vancouver lawyer with much knowledge of real estate law and 25 years of experience.

Connect the dots. Chronology can not be strictly adhered to because of the mass of information.

Chief Justice McEachern used to be a member of a particular law firm. A court case arose that lasted 374 days in the Supreme Court, involving the Gitzan Wet'suwet'en Hereditary Chiefs in land claims. The lawyers for the Chiefs were from the same law firm as McEachern used to be with. These lawyers sold out their clients by agreeing that the territory involved did not belong to the natives, but to the Crown, from the time that the British claimed a colony there! Did the lawyers ask for a different judge? Did McEachern disqualify himself? Need you ask?

Auger continued to be outspoken about this case. In December 1992 the Law Society suspended her right to practice law, without notice and without a hearing, supposedly because her account books were not in order. She complied with all its demands, paid all the imposed fees and penalties, but she was not reinstated. Cram, her lawyer, came into the picture when Auger named a large group of judges and lawyers in her writ of summons, alleging that they had conspired to destroy her law practice and her reputation, to cover up corruption in the form of influence-peddling within the judicial system.

But consider: Cram had previously made a statement that if the truth be known, aboriginals do indubitably own 95% of the province of BC.

Let us go back aways, to the case of a Dr. Gossage, who had been accused of child pornography and sexual assault, indulged in during his practice of medicine. Not only was this man allowed to continue his practice whilst investigation was supposed to be going on, but a lawyer called Peter Leask was appointed as special prosecutor. Leask "managed" to "persuade" the judge to impose a gag order - not only on the allegations but also on the gag order itself!

Then let us move to the case of Mr. Benest, the Burnaby elementary school principal accused of using his pupils for pornographic purposes. Lo and behold, who was the counsel for Benest who succeeded in using delaying and obfuscation tactics to get his client no more than a slap on the wrist? Why, none other than Peter Leask!

And then we come to the grandparents of one child victim in the Gossage case, who hired Cram to represent them in their civil suit against Gossage. They decided to picket Gossage's office to warn other parents, since the judicial system saw fit to let Gossage continue practicing. Suddenly, more facts came to light. At least 30 people contacted Doug Stead, one of the grandparents, some from as far away as Ontario. None of them knew each other. And yet they all told similar stories. A suspicion emerged that Gossage was abusing kids in provincial care, which had to involve collusion. Cram's office was besieged with people giving information. He claimed that he was given pictures of teenage boys "in the company of" judges and evidence that children were taken from reserves and delivered to the Vancouver Club, never to be seen again.

Slide in time to the public statement of Harriet Nahanee, who saw a limousine arrive on her reserve and children with make-up applied being driven away, never to return.

Search your memory for MP Hedy Fry referring on tv to a Canada-wide pedophile ring.

Cram began to air what he knew publicly. He was interviewed by Georgia Straight and on Rafe Mair's show, among others. He was warned by Dr. Wayne Poley at a meeting that something bad would happen to him because of his pursuit of the horrible facts he had uncovered.

So, if we accept the facts so far, we have Cram acting for Auger and possessing all this damning information, not only about judicial corruption but pedophiles in high places within the judicial system.

Sure enough, not only was Auger deprived of her practice but Cram's practice also came under attack. In April 1994 Cram sued on the same grounds as Auger had: that named people conspired to deprive him of the practice of law. At the hearing, the police were present with a machine gun! And guess who was Cram's opponent, acting for the Law Society? Why, none other than our old friend, Peter Leask!

But appearing for Auger at her hearing, also in April, 1994, the court setting was grim. Sheriffs were present in numbers, not usual for civil cases. The plot was to present Cram as suffering from overwork and a drinking problem. Auger was sitting with Cram and without going into details of the set-up suffice it to say that the judge refused to listen to Cram, eventually finding him in contempt and telling him he needed counsel. Cram appointed Auger. She continued to ask the judge to say who had provided him with certain material to read before he heard the case, and to disqualify himself. Very quickly she was grabbed by four sheriffs, handcuffed and dragged to jail. The judge ordered Cram back to the counsel table - at this point Cram had moved to the gallery and was surrounded by friends. Cram refused.

By this time there were over forty sheriffs in the courtroom. The judge ordered them to arrest Cram and many of them wrestled him to the ground, hauling him off to jail too. But a lawyer friend intervened and got Cram released, but only to attend another hearing for the contempt charge. Jack was hauled into the room face down by several sheriffs, then spreadeagled and held down, one sheriff holding him by the throat. The judge apparently relented enough to allow Jack to make his case and by 4 pm that afternoon Cram had laid before Mr. Justice Callaghan details of a coverup by the head officers of the Law Society and by Judges to aid and abet a pedophile and also their allowing a lawyer to continue to practice who had been convicted of heroin possession for trafficking purposes, together with conspiring to destroy both his and Auger's right to practice law.

Adjournment was declared at 4 pm. Cram had not finished his evidence. That night Cram appeared on another radio show to talk about what he had discovered. Just after midnight on arriving home, Cram was attacked by ten police officers and his hands and feet shackled. He was neither read his rights or even informed what the assault was about. Why was an ambulance waiting? Cram was hustled into the ambulance and he believed he was drugged, as he does not remember arriving anywhere, but was detained against his will in the Psychiatric ward at Vancouver General Hospital for a week, during which time he was forcibly injected with a drug or drugs. He was in and out of drug-induced sleep. All attempts by friends and lawyers to contact him were refused.

The "committal" was authorized by two doctors who had just happened (what a coincidence!) to be sitting in the courtroom and had declared on the certificates that they had examined Cram! Now it's committal by remote control!

Cram was released on May 2nd. While he had been detained and drugged the Law Society had obtained a judicial order appointing two lawyers as custodians of his practice and its property. A witness watching Cram's office building saw people holding pictures and negatives up to the light in his office window. Note that the order was signed by Mr. Justice Bruce MacDonald, the same judge who had ordered the arrest of Renate Andres-Auger!

Auger managed to escape during this period and has not been heard of since. Jack Cram has also dropped out of the picture and is now ranching in the interior of the province and refuses to discuss the issue any longer.

Now move sideways in time to the evidence gathered by Rev. Kevin Annett about residential school abuses and huge numbers of murders of native children, portrayed in the media as a few priests with overactive hormones abusing a few children. It was during these hearings that witnesses spoke of **pedophilia**.

Connect the dots....

Satanism, Snuff Porn and the Body Parts Business

Welcome to ITCCS.ORG and The International Tribunal into Crimes of Church and State

Our Mandate: (1) To lawfully prosecute those people and institutions responsible for the exploitation, trafficking, torture and murder of children, past and present, and (2) To stop these and other criminal actions by church and state, including by disestablishing those same institutions.

Memorandum on the Organized Disappearance, Torture, Exploitation and Murder of Women and Children on Canada's West Coast – A Summary from Eyewitnesses

Posted on **February 2, 2011** by **admin**

Posted on February 02, 2011 by itccs

Synopsis

1. An organized system of abduction, exploitation, torture and murder of large numbers of women and children appears to exist on Canada 's west coast, and is operated and protected in part by sectors of the RCMP, the Vancouver Police Department (VPD), the judiciary, and members of the British Columbia government and federal government of Canada , including the Canadian military.

2. This system is highly funded and linked to criminal organizations including the Hell's Angels, the Hong Kong Triad, and unnamed individual "free lance" mobsters from Vancouver and the USA. It is funded in part by a massive drug trade, with which it is intimately connected.

"hooker game", and that the rest of the police force as well as the Mayor and Chief of Police are aware of it. The higher level of the game involves the use of prostitutes in snuff and pornographic films, and in torturing and murdering them. While unaware of the details of the more extreme level of the game, most police know of its existence but do not betray it or its practitioners for fear that their involvement in the lower level of the game will be exposed.

4. The witness claims that the drug most commonly used on victims of the "hooker game" is SCOPALAMINE, a hypnotic barbituate often termed a "rape drug", in which the victim is "zombified", obeying any command, and then is unable to remember the events for some time. However, memory can return, and the fear of this occurring has prompted MICHAELSON and other participants in the more extreme game to murder the victims and dispose of their bodies. MICHAELSON is the key actor in this body disposal system, according to the witness.

5. Soon after the assault of the witness by MICHAELSON in the spring of 2000, she was taken by MICHAELSON to one of the locations of the "hooker game": a "clubhouse" for policemen in either the penthouse of the Century Plaza Hotel or in the basement of the Hotel Georgia in downtown Vancouver . Witness claims that this clubhouse hosts a "pornographic film studio where woman are raped and tortured on film". MICHAELSON is described by the witness as "a pimp and drug dealer for all the Vancouver cops and their friends ... a lot of the dealing goes on at the clubhouse."

6. Witness states that MICHAELSON works out of a North Vancouver RCMP detachment and is on the city drug squad, having access to large volumes of illicit drugs that he sells to policemen and others.

7. At one of the clubhouses described in Point No. 5, the witness was introduced by MICHAELSON to Willy PICTON and Steven PICTON, who ran and continue to run a pornography and snuff film business from Port Coquitlam (alias "Piggy's Palace"). The witness was subsequently taken by Steven PICTON to the Port Coquitlam site (alias "Piggy's Palace") on several occasions to engage in sex and drugs. At this site, she witnessed young girls being drugged and raped, including on film, after being brought to the site by RCMP officers. Witness describes seeing three RCMP officers, including MICHAELSON, at Piggy's Palace, engaged in drugs and in raping women. Witness states that "ten of the twelve recently murdered women were last seen in the company of RCMP guys."

8. At Piggy's Palace the witness also met Jean-Guy BOUDRAIS or BEAUDRAIS, whom witness claims is the serial killer responsible for the murder of many of the women in the downtown eastside of Vancouver over the past ten years. Witness states that BOUDRAIS is a close associate of MICHAELSON, obtains women and drugs from him, and relies on MICHAELSON to dispose of his victims after he has raped, tortured and killed them. Witness says that BOUDRAIS works for a computer programming company tied to the

MICHAELSON in retaliation. On January 9 of either 2003 or 2004, MICHAELSON broke into the Kitsilano apartment of the witness and broke her ribs, jaw and arm with a baseball bat. MICHAELSON then tied her up, put her in trunk of his car and drove her to the policemen's "clubhouse" in the Hotel Georgia basement. MICHAELSON then said to the witness, "Now I'll show you what we do to hookers", and proceeded to torture her with dental instruments, including on her genitalia, branding her cult-style with an insignia. MICHAELSON then told the witness "We own you now", and put her to work as a prostitute and lure to attract other women into the game.

16. The witness went to Vancouver General Hospital for treatment after her torture, and was treated at the Oak street clinic by a Dr. Jean McLENNAN or McLAREN. A report of her injuries was filed by this doctor with the Vancouver Police Deaprtment that same week.

17. The "hooker game" receives judicial protection from at least one judge, a justice GROBBERMAN, who prior to being a judge served in the provincial Attorney-General's office under the very man, Ernie QUANTZ, who organized a judicial cover-up on behalf of several prominent pedophiles during the 1980's. The witness claims seeing other judges and Prime Minister Paul MARTIN at the policemen's clubhouse in downtown Vancouver during the same evening that MICHAELSON and the PICTON brothers were present, and while drugs and prostitutes were being used. Also in attendance that evening were members of the Canadian Security Intelligence Service (CSIS) and Canadian military officers.

18. After she was attacked by BOUDRAIS, the witness phoned the FBI and asked for an investigation of BOUDRAIS, which occurred in 2005. The FBI investigators were misdirected by MICHAELSON to a false witness who shared the same first name as the witness, and as a result the FBI claimed that there was no evidence against BOUDRAIS. VPD detective Rabinovitch who assisted the FBI also claimed that BOUDRAIS could not be found even though he was circulating openly in Vancouver at the same time. One of the FBI investigators told the witness, however, that BOUDRAIS's description matched those of the Green River Killer, a serial rapist and murderer in the USA who is still at large.

19. Witness claims that MICHAELSON provides security for foreign diplomats in Vancouver and film industry stars, including Eddie MURPHY, to whom MICHAELSON introduced the witness in 2002. Witness claims that MURPHY raped and sadistically assaulted her, slicing her skin with a knife and leaving permanent scars on her shoulder and neck. (see videotaped interview) Witness states that MURPHY was also responsible for the death of two women during the years 2002-3 in Vancouver : a 21 year old Asian porn actress and a prostitute, both of whom were provided to MURPHY by MICHAELSON, and whose bodies were disposed of by the latter after MURPHY had tortured and raped them, and then overdosed them on drugs.

20. Witness states that she reported the attack on her by MURPHY to a Detective SCOTT with the VPD, along with the claim of MURPHY's murder of the two women, but when MICHAELSON learned of the complaint he tortured the witness with a knife, carving her

human resources social worker and child apprehension court worker in the Powell River and Zeballos area, the witness claims to have personal knowledge of the allegations made herein. Statement made during the week of 2-7 February, 2006, by telephone.

1. Witness states that she was recently forced out of the coastal community of Powell River , B.C. and had her life threatened because of her firsthand knowledge of the role of local RCMP, church officials and doctors in the murder of local women and children, and in the importation of illegal drugs and armaments from overseas.

2. Witness is a former social and court worker who worked in the aboriginal community and among youth between 1982 and 2004. She was a member of the Powell River United Church until forced from its congregation by ministers Dave NEWELL and Cameron REID after she claimed that local church members were importing drugs and engaging in pedophilia. (Note: REID was one of the two church officials who handed Rev. Kevin ANNETT his summary dismissal notice in 1995 after ANNETT began to uncover church crimes among native people in Port Alberni)

3. Witness has firsthand knowledge that Dr. Harvey HENDERSON of the Zeballos health clinic is deliberately addicting aboriginal people to a lethal drug named Oxycotin, a synthetic heroin that induces suicidal behavior. He is doing so at the behest of officials of the state-funded Nuu-Chah-Nulth Tribal Council (NTC) in Port Alberni, BC, in order for the land of his murdered patients to be bought up cheaply by NTC officers. HENDERSON has himself bought much native land on the Ahousat reserve on Flores Island, which he services as a doctor and where he freely distributes the Oxycotin drug. In 2005, all of the suicides among the Ahousats occurred while HENDERSON was working there. HENDERSON lives in Sayward, BC, north of Campbell River.

4. In 2004, witness observed the unloading of drugs and armaments off a black seaplane in the Okeover Inlet near Powell River, under the oversight of Bob PAQUIN, former officer in Quebec secret police and convicted pedophile, Tracy ELKINS, former officer in the South African army, and Colin McCORMACK and Roland LEWIS, local businessmen and associates of the Mayor, coroner and RCMP. Witness claims that these men operate local drug importation with RCMP protection, and deal drugs to local youth and aboriginals. All three are local Freemasons and members of Catholic Knights of Malta, along with Stu ALFGARD, local coroner and pedophile.

5. Witness claims that a similar drug drop off point is at Bliss Landing seaport and helicopter pad, north of Powell River, where Americans regularly fly in drugs.

6. Witness began to run afoul of this group when, in 1986, her local youth group resolved to confront drug use in Powell River schools, and found immediate resistance to their efforts from the school administration, churches, and social services. Witness then asked parents and local police to support them, which they did; an undercover squad of police began to

GUERIN-JOHN clique is to seize their children and transport them off the reserve, including into pedophile rings connected with the provincial government's Ministry of Children and Families. This clique conducts criminal activities on the Musqueam reserve, including drug dealing, strong-arming of dissidents or critics, illegally selling salmon and other fish as well as cigarettes and alcohol, wrongfully evicting band members from their homes and dis-entitling them of their land and DIA payments.

3. Witness claims that the Musqueam Reserve has functioned as a body-dumping and mass burial site since at least 1989, when he personally observed Willie PICTON deposit and bury large garbage bags in a pit directly opposite the Musqueam First Nation office on the reserve. (See his statement, Exhibit A).Witness claims that he subsequently disinterred the contents of these bags and found numerous bones that upon examination proved to be human, including parts of pelvis, skull and femur. Witness retains samples of these remains in his possession while other samples, including an adult female humerus, are held at Simon Fraser University .

4. Corollary evidence of this allegation was provided by the witness in the form of a letter (Exhibit B) by Musqueam Housing Officer A. Glenn GUERIN dated 29 October 2004, which states that Dave PICTON, brother of Willie, was employed by the Musqueam band under contract for three of four months during 1989 or 1990, to provide land fill for a street extension.

5. Witness states that the activities of Willie and Dave PICTON on the Musqueam reserve were fully known and approved by all the band councilors at Musqueam, including Wendy SPARROW, aka Wendy GRANT-JOHN, federal Department of Indian Affairs official and wife of accused pedophile-drug dealer Chief Ed JOHN, who is domiciled at the Musqueam reserve and owns adjoining Celtic Shipyards.

6. Witness reported the activities of the PICTON brothers at Musqueam in 2002 to the Vancouver police (VPD), after the " Piggy Palace " story was reported in local media. But Ed and Leona SPARROW stopped the subsequent police investigation of the remains deposited at Musqueam by the PICTONs after arranging a cover-up with VPD Constable Scott ROLLINS (Badge #2028) and officer Jodine KELLER. Leona SPARROW was also seen attending parties at the PICTON's "Pig Farm" in company of RCMP.

7. The following media were contacted by the witness and informed of the remains deposited by the PICTONs at Musqueam, but declined from investigating: Mike CLARKE, City TV, Kelly RYAN, CBC radio, Gerald BELLETT, Vancouver Sun, and Karen Urguhart, The Province. Also notified by witness was William MACDONALD, Office of the Police Complaints Commissioner in Vancouver.

8. After more than two years, on November 3, 2004, witness and fellow Musqueam band member Jim KEW made a formal complaint to the VPD Complaints Commissioner about the

GUERIN-SPARROW clique. She then became homeless on Hastings street, was addicted to drugs by CAMPBELL, and then "overdosed" and died. The SPARROW family then received her home and property.

15. Witness claims that GANARJEE's property was seized by lawyer Marvin STORROW of Blake, Cassells and Graydon law firm in Vancouver, who works closely with the SPARROW clique and their relative Chief Ed JOHN. (Note: STORROW represented JOHN in a 2002 BC Supreme Court lawsuit that silenced JOHN's critics and imposed a gag order on any media reporting of the accusations of criminal actions by JOHN.) STORROW has a long history of involvement with the Musqueam band and the SPARROW family (see Exhibit D) and has strong ties with the federal Liberal party. Leona SPARROW who is associated with the PICTONs and concealed their activity at Musqueam (see Point No. 6) has worked for STORROW's law firm.

16. Other lawyers and firms associated with the SPARROW clique and their activities include Lou HARVEY and Smithe-Radcliffe law firm. HARVEY is an old associate of STORROW and has helped to steal and illegally transfer Musqueam land into the control of Squamish politicians working for the federal government.

17. Witness claims that the SPARROW clique evade federal laws limiting the commercial sale of salmon by aboriginal people, and completely monopolize an illegal black market in fish operating out of the Musqueam reserve. Wendy GRANT-JOHN (a former SPARROW) operates her own fish store, Longhouse Seafoods in the Dunbar region of Vancouver, which illegally sells sockeye and other salmon. The enforcement/goon squad silence band criticism of these acts.

18. Similarly, in a written statement dated December 26, 2005, the witness claims "For the record, all the elders whom have died, it's Wendy's family (who) lives in each and every home that comes from another unexpected death ... they (the SPARROW clique) have a group of people monitoring each band member and so they wait for a window of opportunity to strike. They pick targets in the community and slowly tear them apart – deliberately destroy lives."

19. The witness has drawn three separate maps of the Musqueam reserve that identify the location of two major body dumping and burial sites (Exhibit E, 1-3).

Witness #4: Retired aboriginal man in his late fifties, a band councilor and member of the Musqueam band and a friend of Witness #3. Given name is Arthur STOGAN sr, he is a direct descendent of the hereditary chiefs of the Musqueam people. Resides on the reserve, phone **604-263-6295**. His lifelong residence at Musqueam and involvement as a band councilor gives him a personal knowledge of the facts he alleges herein. Initial statement made on videotape during the period 9 May – June 6, 2005, with additional statements made during period of 3 December – 18 January, 2006, in Vancouver.

Chemainus Nation in Oyster Bay, BC, on Vancouver Island. Given name is Steven SAMPSON Jr., he resides on his traditional family land near Shell Beach. He has lived all of his life in proximity with the people described in his statement, and as a traditional chief and a former activist in the American Indian Movement and the Red Power Movement, he has direct and personal knowledge of the facts alleged herein. Statement made during the period 3-19 June, 2005, in Shell Beach.

1. Witness claims that the present leadership of the Chemainus First Nation is deeply involved in illegal activity, and are responsible for murders on the local reserves. This leadership revolves around George HARRIS and George, Ed and Peter SEYMOUR, whom witness claim operate the local drug and child trafficking and child porn networks in conjunction with Nanaimo criminal Willie CURRIE. CURRIE operates a local equivalent of the PICTON "Pig Farm" in a house on Jingle Pot Road in Nanaimo, where he has raped and murdered numerous young girls, including Lisa Marie DEYONG in 2004.

2. Witness states that George HARRIS is closely connected to the GUERIN-SPARROW clique in Musqueam, and engages in illegal fishing and drug importation practices with them across Georgia Straight. The parents of HARRIS, Irene and Lawrence HARRIS, were Catholic church-sponsored "watchmen" who transported children into the Kuper Island Residential School during the 1940's and '50's, and who were descended from collaborating puppet "chiefs" set up by Catholic missionaries in the 19th century.

3. Witness claims that the HARRIS clique have tried to force him and his family off their land for years, through physical intimidation, murder, poisoning their water, and attempting to kill off the SAMPSON blood line through involuntary sterilizations inflicted on both of the witness' sons, Troy and Steve.

Witness #6: Aboriginal woman in her mid-fifties, given name is Bernice WILLIAMS (native name SKUNDAAL), of Haida and Nuu-Chah-Nulth ancestry. Member of the Downtown Eastside Womens' Centre in Vancouver, and an activist since the 1970's with native and womens' groups across B.C. Statement made on April 3 and April 28, 2006, in Vancouver, B.C.

1. Witness claims that a Vancouver police officer named Dave DICKSON is responsible for the rape and murder of numerous aboriginal women in the downtown eastside. DICKSON holds a senior position of responsibility in the Missing Womens' Task Force and is very prominent in the downtown eastside of Vancouver, serving on community liaison boards.

2. Witness claims that she has been attacked on several occasions by policemen and women associated with DICKSON because of her investigation into the missing women. In February, 2006, witness was attacked without warning by five policemen in an alley of the two hundred block east Hastings, was struck in the head, pepper-sprayed and handcuffed, and was being forced into a police van for a "midnight ride", during which she expected to be

Common Law Community Training Manual

Establishing the Reign of Natural Liberty:
The Common Law and its Courts

A Community Training Manual

Issued by The International Tribunal into Crimes of Church and State (Brussels)

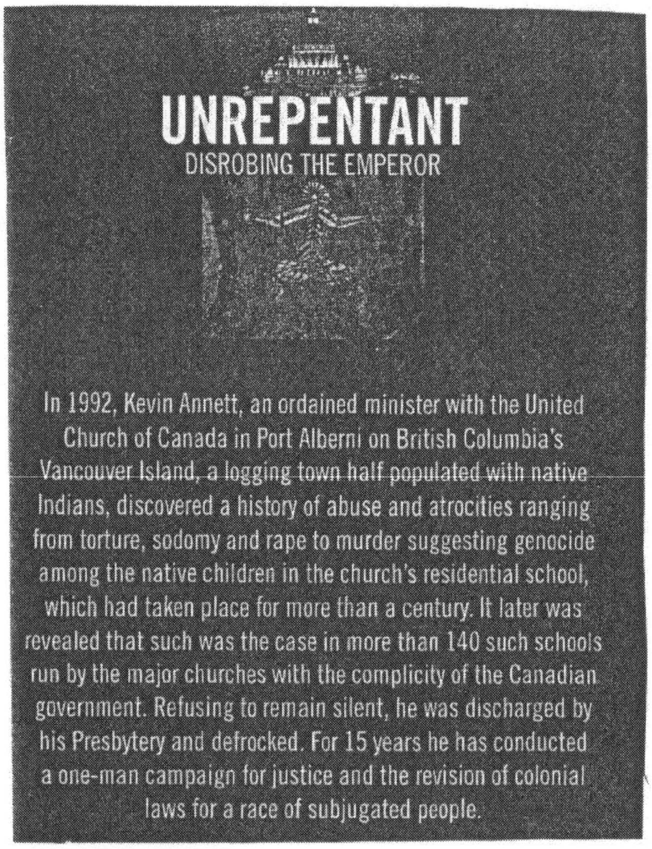

UNREPENTANT

DISROBING THE EMPEROR

In 1992, Kevin Annett, an ordained minister with the United Church of Canada in Port Alberni on British Columbia's Vancouver Island, a logging town half populated with native Indians, discovered a history of abuse and atrocities ranging from torture, sodomy and rape to murder suggesting genocide among the native children in the church's residential school, which had taken place for more than a century. It later was revealed that such was the case in more than 140 such schools run by the major churches with the complicity of the Canadian government. Refusing to remain silent, he was discharged by his Presbytery and defrocked. For 15 years he has conducted a one-man campaign for justice and the revision of colonial laws for a race of subjugated people.

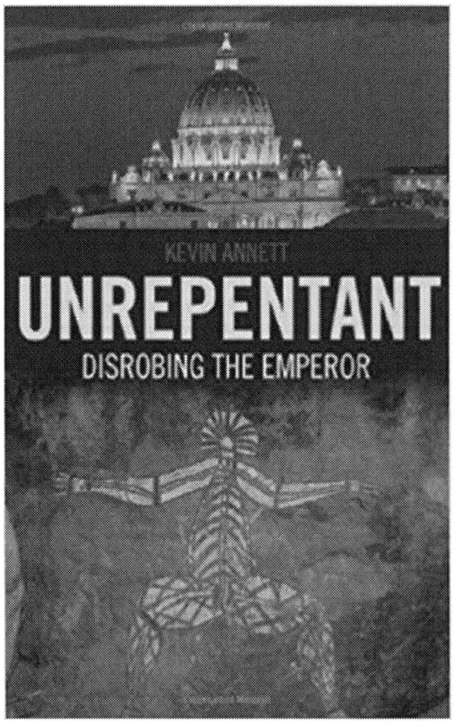

POPULAR COP IS A SERIAL KILLER!

Witness claims that a senior Vancouver police officer named Dave DICKSON is responsible for the rape and murder of numerous aboriginal women in the downtown eastside. DICKSON holds a senior position of responsibility in the Missing Women's Task Force and is very prominent in the downtown eastside of Vancouver, serving on community liaison boards.

From Kevin Annett: Eyewitness of Murder

www.kevinannett.com

www.itccs.org

www.hiddennolonger.com

50 000 CANADIAN CHILDREN MURDERED

Hiddennolonger.com

(pdf book)

19. Witness claims that MICHAELSON provides security for foreign diplomats in Vancouver and film industry stars, including Eddie MURPHY, to whom MICHAELSON introduced the witness in 2002. Witness claims that MURPHY raped and sadistically assaulted her, slicing her skin with a knife and leaving permanent scars on her shoulder and neck. *(see videotaped interview)* Witness states that MURPHY was also responsible for the death of two women during the years 2002-3 in Vancouver : a 21 year old Asian porn actress and a prostitute, both of whom were provided to MURPHY by MICHAELSON, and whose bodies were disposed of by the latter after MURPHY had tortured and raped them, and then overdosed them on drugs.

20. Witness states that she reported the attack on her by MURPHY to a Detective SCOTT with the VPD, along with the claim of MURPHY's murder of the two women, but when MICHAELSON learned of the complaint he tortured the witness with a knife, carving her neck and face, *(see videotaped interview)* and threatened to kill her if she pressed charges against MURPHY. Witness then withdrew her complaint. Detective SCOTT subsequently confirmed to the witness that MURPHY was responsible for the murders but they had not enough evidence to prosecute him.

21. Witness believes that MICHAELSON and his associates are *"hunting prostitutes of intelligence"* and are engaged *"in a kind of ethnic cleansing … they target Indians and girls as young as twelve or thirteen."* She

Kevin Annett's David vs Goliath battle to reveal the truth and obtain justice for the victims.
Award winning documentary! Kevin Annett's David vs. Goliath Battle against corrupt Roman Catholic, Anglican & United churches colluding in native land theft with the Canadian government.
Nazi experiments, gang rapes & murders of school children in "the land of the free." A call to Action! The Depopulation Agenda trial run on these children is being enacted on us all!!!
Winner of Best Documentary in New York and Los Angeles.
Canada's gruesome real history. An unholy trinity of churches, government and Weyerhaeuser (MacMillan Bloedel) colluding in native land theft, rape, murder and the genocide of 50,000 to 100,000 children. An evil alliance of RCMP, politicians, British monarchy, crooked lawyers and pedophile priests making Vancouver one of the top 5 child trafficking sites in the world.
Film Directed and Produced by Louie Lawless.
Unrepentant and the Canadian Holocaust
DVD
Unrepentant
and the Canadian
Holocaust
by
Kevin Annett
Award Winning Documentary

To: Director, Indian/Native Studies

RE: Kevin Annett, guest speaker,
Author of 4 books, filmmaker,
Minister, community worker

Kevin Annett gives lectures worldwide
On the residential schools and how they have affected the Canadian aboriginals. He has meticulously researched and documented the Canadian Holocaust for over twenty years. Contact information:

250-591-4573 Canada
386-323-5774 USA

Hiddenfromhistory1@gmail.com email

260 Kennedy Street

Nanaimo, B.C. Canada V9R2H8

UNREPENTANT
Kevin Annett and Canada's Genocide
JUSTICE
www.Hiddennolonger.com
read pdf book:
Hidden From History:
The Canadian Holocaust
www.itccs.org
(activist site)
Contact:
Kevin Annett
250-591-4573

UNRELENTING
Between Sodom and Zion
by Kevin D. Annett
All the Children
Need a Proper Burial
Former minister alleges
officials killed students
Natives
died
in droves
as Ottawa
ignored
warnings

Investigative Report.

A Council spokesman said today,

"All of these accused men have been under investigation for some time. Senator Campbell has been named by police sources in Vancouver as a major suspect in the disappearance of aboriginal women at the notorious Pickton farm. Senator Brazeau has already pleaded guilty in a Quebec court to charges of sexual assault with a deadly weapon and drug trafficking. Denis Lebel, his friend Cardinal Lacroix, and Bishops Hiltz and Bennett have all been named by government and church insiders as active participants in the Ninth Circle ritual killing of children, at secret catholic church facilities in Montreal and Rome. We will be issuing indictments against all of these men, based on sworn testimony."

Kevin Annett will be issuing his own televised statement to the public to accompany the ITCCS media release.

Satanic Serial Killers

Campbell Murders Women & Children

BrutalProof!

Investigative team definitively links top Canadian politicians, churchmen to child trafficking and sacrifices, and to death of investigator – Key ITCCS leaders placed in protective quarantine

Montreal:

After nearly a year of investigations and relying on undercover informants, **the ITCCS has established that at least two Canadian senators, a former cabinet minister in the Harper government and three senior church officials are actively engaged in trafficking children for sexual and sacrificial purposes in the Ottawa-Montreal area.**

The ITCCS has also learned that these same accused men are complicit in the 2014 murder of Ottawa police inspector Kal Ghadban, who was investigating the disappearance of children at the hands of the accused; and **that key ITCCS investigators in Canada, including Rev. Kevin Annett, are also being targeted for elimination by them.**

Above is Senator Campbell, former Vancouver mayor who has shown no sympathy whatsoever for the murdered and missing women and children-mostly aboriginal in which many have been murdered at the Picton Pig Farm as well as in underground tunnels.

Cardinal Lacroix

A Council spokesman said today,

"All of these accused men have been under investigation for some time. Senator Campbell has been named by police sources in Vancouver as a major suspect in the disappearance of aboriginal women at the notorious Pickton farm. Senator Brazeau has already pleaded guilty in a Quebec court to charges of sexual assault with a deadly weapon and drug trafficking. Denis Lebel, his friend Cardinal Lacroix, and Bishops Hiltz and Bennett have all been named by government and church insiders as active participants in the Ninth Circle ritual killing of children, at secret catholic church facilities in Montreal and Rome. We will be issuing indictments against all of these men, based on sworn testimony."

Kevin Annett will be issuing his own televised statement to the public to accompany the ITCCS media

Bishop Hiltz

Bishop Bennett

:cused men are Senators ıpbell and Patrick below)

arper cabinet minister ıel, Quebec Catholic Gerald Lacroix, and Bishops Fred Hiltz and ett.

right of this and below.

ails of the exhaustive investigation by a special were shared this past weekend with the ITCCS l during its closed gathering near Montreal. In ouncil has placed Rev. Kevin Annett and other ıvestigators under a protective quarantine, and d plans to convene a new common law court in ew year to indict and prosecute the six accused men.

l be issuing a full public statement to the is week, along with excerpts from the

Unrepentant, the award-winning documentary film on Indian residential schools found at www.hiddennolonger.com (http://www.hiddennolonger.com/) .

(2) See Annie Parker's complete testimony at www.itccs.org (http://www.itccs.org/) , Important Posts: "Memo on the Organized Disappearance, Torture, Exploitation and Murder of Womena and Children on Canada's West Coast", May 26, 2006: (http://itccs.org/2011/02/02/memorandum-on-the-organized-disappearance-torture-exploitation-and-murder-of-women-and-children-on-canada-s-west-coast-a-summary-from-eyewitnesses/ (http://itccs.org/2011/02/02/memorandum-on-the-organized-disappearance-torture-exploitation-and-murder-of-women-and-children-on-canada-s-west-coast-a-summary-from-eyewitnesses/))

(3) From the testimony of numerous witnesses in closed sessions, and of Frank Martin and Helen Michel, Carrier-Sekani tribal members who testified about the killing of their relatives by Ed John's agents in Prince George, at the IHRAAM Tribunal in Vancouver on June 13, 1998. The author was physically assaulted at the same Tribunal on June 14 by a large man claiming to represent Mr. John, who while clutching the author by the throat exclaimed, "Eddie John doesn't like what you're doing here! He's the one who speaks for Indians, get it?"

(4) From the Indian Affairs RG 10 collection (Indian residential schools), R 7733 file, West Coast Agency reports, January 17, 1940, as quoted in "Hidden No Longer: Genocide in Canada, Past and Present" by Kevin D. Annett, www.hiddennolonger.com (http://www.hiddennolnger.com/) .

(5) From a series of videotaped interviews by the author during 2004 with Les Guerin and Jim Kew, both of whom were residents on the Musqueam Indian reservation during this period. Documents related to these incidents are also on line at www.hiddennolonger.com (http://www.hiddennolonger.com/) .

(6) The involvement of elements of the RCMP and Vancouver city police with the Hell's Angels and the Pickton brothers has been testified to by eyewitnesses including two aboriginal women who were taken to Piggy's Palace by police during 1999 and 2000. Both women were interviewed by the author on his Vancouver Co-op Radio program *Hidden from History* in the summer of 2010, shortly before that program was suddenly cancelled without cause by the government-funded station managers. In addition, a former Canadian Security Intelligence Service (CSIS) operative named Grant Wakefield who was an udnercover informant at Piggy's palace met with the author during 2011 and gave his own eyewitness account of seeing the politicians mentioned and senior RCMP officials participating in the rape and killing of aboriginal women there. See the author's forthcoming book *Unrelenting* for more details. (www.itccs.org (http://www.itccs.org/) , www.KevinAnnett.com (http://www.kevinannett.com/))

Appendix IV

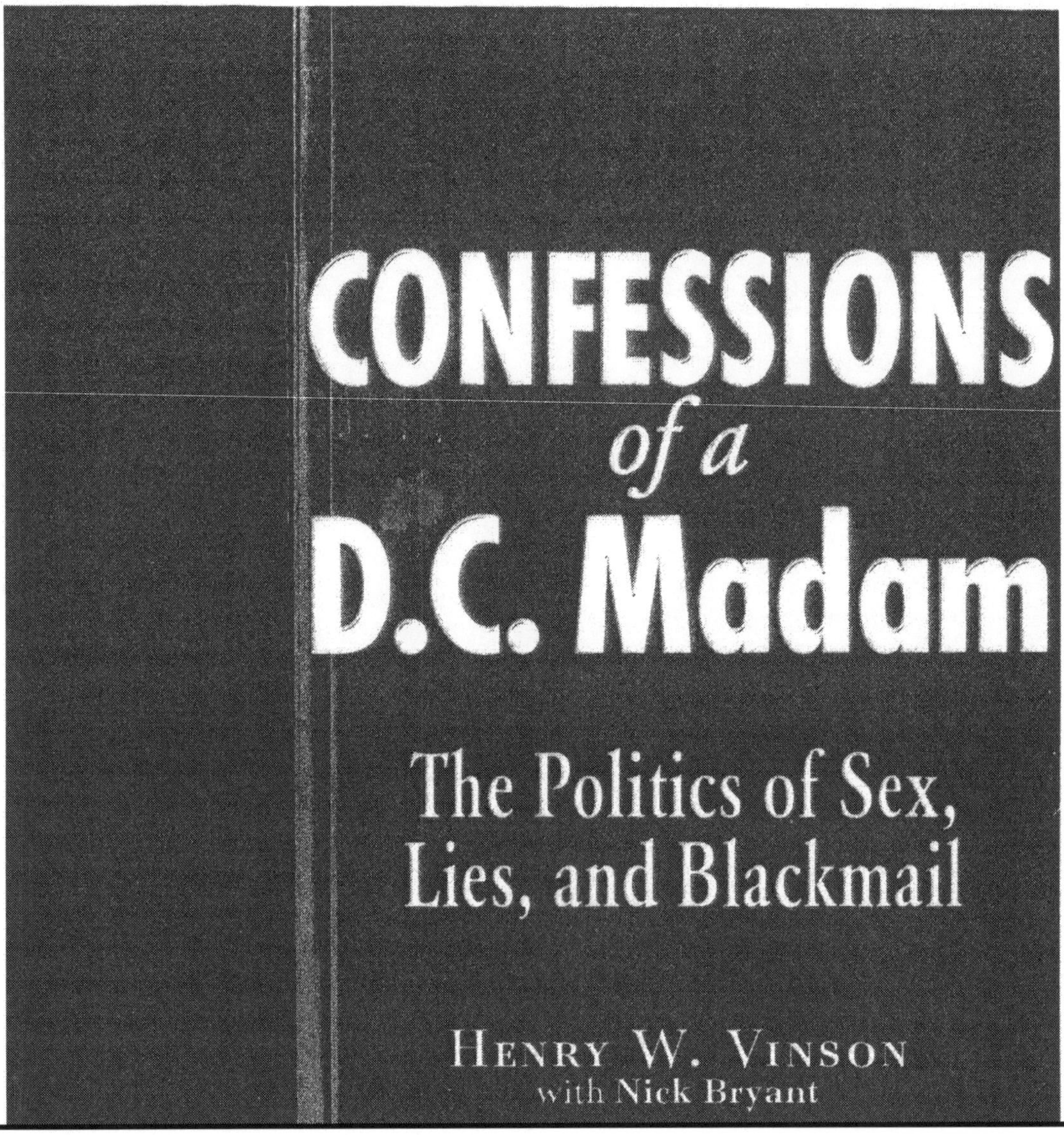

King then made a number of disclosures that I found to be absolutely bizarre. He revealed that he and Spence operated an interstate pedophile network that flew children from coast-to-coast. King also discussed that he and Spence had clientele of powerful pedophiles who actually took pleasure in murdering children. In fact, King seemed to be obsessed with the subject of murdering children. I sincerely thought that I was talking to a pair of psychotics on the run from a psychiatric hospital.

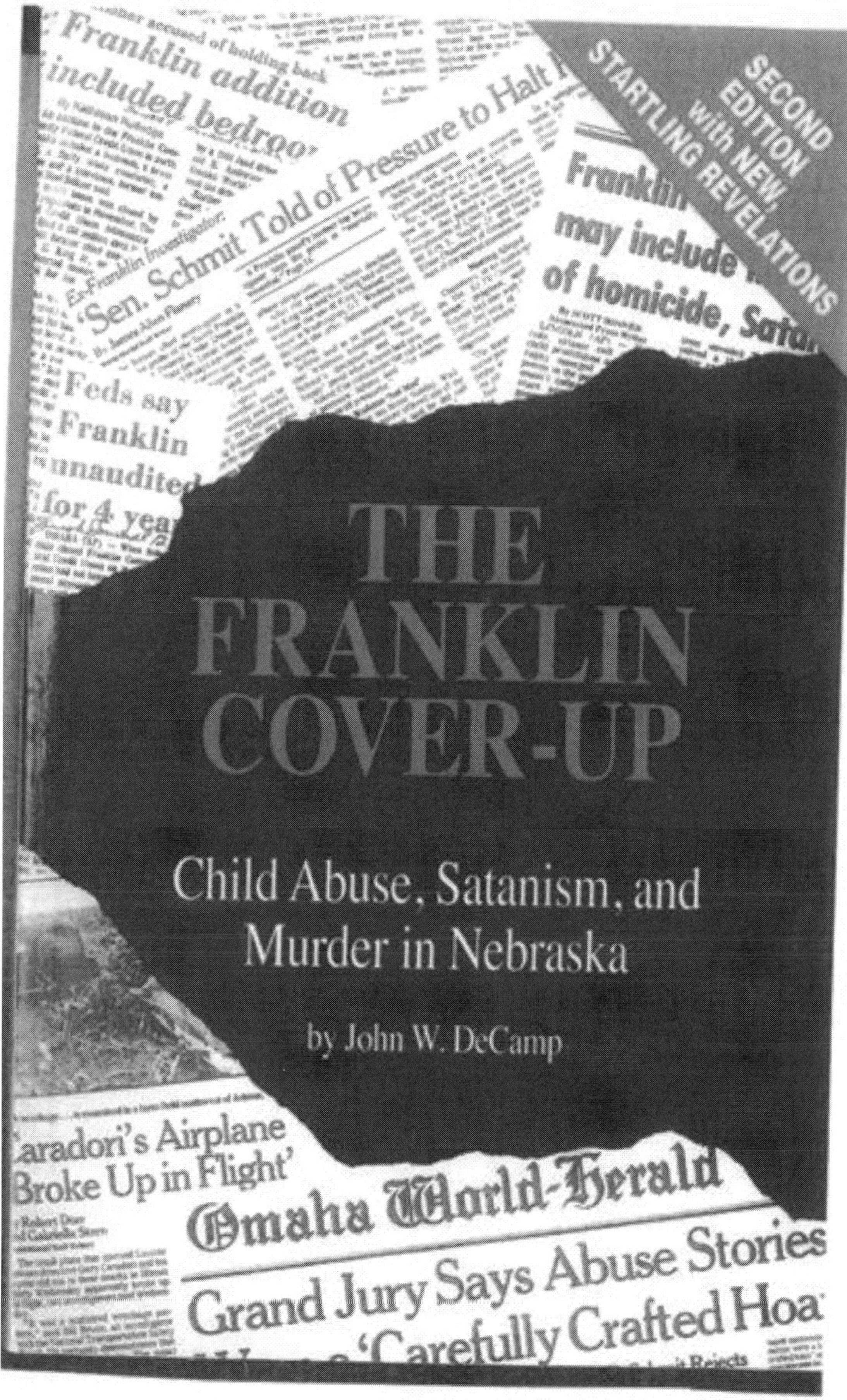

BrutalProof!

Satanic Colonel Aquino & wife Lillith involved in Franklin Cover-Up

-Mark DeMarco once told Stephen Williams he knew a beautician from Darte's Funeral Home, where Kristen French was prepared for burial. He said the beautician claimed Kristen's head had been shaved and her tendons cut---a sure sign a ritual satanic abuse.

This is an ancient ritual sacrifice to the evil God Moloch, the god of money and credit- a demon!!! My God these people are evil! Butter does not melt in their mouths; they have hearts and souls of ice. For the survivors "sorry" is not enough. I know what it feels like to have your life and soul destroyed. Justice is only a small beginning, but JUSTICE must be done. In Canada Justice really means kids are just-ass for pedophiles. After all the pedophiles gleefully took turns raping little boys in these schools and girls to DEATH! Now another survivor mentions his brother was cattle prodded to DEATH, electrocuted and dies screaming for help. Evil!!!

Update: From independent journalist Irene Mack: "The three main LNG pipelines run straight through the Highway of Tears, from west to east through the biggest killing zones. Pacific Northern Gas Company, Prince Rupert Gas Transportation and West Coast Gas Transportation connect the coastal ports to Tumbler Creek and Fort St. John. All of it is on lands still occupied by native groups that have resisted signing deals with the companies." To quote a local white politician from the Terrace region, "We've been telling the Mounties for years that the disappearances of the native families are targeted killings by professionals. In the Carrier-Sekani region it's common place that anyone who speaks out against the backroom corporate deals with the Chinese gets a one way trip to the lake. But I stopped going to the Mounties when I realized they were the ones taking people to the lake."

Significantly, one of the first murdered native women to make the headlines, Wendy Poole of Moberley Lake, was the daughter of political activist Chief Art Napolean who led the fight to stop the surrender of his Saulteaux Cree lands to multinationals. Wendy Poole's body was found dismembered and missing body parts and organs. The RCMP refused to investigate her death.

Wendy's organs were missing for a reason. For the profit-led assault that killed her also involves the Chinese military: specifically, the same Generals who operate China's infamous organ-trafficking industry and have exterminated large swaths of China's own indigenous tribes, the Uyghur Muslims.

One of the most notorious of these officers, former Chinese security chief General Zhou Yongkang, is a major share holder in the hundreds of army-run hospitals across China where prisoners and political dissidents are killed and their organs transplanted into paying recipients. This same consortium of hospitals is now investing heavily in the British Columbia retirement home and health care industries, led by the Beijing-based Anbang Insurance Group.

The holding company of this entire operation, Cedar Tree Investments, owns big sections of downtown Vancouver and is described by one business journalist as "a thinly cloaked Triad (Chinese Mafia) operation that is grabbing up real estate and LNG deposits all over the province and especially up north."

To say that the British Columbia and federal governments are holding the coats of these criminal conglomerates is to understate things. Prime Minister Trudeau just recently lifted restrictions on Chinese takeover investment in the health care field, while Beijing operates "special advisory groups" directly out of B.C. Premier Christy Clark's government office. Clark is even jokingly but not inaccurately referred to by one Chinese lobbyist as "our local office manager".

Over forty years ago when I first learned of how easily people go missing in Vancouver, a worldly-wise TV journalist named Jack Webster warned me, "Don't ever expect to find out who's responsible because nobody wants you to know". Jack might have added, "especially the rich boys who are responsible."

General Zhou Yongkang and his friends need have no such fear. Canada's latest whitewash of its own domestic war crimes known as the Missing Womens Inquiry is ensuring that no names will ever be named and no mass grave sites ever unearthed. And Canadians, with their peculiar talent to blithely look past the evidence of their own backyard malfeasance, are giving their usual blessing to the whole charade.

Business is business, after all." Excerpt from article written by Kevin Annett titled: Missing People, Fake Inquiries and the China Connection: What Price this Profit? Itccs.org

General Zhou Yongkang

Supervisor of Serial Killings

An Excerpt From Kevin Annett's Writing on Pickton's Murders

Let Willie Pickton Speak: Revealing the Bigger Picture of Canada's Genocide

Posted by [illegible] on February 22, 2016

by Kevin D. Annett

"Pickton was the straw man set up for everyone to gawk at and hate while the real killers got away. The arrangement was vast and orchestrated from the very top". – Grant Wakefield, former CSIS agent and undercover operative at the "Piggy's Palace" killing site, August 4, 2011

"It's not just our women who are going missing. Whole families are disappearing, starting with the children. Our northern communities are being wiped out for their land by big corporations and their hired RCMP thugs. It's the residential school genocide taken to its next step." – Carol Martin, Vancouver, September 12, 2008

I've never met the alleged serial killer Willie Pickton, but he and I have this much in common: we have both just published books that have Canada's power brokers worried.

Willie's book, ***Pickton in his Own Words***, claims that he was framed by the RCMP for the murder of dozens of mostly aboriginal women. My own book, ***Murder by Decree: The Crime of Genocide in Canada***, shows that such organized race killing is endemic to this nation and carries on today.

- **Note: Pickton in his Own Words has been removed from circulation from amazon.com and all other book sellers. Grant Wakefield is a former Canadian Intelligence Service Agent who is apparently retired. The only person reporting on these crimes is Kevin Annett who lives under death threats and in hiding and has been victimized by an onslaught of discrediting campaigns run by Gov't Trolls. Kevin Annett's *book Murder By Decree: The Crime of Genocide in Canada* is available.**

Zionist Party

'UNCLE EVELYN' DE ROTHSCHILD, HEAD OF THE HOUSE OF ROTHSCHILD AND INTERNATIONAL JEWRY, ATTENDS A ROYAL BIRTHDAY PARTY

The monster logo "666" is plastered ALL over the sidewalk at Vancouver Island University. Bodies are buried in fenced in areas shown at Vancouver Island University, Nanaimo, B.C. Canada. (Next Page.) The Green Monster Logo is 666 In Hebrew.

Note: hiddennolonger.com is no longer being used as the referenced website but has been replaced by murderbydecree.com.

The Franklin Coverup Scandal

The Child sex ring that reached Bush/Reagan Whitehouse

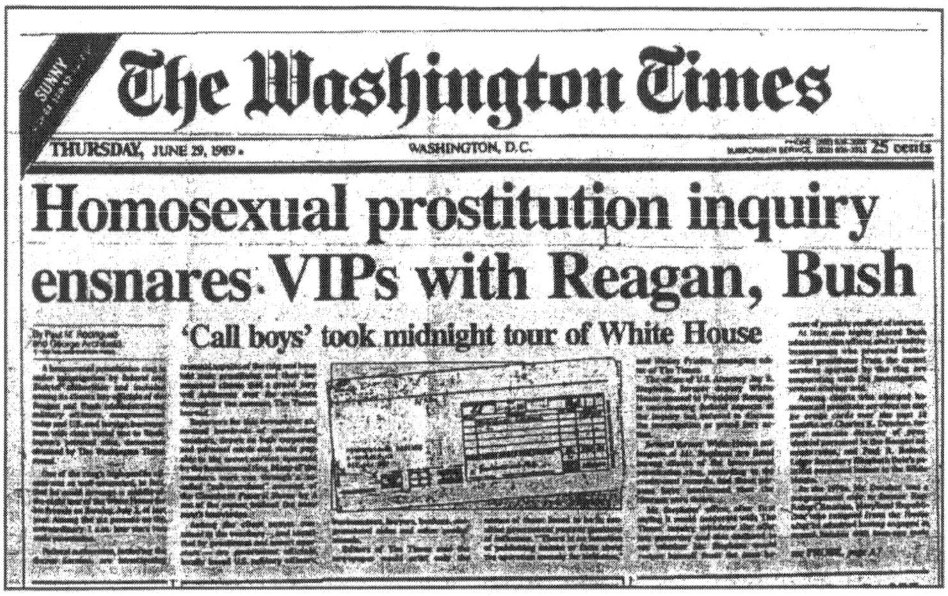
SUNNY

The Washington Times

THURSDAY, JUNE 29, 1989 · WASHINGTON, D.C. · 25 cents

Homosexual prostitution inquiry ensnares VIPs with Reagan, Bush

'Call boys' took midnight tour of White House

Click on the image above to see large scans of the above newspaper.

This was the biggest scandal in the history of the U.S.A history. The story received some newspaper coverage but there was a TV News Media blackout on the subject. For this reason, most Americans have never heard of it.

Former republican Senator John Decamp was involved in the production a documentary called "Conspiracy of Silence" it was to air May 3, 1994 on the Discovery Channel. This documentary exposed a network of religious leaders and Washington politicians who flew children to Washington D.C. for sex orgies. At the last minute before airing, unknown congressmen threatened the TV Cable industry with restrictive legislation if this documentary was aired.

Almost immediately, the rights to the documentary were purchased by unknown persons who had ordered all copies destroyed. A copy of this videotape was furnished anonymously to former Nebraska state senator and attorney John De Camp who made it available to retired F.B.I. chief, Ted L. Gunderson. While the video quality is not top grade, this tape is a blockbuster in what is revealed by the participants involved. You can purchase a VHS copy at this link. Or you can view an online copy at this page. Franklin Cover up video page

Boy prostitutes 15 years old (and younger) were taking midnight tours of the Whitehouse. There are 19 more Washington Times articles in full text about this case available here at this link.
Newspaper scans or text are not for commercial use. Solely to be used for the educational purposes of research and open discussion.

GOOGLE: UNREPENTANT
CONSPIRACY OF SILENCE
www.JusticeforJohnnyGosch.com
www.1-Free-dvd.com

THE FRANKLIN CASE

Paul Bonacci

BrutalProof!

FILED
U.S. DISTRICT COURT
DISTRICT OF NEBRASKA
97 JUN 11 PM 3:21
NORBERT H. EBEL
CLERK

218

IN THE UNITED STATES DISTRICT COURT
FOR THE DISTRICT OF NEBRASKA

PAUL A. BONACCI,	)	4:CV91-3037
	)	
Plaintiff,	)	
	)	
vs.	)	MEMORANDUM AND ORDER ON
	)	MOTION FOR SUMMARY JUDGMENT
CITY OF OMAHA, et al.,	)	OF DEFENDANTS CITY OF OMAHA,
	)	ROBERT WADMAN, AND MICHAEL
Defendants.	)	HOCH

Counts III and IV state the claims against the City of Omaha, former Police Chief Robert Wadman and Police Officer Michael Hoch. Count III alleges deprivation of civil rights of due process, equal protection, and unreasonable seizures; Count IV alleges conspiracy.

Three subparagraph of paragraph 49 of the second amended complaint, filing 139, describe the plaintiff's claim of due process violations:

> "a. The rights under the due process clause of the 14th Amendment the Fourth Amendment, and the 'self-incrimination clause' of the Fifth Amendment to be free of the objectively unreasonable, intentional and unjustified infliction of extreme emotional distress, deliberate and unjustified assaults, detentions, and coercive, heavy handed and outrageous custodial interrogations;
>
> . . . .
>
> d. The right under the Due Process Clause of the 14th Amendment to be free of deliberate police department policy to refuse to enforce laws prohibiting child prostitution and pornography, delinquency, drug abuse when youths such as Plaintiff were the targets of special police department attention;
>
> e. The right under the Due Process Clause of the 14th Amendment to be free of deliberate police department policy to prevent the Plaintiff from alternative means of escaping his circumstances of child prostitution, pornography, drug and sex abuse . . ."

The equal protection claim is stated in subparagraphs of paragraph 49 as follows:

> "b. The right under the Equal Protection Clause of the 14th Amendment to be

Copies mailed on 6-11-97

218

free from arbitrary, discriminatory and unjustified mistreatment because Plaintiff was a member of a group of youths the police department wanted to stay under the control of Larry King and Alan Baer;

c. The right under the Equal Protection Clause of the 14th Amendment to receive from law enforcement officials their protection from child abuse, neglect and delinquency which Plaintiff suffered because he belonged to the group of children the Police Department wished to stay under the control of Larry King and Alan Baer;

. . . .

f. The right to be free under § 1985 of Title 42 of the United States from conspiracies against him that have the purpose of depriving the Plaintiff of his equal protection from the laws of the United States . . ."

In support of the motion these moving defendants have submitted filing 204, consisting of defendant's Exhibit A, an indictment in the ***State of Nebraska v. Paul A. Bonacci***, in the District Court of Douglas County, Nebraska, Docket 127, p. 193; and defendant's Exhibit B, comprising excerpts from the deposition of the plaintiff, Paul Bonacci. The plaintiff has submitted the declaration of plaintiff, Paul A. Bonacci, dated March 29, 1996.

Count IV recites the plaintiff's claims of conspiracy, pursuant to 42 U.S.C. § 1985(3) and § 1986. Second Amended Complaint ¶¶ 50-54.

Rule 56 of the Federal Rules of Civil Procedure in subparagraph (b) says:

> "A party against whom a claim . . . is asserted . . . may, at any time, move with or without supporting affidavits for a summary judgment in the party's favor as to all or any part thereof."

In subparagraph (c) the rule says:

> ". . . The judgment sought shall be rendered forthwith if the pleadings, depositions, answers to interrogatories, and admissions on file, together with the affidavits, if any, show that there is no genuine issue as to any material fact and that the moving party is entitled to a judgment as a matter of law. A summary judgment, interlocutory in character, may be rendered on the issue of liability alone although there is a genuine issue as to the amount of damages."

Subparagraph (e) includes the following:

> "Supporting and opposing affidavits shall be made on personal knowledge, shall

set forth such facts as would be admissible in evidence, and shall show affirmatively that the affiant is competent to testify to the matters stated therein. . . . When a motion for summary judgment is made and supported as provided in this rule, an adverse party may not rest upon the mere allegations or denials of the adverse party's pleading, but the adverse party's response, by affidavits or as otherwise provided in this rule, must set forth specific facts showing that there is a genuine issue for trial. . . ."

In ***Anderson v. Liberty Lobby, Inc.***, 477 U.S. 242 at 250 (1986), the Court said:

"There is no requirement that the trial judge make findings of fact. The inquiry performed is the threshold inquiry of determining whether there is the need for a trial--whether, in other words, there are any genuine factual issues that properly can be resolved only by a finder of fact because they may reasonably be resolved in favor of either party."

I. WHETHER THE PLAINTIFF'S TESTIMONY HAS CREDIBILITY

In an earlier memorandum on a motion for summary judgment by the defendant Alan Baer I reviewed the plaintiff's testimony by deposition, the only testimony offered that could be considered to have been in support of the plaintiff's position. The plaintiff's testimony was that he had been hypnotized sometime between November 18, 1989, and October 21, 1992, when he was incarcerated, which was at least three and one-half years after he claims to have been last sexually abused. He also testified that he was hypnotized once or perhaps twice after that. I make the same observations now as I did relative to Baer's motion.

The plaintiff's testimony by deposition includes this as to his having been hypnotized:

"Q. At some period of time when you were incarcerated, you were hypnotized; is that correct?

A. Yes.

Q. Tell me about that.

A. I believe the first time was one -- about the week after Dr. Mead had diagnosed me with MPD, he -- the next week he came in, he wanted to, wanted me to close my eyes, and when he did, he said -- I don't know, I can't remember what he said, but it brought out one of the other personalities.

And I didn't know that that's what he was trying to do, but -- and I guess he spoke to the personality for a while.

And then later on, I was hypnotized with, I think it was -- Detective Hoch was

Very Important! Read

there, and I think there was another lady, but I'm not sure.

Q. Do you have any particular recollection of those circumstances?

A. Not really. Detective Hoch wanted to find out how accurate some of the things that I had related to him were, how -- not whether they were the truth or not, but how much of them may have been added in, you know, stuff may have been added in by personalities that maybe don't deal completely with reality, you know, may have added stuff, like things that happened that didn't really happen, but to them, they did. And -- 'cause there was distortions and stuff, which I guess happens quite a bit with MPDs when they're first trying to go through the memories.

Q. And you have not been hypnotized since then --

A. No.

Q. -- that you're aware of?

A. Well, yes, and it was with Densen-Gerber, and that was in Lincoln."

Bonacci Deposition 1874:18-1876:5

"Q. You did an interview with Judith (phonetic) Densen-Gerber?

A. Yeah."

Id. 1876:16-18.

Q. I'm sorry, thank you. And you were hypnotized during part of that?

A. I think, yeah, at one point, I was put under hypnosis. I --

Q. Have you ever been told, Paul, that you give different responses under hypnosis than you do when you're in a nonhypnotic state?

A. No.

Q. Do you believe that you give different answers when you're under the influence of hypnosis?

A. Humm. I believe some of the stuff that was given under hypnosis may have been more, more accurate, because it takes out a lot of the, more of the distortions that happen by the different personalities all coming out at the same time. They can specifically go to one personality. You know, they used to be able to do that, anyway, and get things -- ' cause it slows your mind down a little bit."

Id. 1877:1-20

"Q. And other than the incident you described where Dr. Mead -- or, not Dr. Mead, Dr. Densen-Gerber supposedly hypnotized you which was recorded on videotape, had you been actually hypnotized by the psychiatrists up till then?

A. By Dr. Mead, I know I was. Dr. Stoller, I remember very little of that meeting, though.

Q. What's your definition of hypnotized?"

Id. 2006:16-24

Very Important! Read

"THE WITNESS: I'm not sure.

BY MR. DeCAMP:

Q. So far as you understand, what does hypnotized mean?

A. When the psychiatrists or whatever kind of make you, like, ah, close your eyes, and then it's like all of a sudden -- you listen to whatever they're saying. All of a sudden, it seems like you just go somewhere else. That's the way it felt to me, like I went somewhere else, like I was --

Q. What exactly did Dr. Mead do that you understood was hypnotizing you?

A. Oh, basically, he had me close my eyes, and he would talk and count, and he, he told me that because of the MPD and stuff, that it wasn't really him hypnotizing me, that MPDs were able to do that all on their own without really too much help, they're very easy to hypnotize or something, I guess. And that's about all I , I know. I don't understand what he did.

Q. When he told you to close your eyes, was it then that the other personalities would come out?

A. No, it wasn't right then. He would talk for a little while and stuff, and then he would -- I don't, I don't know. It's like -- 'cause it's -- there's a point where I just -- I can't remember, ' cause it's like I lose track of what went on after that."

Id. 2007:1-2008:5.

That raises the flag of ***Sprynczynatyk v. General Motors Corp.***, 771 F.2d 1112 (8th Cir. 1985), which said at page 1122-23:

> "We adopt a rule which requires the district court, in cases where hypnosis has been used, to conduct pretrial hearings on the procedures used during the hypnotic session in question and assess the effect of hypnosis upon the reliability of the testimony before making a decision on admissibility. The proponent of the hypnotically enhanced testimony bears the burden of proof during this proceeding. In addition, we adopt a version of the [***State v. Hurd***, 86 N.J. 525, 432 A.2d 86 (1981)] safeguards to the extent that the district court should consider whether and to what degree the safeguards were followed when making its determination that the hypnotically enhanced testimony is sufficiently reliable. Other factors the district court should take into account are the appropriateness of using hypnosis for the kind of memory loss involved, and whether there is any evidence to corroborate the hypnotically enhanced testimony. The district court must then determine whether in view of all the circumstances, the proposed testimony is sufficiently reliable and whether its probative value outweighs its prejudicial effect, if any, to warrant admission. Ultimately the district court must decide whether the risk that the testimony reflects a distorted memory is so great that the probative value of the testimony is destroyed.
>
> By our ruling today we place this hypnosis evidentiary problem directly within the control of the district court. We think the better approach is for the district court and not the jury to make the preliminary determination of admissibility as is the case with other evidentiary questions. ***See*** FED.R.EVID. 104(a). It is our hope that this case-by-case method of determining the admissibility of hypnotically enhanced testimony will guard against the problems of hypnosis, especially undue suggestiveness and confabulation, but also allow for the inclusion of reliable refreshed memory which hypnosis can at times under certain circumstances produce. In sum, we hold that the district court should, before trial, scrutinize the circumstances surrounding the hypnosis session, consider whether the safeguards we have approved were followed and determine in light of all the circumstances if the proposed hypnotically enhanced testimony is sufficiently reliable and not overly prejudicial to be admitted."

There is no evidence before me of the details of the hypnosis. There is no way that I can tell the effect, if any, of the hypnosis upon the reliability of the testimony of the plaintiff. I do not know what safeguards were utilized. The burden is upon the plaintiff and there has been no evidence presented on his behalf to the effect that his testimony was either unaffected or affected to such a small extent that the probative value of his testimony was not destroyed.

The plaintiff cites ***United States v. Reynolds***, 77 F.3d 253 (8th Cir. 1996), in connection with his argument that expert testimony is not necessary when expert evaluation of the credibility of the testimony is not called for or relevant. That statement is true enough, but does not apply, because in the present case without ***some*** evidence to the effect that Bonacci's testimony was

Very Important!
Read

either unaffected or nominally affected I cannot reasonably determine the effect of his hypnosis, if any, upon the reliability of Bonacci's testimony. I do not know what safeguards were taken during the hypnotic session or sessions. I might be highly benefited by expert testimony on the subject; perhaps lay testimony on the subject would be helpful. There simply is none, unless it be the declaration of Bonacci that was attached to the plaintiff's brief.[1] In the plaintiff's declaration he says, "Dr. Mead however had little to do with refreshing any memories involving the police department." That is of little value to the plaintiff. The question is the reliability of the plaintiff's testimony, which includes both his deposition and his declaration, which were given after the occasions when he was hypnotized by Dr. Mead and again by Dr. Densen-Gerber and, possibly, by Dr. Stoller. With one, two or three sessions of hypnosis involved, with my having no information from any of those doctors as to the safeguards taken or the techniques used, and with the plaintiff's acknowledging that Dr. Mead brought out one of the other personalities[2] and acknowledging that personalities do contradict others, the unsupported testimony of Paul Bonacci after hypnotism is of doubtful reliability. It should be noted, also, that there were, according to Bonacci's testimony, dozens of persons involved in the matters he brings before the court as claims against these moving defendants, yet there has been not one word of evidence by any of those persons to support Bonacci's claims. That does not mean that the claims are all false, but it does mean that Bonacci's hypnotized testimony is highly problematic.

There are also other reasons to question the credibility of the plaintiff's testimony.

Bonacci was addicted to illegal drugs, according to his testimony, extending into 1984. He said:

"Q. Well, going back to this little chronology of what you were involved with between the period of 1980 and '84, as I understand your testimony, at some -- during this period of time, you were acting as a drug runner at the behest of Larry King; is that correct?

A. Yes.

Q. And you took hundreds of trips which you've described in your earlier testimony.

A. Yes.

---

[1] NELR 7.1(a)(2) requires that evidentiary materials in support of motions be filed with the clerk and <u>not</u> be attached to a brief, because briefs are not filed. The declaration of the plaintiff was attached to a brief and has not been filed, but I shall cause it to be filed.

[2] The plaintiff is a victim of Multiple Personality Disorder (MPD).

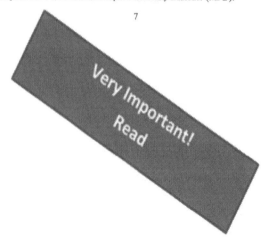

Very Important!
Read

218

Q. You were also involved in the scavenger hunts which you have described at length in your earlier testimony during the period of 1980 to '84 -- .

A. Yes.

Q. -- is that correct? You were also yourself using multiple drugs during this period.

A. Yeah. On and off, yeah.

Q. Well, you described a period earlier today when you had to take uppers every day.

A. Yeah.

Q. Is it fair to say that you were fairly consistently using some drug during most of the period between '80 and '84?

A. Yeah, mostly from about '83 till '84 was when I got stuck on it every day where I had to take uppers in the morning and then downers to put myself to sleep.

Q. So it was at its zenith during '83 to '84, but you also took drugs during the earlier period of time?

A. Yeah. That's why I don't remember my tenth grade.

(An off-the-record discussion was had between the Reporter and the witness.)

THE WITNESS: I say that's why I don't remember my tenth grade year in school and my grades prove it."

Id. 934:15-936:1

The last time the plaintiff says he remembers being sexually abused was in March of 1986. *Id.* 948:4-17.

More problematic than the addiction is the mental condition known as Multiple Personality Disorder (MPD). He testified that he had within him, all at the same time, many distinct personalities. Bonacci Deposition 6:5-8:20, Exhibits in Support of Motion for Summary Judgment (on Behalf of Alan Baer), filing 187. He testified in his deposition after being sworn under 14 different personalities distinct from the primary personalty, Paul Bonacci. *Id.* 9:1-10:23. He testified that the combination of multiple personalities and the drugs and events of his life on occasion cause him to confuse people or events. *Id.* 1154:3-12. When he was questioned about whether he was satisfied that a person he had identified with some particular material was the same Gary Kerr that is on television locally, he said:

Q. And how do you know that that's the way Wesley feels?

A. Because before I thought he integrated, that's exactly what he said."

Id. 736:9-737:7.

One of the strange features of Mr. Bonacci's testimony occurred as follows:

"BY MS. HAHN:

Q. Let me ask you first, you have answered a series of questions under the persona of West Lee.

A. Yes.

Q. Are the answers that you have given to those questions within the last half an hour true and accurate answers?

A. Yes.

Q. Are they complete answers?

A. Yes.

Q. All right. Now I'm going to ask you, what triggered the arrival or development or birth of your personality West Lee in 1974?

A. I cannot give that information under direct orders.

Q. Orders by whom?

A. I cannot say:

MS. HAHN: Mr. DeCamp, would you please instruct your client that he has to answer these questions?

MR. DeCAMP: Yes. You're supposed to answer these questions. Does this have to do with Monarch?

THE WITNESS: Yes.

MR. DeCAMP: If I use the code, will that help, that I just obtained in the last hour? D-6 41 3782 Program XPY Eagle Alex Hope. Please go ahead and

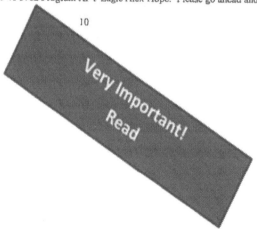

Very Important! Read

answer all questions.

THE WITNESS: I was created by a government program.

BY MS. HAHN:

Q. Which government program?

A. Monarch.

Q. And what is Monarch?

A. Monarch is an operation that was created by the United States Government to create spies for other countries. They use children for the purpose that they're easily integrated into multiple personalities because they can dissociate.

Monarch is a program that is run by Michael Angelo Aquino who was an Army Reserve Colonel at Presidio. He is also the leader of the Temple of Set. He is also -- he also runs a child day-care center. He also is involved in human sacrifice.

Q. Is he employed by the United States?

A. Yes.

Q. At what facility?

A. Presidio, California.

Q. Is that in the San Francisco area, the Presidio --

A. Yes.

Q. -- Naval base?

A. Yes.

Q. Do you know what rank Michael Aquino holds?

A. He was a colonel.

Q. Is he currently employed there?

A. I am not aware of the current situation.

Very Important!
Read

Q. Now, describe the program again, the Monarch program.

A. Monarch, as I said, was a program that used children to make multiple personalities for future use as spies and as a way to take over the United States Government."

Id. 1044:6-1046:23.

The testimony of the plaintiff in many respects is bizarre. Multiple personality disorder is a cruel mental condition. Its effects are stunning. Although the plaintiff believes that his personalities are probably wholly integrated, there is no psychiatric testimony before me that assesses his present condition or what impact the multiple personalities and their differing recollections have had on the plaintiff's ability to recall and testify accurately the awful events that have prompted this lawsuit. In no way do I say that those events or some of them never happened. My concern is what to do with the evidence that is before me as it impacts a motion for a summary judgment. The Eighth Circuit Court of Appeals has already spoken with respect to hypnosis and that, alone, may make Mr. Bonacci's testimony outside the realm of usefulness in opposing this motion. Piled on that is the matter of the addiction, which by the plaintiff's own testimony has harmed his ability to remember, and the multiple personality disorder, which tricks him, covers for him, and disputes him. Without expert testimony to help evaluate the ability of Paul Bonacci, whether partially or wholly integrated, to tell the truth in a reasonably accurate way, I cannot say that the testimony is sufficient to show any support for the claims against these moving defendants.

I am troubled, as I was about the claims against Alan Baer, that all claims against the City of Omaha, former Police Chief Robert Wadman, and Police Officer Michael Hoch be disposed of in summary fashion. I do not know whether there is expert testimony available regarding the possible effect of hypnosis, drug addiction and multiple personality disorder, but there is none that has been presented to me. There is not even evidence by any nonexpert that corroborates anything alleged in the complaint against these defendants. Under such circumstances, a dismissal of all claims against these defendants is necessary.

On former occasions I have been critical of the quality of the representation of the plaintiff by his counsel. That is not so relative to this motion. Counsel responded. Even though the response has not saved the plaintiff from a summary judgment, I am appreciative of the effort.

I find that the plaintiff's evidence is so unreliable that it would not allow a reasonable factfinder to return a verdict for the plaintiff against these moving defendants and, therefore, that summary judgment is in order.

II. IF THE TESTIMONY OF THE PLAINTIFF COULD BE ACCEPTED, THERE STILL WOULD BE NO ISSUE OF MATERIAL FACT WITH RESPECT TO THE CLAIMS AGAINST THESE MOVING DEFENDANTS

In the event it later is determined that the plaintiff's testimony should have been deemed of enough reliability to enable it to be weighed in the balance on this motion, I am persuaded that there is no genuine issue of material fact with respect to the claims against these defendants.

The claims against these moving defendants are set out in Counts III and IV.

Count III asserts that the Omaha Police Department established the "practice" of allowing prostitution for pay for certain homosexuals in the Omaha area. As a result, it charges, Alan Baer, Larry King and Peter Citron and others "were able to solicit young males for prostitution . . . to keep the young males within the homosexual services for pay circles . . ." (¶ 25). It alleges that the plaintiff "frequently saw uniformed Omaha Police Department officers present at the sex parties . . . . These officers appeared to allow the illegal activity to continue. . . ." (¶ 28). As a result, it is alleged that the plaintiff experienced "severe emotional distress . . ." (¶ 30). The Omaha Police Department maintained a policy "of keeping him and other children silent about the illegal activities of Alan Baer, Larry King and Harold Andersen." (¶ 31). It asserts that Wadman, Hoch and Bovasso "failed to act to protect Plaintiff . . ." (¶ 40). It alleges that in November 1989, Hoch and Bovasso subjected the plaintiff to "long hours of brutal interrogation involving threats, intimidation, physical and mental abuse and other outrageous conduct." (¶ 45). Violation is alleged, therefore, of the right under the Fourteenth Amendment's due process clause to be free of emotional distress, assaults, detentions and custodial interrogations and violation of the equal protection clause of the Fourteenth Amendment to be free from mistreatment because the plaintiff was "a member of a group of youths the police department wanted to stay under the control of Larry King and Alan Baer." (¶ 49b). It also alleges the violation of the right under the equal protection clause of the Fourteenth Amendment to receive "protection from child abuse, neglect and delinquency which Plaintiff suffered because he belonged to the group of children the Police Department wished to stay under the control of Larry King and Alan Baer." (¶ 49c).

Additionally, it alleges violation of the due process clause of the Fourteenth Amendment "to be free of deliberate police department policy to refuse to enforce laws prohibiting child prostitution and pornography, delinquency, drug abuse . . ." (¶ 49d). It also alleges violation of the due process clause of the Fourteenth Amendment "to be free of deliberate police department policy to prevent the Plaintiff from alternative means of escaping his circumstances of child prostitution, pornography, drug and sex abuse." (¶ 49e). It also alleges the claim under Section 1985 of Title 42 "from conspiracies against him that have the purpose of depriving [him] of his equal protection from the laws of the United States." (¶ 49f). That claim also is asserted under 42 U.S.C. § 1986 "to have those conspirators who were aware of the conspiracy alleged herein to take necessary steps to thwart the aims of the conspiracy." (¶ 49g).

Count IV asserts that the moving defendants, among others, were in a conspiracy "to continually threaten, abuse, and punish Plaintiff as specifically described in Count III above." (¶ 51). Thus, the two counts may be considered together, because they both assert the conspiracy that is the sole subject of Count IV.

A. DUE PROCESS

1. Evidence Regarding the Defendant Robert Wadman

The plaintiff says he last remembers being abused in March of 1986. Bonacci Deposition 948:4-8, filing 205. He first was able to identify Robert Wadman as Robert Wadman in about 1990, when somebody showed him a picture of Robert Wadman. *Id.* 1123:1-25. Sometime later somebody identified that picture as Robert Wadman. *Id.* 1124:22-25. In the five times that Bonacci saw Wadman, other than once at church, once at Adventureland, and once in a bathroom, Bonacci did not "remember seeing him actually doing anything, but the fact that what was going on that was illegal was right in front of everybody." *Id.* 1131:6-12. On the occasion when he saw him in a bathroom Bonacci was "so stoned and drunk, [he wasn't] really sure it was him. . . . *Id.* 1130:18-25. These incidents happened between 1983 and late 1985, when Bonacci was around 15 years old. *Id.* 1132:6-13. Bonacci's memory of Wadman "is really vague because of the fact of the drugs and stuff, but I know that he was there because there are certain things that he said. . . . *Id.* 1160:2-5. Bonacci never really had any direct contact with Mr. Wadman. *Id.* 1162:8-10. He just saw Wadman places. *Id.* 1162:11-12.

Bonacci never saw Wadman talk to Peter Citron or Larry King or Alan Baer or Michael Hoch or Officer Bovasso or have any information of any other type of communication between Wadman and any of the other defendants, except that he saw someone he thought was Robert Wadman having a conversation with Alan Baer in 1984 but heard none of the contents of the conversation. *Id.* 1900:22-1903:7. Bonacci has never been in a room where Robert Wadman gave orders or instructions to members of the Omaha Police Department and nobody ever told him that that happened. *Id.* 1931:13-1932:4. He has no information of any conversation between any of the moving defendants. *Id.* 1904:3-1905:17..

2. Evidence Regarding Defendant Michael Hoch

Bonacci first met Michael Hoch in 1989 in November. Bonacci Deposition 1112:19-25, filing 205. By then, Bonacci had not participated in or been the subject of any sexual abuse by anybody for a couple of years prior to that. *Id.* 1113:1-6. It is the manner in which Hoch dealt with him with respect to questioning and investigation of Bonacci's claims that Bonacci says was the basis of violation of his constitutional rights. *Id.* 1115:2-7. Hoch lived near Peter Citron and "kept telling me to take stuff back about people." *Id.* 1115:11-12. Hoch threatened that if Bonacci told "this stuff to the grand jury, you'll be going to prison for a long time." *Id.* 961:10-20.

3. Evidence regarding the Defendant City of Omaha

On April 21, 1986, Bonacci reluctantly reported to two police officers, who had been called to Northwest High School by a school counselor, that he had been abused by a number of adult males. Bonacci Deposition 1168:8-16, filing 205. Bonacci did not get an opportunity then to tell his story. He broke down, because he was terrified. *Id.* 1141:5-22. He does not actually know whether there was any investigation that was undertaken of his complaints. *Id.* 1139:15-22. Bonacci admits that "in '86, I was told that some of the guys that had abused me and stuff had gone to prison . . ." *Id.* 1923:2-4.

As for the claim that there was a policy of protecting wrongdoers by being lenient with boys such as Bonacci, the plaintiff acknowledges that he does not know whether there was such a policy:

> "All I know is, like I said, I made -- I made phone calls to somebody, and everytime they said that they would call or get hold of someone and they would have that situation taken care of.
>
> I don't think there was actually a policy that was written down or said by the chief and stuff, but like you said maybe there was someone that somebody knew within the Police Department that had authority that could just do that."

Id. 1696:22-1697:5.

The declaration of Bonacci, that was attached to the plaintiff's brief, supplements the deposition to some extent, but portions of it are pure speculation. For example, at paragraph 6 he says:

> "In my opinion the police who were regulars working or cooperating with Baer left us alone because we were 'Baer Boys' and because we were young, under age male prostitutes."

and at paragraph 3 he says:.

> "Whenever I was on the Run with the group of underaged boys there, the police who were the regular patrolmen there would leave us alone. The regular officers who were cooperating with Baer would instead harass and try to run off the men on the Run. Police told us to cooperate with Baer and them or we would be in trouble."

4. Analysis

None of the testimony, whether by deposition or by declaration, shows that the City of

Omaha had any kind of policy alleged in the second amended complaint of violating any constitutional right of the plaintiff. In the absence of such evidence there can be no liability on the part of the municipality. ***See Leatherman v. Tarrant County Narcotics Intelligence and Coordination Unit***, 507 U.S. 163 (1993). Bonacci's testimony that "police" told the boys Bonacci was with to cooperate with Baer and them or the boys would be in trouble is not evidence of any kind of policy of the City of Omaha. His testimony that "police officers" would force him to have sex with them is not evidence of any official policy of the City of Omaha. The fact that Bonacci "had occasional contact with persons threatening [him] on Alan Baer's behalf" is not evidence of any official policy of the City of Omaha. Evidence that Bonacci would avoid arrest by indicating that Alan Baer or Larry King was involved does not show an official policy of the City of Omaha. The fact that he was released after he had been arrested when he told Robert Wadman that he knew Alan Baer does not show an official policy of the City of Omaha. The fact that police officers promised to follow up interviewing Bonacci, but did not, does not show an official policy of the City of Omaha.

Furthermore, the defendant City of Omaha accurately argues that plaintiff has testified that the last time he was abused was in April 1986 and that any relevant policy would have to predate April 1986. The plaintiff, however, was never in the custody or control of the City during that time period.

The due process claims against these defendants for failing to protect the plaintiff are not supported by the evidence. The duty of any of them to protect Bonacci is limited to one of two circumstances: when the state limits his ability to care for himself in a custodial or other setting and when the state exposes him to danger that he would not have faced otherwise. ***Kennedy v. Schafer***, 71 F.3d 292, 294 (8th Cir. 1995). The evidence, sympathetically but objectively read, does not support either of these in this case. The plaintiff argues that the police officers cooperated with Bonacci's abusers or allowed him to continue his prostitution activities and thereby fostered and helped "trap the Plaintiff in the dangerous world of child prostitution." Plaintiff's Brief, last page. The evidence does not support that argument. It is the defendants who are sued, not "the police." Whatever some unnamed police person may have done is not attributable to these defendants, because nothing in the evidence ties the defendants to them--that is, it is not shown by any of the testimony that either the defendant Wadman or the defendant Hoch are the ones who "helped trap the Plaintiff" or "cooperated with his abusers or allowed him to continue his prostitution activities." Plaintiff's brief, last two pages.

The plaintiff appears to be making two due process claims against the defendant Hoch. In 1989-90 criminal charges were brought against the plaintiff. He now alleges that Officer Hoch told the judge at the preliminary hearing that Bonacci had made some statements at the time of his arrest. Bonacci Deposition 967:12-23, 969:1-20, filing 205. Bonacci does not know and is unable to describe the contents or the subject matter of Hoch's comments, but thinks that he would not have been held in jail if Hoch had not made reference to a statement. How that is a denial of a constitutional right of due process has not been explained. Bonacci did later enter a guilty plea to three counts of sexual assault on a child. ***Id.*** 1322:1-1323:4; 1713:2-1716:12. The second claim relates to an investigation by Officer Hoch of claims made by the plaintiff against a number of Omaha citizens, alleging an involvement in child abuse and other crimes. The plaintiff alleges that Hoch told the plaintiff that if he did not take back what he had said about Peter Citron and Larry King and told these things to a grand jury, the grand jury would indict him for perjury. He says he felt threatened by Hoch's request that he take back what he had said about Peter Citron and Larry King. He also charges that Hoch did not make a good effort to understand multiple personality disorder. *Id.* 1113:7-1120:4; 970:17-971:7.

Bonacci testified that Officer Hoch spent many hours with him at the Omaha Correctional Facility to obtain information with which to investigate Bonacci's claims of child abusers and molesters. *Id.* 971:23-972:12. Officer Hoch drove him around Omaha to identify locations of illegal activity and Bonacci knew that police officers had contacted several of his friends. *Id.* 976:7-12.

On June 26, 1990, about four months after Hoch last spoke with plaintiff the plaintiff did testify before the grand jury. He was indicted for perjury. Defendants' Exhibit A, Indictment, filing 204.[3] The evidence does not suggest that he somehow has been damaged by Hoch's saying that if he testified, he would be indicted for perjury. It can be taken for granted that Hoch did not control the grand jury.

The evidence does not show a failure on the part of the defendants to provide due process of law.

There evidently is also a claim that the "police" are responsible for loss of some pages of the plaintiff's diary. The declaration at paragraph 11 says:

> "Police searched my grandmother's home and seized my personal belongings. The police took a diary of mine. When I saw it again several pages had been removed. In the diary I indicated meetings with child abusers and attendance at sex parties."

That statement does not point at any of the defendants and, if it had, it would not have constituted a constitutional violation, but, at most, a claim under state law for conversion or negligence. *See also,* Deposition of Bonacci, p. 431, filing 205.

B. EQUAL PROTECTION

The plaintiff's equal protection claim asserts that he is in a class of persons of abused and

---

[3] No evidence of the indictment's being dismissed has been presented to me, but I am confident that it was dismissed. The plaintiff's brief says that it was dismissed by the Douglas County prosecutors in 1991.

neglected children. As to the defendants Hoch and Wadman, the only kind of conspiracy that can be considered to have been claimed in Counts III and IV under 42 U.S.C. § 1985 is in subparagraph (3). As to it, the Court in ***Bray v. Alexandria Women's Health Clinic***, 506 U.S. 263 (1993), said:

> "Our precedents establish that in order to prove a private conspiracy in violation of the first clause of § 1985 (3), a plaintiff must show, *inter alia,* (1) that 'some racial, or perhaps otherwise class-based, invidiously discriminatory animus [lay] behind the conspirators' action,' ***Griffin v. Breckenridge***, 403 U.S. 88, 102 (1971), and (2) that the conspiracy 'aimed at interfering with rights' that are 'protected against private, as well as official, encroachment,' ***Carpenters v. Scott***, 463 U.S. 825, 833 (1983). . . ."

Id. at 267-68.

The Court in ***Bray*** also said:

> "Our discussion in ***Carpenters*** [***supra***] makes clear that it does not suffice for application of § 1985(3) that a protected right be incidentally affected. A conspiracy is not 'for the purpose' of denying equal protection simply because it has an effect upon a protected right. The right must be '*aimed at,*' 463 U.S., at 833 (emphasis added); its impairment must be a conscious objective of the enterprise. Just as the 'invidiously discriminatory animus' requirement, discussed above, requires that the defendant have taken his action 'at least in part "because of," not merely "in spite of," its adverse effects upon an identifiable group,' ***Feeney,*** 442 U.S., at 279, so also the 'intent to deprive of a right' requirement demands that the defendant do more than merely be aware of a deprivation of right that he causes, and more than merely acceptance; he must act at least in part for the very purpose of producing it. . . ."

Id. at 275-76.

What "invidiously discriminatory animus" that is "class based" is not identified in Count IV. Count III, to which Count IV references, points to a group of young males for prostitution as the "class" involved. I have no reason to think that a group of young male prostitutes are within the term "otherwise class based" mentioned in ***Bray***. It may be a group of victims, as pleaded, but that does not bring it within the purview of Section 1985.

It is fair to say that the United States Supreme Court has denied protection to all non-racial classes it has addressed. The Court of Appeals for the Eighth Circuit, on the other hand, has extended protection to classes other than those racially based, but thus far each such case has involved a conspiracy to strip of equal protection of the laws a member of a traditionally disadvantaged class. For example, ***see Action v. Gannon,*** 450 F.2d 1227 (8th Cir. 1971); ***Conroy v. Conroy***, 575 F.2d 175 (8th Cir. 1978); and ***Shortbull v. Looking Elk***, 677 F.2d 645 (8th Cir.) ***cert. denied*** 459 U.S. 907, 103 S.Ct. 211 (1982). Persons who are young male prostitutes, even those held into the group against their will by threats and physical force, are not traditionally disadvantaged persons. Victims, yes; traditionally disadvantaged, no.

Whatever interpretation of Section 1985(3) is given, there is no evidence of a conspiracy to which the defendants Wadman or Hoch was tied. Without evidence of a conspiracy involving these defendants, or one of them, there can be no cause of action against them under Count IV, which is limited to conspiracy, or under that part of Count III that asserts conspiracy.

IT THEREFORE IS ORDERED that (1) the declaration of plaintiff Paul A. Bonacci, shall be filed by the clerk, and (2) the defendants' motion for summary judgment, filed on behalf of the defendants City of Omaha, Robert Wadman, and Michael Hoch, filing 203, is granted as to all claims.

Dated June 11, 1997.

BY THE COURT

Warren K. Urbom

United States Senior District Judge

Bush & MKULTRA Satanic killer who Bush pardoned while Governor, BOTH in same cult in '80s

author: repost

Bush covers up likely MKULTRA issues. Plus, Bush himself has been associated with mass murder Satan cult rings at Brownsville, Texas. And this connects him to the very person he "pardoned" while governor of Texas--Henry Lee Lucas, for ritualized killings and cannibalism. They both were associated with Brownsville, TX, cults.

Bush's Wild Years: in the 1980s, Bush and serial killer Henry Lee Lucas in TX Satan cult, George W. Bush investigated for six months for mass murder of 17 people who were skinned in the cult--until VP Poppy Bush told then to drop the case.

"Bush, telling reporters and critics to 'stick to the issues that matter', Republican presidential candidate George W. Bush declined to answer questions Monday concerning his alleged involvement in a 1984 Brownsville, TX, mass murder, in which 17 people were ritualistically murdered and skinned. 'I will not stoop to discussing that,' said Bush....

Bush, the son of a billioniare, was strangely living in the most impoverished place in America, Brownsville. Bush was living nearby to and also inside the headquarters of a Satanic Cult of which he was a member. Bush disappeared for three days during which ALL of the other of his fellow Cult Members were slaughtered. After he reappeared he could not explain where he had been.

The local prosecutor continued to pursue Bush, sole Cult survivor, on mass murder charges for six months thereafter, heavily pressured by Daddy Bush to stop the investigation.

Bush nationalizes principles learned in Brownsville, Texas, Satan cult in '80s

BrutalProof!

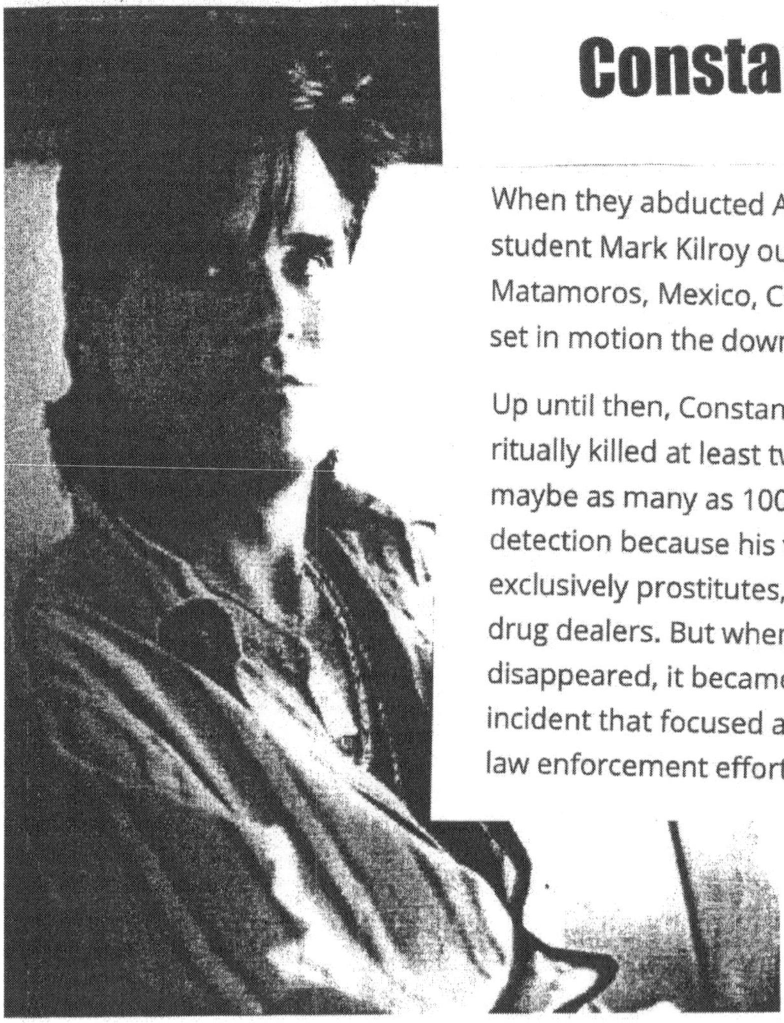

Constanzo

When they abducted American college student Mark Kilroy outside a bar in Matamoros, Mexico, Constanzo inadvertently set in motion the downfall of his bizarre cult.

Up until then, Constanzo and his cult had ritually killed at least twenty people, and maybe as many as 100. He had escaped detection because his victims were almost exclusively prostitutes, homeless people and drug dealers. But when Mark Kilroy disappeared, it became an international incident that focused attention on Mexican law enforcement efforts.

Mark Kilroy

Rense.com

Middle-Finger News - Updated Bush Details

Sticking It To The Poobahs
News Hot Enough To Fry Radio Stations

Accused Mass-Murderer Became President!

By Sherman H. Skolnick and Lenny Bloom
www.cloakanddagger.ca
www.skolnicksreport.com
www.rense.com/Datapages/skolnickdatapage.html
7-15-4

The following is an item from Sunnyvale Ca. from the 2000 election.

"**SUNNYVALE, CA** - Telling reporters and critics to 'stick to the issues that matter', Republican presidential candidate George W. Bush declined to answer questions Monday concerning his alleged involvement in a 1984 Brownsville, TX, mass murder, in which 17 people were ritualistically murdered and skinned.

'I will not stoop to discussing that,' said Bush during a campaign stop at a Bay Area software-packaging plant. 'We've got people across this country without health care, a broken educational system, taxes that are way too high, and all you want to talk about is something THAT MAY OR MAY NOT HAVE HAPPENED 16 years ago? I'm sorry, but I find that offensive.' " (Emphasis added).

Bush, the son of a billioniare, was strangely living in the most impoverished place in America, Brownsville; living nearby to and also inside the headquarters of a Satanic Cult of which he was a member. Bush disappeared for three days during which ALL of the other of his fellow Cult Members were slaughtered. After he reappeared he could not explain where he had been. The local prosecutor continued to pursue Bush, sole Cult survivor, on mass murder charges for six months thereafter, heavily pressured by Daddy Bush to stop the investigation. For asking these questions the reporters were threatened with reprisals later by Bush and thereafter have feared for their life. Currently, as to 2004, Bush and Kerry have long been members of a Satanic Cult, Skull & Bones (Yale).

MORE DETAILS

Following the attempted assassination of President Ronald W. Reagan, ahortly after his inauguration, 1981, George Herbert Walker Bush, as Vice President, on a day to day basis, until the end of Reagan's second term, 1988, actually ran the White House. In 1988, Daddy Bush was himself elected President, actually Bush's third term.

In so doing, the elder Bush was violating the U.S. Constitution, 22nd Amendment, restricting the President to two terms.

During that time, and even before, Daddy Bush and son George W. Bush, had financial and satantic cult links with the drug trafficking from Colombia through the Brownsville/Matamoros area. Brownsville is in the U.S. right smack on the Mexican border above Matamoros, Mexico.

At one time Daddy Bush owned Texas Commerce Bank implicated in the drug traffic through their branch in Venezuela. That unit, starting about 1979, was run by Jeb Bush living in Venezuela with his latino wife. They laundered the drug proceeds from Colombia and from there, through Mexico to the U.S. The Bush Crime Family has for many years been business partners with the co-founder of the Medelin, Colombia drug cartel, Carlos Lehder. [See, the website series, www.skolnicksreport.com "The Chandra Levy Affair".]

This was convenient to Daddy Bush having been with the CIA since 1959, through their adjunct, principally owned by the Bushies, Zapata Petroleum, later called Zapata Offshore, still later their interests joined with Pennzoil which by an induced bankruptcy took over Texaco. [See, "Oil & Honor--- The Texaco-Pennzoil Wars" by Thomas Petzinger, Jr., 1987, G.P. Putnam's Sons.]

The satanic cult mass-murders revolved around in the Brownsville/Matamoros area. Among those involved were El Padrino Cult; and located outside Matamoros, Rancho Santa Elena, having human sacrifice chambers; and the satanic ritual sacrifices and mind control conducted by Aldolfo De Jesus Costanzo with others. The Bush Crime Family with their dope trafficking, Colombia through Matamoros, Mexico/Brownsville, Texas, were interlocked with these situations.

The ranch was reportedly involved in snuffing out dozens and dozens of primarily latinos useful as "mules" in the drug trade and controlled through sexual satanic rituals and mind-control.

In the 1980s, Daddy Bush, actually running the White House, and former head of the American secret political police, was in perfect position to be part of the drug trafficking. The elder Bush was the head of the South Florida Anti-Drug Project, supposedly clamping down on drug trafficking from Colombia to Mexico.

During the 1980s, U.S. drug enforcement was near totally compromised and corrupted. A huge, heavy opus, mentioned in a moment, tells how the top people in the elite units of U.S. drug enforcement actually worked the other side. From time to time, they went to parties at palacial estates in Mexico and elsewhere owned and operated by the major druglords. The drug police rubbed elbows there with movie stars and bigshots from Hollywood, users as well as traffickers with dope. [In recent years. George W. Bush, William Rockefeller Clinton, and Mexico President Vicente Fox have visited and stayed at the estates of Mexico's major druglords.]

For naive, poorly informed persons to risk their neck reporting druglords to the drug police is both tragic and laughable. [See that very thick book about the top drug enforcers, being for sale and totally corrupt, "The Underground Empire---Where Crime and Government Embrace", by James Mills, Doubleday, N.Y., 1986.]

One of those convicted of the satantic cult mass murders in the Brownsville/Matamoros region and elsewhere was a fellow named Lucas. When George W. Bush was Governor of Texas, he mysteriously granted clemency to this mass-murderer. Yet, there was no basis in law or fact for the Governor to so favor Lucas, other than the Bush Crime Family was in business with him in respect to the drug trafficking and satanic cult operations of the Brownsville/Matamoros region.

With terrible-to-look-at pictures, the horrors of the one or more satanic cults so operating in the Brownsville/Matamoros region are detailed in a little-known, hard to locate book, "Hell Ranch" by Clifford Linedecker.

By 1999, some reporters had attempted to question George W. Bush as to some of the foregoing, while Bush was planning to run for President in the U.S. 2000 Election. As the head of an investigative group and Founder/Chairman, since 1963 of the Citizen's Committee to Clean Up the Courts, Skolnick began relating, on various radio talk shows, the problems the reporters were having in confronting George W. Bush with his apparent complicity in the satanic cult mass murders in the Brownsville, Texas area.

Quite some time thereafter, several websites did acts in some ways relating to all this. They palmed off as apparent jokes and parodies, purported stories about the Brownsville/Matamoros horrors. Whether their purpose was reputed damage control for the Bush Crime Family or to simply somehow make jokes about the satanic mass murders, remains for such website handlers and operators to explain.

These websites apparently gave the impression to poorly-informed, naive people that the whole series of events in the Brownsville/Matamoros region were purely imaginary, and never occurred and there was no complicity of the Bushies including George W. Bush.

Obviously to detail all the persons and entities involved with the satanic cultists, human sacrifice locations, and drug-traffickers and mind-control dictators, in the Matamoros/Brownsville region would and could fill a series of encyclopedias on the dope business, satanic cults, corrupted dope enforcers, and related topics.

[A book that does go into many related details is "The Strength of the Wolf---The Secret History of America's War on Drugs" by Douglas Valentine, Verso Books, 2004, New York. The American CIA needs the druglords to be able to penetrate otherwise hard to spy on nations, is a theme of the book.]

[Loads of details of the Bush Crime Family are in the extensive website series, "The Overthrow of the American Republic", www.skolnicksreport.com with two linked sites.]

IS GEORGE W. BUSH's current opponent for President, JOHN F. KERRY different than Bush? Both are satanic cultists, members of Skull & Bastards Society.

Knowledgeable sources contend that concealed, in part, by Kerry's divorce from his first wife and his silence about his episodes in England, are some horrors equal to the foregoing. With the help of entertainers, Kerry in London, England, reportedly engaged in sexual perversions with 13 year old girls and even with those much younger; with Kerry somehow complicit in porno snuff rituals. That is, where after the weirdo event, the victim, whether three years old or thirteen, becomes a human sacrifice, and is killed on camera. This type of thing originally was a specialty from Argentina. Will the newsfakers ever ask Kerry to explain?

Love for Humanity
"You're beautiful!"
LOVE
After Meditation

Recovery Plan For USA

1. Reinstate FDR's Glass-Steagall to protect us from bankster bailins/outs
2. Create Nat'l Credit Bank for large infrastructure projects (China & Russia are already doing this with AIIB)
3. Fusion development for greater energy-flux-density & desalination
4. Abraham's Greenbacks-we don't need to pay interest on debt when we are supposed to be printing our own money
5. Explore TESLA TECHNOLOGY OF FREE ENERGY
6. Government can help fund small, organic farmers with seeds, equipment and training

rense.com

Edgar Cayce - 'Russia - The Hope Of The World'

By Jeff Rense
7-14-8

The readings of America's greatest psychic remain an extraordinary body of data which often stagger the reader with its prescience and projections of future events. Many years ago, during the cold war, I remember reading about how Cayce claimed - while in one of his self-induced trance sessions - some remarkable things about Russia.

Today, much of the world views Russia and the brilliant leadership of Vladimir Putin as the only hope of stopping the malignant and deadly spread of
world zionism. The signing of the new Russian-Iranian strategic gas and oil agreement on Sunday, July 13, further seems to underscore that any attack on Iran may bring Russia directly and immediately into the conflict on the side of peace and the preservation of a free and independent Middle East and - some would argue by extension - the world.

The following two excerpts from Edgar Cayce readings are quite extraordinary by any measure.

FIRST -

In this first short example, Cayce - in the 1930s - indicated the 'sins' of the key nations:

America - has forgotten "in God we trust"
England - conceit

France - lust
China - isolationism
India - internalization of knowledge
Italy - dissensions

He said "Russia will become beacons of hope for the world." The statement about the 'conceit' (of the Zionist London Banksters?) in England is extraordinary. Just look at the Zionist conquest of Europe under the EU. The comment about America having forgotten "in God we Trust" is beyond eerily accurate. Remember, these statements were made in the 1930s

SECOND -

In this, more detailed account of his prowess, Cayce makes a number of nearly breathtaking projections -

Cayce predicted the beginning and end of both the First and Second World Wars, and the lifting of the Depression in 1933. In the 1920s, he first warned of coming racial strife in the United States, and in 1939 he predicted the deaths of two presidents in office;

"Ye are to have turmoils -- ye are to have strife between capital and labor. Ye are to have a division in thy own land, before ye have the second of the Presidents that next will not live through his office... a mob rule!"

President Franklin D. Roosevelt died in office in April 1945. In November 1963, President John F. Kennedy was assassinated in Dallas, Texas, when racial tensions in the United States were at their height.

"Unless there is more give and take and consideration for those who produce, with better division of the excess profits from labor, there must be greater turmoil in the land."

In October 1935, Cayce spoke of the coming war in Europe. The Austrians and Germans, he said, and later the Japanese, would take sides.

"Thus, an unseen force, gradually growing, must result in an almost direct opposition to the Nazi, or Aryan theme. This will gradually produce a growth of animosities. And unless there is interference by what many call supernatural forces and influences -- which are active in the affairs of nations and peoples -- the whole world as it were... will be set on fire by militaristic groups and people who are for power expansion."

(This 'unseen force' is clearly the Zionist banking cartel and its forcing the US into WWII against Germany via the chicanery of FDR and the London and Wall Street Zionist banksters. Few remember that the Bolshevik Communist Zionist Jews were within a few weeks of a massive invasion of Germany and all of Europe when Hitler beat them to the punch with Operation Barbarosa, hoping to destroy Communism/Bolshevism once and for all.)

Through Russia, Cayce said "comes the hope of the world. Not in respect to what is sometimes termed Communism or Bolshevism -- no! But freedom -- freedom! That each man will live for his fellow man. The principle has been born there. It will take years for it to be crystallized; yet out of Russia comes again the hope of the world."

Cayce also predicted the possibility of a THIRD World War. He spoke of strifes arising..."in Libya, and in Egypt, in Ankara, and in Syria; through the straits around those areas above the Persian Gulf."

Later on, when asked in June 1943 whether it would be feasible to work towards an equitable international world currency or a stabilization of international exchange levels when the war (WW II) had ended, Cayce replied that it would be a long, long time before this would happen. Indeed, he said, "there may be another war (WW III) over just such conditions."

It does not get much more clear than that. The final paragraph from 1943 points to the world financial criminal cartel, doubtless the City of London banking and financial controllers, preventing the true and equitable stabilization of world economics after WWII ended. Today's 'exchange levels' are being set by the world's 'currency' masters - the oil and energy and banking cartels - and the control and manipulation of it all by this now not so 'unseen' force.

Cayce was peerless in his visions, and it appears that Mr. Putin and Russia are standing in the breach in terms of preventing, for the moment, the 'unseen force' (world Zionism) from taking total control of the West.

Russia is the only obstacle ('the hope of the world') to that, and the Bush/Cheney/Zionist cabal is unarguably attempting to force Russia into a war with the phony Bush protect-Europe-from-Iran 'missile shield' in Eastern Europe deployment efforts. Russia is now saying it will respond 'militarily' to such a deployment.

Putin For President!

- **GMO's Banned!**
- **Supports Organic Farming!**
- **Wipes Out Terrorism!**
- **No Illegal Immigration!**
- **Prosecutes Financial Criminals!**
- **Jails Banksters and Oligarchs!**
- **Arrest Warrant for Soros! (Mr. Evil)**
- **Guards His Borders!**
- **Builds Infrastructure!**
- **Protects His People!**
- **Puts His Country First!**
- **Works With BRICs Nations!**

BrutalProof!

"

The Pacific Ocean is broad enough to accommodate the development of both China and the United States, and for our two countries to work together to contribute to security in Asia. These are mutually complementary efforts instead of mutually exclusive ones. China and the U.S. should continue to enhance dialogue and coordination on Asia Pacific affairs, and respect and accommodate each other's interests and concerns in this region, and develop inclusive coordination....

We welcome the active participation of the United States and other relevant countries so that together we can promote and share prosperity and peace in Asia Pacific. China is ready to work with the United States to make efforts in a number of priority areas and putting into effect such principles as non-confrontation, non-conflict, mutual respect, and win-win cooperation. And with unwavering spirit and unremitting efforts, we will promote new progress in building a new model of major-country relations between the two countries, so as to bring greater benefits to our two peoples and two countries.

Chinese President Xi Jinping
Beijing, China · November 12, 2014
Joint Press Conference with President Obama

LAROUCHE | PAC

Lyndon LaRouche Political Action Committee
larouchepac.com facebook.com/larouchepac @larouchepac

A New International Order for Mankind

WHY THE UNITED STATES MUST JOIN THE BRICS

Table of Contents

Cover Image: Roberto Stuckert Filho, Agência Brasil

INTRODUCTION

LaRouche: There Are Only Two Alternatives for Mankind

The following is a transcription of remarks made by Lyndon LaRouche on December 1, 2014.

The United States' establishment under its Constitution is unique. There is nothing in the rest of the world which corresponds to the intention of the U.S. Federal Constitution. We are an entity of our own making, our own type, as contrasted with practically every other nation on the planet.

But what has happened is, there's been a change in the process, a global change, that the United States is now, essentially, ruined by bad Presidents, especially the past two sets of Presidencies. What we need to do is return the United States *to being the United States* in its original Constitutional form. We don't need to make any changes from that principle.

But now, the rest of the world is a little bit different: What you have, for example, with the role of Russia, and its relationship to the BRICS formation. What's happened is, that large nations, and to some degree smaller ones, as opposed to Europe in general, have emerged as major forces. That is, those nations as a group, represent a power, one of the greatest powers on the planet, in terms of political power. And that power is growing. What China's doing, for example, in terms of space, in terms of the development of the organization of the space system, within Johannes Kepler's specifications, that's unique.

So, we have to recognize that the United States is actually a *very large* part in its own right of what the new world order ought to be. But right now, we have a collection of nation-state systems which are very large, and they vastly outnumber us.

What's happening with the British Empire's role, is, we were creating a pseudo-world system, and that's what the problem is. If we in the United States get rid of Obama and the Bushes and so forth, get rid of that kind of filthy government, then we can readily come into a certain kind of accord with these other nations which dominate the planet right now, which essentially are the dominant features of the planet, in Asia, in South America, and so forth.

So therefore, what we want to do, is we want to clean up our mess at home. But we have to also find out, how are we going to relate to these BRICS-types of nations; how are we going to relate to the Russia-China agreement, and so forth; how are we going to take all these large entities which will largely dominate the planet, and *include* the United States, as a very important element of that combination of nation-states? And that's what we have to do.

Therefore, we have to clean up the United States, to return it to its principle, get *rid* of all this stuff, like what the present Republicans seem to be doing right now—get rid of that! Get rid of Obama. Get rid of that stuff! And once we do, we simply have to reestablish the principle of the national Union.

Because we will find then, that what will happen, is we will be a relative minority on the planet, relative to the large complexes such as in South America, what will come up in Africa eventually, what will happen in Eurasia generally. And Europe, old Europe, and so forth, will be small: the United States will be a very large entity, but not the biggest entity on the planet politically or otherwise.

A New Conception of Sovereignty

So we're going to have to come to a new arrangement in which we have *a new conception of what national sovereignty is.* That question has not been posed clearly, as far as I can see, thus far. It's important that we *foresee* where we're going, or where we should be going. And that's my concern. From my standpoint, I can see clearly where the United States must be going right now.

Just simply take this new arrangement, which is not a simple sovereignty. It is something new. It is not the

Lyndon LaRouche has provided the intellectual and political leadership in the fight for a new international economic order for the planet. The profound impact of LaRouche's leadership is clearly reflected in the current actions being taken by the BRICS and others to create a new global financial architecture and strategic alliance among nations.

old notion of sovereignty. It's a notion of a certain characteristic right of people, to have their own government, their own system, and to have these systems of government, the new systems typified by the BRICS, to come into concert with the United States under what I've been pushing for now: And let it flow!

Because we're going to find that, as is shown to us by what is being done by China in its space program, in which China has taken steps into nearby space in the direction of Johannes Kepler—we're going to find out that the idea of what a human being is, as opposed to an animal, which is not clear generally, yet, is going to change. What China is doing especially with the space program, is going to *change the way we define the meaning of mankind*, and a lot of other things.

A Peaceful Revolutionary Change

So, just get ready to see those changes, folding into the system we have today. I would say that within maybe a couple of decades at least, to a couple of generations, you'll find that the idea of what mankind is, what sovereignty is and so forth, is going to go through a revolutionary change. But it will be a *peaceful* revolutionary change, and a profitable one.

We just have to proceed step by step, to march in that direction, and to reach the goals which that direction points out.

Lyndon LaRouche also addressed this topic during a discussion which he led on November 29, 2014.

The international system as it has been heretofore, is dying, and there are only two alternatives: general thermonuclear war, or a kind of unity among nations which we see coming out of the BRICS and similar kinds of fora. In other words, the only way that you can maintain society, now, on a global scale, is *on a global scale*. And that means you have to affirm the fact that the nations are all working, very much as Russia and China are. The Russia-China alliance is a measure of what's coming, and we're just a click away from that result.

If you want to be sane, with the bankruptcy of the United States, the bankruptcy of Canada, the bankruptcy of the European nations, the Western European nations—they're all bankrupt! And they're never going to come out of that bankruptcy, as the kinds of nations they've been treated as so far.

What's going to happen is, you're going to have the kind of system which the BRICS represents. The world system will be, in languages and so forth, language practice and so forth, will be somewhat differentiated. But the intention, to be accomplished, of what is to be accomplished, will be more and more unified. Languages will still be used, as such, but the principle, the intention will be unified. You're getting that tendency in South America now. It's much stronger there than other places. The Russia-China relationship is typical of this.

The present system, which dumb Americans believe in still, is dying, and it's waiting to be pushed off the boards, into maybe an empty swimming tank, which would probably make a mess of things. We're going into a new system where mankind will be a unified system, unified in practices, by means of practices which effect that.

There will be a dividing line in which the distinction is clear. You will still have cultures, national cultures, which may be unique and have unique characteristics of their own, but they'll all be part of the same kind of process which is trying to find its general unity.

We are now saying, we're going to a new system. Because we need to have close collaboration with our ally, China, and with other nations, which are close allies, in principle, in intention.

And gradually, we're going to find more and more agreement, more and more integration based on the search for realization of necessary revolutions in practice. And we're going to all be united by the principle of Johannes Kepler.

I. The BRICS: A New International System Has Been Established

The leaders of the BRICS nations appear with Ibero-American heads of state during the Fortaleza Summit in July, 2014.

Whether Americans are aware of it or not, a new international system has been established on this planet, which is now defining the future of the human race. In less than one year, an alliance of nations around the BRICS (Brazil, Russia, India, China, and South Africa) has been created, which has built a parallel economic order with giant steps, one which is dedicated exclusively to the building of the productive economy, in opposition to the current bankrupt trans-Atlantic system of the British Empire, centered on the City of London and Wall Street banks. That bankrupt system is committed to the maximization of speculative monetary profit, and has brought the world to the brink of global economic disintegration and war.

The new system represents a power center based on economic growth, and above all, on leading-edge technologies—a concept of power which belongs to the future, as opposed to preserving the past. It is based on providing credit for high-technology development projects; on educating and training youth to meet the growth challenges of the future; on full respect for national sovereignty, banishing the imperial policy of regime change and war; and on explicit promotion of the common good among nations—the Westphalian principle.

This new system today represents about four billion people, more than half of humanity, and it is being undertaken by the very peoples whom the genocidal advocates of population reduction within the British Empire have slated for extinction. The majority of mankind has stood up to be counted, proclaiming for all the world to hear that the greatest wealth that humanity has, is its own growing population, and their creative minds.

America, are you listening?

A New Global Order

The current world order will not continue to exist in its present form. The future global order is not a mere extension of the present petty geopolitics of narrow nationalistic self-interest and competetion for unilateral control over the planet, but an entirely new ordering of relations among peoples. Mankind must unite as a single creative species to conquer common challenges which face us all, and expand our role and influence throughout the solar system and beyond. National cultures and languages will still be unique and differentiated, but they must converge towards a singleness of intention for a common unified mission.

The ideology of "winner take all" must be replaced with one in which "all are winners," as Chinese President Xi Jinping has so eloquently said.

This mission-orientation defines the BRICS system. Nations which have previously been pulled apart along ethnic or geographical lines by imperial machinations, are now putting differences behind them and establishing an entirely new idea of cooperation for the mutual benefit of all. They are explicitly creating an *inclusive* (as opposed to exclusive) framework of partnership in order to build a new model of relations among nations, one based on the principles of non-confrontation, non-conflict, mutual respect, and win-win cooperation, as the Chinese President has stated.

The United States has been invited by these leaders to be a part of this new system, as opposed to continuing to be the instrument of the dead British Empire vainly seeking to halt the emergence of this new global order. Ironically, the revolution now being effected by the BRICS nations and their allies, is the child of that system which *we* originally fought our own American Revolution against that same British Empire to bring into existence, when our own republic was born.

The True American System

The new system that the BRICS and its allies are building is a modern version of the American System of Political Economy, on which our nation was founded—and yet President Obama remains aggressively opposed to this new system.

Under the war-time propaganda machine of the mass media that Obama and his British Empire controllers have unleashed, we would be led to believe that China is our number one enemy, and that Russia must be crushed through economic sanctions and war. Under the pretext of "democracy" and "human rights," our government is committing acts of aggressive warfare across the planet under the rubric of "colored revolutions" to overthrow the regimes of any nation which fails to acquiesce. Every day, our supposedly free press feeds us enemy images of the Chinese and Russian presidents as "strongmen" with dictatorial and imperialistic ambitions. We are told that for ourselves to survive as a great power on this planet, we must prevent the rise of any other power which would challenge us—precisely the type of geopolitics that led to the First World War one hundred years ago, and now threatens to lead to a third, this time thermonuclear world war.

The United States must radically change its path, if we and the rest of mankind are to survive. The leaders of the BRICS have directly and repeatedly extended their hands of cooperation, offering concrete opportunities for the United States to join this new alliance, while also making very clear that they will defend themselves at all costs and do not intend to surrender in the face of threats and intimidation. We as a nation must force a radical change in the policy of our government and reciprocate these offers of cooperation in the immediate days and weeks ahead—or else face the inevitability of a global war which will threaten human extinction.

Two Opposing Systems

This new system announced itself to the world on July 16, 2014, in Fortaleza, Brazil, when the leaders of the BRICS declared that they were creating a new international economic order with the formation of the New Development Bank—a direct echo of Lyndon LaRouche's idea of an International Development Bank (IDB), which he originally proposed in 1975.[3]

In the days following this announcement, a summit between the BRICS and Unasur (Union of South American Nations), in addition to numerous bilateral meetings with the leaders of Ibero-America, solidly brought South America into the BRICS alliance. The BRICS countries alone represent 43% of the world's total population; when Ibero-America is added in, they represent 48% of the human race, and one-third of the Earth's land area.

At the BRICS summit, Chinese President Xi Jinping summarized the BRICS policy:

> History tells us the law of the jungle isn't the way of human coexistence. Every nation should obey the principle of equality, mutual trust, learning from each other, cooperating and seeking joint benefits... for the construction of a harmonious world, sustained peace, and joint prosperity.

In the course of the summit, Argentine President Cristina Fernández de Kirchner, a close ally of the BRICS, elaborated:

> We are posing a new global financial order, one that is not just fair and equitable, but indispensable... What we demand from the world, is precisely the creation of a new global financial order which will permit sustainable and global economic growth... Thus, the appeal to all nations is to join forces in this real crusade for a new global political, economic and financial organization.

3 *See Appendix: LaRouche's Role in Shaping Current World History*

Lyndon LaRouche summarized the significance of the process that had been unleashed:

> The BRICS and allies are building a world system based on real value, not phony paper value. They are deciding what real value is, and they are imposing it, which is the cost of the productive powers of labor in a changing situation.

The underlying problem that we have to deal with today, LaRouche elaborated, is the "asymmetry of value in the world," which is coming from two distinct systems that are operating with a different logic and different metrics: They are totally incompatible.

The first system is the trans-Atlantic system: "these bastards," LaRouche stated, "who hold pieces of paper that they say are worth quadrillions, and they're prepared to kill for that," as the case of Argentina's battle against the vulture funds attests. This financial paper is absolutely worthless.

On the other side, we have an emerging system, incompatible with the first, which is building a market based on real value. And real value, LaRouche elaborated, comes from, and is measured by, the development of the productive powers of labor—that is, through the introduction of scientifically created new technologies, implementing productive processes which increase the energy-flux density through the physical economy in such fashion as to immensely increase the productive powers of labor. That new system will create a process whereby the increase in energy-flux density will itself increase at an accelerating rate.

New Silk Road Becomes the World Land-Bridge

The orientation of this new international alliance was best expressed by Indian Prime Minister Narendra Modi, when he told the BRICS summit:

> The uniqueness of BRICS as an international institution [is that] for the first time, it brings together a group of nations on the parameter of "future potential," rather than existing prosperity or shared identities. The very idea of BRICS is thus forward-looking... Excellencies, we have an opportunity to define the future—of not just our countries, but the world at large... I take this as a great responsibility.

Russian President Vladimir Putin struck a similar note in comments to the press on July 17, evaluating the results of his trip: "The BRICS are all young states, and the future belongs to the young."

But the Fortaleza summit of the BRICS was merely a crucial inflection point in a process which began a year prior, and has continued to accelerate in the months since.

In September 2013, the newly elected President of China Xi Jinping traveled to Kazakhstan and announced that China was adopting a Eurasian development policy which he called the "New Silk Road Development Belt."

> To forge closer economic ties, deepen cooperation and expand development in the Euro-Asia region, we should take an innovative approach and jointly build an "economic belt" along the Silk Road.

One month later, President Xi traveled to Indonesia to announce the "Maritime Silk Road" policy, as a complement to the Silk Road Development Belt. Then at a summit meeting between Russian President Vladimir Putin and Chinese President Xi on May 20, 2014 in Shanghai, extensive plans for collaboration of the two great powers were signed, including a 30-year natural gas agreement, and 46 additional bilateral accords. They stated that their goals included, among others:

> Increasing the effectiveness of collaboration in high-technology areas, priority projects in the international use of nuclear energy, civil aviation, and a program of cooperation in basic research on space flight, satellite observation of the Earth, satellite navigation, and research into deep space and manned space travel... Russia recognizes the enormous significance of the Chinese initiative for the building of the "Silk Road Economic Belt."

The revolution in the global financial architecture then continued after the July 16, 2014 BRICS summit, at the APEC meeting in Beijing in November. There, President Xi extended his most explicit offer to the United States to join the new system, at a joint press conference with an extremely uncomfortable President Obama.

> We welcome the active participation of the United States and other relevant countries, so that together we can promote and share prosperity and peace in Asia Pacific.[4]

At the APEC summit, another half dozen nations joined the BRICS revolution, bringing another half billion people into the new architecture. Some four billion people have now been swept up in that new dynamic.

America, are you listening?

4 See full quote from Xi Jinping on inside front cover of this pamphlet

WHAT YOU NEED TO KNOW:

NEW INTERNATIONAL FINANCIAL ARCHITECTURE

A new financial architecture has been formed among the BRICS nations along with an extensive network of other countries who now are gaining access to credit for development that has been denied to them for decades by the International Monetary Fund and World Bank. With the creation by the BRICS of a parallel economic order to rival these formerly hegemonic global financial institutions, the IMF's regime of usurious loans and murderous conditionalities is no longer the only game in town. Great infrastructure and development projects that have been on the books for years are already blossoming across the planet, nourished by the productive credit being provided by the array of institutions that have been created by the BRICS over the past six months.

A purely Hamiltonian approach to credit is governing the establishment of this new financial order, with a whole raft of new credit institutions that have been established since the BRICS revolution. These new institutions include:

- **The BRICS New Development Bank (NDB)**
  - Officially agreed to at the BRICS summit in Fortaleza, Brazil in July 2014
  - Financing infrastructure and development projects in BRICS and other developing nations
  - Headquartered in Shanghai, China with the first rotating presidency held by India
  - Initial authorized capital of $100 billion, with an initial subscribed capital of $50 billion
  - Initial capitalization to be equally shared among the bank's founding members
- **The BRICS Contingent Reserve Arrangement (CRA)**
  - Officially adopted at the Fortaleza summit of the BRICS in July 2014
  - Initial captial of the Contingent Reserve Agreement will be $100 billion
  - Intended aim to "help countries forestall short-term liquidity pressures"
- **The Asian Infrastructure Investment Bank (AIIB)**
  - First proposed by President Xi Jinping during his trip to Indonesia in October 2013
  - Officially founded on October 24, 2014 with twenty-one founding members
  - Plans to begin infrastructure investment operations by the end of 2014
  - Issuing credit of $50-100 billion annually for major infrastructure projects based in Asia
- **The New Silk Road Fund**
  - Financing for projects related to the New Silk Road Economic Belt across Eurasia
  - China has announced plans to provide up to $60 billion for infrastructure projects
  - Also announced plans to establish a Marine Silk Road Bank for maritime development
- **The Development Bank of the SCO**
  - A development bank specifically for Shanghai Cooperation Organization (SCO) members
  - Finalized on September 12, 2014 at the annual summit of the SCO in Dushanbe, Tajikistan
- **The Sino-Latin American-Caribbean Cooperation Fund**
  - Sino-Latin American-Caribbean Cooperation Fund of $5 billion for investment in development
  - Discussed at the July 17, 2014 meeting of CELAC with Chinese President Xi Jinping
  - Scheduled to become operational by 2015, plus numerous other financing offers
  - Plus additional fund to finance infrastructure, starting at $10 billion and rising to $20 billion
  - Offers of preferential credit line for CELAC from a Chinese bank as well, as large as $10 billion

BRICS LAUNCH GLOBAL DEVELOPMENT

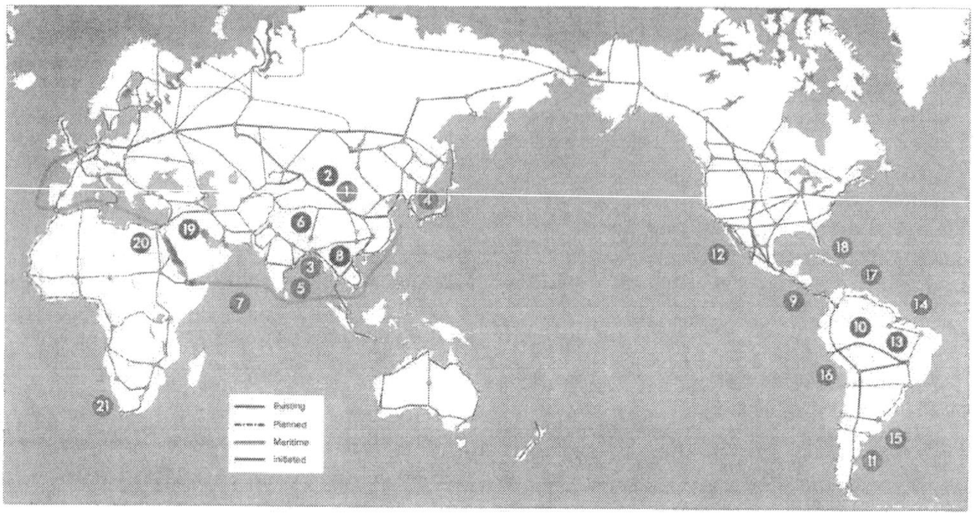

The BRICS revolution has unleashed a veritable explosion of agreements on new major infrastructure projects which, taken as a whole, constitute a fulcrum for lifting the entire planet onto a new trajectory of development. This map presents selected highlights from among those projects, which are proceeding at a dizzying pace:

EURASIA

1 China-Russia New Silk Road Development

In September 2013, President Xi Jinping announced the New Silk Road Development Belt to develop Eurasia. This policy has also been endorsed by Russia. At a joint summit with President Putin in May 2014, the two heads of state issued a joint communiqué, stating: "Russia recognizes the enormous significance of the Chinese initiative for the building of the Silk Road Economic Belt." Xi Jinping and Putin also signed a $400 billion, 30-year agreement for Russia to supply natural gas to China.

2 China-Russia Rail, Nuclear, Space Cooperation

Russian Railways has announced negotiations with Chinese companies to construct a high-speed rail line between Moscow and Kazan, as part of the Eurasian High-Speed Corridor. Russia's Rosatom nuclear company has signed a Memorandum of Understanding with China on the joint development of floating nuclear power plant technologies. The two nations have also reached agreements for cooperation on flood-control on the Amur River, and on exchange of visits to their respective international space stations.

3 China-India Joint Economic Projects

During his state visit to India in September 2014, Chinese President Xi Jinping concluded more than ten significant economic deals with Indian Prime Minister Narendra Modi, and pledged to settle long-standing border disputes. Among the projects is collaboration in nuclear science, particularly in developing thorium-fueled nuclear reactors. China is working on a pebble-bed solid fuel 100-MW demonstrator reactor to be completed by 2024. Talks also took place on the Bangladesh-China-India-Myanmar trade corridor, which would link the Indian port of Kolkata with Kunming, Yunnan's capital.

4 Russia-N. Korea-S. Korea Development Project

On July 18, 2014, Russian, North Korean, and South Korean officials opened the port of Rajin, a state-of-the-art port, built by Russia, connecting to the recently completed rail line from Rajin, North Korea to Russia. China and South Korea also signed a Free Trade Agreement at the APEC summit in November.

5 India-Japan High-Speed Rail

Indian Prime Minister Modi on September 1, 2014 signed an agreement with Prime Minister Abe in Tokyo, whereby India will receive Japanese financial, technical, and operational support to build bullet trains.

6 India-Nepal Hydropower Accord

On September 19, 2014, India and Nepal signed an agreement for the Indian company GMR to construct a 900-MW hydropower project on the Karnali River in Nepal.

SOUTH AND SOUTHEAST ASIA

7 China-ASEAN Maritime Silk Road and AIIB

On August 10, 2014 the ASEAN foreign ministers met in Myanmar, along with representatives of China, India, Russia, the United States, the EU, Japan, South Korea, and Australia. China and ASEAN reached an agreement to deepen their strategic partnership, including joint work on China's 21st Century Maritime Silk Road, as well as projects in the Mekong River development area.

China also welcomed all ten ASEAN nations to join in the Asian Infrastructure Investment Bank (AIIB) as founding members. Thailand has already accepted that invitation, as has Indonesia.

8 Singapore-China Economic Corridor

Planning sessions are underway for a rail, highway, and development corridor from Nanning and Kunming in China, going south through the Indochina peninsula, connecting China, Vietnam, Laos, Cambodia, Thailand, Malaysia, and Singapore.

IBERO-AMERICA

9 Nicaragua-China Inter-Oceanic Canal

Nicaraguan President Daniel Ortega has announced the route of the Great Inter-Oceanic Canal connecting the Pacific and the Caribbean, which will allow the passage of large ships currently unable to fit through the Panama Canal. Top Chinese water management, rail, aviation, and port design companies are partners in the project.

10 Brazil-Bolivia-Peru-China Transcontinental Railroad

China, Brazil, and Peru have agreed to initiate feasibility studies on the construction of a transcontinental rail line linking Brazil's Atlantic coast with Peru's Pacific coast. Bolivia has also asked China for help in developing the Bolivian portion of an alternative transcontinental rail route Brazil-Bolivia-Peru.

Peruvian President Ollanta Humala has also met with President Putin and received offers of Russian help to construct a trans-Andean rail tunnel, which will dramatically shorten travel time from the coast to the interior of the country, and aid the construction of a transcontinental rail link across South America.

11 Argentina-Russia Nuclear Cooperation

During his state visit to Argentina on July 12, 2014, Russian President Putin signed energy, aerospace, agriculture, communications, and military cooperation agreements with President Cristina Fernández de Kirchner. On nuclear energy, Rosatom has submitted a proposal to participate in the construction of Argentina's Atucha III nuclear plant.

12 Mexico-China Rail Projects

After attending the November APEC summit in Beijing, Mexican President Enrique Peña Nieto met with China's Xi Jinping and signed agreements totaling $7.4 billion, including funding for rail and energy projects. Among the rail projects China is bidding to participate in are:

a) a trans-Isthmus industrial corridor, connecting the ports of Coatzacoalcos on the Gulf of Mexico and Salina Cruz on the Pacific;

b) a high-speed rail line from Mexico City to Querétaro, the first in all Ibero-America; and,

c) a Nayarit-Chihuahua-New Mexico rail project, to link Mexico's west coast, through a new deep water port to be built in Nayari, to the U.S. rail grid.

13 Brazil-China Scientific & Military Cooperation

In a July 17, 2014 meeting, Presidents Xi and Brazil's Dilma Rousseff consolidated a "truly strategic partnership," deepening their space cooperation, including joint satellite work with Africa; the sale of Brazilian jets to China; intensified scientific and educational exchanges; and Chinese construction of Brazil's Rio Tapajos hydroelectric project.

14 Brazil-Russia Trade, Military, Nuclear Cooperation

In a July 14, 2014 meeting in Brasilia, Presidents Putin and Rousseff signed seven bilateral agreements including an anti-air defense system; an agreement to expand facilities for Russia's GLONASS satellite navigation system in Brazil; and an MoU to expand bilateral cooperation in nuclear power.

15 Argentina-China Infrastructure Cooperation

During his July 18-21, 2014 visit to Argentina, President Xi signed nineteen agreements with President Fernández in the areas of nuclear energy, infrastructure, communications, transportation, and agriculture. They included $2 billion in preferential financing for Argentina's fourth nuclear reactor, the 760-MW Atucha III; and an $11 billion currency swap agreement between the two central banks, part of which has already been disbursed.

16 Bolivia-Russia Nuclear & Development Cooperation

On July 16, 2014, Russian President Putin offered to cooperate with Bolivia for the development of a "comprehensive nuclear energy program" for peaceful purposes. Chinese President Xi offered assistance to Bolivian President Morales in building Bolivia's second satellite.

17 Venezuela-China Economic & Energy Cooperation:

During President Xi Jinping's July 22, 2014 visit to Caracas, Venezuela, the two countries signed 38 bilateral accords in the context of the "comprehensive strategic alliance" between them.

18 Cuba-Russia-China Cooperation

On July 11, 2014, President Putin signed ten agreements with the Cuban government, including the modernization of the port of Mariel, and exploration for offshore oil deposits.

Chinese President Xi Jinping visited Cuba July 23-24, 2014, and signed twenty-nine agreements for energy, transportation, science, agriculture, telecommunications, and infrastructure development, including a credit line for construction of a multi-purpose terminal at the port of Santiago de Cuba.

AFRICA

19 Egypt's New Suez Canal

On August 5, 2014, Egyptian President Abdel Fattah el-Sisi announced the construction of a second Suez canal, which will run parallel to the existing canal, and double its capacity. The 45-mile canal will be dug in just one year. The overall project includes the development of the canal corridor, including new ports and industrial and economic zones along the canal. Russia has agreed to establish an industrial zone as part of the project. Six tunnels under the canal, with four designated for road traffic and two for railways, will be built at an estimated cost of $8 billion. The completion of these tunnels will be key to developing the rail and road links between Africa and Eurasia. The project has been entirely financed by issuing domestic bonds, denominated in Egyptian pounds and sold only to Egyptians.

20 Egypt-Russia Nuclear Cooperation

Following the meeting between Russian President Putin and Egyptian President Abdel Fattah el-Sisi in Sochi, Russia, on August 12, 2014, at which they discussed Egypt establishing trade agreements with the Eurasian Customs Union, Putin also expressed readiness to support Egypt's construction of a nuclear power plant at Dabaa. President el-Sisi had met with Chinese Foreign Minister Wang Yi on August 3, 2014, who transmitted a message from President Xi Jinping inviting Egypt to join in China's development of the New Silk Road Economic Belt.

21 South Africa-Russia Nuclear Cooperation

On August 28, 2014, President Jacob Zuma met Russian President Putin near Moscow, and Putin offered assistance for a comprehensive nuclear energy industry in South Africa, in light of President Zuma's June announcement that South Africa will greatly expand its nuclear program.

SEE:
The World Landbridge:
Online Interactive Map
larouchepac.com/world-landbridge

II. The Imperial System is Dead and Must Now Be Eliminated

Even the foregoing abbreviated summary of the explosive development process that the BRICS have unleashed on the planet, makes clear the stunning potential this offers for bringing humanity to the highest level of cooperation and development ever achieved. But it is not enough to simply offer and build that option, and hope for the best. The British Empire, whose very existence is threatened by this process and is fighting it to the death, must be eliminated, and the centuries-old oligarchical principle of empire banished from the planet once and for all.

That Empire, with its operational centers in the City of London and Wall Street, has made it clear—much as Milton's Satan in *Paradise Lost*—that it prefers to bring down the world, both economically and militarily, rather than tolerate losing control, not simply to another power bloc, but to an entirely different conception of man.

Financial Cancer

Start with the basics of their international financial system. This system, in which mere money, rather than physical wealth, is considered valuable, is reaching a limit to its ability to loot from the physical economy. The result of this is an enormous speculative bubble that is beyond bankrupt, totaling some $2 quadrillion in worthless financial assets that cannot conceivably ever be paid, a hyperinflationary growth of worthless debt that LaRouche originally warned in 1971 would be the inevitable consequence of the dismantling of FDR's Bretton Woods system.

How in the world did we ever allow this to happen? With the end of the fixed exchange-rate Bretton Woods system in 1971, international financial interests unleashed global speculation on national currencies and futures markets, which left a wake of devastation across the Third World, in particular. Then in 1999, these same financial interests induced the United States to jettison FDR's 1933 Glass-Steagall law, which had strictly separated commercial banks from speculative investment banks. That unleashed rampant speculation in derivatives, which came to represent some 90% of all world financial assets. Between the 1999 repeal of Glass-Steagall, and the 2008 blowout of the world financial system, total financial instruments soared from about $260 trillion to a staggering $1.4 quadrillion—a five-fold increase in a decade!

That was bad enough. But then, the "solution" put in place by Wall Street and London in 2008 to try to save their system, made everything far, far worse. Hyperinflationary "Quantitative Easing" (QE) was launched, which to date has added about $9 trillion in worthless money to the bubble, in an attempt to bail out the banks. This bail-out accelerated dramatically in 2013 and 2014, raising total world financial aggregates from about $1.5 quadrillion at the end of 2012, to nearly $2 quadrillion today—a 33% jump in only two years.

WORLD FINANCIAL AGGREGATES (QUADRILLION $)

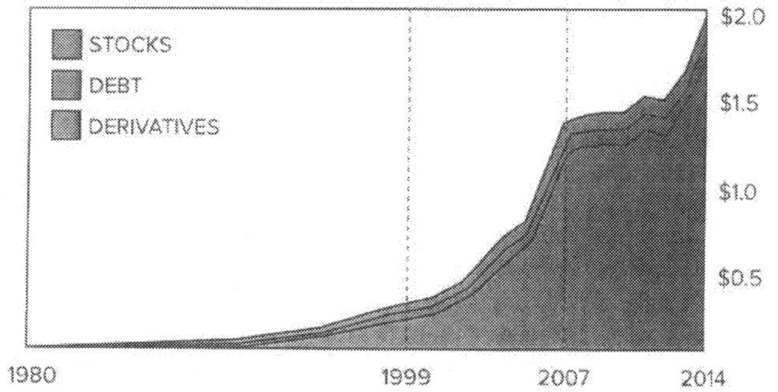

The hyperinflationary growth of total global financial aggregates over the period 1980-2014, measured in quadrillions of dollars. The vertical lines in 1999 and 2007 mark the repeal of the Glass-Steagall Act and the global financial crisis, respectively.

BrutalProof!

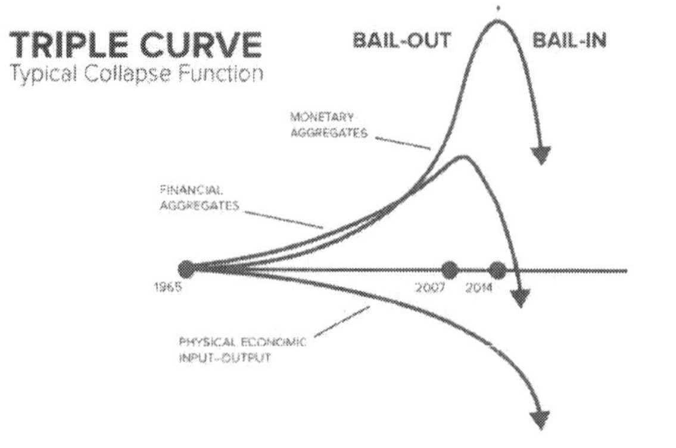

An updated version of a heuristic graphic first developed by LaRouche in 1996 to demonstrate the inevitability of the collapse of the speculative financial system.

At the same time that they have fed the cancer relentlessly with every imaginable form of bail-out, the British Empire has also used its bail-in fraud, codified in the Dodd-Frank bill in the U.S., to loot the population to the bone, stealing everything—from people's bank accounts, to their pensions, to their insurance, to their very livelihood. In Europe, youth unemployment has soared across the Eurozone, hitting over 60% in Greece and Spain.

The United States is no better: more than half of the states have real youth unemployment rates exceeding 30%. On Obama's watch, the number of Americans below the official poverty line rose from 37 million to 48 million. The southwest portion of the country is suffering such devastating drought—aggravated by decades of neglect to build new infrastructure as well as the destruction of that which had already existed—that it is dying from lack of water.

In short, we are in the final phase of a general breakdown crisis of the economic system as a whole in which we are facing the simultaneous explosion of fictitious speculative financial values, while the actual physical economy, on which the lives of the population depends, has been intentionally shattered. Lyndon LaRouche's "Triple Curve Typical Collapse Function" is the best representation of the deadly process now underway—and why it cannot continue.

The physical economy has been so decimated, that one would almost think that it is the result of an intentional policy of the British Empire to kill people off—which in fact it is. The stated policy of the British Queen, her consort Prince Philip, and their imperial spokesmen, is to rapidly reduce the population of the planet from some seven billion human beings today, down to one billion or less. Prince Philip himself has stated this policy unequivocally, when he bragged:

> In the event that I am reincarnated, I would like to return as a deadly virus, in order to contribute something to solve overpopulation.

Compare that bestial, genocidal outlook, with the optimism and love for mankind emanating from the BRICS, as was stated succinctly by Indian Prime Minister Narendra Modi in his September 28, 2014 speech before a crowd of over 20,000 assembled in New York City's Madison Square Garden:

> Youth with competence and capabilities can make their own future. We do not have to look back. There is no reason for pessimism... We have a combination of things that no other nation has, and with this comes responsibility... 1.2 billion people is a blessing from God. People are the face of God.

Prime Minister Modi then posed a challenge to not only the people of India, but the entire world: "Let us make development a mass movement."

Wall Street and London Declare War on China's "New Marshall Plan"

On the same day that Xi Jinping was offering the United States to join the New Silk Road, an editorial appeared in the *Wall Street Journal* denouncing Xi for the heinous crime of "attempting to out-American the Americans," by launching a new Marshall Plan, making the outlandish claim that this "suggests Chinese leaders want to resurrect the imperial tributary system." This echoes a similar article penned earlier in *Foreign Affairs* titled "China's Imperial President" which calls for all-out military and economic warfare against China.

The irony, of course, is that while China and the BRICS, in fact, *are* emulating the Hamiltonian "American System" of economics and bringing development to the world, we are being used by our own historic enemy, the British Empire, to attempt to start WWIII to crush this new economic order, all while we go down on the empire's sinking financial Titanic.

Map depicting the encirclement of Russia and China through advanced placement of troops and military hardware on their borders.

Thermonuclear World War III

Rather than see humanity dominated by the outlook, policies, and economic system expressed by Prime Minister Modi and the BRICS, the British Empire and its allies within Europe and the United States have launched a series of so-called "color revolutions" and other forms of unlawful regime change against any country that dares to jump from the sinking trans-Atlantic financial Titanic, acting to create the conditions of chaos and warfare under which they believe they can maintain global political control. Moreover, they are fully prepared to launch open war against Russia and China in particular, which, in this day and age, can only mean global thermonuclear war, threatening the exitinction of the human race.

As the founder of the Schiller Institute Helga Zepp-LaRouche wrote recently:

> The danger of an intentional—or even an accidental—thermonuclear world war has grown dramatically. The attempt, fed by geopolitical motives, to associate Ukraine with the EU, and thus bring it, de facto, into the NATO sphere of influence, has triggered a series of escalating confrontations, which, in the worst case, could end in the extinction of the human race. But in addition, nearly the entire Near and Middle East is burning; set off by wars built on lies, against so-called rogue states, the seeds of violence were sown that have called to life a million-headed hydra, which not only has leveled the Cradle of Civilization to the ground and created there a Hell on Earth, but also has become an existential threat to the West... There are also geostrategic conflicts breeding in the Pacific, which have the potential to set loose regional wars and beyond.

Time is rapidly running out for the United States to join with the BRICS to put a final end to the British Empire, before that empire succeeds in wiping out the entire human species through economic devastation and global thermonuclear war.

III. Concrete Opportunitites for the United States to Join BRICS

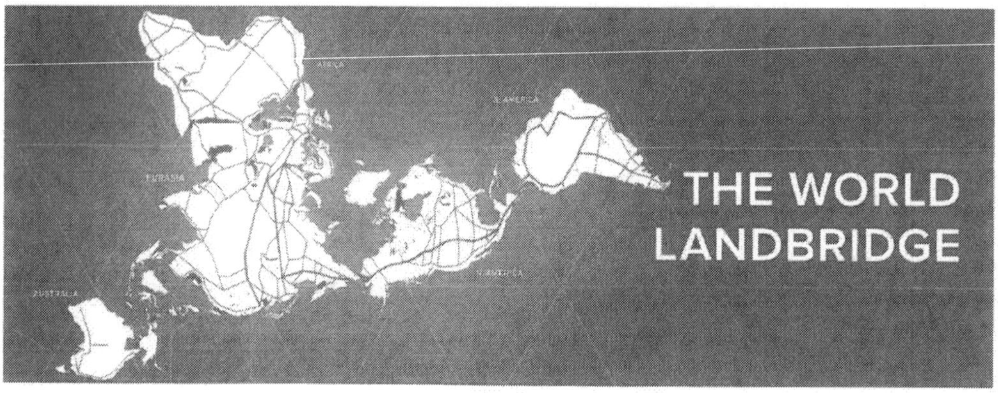

A series of concrete offers have been presented to the United States to collaborate with Russia and China in a new era of global, and interplanetary, development. In addition to the recent offers from Presidents Putin and Xi Jinping regarding the open and inclusive nature of the Silk Road Fund, the Asian Infrastructure Investment Bank, and other BRICS-related new economic institutions, there has been a series of other proposals for cooperative development. Leading the list are proposals for joint projects in Arctic development, space development, and advanced forms of nuclear power.

The Bering Strait Rail Connection

Perhaps one of the most immediate and obvious places for the United States to join in this alliance for development would be to take up the offers from both Russia and China to collaborate in the construction of high-speed rail connections through Alaska and into Siberia, via 50–60 mile tunnels constructed under the Bering Strait. Connecting Russia's transiberian rail lines with those of Canada and the United States, thus linking the entire North American landmass with the vast Eurasian continent, would be the keystone connection to extend China's New Silk Road into the beginnings of a true World Landbridge.

In addition to vastly increasing the volume and speed of trade and transport between the Americas and Asia across the Pacific Ocean, this project would provide a critical driver program for the development of the immense resource potentials of the Arctic and Siberian regions. Massive mineral and hydrocarbon deposits typify the incredible resource potential of these undeveloped northern regions, but to access and develop these regions will require an advanced high technology infrastructure program with significantly increased levels of energy flux density—a critical technological driver program for all the nations involved in such an endeavor.

While the idea for such a rail connection goes back to the 19th century, Lyndon and Helga LaRouche have been central in the fight for this Bering Strait project since the early 1990s.[3] The Russian government has presented plans to extend its rail lines up to the Bering Strait, and government officials have repeatedly advocated building the Bering Strait connection.

Typical of such efforts, in 2007, Lyndon and Helga LaRouche were invited to participate in a Moscow conference titled, "Megaprojects of Russia's East: A

3 See *Appendix: LaRouche's Role in Shaping Current World History*

Transcontinental Eurasia-America Transport Link via the Bering Strait," organized by the Russian Academy of Sciences, in conjunction with other governmental ministries and Russian corporations.

In 2014, Chinese government media began to run reports of China's interest in constructing this Bering Strait rail connection, as reported in *China Daily* and by RIA Novosti, as well as the *Guardian* and elsewehere.[4]

If the United States joins with Russia and China in this great project, the Bering Strait rail connection will truly transform the New Silk Road into the World Landbridge.[5]

Lunar Development and Helium-3

The brilliant success of China's lunar program has drawn renewed attention to the Moon. The development of the Moon is one of the most important steps in mankind's development of the Solar System, and China is not the only nation interested in this. Russia has repeatedly expressed its intent to develop permanent operations on the Moon, as has the United States before Obama dismantled the U.S. lunar program.

A joint U.S.-China-Russia program to develop the Moon can provide mankind with the platform to begin to develop and control the entire Solar System. The ability to use the resources available in space—on the surface of the Moon and asteroids, for example—will completely revolutionize mankind's relationship to the Solar System. Therfore, initial resource development and industrialization of the Moon will be critical.

Perhaps most important will be the development of the unique fusion fuel which is nearly absent from the Earth, but quite abundant on the Moon: helium-3. Leading scientists in China, Russia, and the U.S. have spent decades investigating the immense benefits of developing the helium-3 resources from the Moon, making this endeavor an ideal point of collaboration.

The development of advanced thermonuclear fusion capabilities with lunar helium-3 will radically transform the economy back on Earth, as well as revolutionizing mankind's relationship with the Solar System as a whole. For example, fusion-powered rocket propulsion can cut the travel time between Earth and Mars down from the present range of 5–10 months to a range of potentially 5–10 days.[6]

"When obtaining nuclear power from helium-3 becomes a reality, the lunar resources can be used to generate electricity for more than 10,000 years for the whole world."

Ouyang Ziyuan, father of Chinese lunar program
Xinhua News Agency, November 2012

"One of the most significant contributions of the Apollo missions was confirming the presence of helium-3 on the moon."

Harrison Schmitt, Apollo 17 astronaut
Apollo 40th Anniversary, October 2012

"There is water on the Moon, and there is helium-3, which is better than any other energy source existing on the Earth... One day, we will run out of oil and coal, and mankind will need energy. Then, we will start supplying it from the neighboring planet."

Alexander Volkov, Russian cosmonaut
All-Russia Science Festival, October 2014

"We are planning to set up a permanent station on the Moon. The industrial mining of helium-3, a rare isotope, is expected to begin on the Moon."

Nikolai Sevastyanov, former head of Energia
Energia Official Statement, March 2006

"I predict by the next two decades, we could see missions being carried out to tap the resources [such as helium-3] in the Moon."

A. Sivathanu Pillai, Indian aerospace scientist
Indian Express News, October 2014

Strategic Defense of Earth (SDE)

Fusion technologies will also be critical for the defense of Earth from rogue asteroids and comets, a challenge which top-level Russian officials have repeatedly raised as something that Russia and the United States should collaborate in overcoming.

Mankind not only has no existing or demonstrated defense from potentially hazardous asteroids or comets, but we do not even know the location of the vast majority of the asteroids in our immediate neighborhood, as was demonstrated quite clearly in the surprise explosion of a small asteroid over Chelyabinsk, Russia in February 2013.

Prior to that wake-up call, in the fall of 2011, Russia's then-Special Envoy to NATO, Dmitri Rogozin, had already proposed that the United States and Russia collaborate in developing the capabilities to defend

4 www.theguardian.com/world/2014/may/08/chinese-experts-discussions-high-speed-beijing-american-railway

5 See the online interactive map of the full World Land-Bridge project at: www.larouchepac.com/world-landbridge

6 For more on lunar helium-3: www.larouchepac.com/lunar-he-3-fusion

the Earth from both the threats from asteroids and nuclear missiles. As a joint program, this was offered as an alternative to the unilateral US–NATO advanced placement of thermonuclear-related military capabilities towards Russia's borders. This proposal for a joint US–Russian "Strategic Defense of Earth" (SDE) was a clear echo of Lyndon LaRouche's original Strategic Defense Initiative (SDI).[7]

Following the Chelyabinsk explosion, this idea has been repeated by multiple high-level Russian officials. For example, Prime Minister Dmitri Medvedev declared:

> The meteorite that fell near Chelyabinsk is a lesson to all mankind. It is necessary to look together for ways to withstand the forces of nature.

Nikolai Patrushev, the Secretary of the Russian Security Council called for asteroid defense to be placed on the agenda of the June 2012 Global Security Summit in St. Petersburg, and at that forum stated:

> If we work on improving [our defense from asteroids], especially on an international scale, this will not be out of reach as it would be for just one country, but it can really be done. So we need to do the forecasting of when and how to influence these [space] objects.

In 2013, Nikolai Patrushev reiterated the proposal for an international program in defense of Earth:

> The Russian Security Council has repeatedly proposed to develop an Intergovernmental Targeted Program to counteract space threats associated with the asteroid and comet danger and the build-up of space trash.

Konstantin Tsypko, representative of the Chelyabinsk Region in the Federation Council, stated:

> It would be logical to hold an international conference with the participation of heads of state to discuss the problem of an asteroid threat to Earth.

And in February 2013, Dmitri Rogozin reiterated his proposal for an "international initiative" to create a system against space threats, saying, "the essence of our idea consists of joining the intellectual and technological efforts of industrial nations," citing Russian, American, Chinese, and European industries as leading examples.

This international initiative for a joint asteroid defense system as an alternative to war was expanded in 2013 by the head of the foreign-affairs committee of the Russian State Duma, Alexei Pushkov, to include China as well:

> Instead of fighting on Earth, people should be creating a joint system of asteroid defense... Instead of creating a [military] European space defense system, the United States should join us and China in creating the AADS—the Anti-Asteroid Defense System.

Creating A Fusion Economy

Collaboration between the United States and the BRICS alliance on the development and mass production of nuclear fission, controlled thermonuclear fusion, and associated high energy flux density technologies will also be critical.

The combined scientific, engineering, and productive capabilities of leading nations can be marshalled to define a global crash program to fully develop the capabilities of the nuclear age. While there is important international collaboration ongoing, including advances being made with the construction of the International Thermonuclear Experimental Reactor (ITER), fusion development has been greatly slowed by the financial and political shortcomings of the old paradigm. Today, not only can we accelerate the development of ITER and other ongoing fusion programs, but an even greater crash effort can be initiated.

The benefits will go far beyond the abundant power provided by nuclear fission and fusion systems. This is mankind's entry into an entirely new domain of physical chemistry, subsuming molecular chemistry with the vast untapped potential of the atomic domain.

Such advances will shatter the absurd framework of economics as a so-called "zero sum game." Completely new resource-bases can be opened up by the development of high energy flux density processing methods. New fusion-era technologies can exponentially increase the productive powers of the labor force, allowing for the production of more wealth with fewer man-hours of manual labor.

Such leaps will be critical for man's development of the full potential of the Arctic, the Moon, and the Solar System more generally.

7 For the full historical background on Lyndon LaRouche's role in the Strategic Defense Initiative (SDI), see: www.larouchepac.com/sdi

IV. A New System: Mankind's Future as a Vernadskian Species

Depiction of the Chinese Chang'e-3 Yutu lunar rover on the surface of the Moon, looking back at Earth. (image: CNSA)

The harnessing of fusion power, the construction of the World Landbridge, the development of the Arctic by means of the Bering Strait rail connection, and the utilization of the moon as the platform to access the inner Solar System are, today, among the most important manifestations of mankind's voluntary self-evolution. These are expressions of the unique characteristic separating the human species from the animals.

Mankind is not, inherently, limited by external ecological, planetary, or even interplanetary boundaries. At any given stage of the development of the human species, certain boundaries will exist, but these boundaries are only to be associated with that particular stage, not boundaries of mankind per se. Fundamentally, mankind is the only living species which defines his *own* boundaries, which he then overcomes and replaces with new ones by means of a continuous process of successive revolutionary scientific and cultural advances.

This was understood implicitly by the great Ukrainian-Russian scientist, Vladimir Vernadsky (1863-1945), who, in the 1940s, demonstrated that the power of human scientific and cultural thought itself had become the most powerful force shaping the biosphere—qualitatively and ultimately quantitatively more powerful than physical, geological, or even biological phenomena. Vernadsky recognized that this was a crucial scientific paradox, because human thought does not possess any measurable amount of energy, mass, or any other such characteristics, yet it is the power of human thought which enables mankind to change his boundaries and increase his power as a geological force.

Promethean Fire

Perhaps the earliest and most distinguishing expression of the unique power of the human mind was man's first use of fire. The understanding and management of fire—providing man the ability to cook his food, generate warmth, protect himself, manage the land, and create new materials and tools—marked the process by which man separated himself from a merely biological, animal-like existence, to willfully self-defining his own existence through the creative action of his mind. The subsequent increases in the power of human scientific thought can be usefully measured by the increases in the *energy flux density* of economic activity, as expressed in the successive transitions to higher and more powerful forms of fire: from burning wood and charcoal, to coal and coke, to petroleum and natural gas, to nuclear fission, and, soon, to thermonuclear fusion, with the prospects of matter-antimatter reactions lying ahead.

At each of these stages, mankind becomes a more powerful geological force, shattering prior economic boundaries and limits. However, the sources of these increased powers are not the new energy supplies or other resources attained, but the revolutionary scientific discoveries which *created* those new resources and enabled their controlled application to the improvement of human economies and the biosphere.

How Much Fuel of Different Types Provides the Same Amount of Energy as a Tank of Gas?

FUEL SOURCE	AMOUNT OF FUEL
Combustion of Wood	300 Pounds
Combustion of Coal	200 Pounds
Combustion of Gas	16 Gallons (Gas Tank)
Typical Nuclear Fuel	1 Paperclip*
Deuterium-Tritium Fusion	1 Grain of Rice*
Matter-Antimatter Reaction	1 Flea Egg*

**Equivalent amount of weight (To provide the same amount of energy as an average tank of gasoline, more or less weight of various different fuel types is required, because of their differing energy densities. The value for typical nuclear fuel would be significatly higher with the use of reprocessing and breeder reactors.)*

But to truly approach the core of the issue, it is not any particular level of scientific knowledge or culture which makes us human; it is man's ever-existing ability to create *new* levels. The secret of mankind is his potential to transform society from one stage to the next. It is that process of revolutionary transformation, per se, which is the substance of the distinction of man from beast, *making the continual realization of the ever-existing potential for successively higher transformations the absolute requirement for healthy human society.*

"

Nuclear energy is the fire of the twentieth and twenty-first centuries: It is the fire which our ancestors had 20,000 years ago, which allowed them to make philosophy, technical science, culture, agriculture. Knowledge of the atom... is the sacred fire of the twentieth and twenty-first centuries, as fire was for the pre-agricultural civilizations of 20,000 years ago...

Let us break the mental and colonial chains; break them! Let us dare to leave the cave, as our ancestors did 20,000 years ago. Let us dare to assume our responsibility before the world, before our history and our society. Knowledge of nuclear energy is knowledge of the ABCs of nature.

Álvaro García Linera,
Vice President of Bolivia
August 21, 2014

The Future of Science

The practice of scientific discovery and classical artistic composition reveals the most fundamental and universal aspects of humanity. Modern science began with the father of the Golden Renaissance, Nicolaus of Cusa (1401-1464), and his follower Johannes Kepler (1571-1630), who propelled mankind into the heavens with his discovery of the harmonic principle of universal gravitation. This Renaissance-rooted scientific current grew to eventually lift mankind into the nuclear age, with the discoveries of Max Planck and Albert Einstein revolutionizing the most basic conceptions of physics. When the work of Planck and Einstein is viewed from the standpoint of the discoveries of Vladimir Vernadsky and LaRouche, we can see that mankind is currently on the verge of an entirely new scientific era concerning man's understanding of himself and his relationship to the universe.

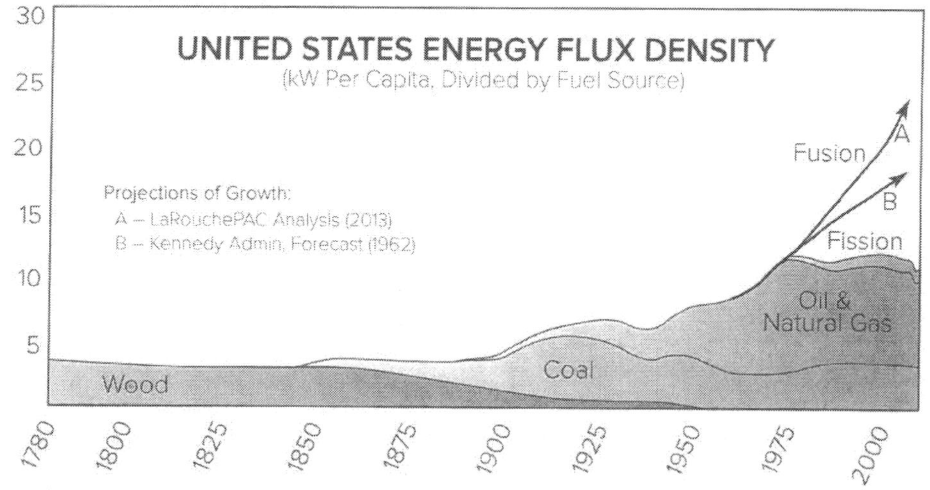

From US EIA and "Civilian Nuclear Power, a Report to the President" submitted to JFK by Leland Haworth.

Per capita power consumption for the United States from 1780 to 2010, divided by the major sources of power. The general growth trend is clear, until 1970, when the zero-growth insanity took over the United States. Two projections indicate what could and should have happened. Curve A is a 1962 projection made by the John F. Kennedy administration, which focused on the then-coming role of nuclear fission power. Curve B is an estimation of what were possible had the Kennedy vision been pursued, followed by the development of controlled thermonuclear fusion (following the 1970s realization of the feasibility of fusion).

No longer can we view the universe as composed of sense perceptual conceptions of space, time, energy, and matter. These become shadows, expressions of an interconnected medium which is organized by universal physical principles, as Kepler was the first to demonstrate. As China's space program takes us into Kepler's Solar System, we will be increasingly forced to think in terms of principle, and discard any remaining false sense-perceptual ideas of mankind's relation to the cosmos.

The economic development of the Solar System and the understanding of the subsuming role of our galaxy will require a series of new scientific revolutions: *recognizing the universe as fundamentally composed of a nested hierarchy of discovered universal physical principles governing processes of anti-entropic development.* Kepler and Cusa were the first to provide indications of this, and Vernadsky and LaRouche have presented the most developed conceptions so far.

Our Solar System is not a collection of objects floating in a large volume of space—it is a process of development, governed by a universal physical principle. Man must begin to think of his relation to the universe in these terms. While the economic development of the Solar System will require placing people and objects in certain locations, that will be merely a secondary effect, a shadow of the primary, determining factor: the increasing power of human scientific and cultural thought to envelope, organize, and reshape the Solar System as a single process of development.

We will still measure shadows, but we will recognize that it is the immortal contributions of individuals and societies which govern the process of development which gives rise to the future. We will recognize that the true nature of man's existence is not found in the biological flesh of the individual, but in the expanding principle of the creative improvement of the universe which is mankind.

SEE: The Vernadsky Project
www.larouchepac.com/vernadsky

Appendix: LaRouche's Role in Shaping Current World History

When the leaders of Russia, China, India, Brazil, and South Africa (BRICS) declared in July 2014 that they were creating a new international economic order with the formation of the New Development Bank (NDB), they were implementing an idea which had been originally conceived of and proposed by Lyndon LaRouche forty years prior, in 1975, in the form of the International Development Bank (IDB).

Soon after the dismantling of the original Bretton Woods system in 1971 with the decision to eliminate fixed exchange rates among currencies and floating the U.S. dollar, Lyndon LaRouche declared that the then-existing IMF system had become an instrument of murderous financial warfare against so-called developing countries and would inevitably go bankrupt. To replace it, LaRouche proposed that a new credit institution be established to facilitate long-term, low-interest credit for capital investment to overcome the underdevelopment of Africa, Latin America, and large parts of Asia. This would be the basis for a new international economic order, premised on "a sweeping financial reorganization of the world monetary system, involving an orderly process of debt moratoria and the establishment of an institution such as the proposed International Development Bank (IDB)."

Within a year following LaRouche's proposal, the Non-Aligned Movement representing eighty-five nations and two billion people met in Colombo, Sri Lanka and issued a unanimous declaration calling for "complete restructuring of international economic relations" and "the establishment of the new world economic order." This included a call for a Bank of the Developing Countries, alternately called a Development Bank for the Third World.

Immediately following the Colombo Summit, the Foreign Minister of Guyana, Frederick Wills, addressed the United Nations General Assembly, and called for the establishment of a new international economic order through the creation of an international development bank and a debt moratorium, saying:

> The IMF and the Bretton Woods monetary system must give way to alternative structures like international development banks... The crippling problem of debt and the servicing of debt has assumed a special urgency. We cannot afford to mortgage the future of unborn generations to the obligations of burdensome capital repayments and crushing debt servicing. The time has come for a debt moratorium.

In the years immediately following, LaRouche became the focal point of efforts internationally to combat the murderous policies of the IMF system and bring into existence a new international economic order. LaRouche developed close relationships with the heads of state of many leading developing countries, including Prime Minister Indira Gandhi of India, and President José López Portillo of Mexico, meeting with them personally numerous times.

At the request of President López Portillo, LaRouche updated his original IDB proposal with a major policy document titled *Operation Juárez*, in which he proposed that the nations of Ibero-America use their collective strategic leverage as debtor-nations to unite in a common bloc and unilaterally declare a restructuring of their debts and the establishment of a new monetary order. The formation of a shared development bank among these nations, he said, would serve "as a coordinating agency for planning investments and trade-expansion among the member-republics." LaRouche stated:

> This bank will soon become one of the most powerful financial institutions in the world. If a sufficient portion of the Ibero-American nations enter into such an agreement, the result is the assembly of one of the most powerful economies in the world from an array of individually weak powers... The Ibero-American continent could rapidly emerge as a leading economic power of the world, an economic super-power.

Immediately following the publication of Lyndon LaRouche's *Operation Juárez*, President López Portillo addressed the United Nations General Assembly:

> The most constant concern and activity of Mexico in the international arena, is the transition to a New Economic Order... It is imperative that the New International Economic Order establish a link between refinancing the development of countries that suffer capital flight, and the capital that has fled... Let us not continue in this vicious circle: it could be the beginning of a new medieval Dark Age, without the possibility of a Renaissance... We cannot fail. There is cause to be alarmist. Not only the heritage of civilization is at stake, but also the very survival of our children, of future generations and of the human species.

How The
INTERNATIONAL
DEVELOPMENT
BANK
Will Work

IDB

$1.00

Policy document published by Lyndon LaRouche in 1975 detailing his proposal for creating an International Development Bank (IDB), a policy now being echoed by the BRICS.

The following year, Prime Minister Indira Gandhi hosted the New Delhi Summit of the Non-Aligned Movement, in which she began her keynote speech warning of the double-threat that humanity faced:

> Humankind is balancing on the brink of the collapse of the world economic system and annihilation through nuclear war.

The solution, Gandhi declared, was to convene "an international conference on money and finance for development [to] suggest comprehensive reforms of the international monetary system to facilitate the mobilization of developmental finance for investment in vital areas of food, energy and industrial development." She concluded her speech:

> The eyes of the world are upon us. Let us decide here to usher in a New International Economic Order, to call for an International Conference on Money and Finance for Development.

The declaration adopted at the summit, called the New Delhi Appeal, echoed Indira Gandhi's demands:

> A thorough-going restructuring of the existing international economic order through a process of global negotiations is necessary. Non-aligned countries are committed to strive for the establishment of the New International Economic Order based on justice and equality. We propose the immediate convening of an international conference on money and finance for development, with universal participation, and a comprehensive restructuring of the international monetary and financial system.

At the same time, LaRouche was working with another head of state, U.S. President Ronald Reagan, to bring an end to the other existential threat facing the human race, "annihilation through nuclear war" as Indira Gandhi had warned. On March 23, 1983, only days after the summit in New Delhi, President Reagan shocked the world by announcing the Strategic Defense Initiative (SDI), committing the United States to a crash program for the development of missile defense technology to "free the world from the threat of nuclear war."

The policy unveiled in this historic announcement had come as the result of years of effort by LaRouche personally, developing the programmatic outlines of such a policy over the span of nearly a decade, and engaging in direct back-channel negotiations with Soviet representatives over the immediately preceding months—negotiations which LaRouche had conducted personally on behalf of and at the behest of leading members of Reagan's national security team, reporting directly to the closest advisers of the President.

LaRouche had been advocating a Manhattan Project-style crash program for the development of a joint space-based missile defense system based on new physical principles since the mid-1970s, in the context of his campaign for a new international economic order. The key principle behind such a crash program was economic at its core, as well as strategic. LaRouche emphasized that human survival depends fundamentally on constant up-shifts in technology and the energy flux density of power sources utilized in the productive process. A full-scale crash program for the achievement of thermonuclear fusion would be accompanied by a general surge in productivity which would be more than sufficient to lift the entire human species out of poverty. Such a global driver would be financed through credit provided by the International Development Bank and related institutions.

When the Andropov government rejected Reagan's offers of cooperation, LaRouche warned that the East bloc economies would collapse under the weight of the Soviet Union's desperate military buildup by the end of the 1980s. LaRouche repeated this warning in a televised press conference in West Berlin in October 1988, in which he forecast the imminent breakup of the Soviet system and proposed a kind of Marshall Plan for the industrialization of Eastern Europe.

With the fall of the Berlin Wall, Lyndon and Helga LaRouche immediately moved to put this plan into action, proposing to use the modernization of Eastern Europe as the "locomotive" for the economic development of Eurasia. The concept took the form of the "Productive Triangle" linking together Paris, Berlin, and Vienna through development corridors. LaRouche proposed that such a development driver could be the cornerstone of a new, more just international economic order to replace the equally bankrupt and decayed Western free market system, which he warned was also on the verge of collapse.

Helga Zepp-LaRouche appearing at a press conference in December 1998 with José López Portillo, the former President of Mexico, who stated: "It is now necessary for the world to listen to the wise words of Lyndon LaRouche."

Following the official dissolution of the Soviet Union the following year, Lyndon LaRouche expanded the concept of the "Productive Triangle" to include the former Soviet territories in Russia and central Asia, as well as China, stretching all the way from the Atlantic to the Pacific coast. This proposal, which became known as the "Eurasian Landbridge" or the "New Silk Road," would economically integrate the entire Eurasian continent, maximizing the productive potential of its territory and peoples for the common benefit of all, and resolving the artificially imposed strategic divisions among the great powers through the promotion of development in their mutual interest.

Helga Zepp-LaRouche, known as the "Silk Road Lady," pictured during a trip to China in 1998 at the Eastern Terminal of the Eurasian Landbridge.

In 1995, Helga Zepp-LaRouche traveled to China to attend the "International Symposium on Economic Development of the New Euro-Asia Continental Bridge," sponsored by the Ministry of Foreign Trade and Economic Cooperation of the People's Republic of China. In 1998, Helga Zepp-LaRouche returned to China to participate in a second conference on the Eurasian Landbridge, called "Asia-Europe Economic and Trade Relations in the 21st Century and the Second Eurasian Bridge." Through her role in promoting the concept of a New Silk Road internationally, she became known as the "Silk Road Lady." Over the past year, Helga Zepp-LaRouche has returned to China twice to participate in several high-level seminars on the Landbridge, as well as being interviewed by numerous Chinese national media, both television and print, in which she has been recognized and celebrated as an original champion of the Eurasian Landbridge idea.

With the announcement of China's "New Silk Road Economic Belt" in September 2013 by President Xi Jinping, the Eurasian Landbridge became official policy of the largest nation on the planet. In the year since this initiative, the full scope of the new international order, first proposed in 1975 by Lyndon LaRouche, has come into focus around the BRICS, and now half of humanity is in the process of adopting the policies which Lyndon and Helga LaRouche have conceptualized and fought for over the past forty years.

The role of Lyndon LaRouche and his wife Helga Zepp-LaRouche in providing the intellectual and political leadership for over four decades in the fight for a new international economic and strategic order for the planet, to end the historic imperial control of monetarism and unleash mankind's creative powers as a species, is a testament to the power of human reason in shaping the history of mankind. It is an example of the dedication and leadership that every citizen must emulate if we are to follow through on the opportunity which has been given mankind to survive in the immediate future ahead. That survival is by no means guaranteed, but the very fact that the opportunity for survival now exists, is the direct result of the efforts of the LaRouche movement and its allies around the globe.

It is now incumbent on the American people to act, and bring the United States decisively into this new international order, fulfilling our republic's original mission for mankind and finally eliminating from this planet the system of empire, once and for all.

SEE: LaRouche's 40-Year Record: A New International Economic Order
www.larouchepac.com/new-economic-order

“

We seek not the worldwide victory of one nation or system but a worldwide victory of man. The modern globe is too small, its weapons are too destructive, and its disorders are too contagious to permit any other kind of victory.

President John F. Kennedy
January 14, 1963 · State of the Union

SIGN THE PETITION:

THE UNITED STATES & EUROPE MUST HAVE THE COURAGE TO REJECT GEOPOLITICS AND COLLABORATE WITH THE BRICS

In today's nuclear age, the consequence of a geopolitical policy of confrontation with Russia and China can only be the thermonuclear extinction of the human race. Therefore, every effort must be made to cooperate to solve the multiple crises facing humanity.

The BRICS nations (Brazil, Russia, India, China, and South Africa) have united to pursue a policy of economic development not just for their individual countries, but for the benefit of the people of all nations. To that end, they have created a New Development Bank (NDB) to invest billions in necessary development projects.

China recently initiated the Asian Infrastructure Investment Bank (AIIB), joined by over twenty Asian nations as founding members, and has set up a Silk Road Development Fund.

At the APEC conference in Beijing, Chinese President Xi Jinping invited President Obama to join the efforts of China and other Asian nations, including Russia, in the development of the New Silk Road.

These initiatives are not geopolitical in nature. Contrary to the Transpacific Partnership (TPP) advocated by Obama, which excludes Russia and China, the BRICS-related initiatives, including the Chinese-proposed Free Trade Area of the Asia Pacific (FTAAP), are inclusive. They are based on the concept expressed by the late Pope Paul VI that the "new name of peace is development." Thus, in Australia at the recent G-20 meeting, both Xi Jinping and Indian Prime Minister Modi spoke of the twin goals of achieving global peace and ending poverty through economic development."

There is no problem in the world that cannot be solved by such an approach, and conversely, no problem that will be solved without it.

Such cooperation between the U.S., Russia, China, India, and South Africa, among other nations, is necessary to defeat the Ebola pandemic in Africa.

The terrorist threat represented by ISIS and Al-Qaeda is aimed equally at Russia, China, and India, as well as the U.S. and Europe. It can only be defeated through a new security architecture based on cooperation.

The policy of conducting "color revolutions" under the pretext of democracy, represents a policy of war, even if that term is not used, because its aim is to topple governments with the aid of foreign money. It has to stop. The campaign to impose sanctions on Russia for its opposition to such "color revolutions" and to a Nazi coup in Ukraine, is only exacerbating the global crisis. An approach based on mutual cooperation to achieve the common ends of mankind throughout Eurasia and beyond, would instead create the basis for global peace.

While the United States has abandoned the Kennedy space program, the Chinese are committed to a lunar program focused on the exploitation of helium-3 for the purpose of generating unlimited fusion energy. With collaboration between the U.S., Europe, Russia, China, and India, among other nations, man could finally realize Johannes Kepler's vision of mastery of the laws of the solar system for the benefit of man.

Only such an approach would restore the United States and Europe to their original purpose as expressed in the European Renaissance and the American Revolution, a purpose which the United States and Europe have increasingly abandoned, and the rest of the world has now adopted and is now urging them to readopt.

We therefore call upon the United States and Europe to abandon the suicidal geopolitical policies of the past which led to the two previous World Wars and are leading to a third, and to build a future for all humanity by readopting the principle of the Treaty of Westphalia, by basing foreign policy on the principle of the "benefit of the other," which ended the Thirty Years War in Europe, and on John Quincy Adams' concept of a "community of principle among sovereign nation states."

That is the only course coherent with the true nature of man as the only creative species. Any other course is based on a concept of man as an animal, and leads to human extinction.

As patriots of our own nations, and as citizens of the world, we call on our fellow citizens and the leaders of our nations to have the courage to break the current cycle of escalating bestiality, by accepting the generous offer to collaborate with the BRICS.

TO SIGN THE PETITION, VISIT: LAROUCHEPAC.COM/PETITION

Made in the USA
Las Vegas, NV
15 February 2021

17933520R00219